D1609955

# HEBREW IDEALS
## in GENESIS

# HEBREW IDEALS
# in GENESIS

### Study of Old Testament Faith and Life

by
James Strahan

KREGEL PUBLICATIONS
Grand Rapids, Michigan 49501

**Library of Congress Cataloging in Publication Data**

Strahan, James, 1863-1926.
  Hebrew Ideals in Genesis.

  Reprint. Originally published: Hebrew Ideals
From the Story of the Patriarchs. Edinburgh:
T. & T. Clark, 1902-1905.
  Includes index.
  1. Bible. O.T. Genesis — Commentaries.
I. Title.
BS1235.S75        1982        222'.1107        82-7785
ISBN 0-8254-3729-6                               AACR2

*Printed in the United States of America*

# CONTENTS

*Foreword* . . . . . . . . . . . . . . . . . . . . . . . . . . . . . . . . . . . *vii*
*Preface* . . . . . . . . . . . . . . . . . . . . . . . . . . . . . . . . . . . . . *ix*
Ideals               Genesis 12-50 . . . . . . . . . . . . .  13
Separation           Genesis 12:1 . . . . . . . . . . . . . .  18
Blessedness          Genesis 12:1-3 . . . . . . . . . . . . .  24
Worship              Genesis 12:4-9 . . . . . . . . . . . . .  30
Truth                Genesis 12:10-20 . . . . . . . . . . .  37
Decision             Genesis 13 . . . . . . . . . . . . . . . .  43
Warfare              Genesis 14:1-16 . . . . . . . . . . . .  53
Peace                Genesis 14:17-20 . . . . . . . . . . .  60
Assurance            Genesis 15 . . . . . . . . . . . . . . . .  71
Grace                Genesis 15:18 . . . . . . . . . . . . .  78
Patience             Genesis 16 . . . . . . . . . . . . . . . .  85
Compassion           Genesis 16:7, 10, 13 . . . . . . . .  91
Power                Genesis 17 . . . . . . . . . . . . . . . .  97
Hospitality          Genesis 18:1-15 . . . . . . . . . . . . 107
Education            Genesis 18:16-19 . . . . . . . . . . . 112
Intercession         Genesis 18:23-32 . . . . . . . . . . . 119
Mercy                Genesis 19:1-14 . . . . . . . . . . . . 126
Judgment             Genesis 19:15-29 . . . . . . . . . . . 130
Integrity            Genesis 20 . . . . . . . . . . . . . . . . 139
Laughter             Genesis 21:6 . . . . . . . . . . . . . . 142
Tears                Genesis 21:11-17 . . . . . . . . . . . . 146
Aspiration           Genesis 21:22, 31 . . . . . . . . . . . 152
Discipline           Genesis 22:1-3 . . . . . . . . . . . . . 157
Sacrifice            Genesis 22:6-18 . . . . . . . . . . . . 167

| | | |
|---|---|---|
| Pilgrimage | Genesis 23 | 175 |
| Love | Genesis 24 | 181 |
| Heaven | Genesis 25:7-10 | 195 |
| Birthright | Genesis 25:12-34 | 203 |
| Meekness | Genesis 26 | 213 |
| Blessing | Genesis 27 | 219 |
| Bethel | Genesis 28 | 229 |
| Love | Genesis 29:1-30 | 239 |
| Memory | Genesis 29:31-31:55 | 243 |
| Wrestling | Genesis 32-33:17 | 250 |
| Purity | Genesis 33:18-34:31 | 262 |
| Restoration | Genesis 35 | 269 |
| Dreams | Genesis 37 | 277 |
| Virtue | Genesis 39:1-19 | 285 |
| Inspiration | Genesis 39:20-41:39 | 295 |
| Honor | Genesis 41:40-57 | 304 |
| Conscience | Genesis 42 | 309 |
| Brotherhood | Genesis 38, 43, 44 | 316 |
| Attainment | Genesis 45:26-46:34 | 329 |
| Service | Genesis 47:1-48:20 | 332 |
| Farewell | Genesis 48:21-50:13 | 340 |
| Faith | Genesis 50:14-26 | 351 |
| *Index of Ideals* | | *359* |

# FOREWORD

*Hebrew Ideals in Genesis* is one of the most valuable studies of Genesis to appear in this century. It is valuable because it accomplishes what many commentaries fail to accomplish — the penetrating of the heart and spirit of the people and events in Genesis, and the relating of these "ideals" to life today. "The Book touches existence at every point," the author wrote in his first chapter; and had the word been in vogue at that time, he might have subtitled this book "an existential approach," for that is what it is.

Genesis is a window that permits us to examine patriarchal life. But the longer we look, the more we realize that Genesis is also a mirror that reflects our own hearts and lives; and it is here that Strahan's great book assists us. He reminds us of the things that matter most. He lifts us above the purely local and temporal and introduces us to the timeless and universal. A glance at the chapter headings in the table of contents will convince you that this book deals with the essential and the eternal, for Strahan discusses "Separation," "Worship," "Hospitality," "Integrity," "Laughter," "Dreams," and forty other themes. You can be sure that these subjects are not mentioned in the critical commentaries, and they are probably not investigated with any depth in the devotional and sermonic commentaries. Strahan stands alone.

I appreciate the scholarship in this book, although the author very wisely does not parade his learning. I also appreciate the sympathy and sensitivity of the author as he enters into the lives of the people described in Genesis. His amazing ability to state the heart of the matter in a few precise paragraphs repeatedly overwhelms me as I use this book. He has spiritual vision; he sees what all of us need to see but often cannot. It is no wonder that Alexander Whyte, that prince of Scottish preachers, said of *Hebrew Ideals in Genesis*, "Let that fine piece of evangelical scholarship be in every home."

James Strahan (or Strachan) was born in Fyvie, Scotland, on May 1, 1863. Early in life he dedicated himself to the ministry. He received training at the University of Aberdeen, New College in Edinburgh, and the Universities of Tubigen and Berlin. He was licensed to preach by the Free Church, Edinburgh, in 1889, and ordained on April 22, 1890. He was a tutor in Hebrew at New College, as well as a Cunningham Lecturer. One of his fellow lecturers was James Moffatt. "You have no idea of the brilliancy of the lectures Strahan is giving," Alexander Whyte wrote to a friend.

Strahan was greatly influenced by his professor and close friend, A. B. Davidson. In fact, *Hebrews Ideals in Genesis* is dedicated to the memory of Davidson, "O sweet and virtuous friend " Strahan taught Hebrew and Biblical Criticism at Magee College, Londonderry. It is interesting to note that he married Catherine Evangeline Booth-Clibborn, the granddaughter of General William Booth who founded the Salvation Army. Strahan died March 27, 1926.

*Hebrew Ideals in Genesis* is perhaps his best book. He also wrote: *The Captivity, Pastoral Epistles, The Book of Job* (one of the best studies of this difficult book) and the official biography of A. B. Davidson.

This is not simply a book to refer to when you study to preach from Genesis. It is a book to read with care, to digest, to appreciate and appropriate. It is also a book to imitate, for James Strahan in these pages shows us how to transform ancient history into present reality. He teaches us that the Bible is a living book, with living ideals that still apply today. *Hebrew Ideals in Genesis* has enriched my own life and ministry, and I am sure it will enrich yours as well.

July 1982

WARREN W. WIERSBE

# PREFACE

## Genesis 12:1-25:11

THIS handbook is an attempt to give, not a critical analysis of documents, but a sympathetic interpretation of ideals, and it is written for the purpose of instructing and stimulating young minds.

There are plenty of learned critical works on Genesis. The best are those of Dillmann, Delitzsch, Gunkel, and Ball. To add another to the number would be wasteful and ridiculous excess. My commission was to write something simple. That is more difficult, and at present more needful. Criticism has had its innings, and the time is come for appreciation. Analysis must lead to a new synthesis.

It is sometimes said that "vast tracts of Scripture, and especially of the Old Testament, which were luminous and comfortable to our fathers, are bare desert to the younger generation of preachers." If there are such tracts, I believe they can all be reclaimed. Genesis, at any rate, should not be allowed to become desert; and rightly cultivated it will always rejoice and blossom as the rose. My conviction is that when criticism has done its worst, or, as I for one prefer to say, its best, Luther's words will be as true as ever : *Nihil pulchrius Genesi, nihil utilius.*

A word should be said as to the divine name. I do not care to use the discredited form *Jehovah*, which was unknown till it was coined by an erring scholar in the sixteenth century. Some authors are beginning to write *Yahweh*, even in popular books. I shall not follow this practice till we begin to say *Yoseph* and *Dawid*. If we are to be guided by analogy, we may agree to write *Jahveh*. Meantime in this text-book I generally use the familiar form *LORD*, like the Authorised and Revised Versions.

## Genesis 25:12-50:20

THE purpose of this study was indicated in the first part. The main portion of Genesis was probably written in the ninth or the eighth century B.C. I assume that it mirrors the period to which it belongs. It is true to the highest moral sentiments of the age. It faithfully represents the supreme type of excellence to which the best men were then tending. It is in harmony with their beliefs, feelings, aspirations. It is written to take possession of human life, to make certain great ideals current, to commend the highest principles of action and rules of conduct. At the same time it does not so much recount the acts of human beings, as reveal the thoughts of a Divine Intelligence bent on the regeneration of the world. Its one Hero is God.

It is not my purpose to get *behind* the narratives in Genesis. That the traditions themselves have a history is certain. Genesis contains traces of primitive belief and practice which the moral sense was discarding. The Book itself has nothing to do with these but to transcend them. They could not bear the light of a growing revelation. Their vitality was gone, their very meaning was forgotten. They are outside the range of this study. 'Everything which survived in Israel merely as a custom that was not understood, may claim an interest from the point of view of archeology and the history of religion in general, but has, strictly speaking, none so far as the religion and theology of the Bible are concerned.'[1]

[1] Prof. Kautzsch.

But the ideals of Genesis are for all time. The conflict of our age is not so much between faith and science, as between old knowledge and new. The elemental things of life—faith and hope and love—are essentially the same to-day as they were a thousand years before the coming of Christ. 'Let the world progress as much as it likes, let all branches of human research develop to their utmost, nothing will take the place of the Bible —that foundation of all culture and all education.'[1] 'The Bible reflects to-day, and will reflect for ever, every wave of human emotion, every passing event of human life—reflect them as faithfully as it did to the great and simple people in whose great and simple tongue it was written. The Bible is going to be eternal.'[2]

J. S.

[1] Goethe.                    [2] Watts-Dunton.

# HEBREW IDEALS
## in GENESIS
### Part One

## IDEALS
### Genesis 12-50

*"The world is ruled by great Ideals, the soul responds to them."*
WESTCOTT.

IDEALS.—"Nothing," said Luther, "is more beautiful than Genesis, nothing more useful." Genesis is not a bare record of facts, but a book of ideals. It embodies in living and attractive forms many of the highest Hebrew conceptions of faith and character and conduct. The story of the Patriarchs displays the ideal of fellowship between God and man. The LORD draws nigh to men in love, chooses them for His service, blesses them with His favour, enriches them with His promises, binds them with His behests. Men are taken into covenant with God, justified by faith, disciplined by trial, perfected through suffering. The story also exhibits the ideal of human fellowship in its various relations—between husband and wife, parent and child, master and servant, warrior and priest, statesman and king, saint and sinner. The Book touches existence at every point. Manners and customs, ethnology and ethics, highways and byways of history, births and weddings and burials, love and war, eating and drinking, laughter and tears—all the sunshine and shadow of life are found in the story. But the ideal is never absent.  Sometimes it is patent in the characters depicted, sometimes it is latent in the tone and spirit of the narrator.  The *dramatis personæ* are men and women of like passions with ourselves ; we are permitted to see them in their frailties, deceits, and deeds of violence ; and inspired writers never spare the saints.  Genesis would have but little value for us if it did not hold the mirror up to nature, before displaying the operations of grace and showing how human characters are ennobled and transfigured and made Godlike.  The Book portrays the failures as well as the victories of the servants of God.  For its purpose is not hero-worship, but encouragement to humble seekers after God, religious discipline, culture of moral sentiment.  No attempt is made to hide the tragedies of life which are the results of sin.  Plain tales of human weakness and folly are told, no censure is passed, no moral appended ; yet the narrator makes his own ideal as clear as daylight.  Here is realism, not of the sort that defiles like pitch, but of the kind which purifies the mind with emotions of pity and fear.  The ideal so shines through the real that we feel " how awful goodness is," and see " virtue in her shape how lovely."  Everything is described as it appears, not to the sensual eye of man, but to the pure eye of God ; and behind all the shortcomings of actual goodness we see the divine potentiality of good.

> " Not in their brightness, but their earthly stains,
> Are the true saints vouchsafed to human eyes.
> Sin can read sin, but dimly scans high grace,
> So we move heavenward with averted face,
> Scared into faith by warning of sin's pains ;
> And saints are lowered that the world may rise." [1]

HEBRAISM.—Modern writers are in the habit of comparing and contrasting the Hebrew with the Greek and the Roman ideals.  They speak of the Hebraic, the Hellenic, and the Roman *spirit*, and say that to understand and sympathise with each of these is to possess the noblest culture.  It would be

[1] Newman.

narrow-minded to deny that in each of them there is something of the Spirit of God ; but the Hebrew spirit has a higher potency for moral and religious culture than either the Greek or the Roman spirit. Where, then, shall we find the essential Hebrew spirit ? If we except the Psalms, no book in the Old Testament contains such a fulness of Hebrew life and thought as the book of Genesis. No book is so rich in materials for constructing the real history of the Hebrews. How they acted, how they thought, how they talked, how they felt ; their public and private life ; what they made of the world—here it is all delineated in classic form. Here are no bare annals or chronicles, no dates or dry-as-dust details ; but here are living and glowing pictures of real life ; here are the action, passion, emotion of actual men and women, who interest us as intensely as our most intimate living friends. Names and places are unessential ; the work and life are all that we need care for. The book is real as nature, true as life ; it enables us to see the Hebrew world in the warm glow of flesh and blood ; it preserves for us, as far as inspired art can do it, the reality of an old faith and civilisation ; and to understand it is to be imbued with Hebrew modes of thought and feeling, to be penetrated by the Hebrew spirit.

CHARACTER.—The book of the Patriarchs is a series of character-studies. It evolves, displays, and rewards character. It is an unsurpassed gallery of portraits, and the study of character is the primary task of the reader as of the writer. Truth is made most attractive when it is embodied in concrete forms. The word must be made flesh, and dwell among men. Abstract virtue is pale and cold as a marble statue. Theoretical morals are impotent. Wise men say that you cannot by any possibility cordialise with an *ens rationis*—a thing which exists only in the mind. We love to see " ideal manhood closed in real men." [1] It is not beautiful abstractions, but good and true men and women, warm and pulsing with humanity, that win our affec-

[1] Tennyson.

tions. The more vividly their characters are depicted, the greater is their power to allure us to whatsoever things are lovely and of good report. We love them even in their weakness, perhaps because of it, and we are drawn to the ideal which they some-times attain and sometimes miss. On the other hand, the study of evil characters gives us that moral insight and practical guid-ance which only contrast can afford us. In Genesis there is no need for moralising or appealing or exhorting, for the story does its own work, the characters speak for themselves, and the moral effect is all the greater. The Bible easily surpasses all other books in skilful and truthful portraiture. " The characters in Scripture," as an eminent student of character has said, " are a literary marvel. It is very hard to write characters in one country to be popular in every land and age. Especially hard in narrative. Hardest of all to create such world-wide and everlasting characters in few words, a bare record of great things done and said. What the whole world outside Palestine could not do, this petty province did on a large scale." Its writers " all achieved a wonder. They sat down to record great deeds done, and great words spoken, and they told them wondrous briefly, yet so that immortal and world-wide char-acters rise like exhalations from the narrative. Written in the East, these characters live for ever in the West ; written in one province, they pervade the world ; penned in rude times, they are prized more and more as civilisation advances ; product of antiquity, they come home to the business and bosoms of men, women, and children in modern days. Then, is it any exaggera-tion to say that the characters of Scripture are a marvel of the mind ? " [1]

PATTERNS.—The narratives in Genesis are to a large extent transcripts from a vivid oral tradition. In times when there was no written word in Israel, tradition was the medium of religious instruction in Hebrew homes. The Divine Spirit made the

[1] Charles Reade.

recital of the sacred stories the means of arousing in the hearts of the young a living interest in the ancestral faith. The old traditions were necessarily recast and amplified again and again in accordance with the advancing requirements of successive ages. Where a sacred writer undertook to collect these traditions and weave them into a continuous narrative, he was animated, not by an antiquarian or æsthetic, but by a religious, motive. The moral and spiritual interest predominated in his mind. He went to work, not as a Percy gathering reliques, but as a man of prophetic spirit, mastered by great religious convictions, seeking to give his people spiritual light and leading by exhibiting to them a divine pattern of faith and duty, and for this purpose he used the sacred traditions which lay ready to his hand, modifying and supplementing them according to his prophetic principles, "breathing into them, or rather eliciting from them, important moral and spiritual truths, without taking away anything of their poetic character and the childlike simplicity of expression which belonged to them as they came from the lips of the people." [1] Sacred history was prophecy teaching by example. " The ancient traditions are moulded into forms of rare grace, dignity, and simplicity under prophetic influence. . . . The peculiar features and essential elements of the religious life are nowhere so vividly portrayed as in the living and breathing pictures of the patriarchs." [2] Genesis is far more than a book of origins. It contains not merely the roots, but the flowers and fruits of Hebrew faith. " The patriarchs are not inferior to the prophets of the eighth cent. B.C. in purity of religious insight and inward spiritual piety." [3] " If any man wishes to get a true idea of the conduct expected in ancient Israel of a just, upright, pious, sensible man, he must not first turn his attention to the Commandments in the Pentateuch. . . . We must first of all study the ideal figures of the Patriarchs, and the traits most prominent in the greatest religious characters of the earlier ages." [4] Thus, while we trace the footsteps of the heroes of faith, we shall be

[1] Dillmann.  [2] R. L. Ottley.  [3] Kuenen.  [4] Schultz.

under the guidance of men of prophetic inspiration. The collected and edited traditions are treasures of moral and spiritual truth for all time, because they are made to embody prophetic ideals, which are set forth for our imitation, admiration, and emulation. ".Look to your progress," says A Kempis, "that if you see or hear a good pattern set, you may be straight on fire to keep it."

## SEPARATION
### Genesis 12:1

> " Thou shalt leave each thing
> Beloved most dearly : this is the first shaft
> Shot from the bow of exile."—DANTE.

REVELATION.—The story of the Hebrews, which is the story of divine grace striving against human sin, begins in heaven rather than on earth. The stream of sacred history rises among the hills of God. Salvation must be traced back to Revelation. It was a divine movement towards the human race that formed the starting-point of a true religion. " The LORD spake unto Abram " (12[1]). " The God of glory appeared unto our father Abraham." [1] " God at the first did visit the Gentiles to take out of them a people for His name." [2] When we raise the question, How did Abram find God? the only adequate answer that can be given is, that God found Abram. God cannot be reached by human effort. It is not only difficult, but impossible, for men, left to their own resources, to find out God, and to retain Him in their knowledge. " If a man is to have aught of God, he can only receive it from God, who communicates Himself in love." [3] The development of a higher religion was due, not to the natural genius of the Hebrew race, but to the supernatural action of God upon the human soul. Abram was called by God ; the voice, impulse, light, inspiration, came to him from God ; he obeyed a summons, and his steps were directed by a

---

[1] Acts 7[2].    [2] Acts 15[14].    [3] Schultz.

wisdom not his own. Revelation is a direct influence of God on the souls of men which teaches them the truth in moral and spiritual things. Religion, which is on the human side a grand discovery, would be impossible but for the divine intervention. "No historian dealing with primitive days ever thinks of man as raising himself to God by his own act. From the first God is the Speaker, man the hearer. God reveals Himself; man reverently calls on His name. The religion of Israel came into existence by God speaking, commanding, and by man obeying and believing."[1] Nothing less than a spiritual vision of the divine glory and a heaven-born impulse towards righteousness is grand enough to break the ties which bind man to the world, and prepare him for the service of God.

DETACHMENT.—The Hebrews were to have impressed upon them the ineffaceable stamp of separateness. "Lo, the people shall dwell alone, and shall not be reckoned among the nations."[2] Abram is "the ideal representative of the life of faith and of separation from the idolatries of an evil world."[3] God's call to him detached him from his heathen environment. It was a command to leave his country, his kindred, and his father's house ($12^1$). The words are terribly clear, sharp, and stern. God is rigorous, severe, exacting in His demands, but this is the sternness of love. Life is so precious for Him, and character so grand, that He deems them worthy of the sharpest sacrifices. Fatherland, kindred, and home are sacred; there is scarcely aught that men will not do for them; the best literature of the world is a record of what men have done for them. There is just one thing which a man must not do even for country, kindred, and home; he must not for their sake lose his own soul. If we have to choose between everything on earth that the heart counts most dear and our obligation to God, the claims of earthly relationship must yield to the

1 Schultz.      2 Num. 23$^9$.      3 Ottley.

superior claims of God and duty, even though the surrender almost breaks the heart. The man who has once heard the divine call, and seen the heavenly vision, will allow no natural craving, no desire for personal pleasure, no prevailing customs, no counsel or entreaty of friends, to come in his way, but in defiance of custom and habit he will yield himself to the will of God. Separation from the world is the crux, the cross of true religion. "It is only with renunciation that life, properly speaking, can be said to begin."[1] But what is essential in this is the detachment of the heart. "Abram's renunciation," as Augustine observes, "was not the bodily removal, but the inward separation of the soul, from his worldly possessions." His change of locality would have effected little, had there not been at the same time a change in the condition of his heart. When God commanded His people to separate themselves, this was but a means to an end. Detachment from the creature is useless unless it leads to attachment to the Creator. God asks not only world-surrender, but self-surrender. The abiding ideal is not abstraction from the world, but protection from its evil; to be in the world without being of it; not to retire from the world, but "rather to retire from the world as it is man's, into the world as it is God's."[2] Religion is no mere negative thing —the quenching of the love of the temporal; it is a positive thing—the love of the Eternal. What we require for unworld-liness is not the pilgrim's staff and scrip, but the pilgrim's spirit of detachment, which we may have in our own quiet homes. Whatever injures the soul and impedes its service of God must be abandoned; and the passion of self-denial, of losing life to save it, of throwing it away in devotion to some high ideal, is what has made saints and martyrs and missionaries.

INDIVIDUALITY.—God's call to Abram individualised him. The summons was, "Get thee out *from* thy kindred," not "*with*

[1] Carlyle.                    [2] Cowley.

thy kindred " (12¹). " Look to Abraham your father," said the
LORD by the prophet Isaiah, " for I called him *alone*." ¹
Individuality was not only a national, but a personal ideal.
" These tales in Genesis teach us that it is an error to suppose
that ancient Israel was conscious only of God's relation to
Israel, for they speak everywhere of God's dealings with
individuals. We should rob many of the tales of all their
charm if we failed to appreciate this fact." ² Not only the
Hebrew race, but each Hebrew was called to be God's servant.
The Hebrew religion endowed every man with the right to say
" I." Aloneness is an essential element of true religion, which
is nothing if not personal. "Solitude is to character what
space is to the tree." As every man enters through the gate of
life alone, and will depart through the gate of death alone, so
in the decisive spiritual crises of life every man is alone. He
must repent and believe alone, he must bear his own burden
alone, he must give account of himself to God alone. There is
a sympathy which unites souls, but the singleness and loneliness of personality remains. " By degrees," said Newman, "we
begin to perceive that there are but two persons in the universe,
our own soul and the God who made it." The deeper a man's
spiritual life, the more lonely, secret, and incalculable it will be.
In all his great experiences Abram was " alone with the Alone,
one with One." ³ So long as a man shields himself behind others,
loses his individuality among the many, God's work cannot be
done in his soul. It is when he isolates himself, and lets God
speak as directly to him as if there were not another person in the
world, that the truth finds him. Nothing but a distinct personal
call addressed to the individual heart and conscience avails
to bring a man into a right relationship with God. " In the
solitary places of the human heart is to be found the meeting-
place of man with God." ⁴

EXPERIENCE.—While the divine call to Abram was sudden

¹ Isa. 51². ² Gunkel. ³ Dean Church. ⁴ James Seth.

and decisive, there lay behind it a moral and spiritual experience. A divine revelation does not dispense with certain qualities of heart and mind in the person who receives it. God does not reveal Himself to the indolent and the debased. His calls are preceded by a season of spiritual unrest and inward questioning, of heart-hunger and unsatisfied desire. "The relations of God to men were never mere objective calls to take a certain place and do a certain duty, there was always a personal element in them ; they were a crisis in the individual religious life. . . . That was the source of the power wielded over the masses of their fellow-men." [1] What conflicts a man has passed through ere God's clear call comes to him, how the providence of God has controlled his life, how his mind has exercised itself on questions of faith and duty, how he has battled with his doubts and fears till the knowledge of the living God has flashed upon his soul and laid a divine compulsion upon his conscience, how he has broken with the religion or irreligion of his fathers, and what he has endured inwardly and outwardly for conscience's sake—all this may remain untold. But his silent struggles and sorrows, known to himself and God, are, like roots and sap working underground, the secret power of his life. Abram is already quitting the land of Chaldea, like Pilgrim leaving the City of Destruction, when without prologue the tale begins. The seventy-five silent years in Ur, like the thirty silent years in Nazareth, are full of significance. The Bible gives us results rather than processes. But in every life of fellowship with God there has been a prevenient grace leading up to a spiritual crisis and victory.

FAITH.—Abram was called to leave a certainty for an uncertainty, to go forth to a land which the LORD promised to show him ($12^1$); and "by faith he obeyed, not knowing whither he went." [2] His faith was the sense of the unseen. By faith he ventured forth into the untried and unknown in obedience

[1] A. B. Davidson.     [2] Heb. $11^8$.

to a divine impulse and in reliance on divine guidance.
"What," said Augustine, "is faith, but to believe what you do
not see?" "Faith is the assurance of things hoped for, the
proving of things not seen."[1] Faith is sure of its destination,
but asks merely light enough for the next step. Its language is,
"He knoweth the way that I take,"[2] and—

> "Keep thou my feet; I do not ask to see
> The distant scene; one step enough for me."[3]

There is a venture, an *abandon*, in true faith, which has been
the secret of all the best lives lived on earth. "The life of
goodness, the ideal life, is necessarily a grand speculation, a
great leap in the dark. But its progress brings with it the
gradual conversion of the speculative peradventure into a
practical certainty."[4] The man of faith acts on the assumption,
which is also the assurance, that the best things which the heart
can conceive are real. He orders his life on the conviction that
God, the soul, and immortality are not imaginations, but facts—
that the ideal is the true. "That blessed thing which the Bible
calls faith is a state of soul in which the things of God become
glorious certainties."[5] Abram was through his faith the prince
of spiritual pioneers and pathfinders. He is called the father
of the faithful; and whosoever steps boldly forth into a dim
future, along an unknown path, taking as guide the known will
of God, in the expectation of finding a land of promise at the
end of the journey, is a partaker of Abram's faith. Not only
prophets, apostles, martyrs, pilgrim fathers, and Christian missionaries, but all who live as seeing the invisible, are of the
family of faithful Abraham.

HEBREWS.—The name "Eber," which is found in the "generations of Shem" ($11^{15}$), is an eponym from "Hebrew," like
Romulus from Rome. "The name *Hebrews* is usually explained

---

[1] Heb. $11^1$.  [2] Job $23^{10}$.  [3] Newman.
[4] James Seth.  [5] F. W. Robertson.

as those who have come from the far side of the Euphrates ;
and this remains the best explanation that has been given." [1]
The name is found for the first time in Gen. 14[13], where Abram
is called "the Hebrew"; and in this passage the Septuagint
has "Abram the *Crosser*." The name was applied by other
tribes to the Shemitic family that crossed the Great River and
settled in Canaan. The supposition that the name was given
by the Canaanites to a tribe which immigrated from the other
side of the *Jordan*, is unfounded. The crossing of the
Euphrates was an epoch-making event, like Cæsar's crossing
of the Rubicon or Columbus' crossing of the Atlantic. "There
is no cogent reason for doubting that the migration of Israel's
ancestors from Mesopotamia was the starting-point of a higher
faith"; [2] and the name "Hebrews" kept those who bore it for
ever mindful of their origin, at once humbling them and filling
them with gratitude. "Your fathers," said Joshua to them,
"dwelt of old time beyond the River, and served other gods." [3]
As Crossers the chosen people emerged from the darkness of
heathenism into the light of revelation, they passed from the
region and state of nature into the sphere of grace. In that
sense all the servants of God are Crossers.


# BLESSEDNESS
## Genesis 12:1-3

"There is in man a HIGHER than happiness : he can do without happiness,
and instead thereof have blessedness."—CARLYLE.

PROMISES.—The summons which Abram received to quit his
home and country was accompanied with seven generous promises (12[1-3]). The LORD did not send him forth to an unknown
land with no prospect but the cheerless one of perpetual exile.
He opened before him a vista of future blessings so immense

---

[1] Dillmann.          [2] Ottley.          [3] Josh. 24[2].

that the sacrifices and hardships of the present were unworthy to
be compared with the glory that should be revealed. As soon as
a man finds God, and consecrates his life to Him, his blessedness
begins. God purposes the highest good of His servants in every
task and trial to which He summons them. His calls are always
upward to a better, richer, fuller life ; and divine promises come
trooping in the footsteps of self-denial. God's commandments
are not grievous, and His promises are exceeding great and
precious. "God calls no man to a life of self-denial for its own
sake."[1] If we only let His sweet, stern spirit have its way with
us, we shall always find how gracious His will is. What looks
like the rigour of law quickly turns out to be the tenderness of
gospel. God's will has reference, first and last, to our best estate
and most assured happiness ; and for what He takes away,
He never fails to give a superabundant recompense. He never
requires us to do anything which it is not for our highest advantage to do. He so governs the world that sin is always loss,
godliness is great gain.

(1) PATRIOTISM.—God first promises Abram a country, calls
him to a land which He undertakes to show him ($12^1$). The
country thus mysteriously mentioned for the first time was to be
the inheritance of the chosen people, the scene of the most
momentous events in human history. God had destined the
land for the Hebrews, and the Hebrews for the land. He was to
make them the most ardent patriots the world has ever known.
Their country has been called "the least of all lands," being
much smaller even than little Greece, scarcely so large as Bel-
gium, and not much greater than Wales. But to the Hebrews it
was "a good land and a large";[2] a land of plenty, "flowing
with milk and honey";[3] "the land which He promised";[4]
"a land for which the LORD careth";[5] "an exceeding good
land";[6] "the land which is the glory of all lands."[7] It was a

---

[1] Henry Drummond.  [2] Ex. $3^8$.  [3] Num. $13^{27}$.
[4] Deut. $9^{28}$.  [5] Deut. $11^{12}$.  [6] Num. $14^7$.
[7] Ezek. $20^{6, 15}$.

land to love, and, if need be, to suffer and die for, as myriads did. To us it is the Holy Land, consecrated by a thousand memories—

> " Those holy fields
> Over whose acres walked those blessed feet
> Which " nineteen " hundred years ago were nailed
> For our advantage to the bitter cross." [1]

(2) NATIONALITY.—The LORD promised to make of Abram a great nation (12[2]). Abram's faith, received and cherished by his descendants, was by God's grace to weld the Hebrews into a great and strong people, who were once for all to give the world a true ideal of nationality. "It is a common Faith, a common Ideal, a common Spirit, which makes a nation. Victory, commerce, art, and science do not make a nation : God makes a nation." [2] The Hebrew kingdom in its palmy days was a theocracy, willingly and gladly governed by Jahveh, Lord of hosts. Theocracy is the ideal government, and nations are great in proportion as they approach the ideal. "Every human society," said Carlyle, "not either dead or hastening towards death, always is a theocracy." Green the historian tells us how essential it is to know " the intimate part religion plays in a nation's history, and how it joins itself to a people's life." A secular nation, based on self-interest, and held together by fear, is from the outset doomed to failure. "For that nation and kingdom that will not know Me shall perish ; yea, those nations shall be utterly wasted." [3] The Hebrews were invincible so long as the LORD was their God and they His people ; they became weak as water when they would not own His ways, and He left them to their own. The greatest empires have fallen to pieces, not for want of power, but for want of character, which means want of faith, want of God. There is nothing which a country needs more jealously to guard than its national faith, and its sense of dependence on God for greatness and prosperity. "Do we not hail in this less the energy

---

[1] Shakespeare.          [2] Charles Kingsley.          [3] Isa. 60[12].

and fortune of a race than the supreme direction of the Almighty?"[1]

> "God of the nations, spare us yet,
> Lest we forget, lest we forget."[2]

(3) BLESSEDNESS.—The LORD next promises that He will bless Abram ($12^2$). God puts pleasure in the forefront of a believer's right relations to Himself. Pleasure is an essential element in true religion. If a man's religion is not giving him pleasure, and more and more pleasure, there is something essentially wrong with his religion. Faith does not subtract from, but indefinitely adds to, the sum of human happiness. It is the reasoned conclusion, or the simple intuition, of the Hebrew thinkers and saints, that life is meant for happiness. Their Scriptures are full of beatitudes. " Happy is the people whose God is the LORD."[3] Blessedness is the keynote of their national songs.[4] It is absolutely certain that God wills us to be happy ; true religion is a well-spring of pure unmingled joy ; and our chief end, our highest good is to enjoy God. None have the same right and reason as believers have to say " Gaudeamus "—" Let us rejoice." The exquisite pleasure called blessedness, the gift of the blessed God to believing men, is a joy unspeakable, a song without words. This blessedness is promised, and must not be pursued for its own sake. God never commands or commends the search for pleasure. To hunt after happiness is the sure way to miss it. Blessedness is the fruit of faith, obedience, and self-denial. True self-surrender cannot be made for the sake of happiness, but once made it always leads on to blessedness. All other kinds of joy, springing from youth and beauty, health and wealth, are soon followed by dull satiety ; blessedness is perennial. It is inseparable from the ideal life of faith.

> "Live greatly ; so shalt thou enjoy
> Unknown capacities of joy."[5]

---

[1] Lord Rosebery.   [2] Kipling.   [3] Ps. $144^{15}$.
[4] Ps. $1^1$.   [5] Patmore.

(4) GREATNESS.—The LORD promised Abram a great name (12²). As "a mighty prince" (23⁶), as "the father of many nations" (17⁴), as "the father of all them that believe,"[1] as "the friend of God,"[2] his name became illustrious above almost all human names ; and to this day it is universally honoured by all Christians, Jews, and Moslems alike. His memory, his example, his spirit live for evermore. His grand ideal life is indestructible. His influence is intact, undiminished, pervasive, enduring. "The righteous shall be had in everlasting remembrance."[3] "We want to know more about this man than we do," said Max Müller, "but even with the little we know of him, he stands before us as a figure second only to One in the whole history of the world."

(5) SERVICE.—God next offers Abram the joy of service. The fifth promise takes rather the form of a command, "And be thou a blessing" (12² R.V.). Abram is to be the channel and bearer of divine blessing to others. He and his descendants are chosen not only for salvation, but for service. Religion is not a possession to keep, but a blessing to share, a light to diffuse, a life to communicate. Elect and highly-favoured men and nations are specially endowed and gifted that they may help and save and bless their fellows. Election is in order to mediation. We are not redeemed just to be happy ; we are saved to serve. "The election of some does not, as many complain, mean the proscription of others. Election was simply a method of procedure adopted by God's wisdom, by which He designed to fit the few for blessing the many, one for blessing all."[4] The believer is so blessed in himself that he has a surplus and overflow of blessing for others. "The greatest felicity that felicity hath," says Hooker, "is to spread and enlarge itself."

(6) PROTECTION.—The next promise to Abram was, " I will bless them that bless thee, and him that curseth thee will I curse " (12³). Jahveh completely identifies Himself with His people

---

[1] Rom. 4¹¹.  
[3] Ps. 112⁶.  
[2] Jas. 2²³.  
[4] Dr. Bruce.

in spirit, purpose, and effort. He makes common cause with them, so that He and they have common friends and common foes. So jealous is He of their reputation, rights, and honour, so close, both in joy and sorrow, is His union and sympathy with them, that whatsoever is done unto them is done unto Him, and will be rewarded or punished accordingly. Their defence is sure ; their lives are sacrosanct and inviolable ; for they are "bound in the bundle of life with the LORD their God."[1] A kindness done to them will in no wise lose its reward ; a word spoken against them, a hand lifted in opposition to them, is an outrage offered to their God, who resents it as His own. "For he that toucheth you toucheth the apple of His eye."[2] "In all their affliction He was afflicted, and the angel of His presence saved them."[3] This is a foreshadowing of the wonderful truth of the mystical union of the Saviour and His followers. "Inasmuch as ye have done it unto one of the least of these My brethren, ye have done it unto Me."[4]

(7) UNIVERSALISM.—The seventh and last promise is the most marvellous of all. God undertakes that in Abram all the families of the earth shall be blessed ($12^3$ $18^{18}$ $22^{18}$). "The sense is little altered if for 'be blessed' we render 'bless themselves,' *i.e.* wish for themselves the same blessings as Abraham and his seed are seen to enjoy."[5] In either case the Hebrew sphere of influence, like the divine purpose of grace, is regarded as conterminous with the human race. The Hebrews were not to be guilty of the exclusiveness which looks down with contempt upon all those who are outside a favoured caste. They were to cherish the largest sympathies, and to realise the wide sweep of the divine purpose. They had not the monopoly of God and His love ; they were not His favourites but His ministers ; His revelation came to them not merely as a message but as a mission ; they held the truth in trust for all mankind ; they were a light to lighten the nations ; through them the LORD'S way

[1] 1 Sam. $25^{29}$.  [2] Zech. $2^8$.  [3] Isa. $63^9$.
[4] Matt. $25^{40}$.  [5] A. B. Davidson.

was to be known upon earth, and His saving health among all nations.[1] The believing Hebrews were not the exclusive people they are sometimes represented to have been. They early recognised God's hand in universal history ; and when they knew the LORD their God to be the God of the whole earth, their monotheism led them straight to universalism. If there was one God, there was one humanity, and all the families of the earth must sooner or later begin to draw together, and ultimately enjoy the blessings of a common salvation. Thus "instead of exclusiveness there was a most expansive liberality in this first call to Abraham. It was connected with a wide purpose of mercy on behalf of mankind at large."[2] Our words of aspiration and prayer—

> "Through the great world far and wide
> Let there be light "—

have a modern ring ; yet they express the very ideal which thrilled the great heart of the Hebrew race in the glimmering dawn of history.

## WORSHIP
### Genesis 12:4-9

> "They have left unstained what there they found,
> Freedom to worship God."—FELICIA HEMANS.

OBEDIENCE.—The fulfilment of the divine purpose of grace depended upon man's response to the revealed will and electing love of God. Abram's characteristic was that in simple unhesitating faith he acted at once and to the fullest on every intimation of the divine will. Divine voices called him, visions beckoned him, instincts urged him ; and "he went, as the LORD had spoken unto him" (12[4]). His new faith was followed and verified by immediate action. As no selfish passion had hindered him from knowing God's will, no weakness hindered

---

[1] Ps. 67[2].                    [2] Thomas Chalmers.

him from doing it. The visions of the mind, the intimations of the conscience, the ideals of the heart, are converted into practice and experience by the actions of the will which issue in obedience. God gave the Hebrews no abstract truth, no light for the mere speculative intellect ; He gave a Revelation, not merely that men might *know* it, but that they might *go* by it. True religion is a willing, cheerful obedience to God. It is only when the will, the controlling faculty, is called into play that religion is actualised. Thomas Fuller more than two centuries ago divided mankind into three classes, intenders, endeavourers, and performers, these making an ascending scale. The Hebrews, whose ideal was to run in the way of God's commandments,[1] most significantly called the divine word a lamp, not unto the eyes, but unto the feet, and a light unto the path.[2] If we bravely advance through the darkness, we shall have the whole way of life illumined ; if we stand still, irresolute and fearful, we only waste the guiding light. Religion is an active progress along a highway revealed by the gleaming light of divine revelation.

> "Make me to go in the path of Thy commandments ;
> For therein do I delight." [3]

POWER.—When Abram was enjoined to leave his home and his friends, he would have given a sorry proof of his affection if he had refused the divine call for fear of displeasing his kindred. But he dared to obey at all costs, thinking only of his duty ; and then his power began. His faith conquered his kindred ; his example moved them to embrace his religion and become his fellow-pilgrims. He did not leave his native land alone. He was accompanied to Haran by his father Terah ($11^{31}$), and to Canaan by his wife Sarah and his nephew Lot ($12^5$) ; and there was a sequel in the migration of his brother Nahor and his household to Haran ($20^{20-23}$). They all shared his faith. It is when a man has the heroism to stand

---

[1] Ps. $119^{32}$.　　　[2] Ps. $119^{105}$.　　　[3] Ps. $119^{35}$.

morally and spiritually alone and independent, that he begins
to exercise a powerful influence over the lives of others. So
long as he is of the world he can do the world no good. Union
with the world is weakness, separation from it is strength.
Our loyalty to truth renders the greatest possible service to
our friends. When we are prepared for conscience' sake to
leave them, impulses of natural affection blend with motives
of spiritual grace to make them resolve to cast in their lot
with us and follow us on to the land of promise. Many a
man has found that by forsaking his friends for a season he
has gained them for ever. Every Pilgrim's Progress has a
sequel. Grace does not run in the blood, but the natural affection of the human heart is the oldest and strongest ally of
divine grace. Nothing is finer than to observe "grace working
together with nature, and example working together with prayer,
to draw forth the most blessed issues which this world can
see." [1]

LIBERTY.—Abram and his people "went forth to go into
the land of Canaan, and into the land of Canaan they came"
(12⁵). "We feel," says Professor Gunkel, "as we read Genesis,
that it has a melody of rhythmic numbers." The sacred words
quoted have a lightsome musical cadence, expressing the cheerful
alacrity with which the pilgrims sped along their way till they
reached their destined goal. There was a will and a way,
a purpose conceived and achieved, a journey bravely begun
and quickly done. Into the land of their dreams the pilgrims
came with a glorious sense of freedom, as men redeemed from
a cruel and evil world. Their manhood was liberated, their
souls were saved, their real life was begun. The old historian
understands his task right well, and gives us the impression
that through the power of faith the most arduous labours are
accomplished with ease. It is no part of his duty to magnify
difficulties or exhibit a pageant of bleeding hearts. What

[1] Kerr-Bain.

though between Chaldea and Canaan there were leagues of desert, a fierce sun overhead, wild beasts and hostile tribes hovering around. By God's grace the dangers are passed, the goal is reached, the labours and difficulties are speedily forgotten. Thus every believer follows the LORD his Deliverer, bating no jot of heart or hope, saying or singing—

> " He my Guide, my Guard, my Friend,
> Leads me to my journey's end."

SOULS.—Abram and Lot took with them " the souls that they had gotten in Haran" (12⁵). These " souls " were slaves, a class frequently mentioned in Genesis. They were " persons," not chattels or soulless machines. As a slave-owner Abram conformed to the ordinary Hebrew practice. Bond-service was one of the institutions of the Hebrews. But it is a significant fact that while a Roman master counted the "heads" of his servants, and an English master counts "hands," a Hebrew master counted "souls." The Hebrew master's servants were not only hands to work for him, and heads to think for him, but souls to be cared for by him and to be saved by God. True religion had the power of refining and sweetening all human relationships, and it breathed a new spirit into the relation between master and servant. It taught that God was the true Lord of human life, and that masters and slaves were alike His servants ; it stirred in the heart a new pity, tenderness, sympathy for weakness and suffering ; it inspired good men with feelings of reverence for the humblest of their fellow-men, and invested the meanest slave with a certain dignity. When the divine saying, " All souls are Mine," was once realised, it proved a grand humaniser. In comparison with pagan slavery, Hebrew bond-service was mild and gentle. When we think of Egyptian bondage, we think of crushing labour and cruel torture ; when we think of Roman slavery, we think of "the sum of all villainies." But the Hebrew master said of his slave, " Did not He that made me make him ? And did not One

fashion us in the womb?"[1]  With such a thought in his heart
he could not handle his servant harshly and ignominiously.
" Hebrew slaves were very humanely treated.  They were really
regarded as members of the family, for whose welfare the
master cared as for that of his own children . . . As co-
religionists they received a kind and paternal treatment."[2]
Thus the Hebrew ideal, without directly condemning the whole
system of slavery, so controlled and limited it as to divest it
of its greatest evils, and ultimately to undermine it.  " To
abolish slavery," says Ewald, " was not to be thought of; but
no ancient religion was ever so emphatically opposed to it,
or at least to all inhumanity connected with it, or made such
preparations for its overthrow."

REST.—Having entered Canaan, Abram passed through it
till he came "unto the place of Shechem" ($12^6$).  He lighted
on a spot which is all loveliness, fragrance, and delight.
Robinson says there is nothing in Palestine to compare with
it for beauty.  Stanley describes it as "a valley, green with
grass, gay with olives, gardens sloping down on each side,
fresh springs rushing down in all directions."  There Abram
and his companions rested and refreshed themselves after
their journey, pitching their tents under the sacred " oak of
Mamre,"—the oak of the Teacher or Oracle,—once the haunt
of some heathen soothsayer who interpreted the murmuring
wind and rustling leaves as the voice of a god.  " Oracles
and omens from trees are among the commonest among all
races. . . . The tree is believed to be the actual seat of a
god, and embodiment of a divine life."[3]  In this spot Abram
worshipped the LORD; it became a real presence-chamber,
where he bowed before his God, and where it was revealed
to him that God would give him the goodly land he had
entered as a personal possession.  This assurance was the
first reward of obedience.  To all His tired servants, worn

[1] Job 31[15].          [2] Benzinger.          [3] Robertson Smith.

with desert marches, God gives seasons of refreshing, "green spots on the path of time," valleys warm and sunny under the smile of heaven, where the memory of their journey and its hardships is obliterated. "He makes me to lie down in green pastures : He leads me beside still waters : He restores my soul." [1]

WORSHIP.—It was neither poverty, nor love of adventure, nor the migratory spirit of his age that impelled Abram to quit his native land. No sooner had he entered Canaan than he showed what had brought him to that distant scene. His first care was to build an altar to the LORD at Shechem ($12^7$). He set up a second on the hill to the east of Bethel ($12^8$), a third at Mamre ($13^{18}$), and at a later time he erected a fourth on Mount Moriah ($22^9$). He came to the new country seeking and finding freedom to worship God. It is important to note the characteristics of his worship. (1) It was *local*, without being limited to one sacred spot. The scene of a theophany was invested with special sanctity. Sacred associations will always make certain places dear to good men and helpful to their devotions ; and memory loves to linger where special mercies have been received. The place where the soul first knew God, where it had a special sense of His presence, where it consecrated itself to Him, will always be specially hallowed. But the Hebrews never speak of God as locally confined like the gods of the heathen. "The multitude of altars scattered over the country, if they did not suggest the positive idea of His ubiquity, suggested, at least, that there was no place where He might not let Himself be found." [2] (2) It was *vocal*. Abram "*called* upon the name of the LORD" ($12^8$). Mental prayer, silent adoration is good ; but vocal prayer does more to awaken and to sustain the spirit of devotion. Children all pray vocally, as nothing helps men so much to retain the childlike spirit through life as daily vocal prayer. (3) It was *simple*. Abram's

[1] Ps. $23^{2.3}$.          [2] A. B. Davidson.

worship was always an open-air service ; and his holy places were marked by nothing more than a rude cairn of unhewn stones, or a heap of earth covered with turf ; yet these were the precursors of all the temples, synagogues, churches, and domes in which his spiritual children have met to commune with God. However grand and inspiring the accompaniments and non-essentials of worship may be, the essence of it is always intensely simple. True worship is an attitude of the soul, a humble, reverent, thankful, adoring posture of the mind. It is entirely irrespective of place ; God cares no more for St. Peter's or St. Paul's than for a hillside. (4) It was *spiritual*. When Abram called upon the name of the LORD, he bowed himself before the Unseen, he lifted up his heart to the living God, without the aid of image or emblem, picture or symbol. He saw "no manner of form." The Godhead was represented by no art or man's device. The Hebrew saint worshipped neither man nor nature, neither stock nor stone ; his adoration went past all visible objects, all the gods of heathenism—sun, moon, and stars ; heaven, earth, and sea ; birds and beasts and fishes —to the Infinite. He worshipped the Invisible alone. Hebrew worship was the triumph of the spiritual over the material. (5) It was *reasonable*. Abram regarded his God, not with slavish terror, but with intelligent, loving reverence ; and the more his knowledge grew, the warmer grew his piety. Growing intelligence, which sooner or later leads all the heathen to become unbelievers in their gods, made the Hebrews ever firmer believers in their God. Reason abolishes false religion, but establishes true religion. God, the highest Reason, seeks a "reasonable service,"[1] and nothing else is holy and acceptable to Him.

[1] Rom. 12[1].

# TRUTH
## Genesis 12:10-20

" The truth, whatever the consequences may be, is what you owe to your country, and to that God whose word is truth, and whose name you have now invoked."—SCOTT.

DEPENDENCE.—Abram had not sojourned long in Canaan before "there was a famine in the land" ($12^{10}$). After tasting the pleasures of Shechem, he had an experience of utter want. He saw the Promised Land turned for a season into a wilderness. God showed him the best for the comfort of his spirit, and then the worst for the trial of his faith. Central Palestine is a tableland in which there are no perennial streams. Its surface is seamed with deep ravines, which are periodically flushed with roaring torrents ; but during the greater part of the year the bare white channels lie blistering in the sun. When the early and the latter rains fall in their due time, God gives healthful, fruitful, peaceful seasons. But drought is a constant menace. Sometimes no rain falls all the year round ; the heaven is as iron, the earth as brass, and no clouds drop fatness on the valleys ; the pastures, cornfields, and vineyards are dried up ; the cattle perish ; and little children cry in vain for bread and water. Three famines are mentioned in Genesis, one in Abram's, one in Isaac's, one in Jacob's time. God had a purpose whenever He turned the fruitful land into a desert. He taught His people by a sign that could not be mistaken that He was the Master of ocean and earth and sky, giving, sustaining, and withdrawing life at His pleasure ; and that His creatures who were dependent upon Him for life and breath were indebted to Him for all other things. "He suffered them to hunger . . . that they might know that man doth not live by bread alone, but by every word that proceedeth out of the mouth of God." [1]

WATCHFULNESS.—When the famine was sore in the land of

[1] Deut. $8^3$.

Canaan, "Abram went down into Egypt to sojourn there" ($12^{10}$).
All through their history Egypt was to the Hebrews the land of
temptation and witchery and danger. When they went thither
of their own accord, they always went down morally as well as
geographically. "Alas for them that walk to go down into
Egypt, and have not asked at My mouth!"[1] As Abram entered
Egypt, he imagined that his life was in imminent danger, and
instead of taking counsel with God and trusting wholly in His
protection, he resorted to scheming. He put his own shrewdness
in the place of Divine Providence. Every human being has his
vulnerable point, his Achilles' heel; and it is singular that a
man's subtlest temptations assail him, not where he is weakest,
but where he is strongest. Abram is called the father of the
faithful; faith was his special grace, his highest achievement,
and the secret of all his triumphs. Yet it was just by unfaithfulness that he erred and sinned. He was not tempted to passion
or lust or pride, hatred or ambition or idolatry. But he was
tempted to infidelity, and succumbed to the temptation. It is
recorded in history that Edinburgh Castle was supposed to be
inaccessible on the precipitous side, and there the defences were
feeble and the outlook careless, while on the weaker sides the
fortifications were strong and the watch was strictly kept. But
it was at the strongest, not the weakest point that the entrance
was effected and the citadel captured. It is also on the strongest
side that the citadel of man's soul is often captured. The weakness of God's servants is most conspicuous where their strength
lies. The sense of security is near akin to the haughty spirit
that goeth before a fall. Abram, the most faithful of men, sinned
by unfaithfulness; Moses, the meekest of men, by anger;
Solomon, the wisest, by folly; Elijah, the most valiant, by fear;
John, the gentlest, by vindictiveness; Peter, the bold, by
cowardice. Unguarded strength is double weakness. "We
are not to walk in all the footsteps of the saints, but only in
the footsteps of their faith."[2]

[1] Isa. $30^2$.     [2] Thomas Chalmers.

TRUTH.—Dillmann rightly observes that in the narrative of the sojourn in Egypt "the author presents Abram in an unfavourable light." We see the hero unheroic, the saint unsaintly. The tone and spirit of the story condemn his prevarication. The question whether the popular tradition ever had a different colour—praising and enjoying the patriarch's cleverness—does not at all concern us. The Bible never suggests that lying is good business and sharp practice to be admired and imitated. Abram's title was "the father of the faithful," and an essential part of fidelity is truthfulness. Our ideal English king, Alfred the Great, had as noble a title as Abram, being called "Alfred the truth-speaker." It is always a sorry, and sometimes a ludicrous, spectacle to see a man of faith attempting to play the part of a shrewd man of the world. The part does not suit him ; he handles but awkwardly the weapons of duplicity which less scrupulous men use as past masters. At the entrance to Egypt, Abram became the victim of fear. He thought that the princes of luxurious Egypt would kill him to get possession of his beautiful wife. His alarms were the offspring of his own imagination. In his trepidation he adopted an unworthy subterfuge to secure his own safety. He devised a scheme which he hoped Providence would aid and abet him in carrying out. His own arrangements took precedence of God's purposes. He trusted his self-activity more than the divine operations. God was to be fellow-worker with him, rather than he with God. The true course in all difficulties is to begin by taking counsel with God, to make sure of knowing His mind and will, and then to go bravely forward in His way, trusting Him to take charge of our life and open the gates before us. "Do not," said a modern hero of faith, "try planning and praying and then planning again ; it is not honouring to God."[1] Abram inverted the moral order of things ; he went in front of God, acting upon the prompting of his own self-will, instead of waiting upon God. If we cannot do a right thing to meet our difficulties, we should do

[1] General Gordon.

nothing. Our hurry and worry only interfere with God's working on our behalf. "In quietness and confidence shall be your strength." By taking one false step Abram quickly involved himself in a labyrinth of errors.

(1) He spoke *untruthfully*. He studied to suppress the truth and suggest what was false. He used words in a sense true, but with intent to deceive. Augustine defends him, pleading that "he spake of his sister, but did not deny his wife ; withheld part of the truth, but did not speak anything false." But the fact remains that he tried to convey a false impression, and succeeded in doing it. Truth-speaking is the representing of things *as they are*. A lie is anything said or done with intent to deceive. Silence may spell insincerity : *suppressio veri suggestio falsi*. We are not bound to gratify every idle curiosity, but we are bound to tell the truth which will materially affect another's moral conduct. The intention to deceive constitutes the essence of lying. "Behold, Thou desirest truth in the inward parts." [1]

> " Even to the truth
> Which but the semblance of a falsehood wears,
> A man should bar his lip." [2]

(2) Abram acted *presumptuously*. He counted on God assisting him to carry out a policy of deceit. Delitzsch represents him as "thinking that he would give the marriage honour of his wife as a sacrifice for his self-preservation." He did not sink so low as that ; he believed that his wife would be preserved from danger for the promises' sake. Still he did good that evil might come ; he thought the end justified the means ; and he was guilty of tempting the Lord his God. The protecting providence of God needs no aid of human sin ; His wisdom requires no supplement from our own wickedness. All tricks of policy, all compromises with error, all silence through fear of consequences, so far from assisting God, are hindrances which He has to overcome before He can help and save us. "The God who delivered

[1] Ps. 51[6].　　　　　　　　[2] Dante.

Abram in spite of his perversity would have delivered him had he committed himself in all fearlessness and truth to His holy keeping."[1]  (3) He acted *faithlessly*.  His anxious, restless, personal action was the opposite of faith.  His divided confidence, his resting partly on God and partly on self, his oscillating between faith and reason, indicated that the simplicity of trust was still too difficult for him.  He must build partly upon the sand and partly upon the rock.  On the few occasions on which Abram's activity took the form of scheming for himself, he fell far below the moral ideal.  Whenever he was content to watch and wait for divine direction, to live by faith, he attained the ideal.  (4) He acted *imprudently*.  His scheme was a blunder as well as a wrong, creating the very trouble which it was designed to prevent.  He would have avoided all danger had he told the simple truth.  Double-dealing is always shortsighted, and the sure precursor of shame.  The wise man is snared in his own craftiness, learning the folly of his wisdom and the feebleness of his strength.  In all self-reliance there lurks a perilous weakness.  It has been said that the raw material of a grossly foolish man is a very cautious man, who scents danger where there is none, and blunders egregiously when all is simple.  The morally right course is always the wisest.  "We too often forget the penetration of sincerity, the depth of simplicity, the cleverness of uprightness, the stategy of straightforwardness."[2]  "Above all things, truth beareth away the victory."[3]  (5) Abram acted *dishonourably*.  Pharaoh treated him well for Sarah's sake ($12^{16}$).  According to the custom of the country, the king sent a rich present to his prospective brother-in-law.  Sheep and oxen, asses and camels, men-servants and maid-servants arrived at the Hebrew camp; and Abram had by his crafty dealing placed himself in such a dilemma that he could not refuse the ill-gotten gain.  He did not keep his hands clean, he accepted gifts on false pretences.  It is well to see him with the blots and blemishes in his character, caused by lack of faith;

[1] Thomas Chalmers.　　　[2] W. L. Watkinson.　　　[3] 1 Esdr. $3^{12}$.

we are to see what the grace of God can make of him. The narrative shows "what the best of men are when they take to their own devices. As the minister of God, Abram is great and noble ; as the architect of his own fortune, he is cowardly, selfish, and false." [1]

DISCIPLINE.—With a fine sense of justice the author represents Pharaoh as speaking the word of truth and righteousness, which is always the word of God. The heathen king condemns the Hebrew patriarch's sin, and administers the judicial and merited rebuke. Deceived and indignant, he puts two or three pointed questions which cut through all quibbles. Abram is struck dumb, feeling that the reproach is just. Pharaoh has the last word ; and with kingly dignity and forbearance he bids the Hebrew behold his wife, take her, and go his way ($12^{19}$). Dishonoured before the royal court, Abram is required to leave Egyptian society as unworthy to be trusted, and with the stern words of rebuke ringing in his ears he turns back to Canaan, escorted on his way by Pharaoh's servants. Defeat and humiliation are wholesome. To be beaten and thwarted and compelled to see our shortcoming and failure—nothing is better than this for the soul. Our reverses drain us of our self-reliance and self-will, and throw us back upon the help of God. We cannot pay too high a price for the lessons of spiritual faith and moral fidelity. God disciplines us that we may learn that in morals as in geometry a straight line is the shortest distance between two given points, and that it is not our own grovelling wit, but simple obedience to the laws of heaven, which conducts us safely through the perplexities and difficulties of life. The purpose of all our defeats is to show us the excellence of the precept : "Trust in the LORD with all thine heart, and lean not upon thine own understanding : in all thy ways acknowledge Him, and He will direct thy paths." [2]

[1] Joseph Parker.      [2] Prov. $3^6$.

# DECISION
## Genesis 13

"Choose well ; your choice is
Brief and yet endless."—GOETHE.

WEALTH.—"Abraham was very rich in cattle, in silver, and in gold" (13²). His possessions were a blessing to him, because he recognised them to be the gift of God, because he had grace and wisdom to use them aright, and because he set his heart upon the true riches. "Say not in thine heart, My power and the might of mine hand hath gotten me this wealth. But thou shalt remember the LORD thy God : for it is He that giveth thee power to get wealth."[1] The man who recognises that his wealth is a loan from God, and deems it his duty and privilege to administer it as a trustee on behalf of others, never fails to get a blessing with it. Wealth in itself has no moral quality. The character is in the possessor, not in the possession. It is the waste and abuse, not the possession and use of wealth, that is to be reprobated. The gifts of God may be consecrated to noble ends, or prostituted to wicked uses. Not money, but the love of money, is the root of all kinds of evil.[2] There is a right, blessed, holy use of wealth ; and the consecration of property is the rich man's ideal. Wealth rightly administered is the means of diffusing immense happiness. Flowing into proper channels it assists the cause of God, of truth, of humanity. Wealth is power, and all power is dangerous if it is not wisely controlled and directed, beneficent if it is rightly governed. "Once get Abram's humble, noble, heavenly mind, and then set your heart upon making riches as much as you like. For the good that you will then be able to do all your days, both to yourself and to other men, will be simply incalculable."[3] But the story of the choice of Abram and Lot inculcates a high-minded indifference to *mere* wealth. While it proves how one man is unharmed by

[1] Deut. 8¹⁷·¹⁸.　　[2] 1 Tim. 6¹⁰.　　[3] Dr. Whyte.

his wealth, it shows how another is almost drowned in his. The purchase-power of riches is easily overrated. Wealth cannot procure "the best gifts." Youth and health cannot be bought. Friendship, peace, blessedness, the love of our fellow-men, the esteem of the wise and good, have no market price. The invaluable possessions are free to the poor as well as to the rich, to the rich as well as to the poor. God is no respecter of persons : "the rich and the poor meet together ; the LORD is the Maker of them all." [1] When Dives, who was punished, not for the possession, but for the abuse of wealth, lifted up his eyes in the place of torment, he saw Lazarus in Abraham's bosom—the man who on earth was miserably poor in blessed fellowship with the man who was "very rich," both enjoying their reward in Paradise.

RESTORATION.—From Egypt Abram returned to the South of Canaan, and advanced by slow steady marches "from the South even to Bethel, unto the place where his tent had been at the beginning, between Bethel and Ai ; unto the place of the altar, which he had made there at the first" (13³·⁴). This is not topography ; it is the story of a penitent soul. The pilgrim labours like the period. The very words are heavy with the yearning of an unquiet spirit to get back to God and itself, to live again the pure ideal life of faith as "at the beginning," to kneel at the altar of Bethel as "at the first." The holy place was the magnet that drew the traveller's soul. His flesh and heart cried out for the living God. Back from the temptations of Egypt, defeated and defiled, he returns to the old trysting-place on the clear heights of Bethel, and calls upon the name of the LORD (13⁴). On holy ground he recollects himself ; seeks restoration of soul in communion with God ; unburdens himself in prayer ; waits for new voices, intimations, revelations ; until at length he realises the blessedness of "the man in whose spirit is no guile, nor fraud is found therein." [2]

[1] Prov. 22².      [2] Ps. 32²

Whenever a blight falls upon a believing Hebrew's life, he can do nothing better than revisit the place where the LORD'S honour dwelleth.

> "O send out Thy light and Thy truth; let them lead me:
> Let them bring me to Thy holy hill.
> Then will I go unto the altar of God,
> Unto God my exceeding joy." [1]

FRIENDSHIP.—"And Lot also, who went with Abram, had flocks and herds and tents" ($13^5$). For a time these two men were inseparable. In Ur of the Chaldees and Haran, in Shechem and Bethel, in Mamre and Egypt, they and their households dwelt together as brethren in unity. Lot had felt the quickening touch of a loftier soul, the stimulus of a magnetic friendship; and the alluring visions of a grand faith had given a spiritual impulse to his pliant will. Lot never did a wiser thing than when he chose as his guide and counsellor and friend the man who for conscience' sake forsook his native land to be a stranger and pilgrim in the earth. "Our wisest plan," says Charles Kingsley, "is to choose our friends, not for their usefulness, but for their goodness; not for their worth to us, but for their worth in themselves; and to choose, if possible, people superior to ourselves. It is wise, it is ennobling to our own character, to choose our friends among those who are nearer to God than we are, more experienced in life, more strong and settled in character. Wise to have a friend of whom we are at first somewhat afraid; before whom we dare not say or do a foolish thing; whose just anger or contempt would be to us a terrible thing. Better it is that friendship should begin with a little wholesome fear, till time and mutual experience of each other's characters shall have brought about the perfect love which casts out fear." Abram was superior to Lot in years, in experience, in character. "Exactly in the degree in which you can find creatures greater than yourself, to look up to, in that degree you are ennobled yourself, and, in that degree

[1] Ps. $43^4$.

happy." [1] Lot was one of those good but weak men to whom, as they cannot stand alone, the sympathy, encouragement, and support of a strong friendship are indispensable. Well it had been for him had he been more conscious of his weakness, had he always realised that " two are better than one ; for if they fall, the one will lift up his fellow." [2]

DESTINY.—The unwisest thing that Lot ever did was to let the bickerings of his servants estrange him from his friend. "There was a strife between the herdmen of Abram's cattle and the herdmen of Lot's cattle" ($13^7$). The great herds got mixed ; the question of precedence at pastures and wells was a source of constant irritation ; the herdmen bandied angry words, giving as good as they got ; and words would soon have led to blows. The flames of strife once kindled burn fast and furiously. It lay with the masters to terminate the unseemly dispute, and this obligation brought out all the moral worth of the two men ; it revealed their true quality and temper. They were both converts from heathenism, and worshippers of the true God. But believing men have still fresh choices to make, choices which serve to show how far they have become detached from the world and holy unto the LORD. One man is indifferent to earthly gain, and avoids everything that can imperil his moral ideal. Another is allured by a vision of earthly happiness, and, hastening to be rich and careless of danger, "falls into a temptation and a snare, and many foolish and hurtful lusts." [3] An unexpected trial proves how men's minds have been growing in the slow course of silent years. Suddenly, stealthily the crisis comes, and before they realise what has happened, they have cast the die, and for good or evil made a decision which seals their destiny.

> " And the choice goes by for ever,
> 'Twixt the darkness and the light." [4]

---

[1] Ruskin.        [2] Eccles. $4^{10}$.        [3] 1 Tim. $6^9$.        [4] Lowell.

BROTHERHOOD.—Abram acted the noble part of a peace-maker. His calm, strong figure rebuked all petty feelings. In the midst of strife he was tranquil and self-possessed, his speech was gentle and courteous. He avoided the causes in which discord originates ; he was free from pride, unkindness, selfishness, and ambition. He lived among the high things of life, and on those altitudes he was calm. Speaking with the meekness of wisdom and the gentleness of faith, he deprecated strife between brethren ($13^8$). The name of brother carries with it a sweet and delectable sound, and is in itself an argument for peace. It is true that the complication of interests strangely relaxes the fraternal tie ; brethren pursuing their fortune by the same path often jostle and hinder one another ; but a common faith originates a true and perfect brotherhood, which nothing should ever be allowed to disturb. The beautiful ideal of brotherly kindness is always a reason for peace. Fraternal discord is an odious spectacle. Strife between those who should be friends is more grievous than an outbreak of plague. If brethren or their households cannot live quietly together, let them quietly separate ($13^9$). "The beginning of strife is as when one letteth out water : therefore leave off contention before there be quarrelling." [1] The world is wide ; there is air and sunshine for everybody ; there is healing in new scenery and surroundings. Quarrels among brethren are always unnatural, and in the presence of unbelievers—the Canaanite and the Perizzite in the land—unspeakably mischievous. There is always a common foe around us, within earshot of our brawling and controversy, rejoicing in our internecine warfare, and watching for our fall. On the other hand, it is beautiful and impressive when men who are united by a common faith and hope live in love and peace. "Behold, how good and how pleasant it is for brethren to dwell together in unity ! " [2]

> " Religion should extinguish strife,
> And make a calm of human life." [3]

[1] Prov. $17^{14}$.      [2] Ps. $133^1$.      [3] Cowper.

RENUNCIATION.—Whether as senior partner in business or as chief of the Hebrew clan, Abram might have dictated terms to his nephew. But he waived his own rights and claims and privileges. He was meek when he might have been masterful. He was actuated by the love which seeks not its own, which rejoices in the promotion of others, and gladly takes the lower room. Out of the fulness of his heart, and not from any thought of being magnanimous, he made the proposal that his nephew should take the choice of the land, and promised to be content with whatever was left (13⁹). He acted, not as one who was painfully denying himself the delights of the world, but rather as one who was unconscious of the existence of any attractions or pleasures which were worthy of his notice. His disinterestedness was the more beautiful in contrast to Lot's self-seeking. In Abram aspiration was predominant, in Lot ambition ; Abram coveted righteousness, Lot success. Abram had given up the world in a passion of holy love to God, and now it was easy to give up what to his nephew seemed an earthly paradise. Life with its alternatives and possibilities presents the inevitable necessity of choice. The freedom of the will, involving the duty of personal decision, is the privilege and responsibility with which God endows every man. It is a critical moment when a man has to make one of the supreme decisions of life. Abram's choice was to have no choice. He could be indifferent to wealth in the consciousness of the value of God's friendship. When "Lot chose him all the plain of Jordan," Abram dwelt in the bare uplands of Canaan (13¹¹. ¹²). Every noble life can be traced to some great renunciation, and every ignoble life to a "great refusal." The alternatives are always essentially the same— duty and pleasure, the austerity of Canaan and the luxury of Sodom. The moral problem is complicated when the choice lies, not between the bad and the good, but between the good and the best. The story of the renunciation of the good and the choice of the best never fails to thrill every generous heart, to which a true example of disinterestedness is an inspiration.

The Greeks had their legend of the choice of Hercules, who preferred the rough path of virtue and spurned the allurements of the way of pleasure. The Moslems have no other tale so fine as that of young Mohammed standing on the brow of Mount Selahie, gazing long with ravished eyes upon the gorgeous city of Damascus, and then turning away with the words, " Man has but one Paradise, and mine is fixed above." But the Hebrews have left us the noblest examples of men who with a light heart renounced all earthly advantages because they knew the things which were superexcellent. Abram's children in modern times are men like Henry Martyn and John Cairns, who lightly abjured the dazzling splendour of the highest rewards and honours, because their hearts were satisfied with the service and love of God.

DECISION.—An important decision is never an isolated act, it is the epitome of a life. The desire which seems to arise in a moment has its roots in our whole past history. Character is condensed into a single concrete act. Hence Lot's choice is full of instruction and warning. He was not slow to seize the advantage offered him by Abram's generosity ; no sense of gratitude, no rush of right feeling, impelled him to reject the magnanimous offer. From the hill of Bethel on which the two men stood, Lot cast his eyes over the broad Circle of Jordan, where, on both sides of the winding river, lay the richest pasture-lands of the country, bringing to his mind the proverbial beauty of Eden and the green fields of Zoar in Egypt. The sweet valley, with its luscious herbage and shining waters, was very alluring to one in whom the lust of the eye was very strong. The picture presented itself to his fancy with a mighty allurement which he could not resist ; it worked like magic, and promised him infinite happiness and joy. His ruling passion was covetousness, and his only course of safety lay in avoiding all the avenues and approaches to this particular sin. But his eye was dazzled, his mind was engrossed, by the outward appearances of things ; and

"Lot chose him all the Plain of Jordan" ($13^{11}$). He was not in the least conscious that a solemn and awful crisis in his life had come; he did not pause to think well over the new paths he must tread; he cast no prescient glance into the future. He did not wait to let God choose for him. It is not the temptations which meet men, but the temptations which they go to meet, that imperil their moral life; and Lot entered the magic "Circle" with open eyes. The character of the men of Sodom was already notorious, the dangers involved in associating with them were apparent; but Lot was resolved to run the risks for the sake of capturing the prizes. Across all moral obstacles he would drive to his goal. "For the sake of gain, do we not put aside all considerations of principle as unseasonable and almost absurd?"[1] Had Lot's vision not been strangely impaired and distorted by avarice, he would have seen, not a well-watered plain, but a whirlpool of iniquity that would suck the strongest into its depths. Had he known the subtle perils of city life, he would have thanked God for the safety of his tent. His fateful decision, his choice which was a mischoice, on the hill of Bethel, illustrates Augustine's well-known history of a temptation in four words: *cogitatio, imaginatio, delectatio, assensio*—a thought, a picture, a fascination, a fall. Lot did not, however, go straight to Sodom; he approached it by a finely graduated process of descent. There was no apparent rashness or impulsiveness in his action; his downward path was so gradual and gentle that it seemed quite natural and safe. The whole history of his declension, from first to last, is summed up in four sentences. He looked toward Sodom ($13^{10}$). He "pitched his tent toward Sodom" ($13^{12}$). He "dwelt in Sodom" ($14^{12}$). "He lingered" in Sodom ($19^{16}$). "Sow a thought," says Thackeray, "reap an act; sow an act, reap a habit; sow a habit, reap character; sow character, reap destiny."

PARADISE.—The Plain or Circle of Jordan was so beautiful

[1] Newman.

that Lot almost doubted if Eden were more fair. As he viewed it from the hills of Canaan it looked "like the garden of the Lord," the lost Paradise of the race ($13^{10}$). It charmed his eye and feasted his imagination. Distance lent enchantment to the view ; but on closer inspection Lot found that the green plains of Sodom were not the sweet fields of Eden. Sin had entered that demi-paradise, and changed it into a pandemonium. The beauty of nature did nothing to save men from impurity of affections, imagination, language, and behaviour. "The men of Sodom were wicked, and sinners against the Lord exceedingly" ($13^{13}$). It was one of many scenes "where every prospect pleases, and only man is vile." Socialists cherish the idea that if man were placed in good surroundings, he must himself become good ; and they clamour for an experiment. As a matter of fact, Nature has often made the experiment. Times out of number she has created for men a perfect environment. She made the Circle of Jordan a dream of beauty and fertility, and gave the people "fulness of bread and abundance of leisure."[1] But the result was not satisfactory. The inhabitants of this other Eden were infamously base. Neither the beauty nor the bounty of Nature restrains the sinful passions of men. An earthly paradise does not produce ideal lives. If the ashes of Sodom or the ruins of Pompeii could speak, they would warn us that in the very sanctuaries of Nature he that is filthy will be filthy still. Man's first and imperative requirement is not the production of a new environment about him, but the creation of a clean heart and the renewing of a right spirit within him. Purity of heart is Paradise restored.

RECOMPENSE.—"Abram's beautiful and glorious example of love to our neighbour"[2] kindled no spark of gratitude in Lot's cold heart. Oftentimes kindness elicits no response ; goodness wins no honour or applause ; charity and self-denial seem to be wasted ; and generosity begins to wear a different aspect when

[1] Ezek. $16^{49}$.     [2] Luther.

its benefactions are accepted as if they were a birthright. Keen is the grief which comes from unrequited affections and unappreciated aims ; and many are tempted to ask, "Why should we be kind to the selfish and the ungrateful?" But there is a high chivalry which refuses to entertain such questions, and nothing will ever prevent the sons of the Most High from being "kind to the unthankful and evil." Love is pure and uncalculating ; it has no selfish aim. Nevertheless, Greatheart has his reward, though not of men. It is God whom he serves and by whom he is requited. Immediately after the departure of Lot the LORD revealed Himself to Abram, and assured him of a recompense. Abram had refused to choose, and was willing to forego every advantage ; but God had chosen for him, and would maintain his lot. God would give the whole of that beautiful land to Abram and his descendants, and make his seed like the dust of the earth ($13^{14-16}$). For all who are generous and self-denying God has prepared an unimagined happiness. There is much to be endured and much to be given up in His service, but whatever He makes it our duty He also makes it our interest to do. We may not always see this, and the world would cease to be a scene of probation if it were always manifestly our advantage to follow the noble and generous course. Virtue does not always carry a material bribe in her hand, and it is the apparent conflict between duty and interest that makes it hard to yield to the pleadings of conscience. But the conflict is only apparent. Our interest is always on the side of duty. The soul of the world is just. God gives measure for measure. "He that watereth shall be watered also himself." [1] "Verily there is a reward for the righteous." [2] The balance soon adjusts itself ; there are equivalents and compensations for all deprivations. No act of self-sacrifice, prompted by love, will pass unrewarded. "Say ye of the righteous, that it shall be well with him." [3] Because God is just, and the world is governed reasonably, goodness and blessedness in the end coincide. We lose nothing by making a sacrifice,

[1] Prov. $11^{25}$.      [2] Ps. $58^{11}$.      [3] Isa. $3^{10}$.

but receive an hundredfold.  Man's ingratitude is a foil to God's grace.  John Calvin said when he was banished from the city of Geneva, which he had loved and served so well, " Certainly, if I had merely served men, this would have been a poor recompense; but it is my happiness that I have served Him who never fails to reward His servants to the full extent of His promise."

## WARFARE
### Genesis 14:1-16

" War is the foundation of all the high virtues and faculties of men."

RUSKIN.

VICTORY.—The fourteenth chapter of Genesis echoes with the din of warfare.  Two campaigns are described in language so terse and vivid that the reader can scarcely avoid catching the excitement of the field.  For the merits of clearness, force, brightness, and simplicity, the narrative style of Genesis has never been surpassed.  This story bears the marks of an ancient date, and some scholars have suggested that it may be a chapter from the lost *Book of the Wars of Jahveh*.[1]  Four kings of the East, *i.e.* from beyond the Euphrates, under the leadership of Chedorlaomer, made war upon the five kings of the Circle of Jordan, who had attempted to throw off the suzerainty of the king of Elam.  The invading army came down the eastern side of the Jordan, harrying the homesteads of the primitive tribes whose lands they traversed, and advanced as far as the Arabian desert.  Thence they turned back, swept round the south end of the Dead Sea, spoiled the oasis of Engedi,[2] and at length encountered the army of the Pentapolis in the bituminous vale of Siddim.  Gaining a complete victory, the invaders entered the cities of the Plain, plundered Sodom, the richest of the five, and retired northwards along the western bank of the Jordan, laden

[1] Num. 21¹⁴.        [2] Or Hazezon-tamar, 2 Chron. 20².

with spoils, and leading many captives in their train.  But their victory was quickly turned into ignominious defeat and disaster. For Abram the Hebrew, receiving tidings that Lot was among the captives, speedily mustered a band of three hundred and eighteen retainers, called his three Amorite confederates to his aid, and hastened in the track of the invaders.  After a pursuit of a hundred and twenty miles he scouted the enemy among the hills of Dan by the springs of the Jordan, and lay concealed till night-fall, when, dividing his slender forces into companies, he made a sudden and impetuous onset, from different sides at once, upon the careless sleepers, drove them in headlong panic, and did not abandon the pursuit till he had rescued all the captives and recovered all the spoils.

WARFARE.—Abram the Hebrew left his people an ideal of noble warfare and high chivalry.  He is the type of all those heroes of faith, mighty men of valour animated by the spirit of God, by whom brave deeds were done for the glory of God and the cause of liberty.  Age after age the story of his prowess was told to infuse into the young Hebrews the spirit of valour, magnanimity, and contempt of fear.  Good men never love war for its own sake ; but so long as the weak and innocent are oppressed by the strong, there will be need for deeds of daring rectitude, and war will be a sacred duty.  " We must look at war with manly eyes," said Martin Luther.  When the tyrant fights for lust of bloodshed, glory, and spoil, God raises up the true hero to lay the tyrant in the dust.  Sympathy for the weak turns peaceful men against their will into men of strife.  Conscience imposes on them the task of war.  The noble impulse to succour the distressed, to liberate the captive, to raise the fallen, has been the motive to heroic deeds in all ages.  The most peace-loving man who willingly turns his own cheek to the smiter, cannot stand quietly by and see his brethren done to death while he has power to rescue them.  Lawless war makes war lawful.  The same law of humanity which requires a nation to punish one

criminal, requires it to repress ten thousand, and that is war. If
we justly punish every thief, we cannot in consistency allow a
whole land to be devastated by a horde of armed invaders.
"Justice and duty require princes to keep themselves armed,
and to enter into defensive leagues, as Abram did, for the
purpose of repelling attacks and incursions."[1]  War is a
stern, serious, tragically earnest business, which never fails
to bring many calamities in its train ; but it is not the worst
evil.  It is better than

> "a peace that is full of wrongs,
> Horrible, hateful, monstrous, not to be told."[2]

The Hebrews believed that in every just quarrel the LORD of
hosts was with them,[3] that they were fighting the battles of the
LORD,[4] whose spirit came upon them to arouse them to action,[5]
who taught their hands to war and their fingers to fight,[6] who
girded them with strength for battle,[7] who went forth with their
hosts,[8] whose right hand and holy arm got Him the victory.[9]
Their true successors are the Christian soldiers of to-day who
contend for justice and liberty and humanity.  Dan, the scene
of Abram's triumph, was the first of many fields of honour in
Canaan—Jericho, Michmash, Bethhoron, Kishon, Mizpah, Jezreel,
Bethbarah, Aphek—where the Hebrews won great victories,
renowned in legend and song.  The memories of battles fought
for liberty are among a nation's best traditions, and consecrate
a land scarcely less than its altars.  The appropriate limits of
the Holy Land—Dan and Beersheba—were a battlefield and a
shrine.  Valour and faith are the springs of all that is most
glorious and inspiring in a nation's history.  "The man is little
to be envied whose patriotism would not gain force upon the
plain of Marathon, or whose piety would not grow warmer
among the ruins of Iona."[10]

1 Calvin.      2 Tennyson.      3 2 Chron. 32⁸.      4 1 Sam. 25²⁸.
5 Judg. 6³⁴.   6 Ps. 144¹.      7 Ps. 18³⁹.       8 Ps. 108¹¹.
9 Ps. 98¹.     10 Samuel Johnson.

BROTHERHOOD.—Abram gives the Hebrews an ideal of true brotherhood and its offices. The invaders "took Lot, Abram's brother's son. . . . And when Abram heard that his brother was taken captive, he led forth his trained men" (14¹². ¹⁴). In ancient days the only protection for life and property lay in a man's willingness to defend his kinsmen, and avenge the injuries done them. Every male relative, every man of the same tribe or people, was a brother.¹ It was the thought of a brother in chains that stirred Abram's heart. There had been no drying up of the springs of his affection, and no selfish indolence repressed his exertions on behalf of his brother. Though he was formally separated from Lot, he was still knit closely to him by natural and spiritual bonds of fraternity. He could not be unmoved by the thought of his brother's suffering, or indifferent to his fate. He counted his brother's welfare as sacred as his own. The same ideal of brotherhood which but lately made him a peacemaker (13⁸), now transforms him into a man of war, intense and ardent, swift to move and strong to smite, with "a brow for a noble cause." Love is changeless, though circumstances modify its offices. "A brother is born for adversity,"² and never asks the question, "Am I my brother's keeper?" Dangers which expose a false and hollow friendship reveal a true brotherhood. In the darkest hours the lamp of love shines the brightest. Abram was ready to seek his brother's welfare by every service and sacrifice which love could inspire. Practical sympathy which is willing to dare and do all things is the proof of brotherhood. Abram might have left his nephew to the consequences of his avarice and selfishness: Lot thought he could do without him, let him try. But Abram was too magnanimous to fail his old friend in time of need ; Lot should feel the grasp of a brother's hand, and know that love is unaffected by the breath of change. It has been said that our moral rank is determined by the returns we make for good and evil. To return good for evil is Godlike ; good for good, manlike ; evil for evil, beastlike ; evil for good,

¹ Gesenius.                    ² Prov. 17¹⁷.

devil-like. There could be no doubt about Abram's moral rank. He forgot his brother's great errors, and thought only of his sore need ; and like some "very perfect gentle knight" of modern chivalry, took his life in his hand and valiantly went forth to redress the wrong.

VALOUR.—Abram the pursuer of invaders, the rescuer of captives, the victor in battle, who made the pride of Eastern kings bite the dust, was the same man who feebly shuffled for his own safety among the princes of Egypt. He was the same, and yet not the same. Out of weakness he was made strong. By the courage of faith the peaceful shepherd was transformed into a military hero, fit for noble enterprises ; by faith he " waxed valiant in fight, put to flight the armies of the aliens." [1]   His valour was derived from a lofty faith in God.   There is a kind of fortitude, much admired among men, which has little moral value ; an instinctive animal courage, a physical delight in danger —the bravery of the savage.   But Abram's valour is much more than strength of nerve, more than reckless defiance of danger ; it is courage of soul, begotten of calm trust in the living God. To this high courage God gives the victory. The first, typical battle-story in the Bible teaches us that Providence does *not* fight on the side of the strongest battalions. "There is no restraint to the LORD to save by many or by few." [2]   He gives the conquest to the weak.   Moral power, the might of right, counts for much in the armies of the living God.   The courage of the mind is always in the long-run more than a match for the courage of the sword. "Thrice is he armed that hath his quarrel just."

SERVICE.—Abram "led forth his trained men, born in his house, three hundred and eighteen, and pursued as far as Dan. And he divided himself against them by night, he and his servants, and smote them" (14[14. 15]).   It was the rank and file who

[1] Heb. 11[34].          [2] 1 Sam. 14[6].

won the battle. Abram's retainers were all first-rate fighting men. They were slaves, born thrall to Abram the Hebrew, but they had none of the qualities of slaves. What's in a name? No freemen ever fought with greater spirit than these serfs. They were "home-born" ($14^{14}$), slaves of the best class, trained under their master's eye from childhood. They loved and trusted their master ; they were loved and trusted by their master. It is true they were not their own, and their labours were not formally requited. But they knew nothing of grinding toil, or burdens too heavy to bear, or the lash of the taskmaster, or the open slave-market, or the other horrors of pagan slavery. They were trained men—trained in habits of obedience, order, respect for authority, mutual trust, and co-operation. Inured to heat and cold, to wind and sun, to hardships and dangers, they were sinewy, vigorous, valorous young men. Best of all, they shared their master's faith. He commanded his household that they should know the way of the LORD ($18^{19}$). True religion does not unfit men for hard fighting. " I know nothing," said Oliver Cromwell, "that will give courage and confidence in battle as a knowledge of God in Christ will." Abram's retainers and Cromwell's Ironsides afford sufficient proof that faith and fortitude go hand in hand.

LEADERSHIP.—Abram displayed high qualities of leadership in the mustering and disposition of his forces. His own trained men were at his beck and call, and his magnetic influence over strangers is evidenced by the ease with which he attracted the Amorite princes to his side.

> " These valiant chiefs their sympathy declare,
> And pledge their faith his righteous cause to share." [1]

When Abram had sighted the enemy, he divided his men into companies, which simultaneously fell upon the enemy by night from different sides, and struck a panic terror into their hearts.

[1] Cædmon.

The Hebrew flockmaster proved himself a born leader of men, an untaught master of strategy. He adopted the tactics afterwards employed by Gideon[1] and Saul,[2] and in other lands by such experts in the art of war as Cæsar and Napoleon. The rapid march, the division of forces, the sudden irresistible onset, enabled him to gain a victory which he could hardly have achieved in a pitched battle. Untutored valour fighting for a good cause has often been more than a match for military science. There are many historical parallels to the Hebrew shepherd's achievement. Cromwell was a common farmer till he was past middle life ; but when he had once taken up arms, he proved himself a consummate leader of armies, the greatest soldier whom Britain has ever produced.

DISCIPLINE.—The men of the East "took Lot, Abram's brother's son, who dwelt in Sodom, and departed . . . and Abram brought again his brother Lot and his goods" ($14^{12.\ 16}$). Lot had the opportunity of terminating his unholy connection with Sodom. The thought of renewing his separation from the world was forced upon him. He had been chastised for his worldliness, had been roused from his false peace and gross content by the rude shocks of war, had seen his imaginary Eden made desolate, and found that "riches certainly make themselves wings and fly away."[3] He had shared the fate of his chosen companions ; and, but for the valour of his tried friend, would have ended his days in heathen captivity. God had troubled, startled, shaken him ; spoiled his pleasure and dissipated his dreams ; vexed his heart and soul. Well for him had he then emerged from Sodom with strong crying and tears. But when the chance of a happy release from worldly entanglements, and of return to the peaceful separate life was presented to him, he let it go. There is a fatal fascination in sin—a kind of insanity, so that, against his reason, against his true interests, a man will follow that which he knows will injure him ; and neither the

[1] Judg. $7^{16\cdot19}$.　　[2] 1 Sam. $11^{11}$.　　[3] Prov. $23^5$.

terror of the LORD drives him, nor the goodness of the LORD leads him, to repentance. Lot had fallen in love with inglorious ease ; Sodom's "fulness of bread and abundance of leisure"[1] had become indispensable to him ; his family had formed pleasant associations in the Circle ; and though his righteous soul was vexed by the evil life of the city, he could not again become a stranger and a pilgrim in the earth. He could not, because he would not. Compromises and compliances had become part of his nature. The shudder of fear passed quickly away, and, like a bird that has been rescued from the fowler's snare and straightway returns to it, Lot went back to Sodom. This is the tragedy of human life that " we see the better course and approve it, but follow the worse."

# PEACE
## Genesis 14:17-20

'' His face wore
The utter peace of one whose life is hid
In God's own hand."—H. A. KING.

FELLOWSHIP. — Abram's return from Dan was marked by events no less striking than the campaign itself. The report of his victory had gone before him, and he received a singular " welcome home." In the vale of Shaveh he was met by Melchizedek, king of Salem, priest of the Most High God, who brought forth bread and wine for the wearied troops, invoked the divine blessing on the conqueror, gave thanks to God Most High who had given the victory, and received from Abram the tenth part of the spoils of war ($14^{18-20}$). The two men who thus interchanged good offices belonged to different branches of the human family, Abram the Hebrew being Shemitic, and Melchizedek, if a Canaanite, Hamitic. Their paths had never crossed before. Abram came from the far East, Melchizedek from no

[1] Ezek. $16^{49}$.

one knew where. But they found a bond of fellowship and brotherhood in their common faith. They believed in El Elyon, God Most High. They were akin, not after the flesh, but after the spirit, and they needed no introduction to one another. " Between simple and noble persons there is always a quick intelligence : they recognise at sight." [1] Abram and Melchizedek were both heroes of faith, kings of men by divine right, born to rule because they had great souls, receiving the homage which is yielded to real superiority not to official claims, exercising an authority that rested on character, laying men under the spell of a great manhood. Theirs was "a kingship of the inevitable kind, whether crowned or not." [2] When they met and looked in each other's eyes, at once soul recognised soul. They embraced in God. What " father or mother or lineage " they had was a matter of no moment ; of one of them it is said that he had none.[3] " If it is a happiness to be nobly descended, it is no less to have so much merit that nobody inquires whether you are so or not." [4] Genius and grace have no genealogy.

> " There is neither East nor West, Border, nor Breed, nor Birth,
> When two strong men stand face to face, though they came from
> the ends of the earth."

As Melchizedek and Abram met, so they parted, grateful for a little of each other's fellowship, yet nobly independent. The best friends in the world are unnecessary to one another ; for each of them El Elyon—God Most High—is enough.

KINGSHIP.—Melchizedek's government at Salem is a miniature theocracy. He is a priest upon a throne, a royal priest or priestly king, a religious as well as a political ruler, having both the temporal and the spiritual power vested in him. He is clothed with the attributes which adorn both offices. Alike his royalty and his priesthood are of the texture of his character. He is a king by his intrinsic excellence, his commanding per-

[1] Emerson.　　　[2] Ruskin.　　　[3] Heb. 7[3].　　　[4] La Bruyere.

sonal influence, his native might and majesty. His claims rest
upon no hereditary descent. He is a true king—the guardian,
the leader, the father of his people. His priesthood hallows his
kingship. He governs wisely, establishes righteousness, loves
peace, observes the moral law in his own person, seeks to have
the lives of his subjects moulded by faith in the Most High, and
so makes civil order and personal conduct an expression of the
will of God. He is the ideal king of righteousness, and he
reigns in the City of Peace. A special sanctity attaches to his
character, a special virtue to his blessing. He is greater than
Abram, for "without any dispute the less is blessed of the
better."[1] The secular and military power is consecrated by the
religious sanctions wielded by the priesthood. These are the few
ideas associated with the name of Melchizedek. He vanishes
and leaves no peer, but not before he has created a new order of
manhood ; and among the Hebrews he begins to have the power
of an endless life. Being dead, he yet continued to speak. He
was not merely a historical figure, but had a significance far
beyond himself. His was the kind of personality that furnished
the Hebrews with their ideals. They were an idealising race.
They viewed the grand figures and events of their history in the
light of God's declared purpose of love, and out of the existing
materials, by a high and sacred use of the imagination, they
fashioned ideals which they believed that time would realise.
Their inspired phantasy, which we call idealism, was justified by
their knowledge of God's power and purpose to perfect whatever
He began. They believed in the succession of grace, and their
great recollections awoke ever greater anticipations. They
seemed always to stand on tiptoe with expectation. They had
a passion for perfection ; every historical character gave them a
glowing hope that a greater was on his way ; and their golden
age of the future was not a fancy picture, but an ideal which
God Himself gave them. Thus, having once caught a glimpse
of Melchizedek, king of Jerusalem, they not only cherished his

[1] Heb. 7⁷.

memory, but predicted the advent of a greater " Priest upon a throne," [1] " a Priest for ever after the order of Melchizedek." [2]

> " The King who reigns in Salem's towers
> Shall all the world command."

PEACE.—" Blessed be Abram of God Most High," said the king of Salem. The Prince of Peace came out to bless the man of war ($14^{19}$). Melchizedek the ideal king loved the reign of gentle peace, and desired the time when wars should cease unto the ends of the earth. Yet he was no advocate of peace at any price. He was " first, by interpretation, king of righteousness, and *after that* also king of peace." [3] He blessed the hero whose good sword was wet with the blood of tyrants. Before the dulcet notes of peace there must often be heard the trumpet tones of war for righteousness. God Most High does not permit peace to be gained or maintained apart from the ends of justice. His priest approves " the slaughter of the kings of the East," [4] and is thankful for the stern arbitrament of war. Strong, firm, inflexible righteousness must lead in mild, merciful, gentle peace. The kingdom of God is first righteousness, then peace and joy. [5] " Righteousness and peace kiss each other." [6] The Hebrew saints never cease to emphasise the fact that there can be no peace without God or with sin. " The work of righteousness shall be peace, and the effect of righteousness quietness and assurance for ever." [7] A peace, or even a truce, with iniquity is monstrous. Blessed is the man of God who lays the usurper low and gives the captive liberty. The " King of Peace" would not have blessed Abram had he not rescued his weak brother from the four Eastern despots, just as He would not bless the European Powers that did not rescue their Armenian brother from the brutal Sultan. He who is after the order of Melchizedek "shall strike through kings in the day of His wrath ... He shall wound the heads over many countries." [8]

---

[1] Zec. $6^{13}$.    [2] Ps. $110^4$.    [3] Heb. $7^2$.    [4] Heb. $7^1$.
[5] Rom. $14^{17}$.    [6] Ps. $85^{10}$.    [7] Isa. $32^{17}$.    [8] Ps. $110^{5, 6}$.

" Blessed be God for the sword when it is wielded by the hands of justice and virtue." [1]

> " The mountains shall bring peace to the people,
> And the hills, *by righteousness.*" [2]

DIVINITY.—Both Melchizedek and Abram believed in " God Most High, Possessor (or Maker) of heaven and earth " ($14^{19. 22}$). Their God was one, and personal. The heathen said there were many gods, each possessing and ruling a bit of the world ; the Hebrews believed that there was one Elohim, God Most High, the Maker and Possessor of all things, the sole Proprietor of the world. Modern men of thought say that behind the sum of things there is only an impersonal Force, of which the world is the necessary result, manifestation, or emanation. But from the Hebrews we learn that God and the world are not related merely as cause and effect ; that God is neither embodied in the world, nor adequately expressed by it. They teach us that the world—heaven and earth—is the possession of a personal Being who created it, who is known to His rational creatures, who is distinct from the world, greater than it, and exalted above it, and who was as truly God before as after the heavens declared His glory and the firmament showed His handiwork. Looking at all the wonders of the world the Hebrews said, " Lo, those are but the outskirts of His ways ; but the thunder of His power who can understand ? " [3] This majestic idea of God, as an infinite, free, self-conscious, personal Being, an idea which is not found in antiquity outside the Hebrew sphere of thought, is the noblest heritage we have received from the Hebrews. It was their greatest achievement, and nothing can ever obliterate the knowledge of it from the minds of men.

THANKSGIVING.—" Blessed be God Most High," said the king of Salem in Abram's presence, " which hath delivered thine enemies into thine hand " ($14^{20}$). When Abram and his

[1] Joseph Parker.    [2] Ps. $72^3$.    [3] Job $26^{14}$.

brave followers returned all dust and sweat victorious from the battle, they were less or more than human if they were not flushed and elated with their success. The excitement of a triumph has often turned good men's heads. But in the quiet Vale of Shaveh the minds of the Hebrews were raised above the tempting joys of victory to high and holy thoughts of God, the Possessor of heaven and earth, their Preserver in the hour of danger. They heard the priest lift up his voice in praise of God Most High, the Giver of victory. The simple *Te Deum* hallowed their triumph, purified and uplifted their hearts. It was as if they took up the strain and said, " Not unto us, O LORD, not unto us, but unto Thy name give glory." [1] They learned to attribute their exploit, not to their own sinewy strength, but to the grace and goodness of their God, for whom and by whom are all things. They suddenly felt that they were on holy ground ; God was near them, and they laid their trophies at His feet. Their passage through the King's Dale, their meeting with the man of God, their partaking of bread and wine, the solemn benediction, the joyful thanksgiving, the dedication of the tithes —all this was to Abram and his young men a real sacrament. Happy is every man who remembers hallowed hours and scenes which have transfigured his life, and made him feel that henceforth he " must be, else sinning much, a consecrated spirit." [2]

LIBERALITY.— In the Vale of Shaveh Abram gave Melchizedek " a tenth of all " the spoils of war as a thank-offering to God, a token of gratitude for help and deliverance in battle. Whenever men are really in the presence of God, and have a warm sense of His goodness, they instinctively wish to present Him an offering of love. The spirit of gratitude naturally finds expression in freewill offerings. Our liberality is an infallible index of the temperature of our religion. Abram's offerings were a pattern to all his descendants. The Hebrews regarded the tithes of their income—whether from the fruits of their fields,

[1] Ps. 115[1].                    [2] Wordsworth.

or from their herds and flocks, or from the spoils of war—as the
LORD'S portion, which they put aside before beginning to use
the rest. The tithe was the first charge upon their income, and
brought a blessing on the rest. They believed that they could
not safely and happily enjoy the bounties of God until they
had gratefully dedicated the first-fruits to Him as too holy for
themselves. The practice taught them habits of forethought
and self-denial for the LORD'S sake. The motive which
prompted them determined the value of their offerings in God's
sight. Gifts of love were to Him pleasing sacrifices, while offerings without love were "vain oblations." [1] The Hebrew "knew
no greater happiness than to draw near his God with offerings ;
no acuter pain and no deeper dishonour than for this to be
impossible or forbidden to him." [2] The invariable Hebrew
practice stands before us with the moral force of a noble
precedent. The tithe is more than an interesting relic of a
submerged antiquity ; it is a present, potent, stimulative ideal.
We who are instructed to lay by us in store as God hath prospered us,[3] cannot let our Christian aim fall below the Hebrew
practice. The giving of a tenth of one's income is a simple,
easy, unencumbered plan. We are not in bondage to law ; every
believer is now a law unto himself ; and God would not accept
our offerings if they were wrung from us by constraint. But
heart-religion changes all the pain and effort of self-denial into
very delight. "Men rejoice when they divide the spoil," [4] but
they have the purest joy when they give the LORD His portion,
the first and the best.

> " Give all thou canst ; high Heaven rejects the lore
> Of nicely calculated less or more." [5]

The Hebrews teach us how close is the connection between
liberal offerings and spiritual blessings. " Bring ye the whole
tithe into the storehouse, and prove Me now herewith, saith
the LORD of hosts, if I will not open you the windows of

[1] Isa. 1[13].    [2] Ewald.    [3] I Cor. 16[2].    [4] Isa. 9[3].    [5] Wordsworth.

heaven, and pour you out a blessing, that there shall not be room enough to receive it." [1]

HONOUR.—The meeting between Melchizedek and Abram was witnessed by the king of Sodom, who had either come back as one of the rescued captives, or had crept out of a hiding-place to meet the returning forces and salute the conquering hero. Melchizedek ignored the king of Sodom, but Abram required to come to an understanding with him. As memorable as the clash of arms at Dan is the moral encounter between these two men in the King's Dale. Abram's instinctive revulsion and high disdain when face to face with the king of Sodom is as expressive as his beautiful reverence for the king of Salem. Having witnessed the interchange of gifts, the king of Sodom thought he would not be outdone in courtesy and liberality, and made a proposal to Abram which seemed to himself generous. " Give me the persons," he said, " and take the goods to thyself" ($14^{21}$). Abram might have replied that it lay with the conqueror to be the divider, that by the law of war both the spoils and the prisoners belonged to the victor. But Abram was in no mood for insisting on his rights; he had determined to relinquish them all. Though he had won a battle and captured the spoils of a whole city, he was resolved to take no reward. He was no mercenary soldier, he had no personal ends to serve, and no shadow of self should darken his victory. His motives were pure : it was brotherly-kindness, not covetousness, which constrained him to take up arms ; and either before or after the battle he had made a solemn vow to God that he would not touch so much as a thread or a shoe-latchet. As a servant of God he must not compromise himself or do anything unworthy of himself ; he must keep his hands clean, and stoop to nothing mean ; he must be above suspicion, and cherish a scrupulous regard for his own good name and the honour of his God. His high self-reverence was a reverence for what

[1] Mal. $3^{10}$.

God had made and redeemed. His manner of using his own name was an expression of noble self-respect. The king of Sodom make *Abram* rich ! Abram had been constituted heir of the whole land by the Possessor of heaven and earth. Abram could not receive any portion of his heritage from man, least of all from a man of Sodom. Having ended his campaign, Abram would go back to his place no richer than he left it. He would be indebted to none but God for wealth and happiness. A modern soldier of this high type was seen in General Gordon, who at the close of his famous Chinese campaign wrote, " I know that I shall leave China as poor as when I entered it, but with the knowledge that through my weak instrumentality upwards of eighty to a hundred thousand lives have been spared. I want no further satisfaction than this." When honours were pressed upon him, he said he did not " care twopence for these things." He accepted a grant of money only to divide it all among his troops ; and bringing home a gold medal, the Empress' special gift, he effaced the inscription, and gave it to God by giving it to His poor.

Vows. — Abram made a solemn vow that he would not enrich himself with the spoils of battle, the treasures of Sodom. He expressed his purpose in the most emphatic language—not a thread, not a shoe-latchet would he take, and with uplifted hand he called on God to hear and remember his vow ($14^{22.\ 23}$). He foresaw a temptation, and forearmed himself against it. He took measures to save himself from himself. While he clearly discerned the path of duty—the will of God—he bound himself to follow it at all costs ; he committed himself to a line of conduct from which he could never turn back. " A vow is an act of self-restraint by which a man keeps himself from falling into evil." [1] Because there is in a vow at once a confession of weakness and a prayer for strength, a wise and good man makes many vows in the course of his life.

[1] Calvin.

Knowing his liability to be assailed by fierce temptations, he fortifies himself in time of moral strength and clear vision for the conflicts that will certainly come, conflicts in which strong human passions are so apt to get the better of reason. If we could always live at a high level, there would be no need for vows ; but as experience teaches us how often we are untrue to ourselves, common prudence bids us determine beforehand what our course of action will be under certain conditions. By making a vow, "not to any creature, but to God alone, we more strictly bind ourselves to necessary duties." [1]

> " Tasks in hours of insight willed
> May be in days of gloom fulfilled." [2]

A vow gives a man firmness and fixity of purpose, and saves him from the misery of an unstable will. Whether we utter our vow in words with the right hand lifted towards heaven, as Abram did, or silently attach our name to a written pledge, in either case we deliberately take upon ourselves a solemn obligation of which God is witness ; and a vow once taken should be faithfully and religiously kept. "When thou vowest a vow unto God, defer not to pay it. Better is it that thou shouldst not vow, than that thou shouldst vow and not pay." [3] An honourable man changes not though he swear to his own hurt.[4] The obligation of our vows, in things right and expedient, is sacred, and the bond indissoluble. And vows are all the more effective if they are often made afresh, till all doubt and danger shall be past.

> " High heaven, that heard the solemn vow,
> That vow renewed shall daily hear."

There is a certain subtle danger connected with all acts of self-devotion. If a man takes a vow or pledge trusting in the strength of his own will, the emphasis of his words, the firmness of his purpose, or the goodness of his intentions—if his vow is a mere

---

[1] Confession of Faith.    [2] Arnold.    [3] Eccles. $5^{4, 5}$.    [4] Ps. $15^4$.

utterance of self-confidence, it will be worth less than nothing
—idle breath or wasted ink. But if he vows with a knowledge
of his utter weakness and an absolute dependence upon Divine
strength, his vow will bring him off more than conqueror.

LIBERTY.—Abram stipulated with the king of Sodom that
his Amorite confederates should have a due share of the spoils
of war (14²⁴). He would not touch the booty himself; he
had a sure sense of his own duty, and would keep his conscience scrupulously clean. But he would not make his action
a standard for other freemen. His own young serfs, who had
fought so bravely and risked their lives so nobly, should have
nothing for their service but "what they had eaten"—and
perhaps everlasting renown. But there was no reason why
the allies should not have their portion of the spoils. Abram
was a law unto himself, but no conscience-keeper for other
men ; and his treatment of his confederates displays a fine
sense of what is just and right and fitting. The Amorites
had no scruples about taking the spoil, and Abram almost
invited them to take it. The man who is most severe—almost
merciless—to himself, is often the most gentle in his judgments
of others, and the last to interfere with their liberty. " I rebuke
not what others do," said Chevalier Bayard, " but I will not
do it myself." Conscience needs to be enlightened, not coerced ;
and only voluntary actions have moral worth. Many questions
of conduct do not admit of categorical answers ; what is right
for one person is wrong for another ; and hard and fast rules
are a poor substitute for personal reflection and decision.
Every free agent must be thrown on his own responsibility,
and make his own moral determinations. " Let every man be
fully persuaded in his own mind." [1]

SELF-CONTROL.—Having given proof of his valour by subduing kings, Abram displays his greatness of mind by con-

[1] Rom. 14⁵.

quering himself. Nothing tries a man like power. What with the blessing of Melchizedek the priest of God Most High, the support of princely confederates, the subservience of the king of Sodom, and the devotion of the brave retainers who formed a lifeguard around their master's person, Abram had reached the highest pinnacle of earthly power. He was a king in all but in name. Here he had his opportunity and his temptation. Had he chosen to follow up his advantage, he might quickly have had the country at his feet. It would have been very pleasant for him to attain his end at once. But his hour was not yet come. He must not march through bloodshed to a throne. God had some better, as yet unknown, way of achievement prepared for him. With the coveted prize—the possession of Canaan—within his reach, he sheathed his sword, quietly disbanded his forces, returned to his herds and flocks, and resumed his old attitude of waiting only upon God. " Better is he that ruleth his spirit than he that taketh a city." [1] God's hand cannot be forced. There is no short cut to the ideal. The first of possessions is self-possession, the noblest conquest is self-conquest.

## ASSURANCE
### Genesis 15

" All great souls are apt to be in thick darkness till the eternal ways and celestial guiding stars disclose themselves."—CARLYLE.

REFLECTION.—No book is so true to life and experience as the Bible, which pictures men in all their changing moods. Human spirits are subtle and delicate, subject to strange alternations of hope and fear. The tides of feeling flow and ebb. Shadows of doubt creep across every soul. The bravest hearts have their " fainting fits." After the elation of victory Abram is seen in an hour of heavy depression. The swift march, the clash of arms,

[1] Prov. 16³².

the shout of victory, the voice of thanksgiving are past, and he is back among the sleeping oaks of Mamre. The unwonted strain is relaxed, and the excitement of action is followed by the dulness of reflection. Everything is "sicklied o'er with the pale cast of thought." What is the net result of the successful war? What progress has been made? The achievement seems pitifully small. The king of Sodom has got back his crown, his people their goods and chattels, and Lot is re-established in the city of ill-fame. Meantime the fierce hatred of the men of the East has been inflamed, and will they not return in overwhelming numbers and take their revenge? Abram has let slip his opportunity of seizing his heritage by the aid of the sword, and no other means seem available. He has striven and not attained. And even if the promised possession were already his, what would it profit a childless man who sits brooding in solitude, whose only heir is a slave? Here is a striking proof of the strange dualism of human character. Abram unabashed before kings, and Abram sick and sad and sore at heart when left to his own reflections, is one and the same man. The strongest soul has its conflicts with doubt and its seasons of dejection. Meditation is heartening only when it keeps God full in view. Faith is the great aid to reflection, delivering the soul from its stupor, and restoring it to the vigour of hope. The verdict of melancholy is always a mistake.

REASSURANCE.—The LORD is very gracious to Abram in his dejection. His word comes to him in a vision of the night, allaying his fears and bidding him hope. Clear above all the bodings and murmurs of doubt and fear the divine voice speaks, giving assurance of safety and blessing. God is to Abram a shield, against which the most powerful enemies will only dash themselves to their own destruction ; and his reward, richer far than all earthly possessions. But it is not easy to overcome a deepseated despondency. "What wilt Thou give me," Abram sadly asks, "seeing I depart (die) lonely, deserted, childless?" (15²)·

The end of life is in sight, and the desire of his heart is unfulfilled ; what to him are all rewards and possessions, no son of his
succeeding ? The divine response is that no stranger, but a son
of his own loins, shall be his heir,—not Eliezer, whom in default of
a real heir he had adopted as a substitute (15⁴). Then still another
message of comfort is given. There is no better tonic for a sick
heart than the sights, breaths, and sounds of Nature. In the hush
of night God leads His servant forth under the cloudless skies,
and bids him look up and tell the number of the stars if he can.
Abram's soul is uplifted, awed, overpowered by the incomparable
glory of the Syrian heavens, and the prophetic voice whispers to
him that so great and so glorious shall his seed be. Abram
accepts the astounding prophecy in faith, his doubt is dispelled,
his hope revived, his soul satisfied. His faith is counted unto
him for righteousness (15⁶).

PROPHECY.—The formula, "the word of the LORD came"
(15¹), is the all but invariable introduction to a Hebrew prophecy.
It virtually puts Abram into the goodly fellowship of the
prophets, and in Gen. 20⁷ he is expressly called a prophet. The
prophet was a man conscious of a supernatural call, quick to
apprehend and welcome and publish the promises of God. He
was God's interpreter, through whom we, God's moral creatures,
have received our rich knowledge of His mind and will. *How*
the word of the LORD came to the prophet, how he apprehended
the promises and purposes of God, we can never fully know. To
Abram the LORD spake in a vision (15¹), in a deep sleep (15¹². ¹³),
by His angel (22¹¹), as a man speaketh to his friend (18¹⁷), and
in unrecorded ways (12¹ 21¹²). To other prophets He spake by
oracles, by the still small voice, by His Spirit. But the secret of
inspiration remains. The relation between God and the prophet
is, as Wellhausen says, "mysterious and irreducible." No one
has succeeded in plucking the heart out of the prophet's mystery.
What we do know is that through the prophets God brake the
silence of eternity, and introduced a new order of things in the

world ; that He gave them a line to sound the hidden depths of His providence, a key to unlock the secret places of the Most High ; that they were the embodied soul and conscience of the Hebrew community ; that the moral and spiritual truths of which they were the bearers came to them, not "from their own hearts," but from the living God, and commended themselves to every pure heart and enlightened conscience ; and that all their ideals were ultimately realised, if not in the details, then in some grander way than ever they anticipated.

PROTECTION.—Abram receives the assurance of safety in the midst of all dangers : he need fear no enemies, however strong and malignant, for God will be his shield (15[1]). If he has mighty foes, he has a mightier invisible Defender. The ancient warrior bore strapped on his arm a shield of brass or of wood covered with leather, armed with which he rushed into battle and turned death aside. In modern warfare the shield is quite unserviceable ; it hangs with bows and arrows in the museum of ancient armour. But "no word ever becomes obsolete which has once deeply touched the heart of humanity."[1] The shield will always be a weapon of spiritual warfare ; God will never cease to be "a shield to all them that trust in Him."[2] The believer's defence is complete ; before and behind, on the right hand and on the left, he is beset by the protective power of God. This was a favourite thought of Luther's, whose famous spiritual battle-song opens with the words—

> " A sure stronghold our God is He,
> A trusty shield and weapon."

"What will you do," Luther was asked, "if the Duke, your protector, should no longer harbour you?" "I will take my shelter," he answered, "under the broad shield of Almighty God." Modern nations, with their immense armies and fleets, are apt to forget how insecure they are without that divine pro-

---

[1] Parker.     [2] Ps. 18[30].

tection. Foolish are they if they " put their trust in reeking tube and iron shard."[1] He who spread His shield over Abram and his little Hebrew army must equally be the "Lord of the far-flung battle-line."[1] He is the ultimate safeguard of all national greatness, and no weapon formed against Him shall prosper.[2] "For the LORD God is a sun and shield."[3]

REWARD.—Abram next receives the divine assurance, "I am thy exceeding great reward"; or perhaps it was, "Thy reward shall be exceeding great" ($15^1$). God is both the Rewarder and the reward of His people. The writings of the Hebrews are full of this great idea. "The LORD is the portion of my inheritance"; "God is my portion for ever"; "I will go unto God my exceeding joy." The LORD communicates to His people not only His attributes, His love, His covenant, but Himself. Since the beginning of history thoughtful men have been asking what is man's *summum bonum*, his highest good, his heart's true ideal. "Power," "wealth," "pleasure," "wisdom," "culture," are some of the answers. The true answer is "God." "I have no good beyond Thee,"[4] said one who had learned the secret. "Lord, give me Thyself," was Augustine's constant prayer; and he adds the exquisite reason, "*Habet omnia qui habet habentem omnia*,"— "he has all who has Him that has all." Slowly or suddenly we rise from delight in God's gifts to delight in Himself. "Unless," says Hooker, "the last good, which is desired for itself, be infinite, we do evil making it our end. No good is infinite but God; therefore He is our felicity and bliss." Every soul has capacities greater than the infinite sea, and only He who filleth heaven and earth, whom the heaven of heavens cannot contain, can satisfy one little human heart.

STARS.—Abram was heartened and reassured by the sight of the stars, which God made a prophecy of the greatness and glory of Abram's posterity, a symbol of the splendour of His own

---

[1] Kipling.     [2] Isa. $54^{17}$.     [3] Ps. $84^{11}$.     [4] Ps. $16^2$.

inheritance in the saints. Among the ancients the Hebrew alone could rightly read the heavens. No sad astrology, no superstitious dread of planetary influences, troubled his thoughts. On him the stars looked down, not with malignity or scorn or pity, but radiant with a message of infinite hope. To him the night glowed with a myriad stars of promise, under which men could not live with desponding hearts. He knew that the incomparable God who created them, and nightly marshalled their host, would do as marvellous things for men in grace. Their glory and their steadfastness reassured his faith. " Lift up your eyes on high," said the prophet, "and see who hath created these, that bringeth out their host by number : He calleth them all by name by the greatness of His might, and for that He is strong in power ; not one faileth."[1] In the clear atmosphere of Palestine the stars shine with a brightness of which we dwellers in northern climes have but a feeble conception ; the Pleiades are not seven stars but a hundred ; and the rings of Saturn are visible to the naked eye. Our knowledge of the heavens has immensely widened since Abram's day, and with the aid of the best instruments a hundred million worlds are now visible, and many more pursue their pathless way through awful space. But the Hebrew reading of the stars remains for ever the right one. "To the intelligent, nature converts itself into a vast promise."[2] Carlyle called the starry heavens "a sair sicht," only because the Hebrew hopefulness was not so strong in him as the Hebrew righteousness. That great host, stretching numberless beyond the range of vision, was set in the heavens, not "to burn and brand his nothingness into man," but the reverse—to illustrate his splendid destiny, to be a shining warrant for all idealism—

> " A world above man's head to let him see
> How boundless might his soul's horizons be,
> How vast, yet of what clear transparency !
> How fair a lot to fill
> Is left to each man still!"[3]

[1] Isa. 40[26].      [2] Emerson.      [3] Arnold.

FAITH.—When Abram received the promise of a great posterity, he believed it because he first "believed in the LORD" (15⁶). Under the stars, in the presence of God, he came back to clear vision, sweet peace, triumphant assurance. Inspired with a sense of God's goodness and faithfulness, he passed from fear to confidence, from sadness to joyousness. His reason might be stunned, his imagination dazzled, by the promise, but God was true, and he reposed implicit faith in God. "Everything in himself and on earth forbade him to hope, but in the place from which the promise came he saw nothing but the strongest grounds for hoping." [1] If the greatness of God's promised gifts almost staggers us, the greatness of the Promiser reassures us, and we believe amid all the improbabilities of nature and experience. God's revealed goodness is a warrant for faith in all good things. If the promises were spoken by any other than God, they would have to be dismissed at once as incredible and preposterous. But nothing is too good to be true if it is promised by God. Once we believe in Him we bid good-bye to all our faint-heartedness. Having such a God, it becomes easy for us to believe the sixty thousand promises which are contained in the Bible, shining like stars of hope in the firmament.

RIGHTEOUSNESS.—"Abram believed in the LORD, and He counted it to him for righteousness" (15⁶). "The great text of the Book of Genesis," exclaims Luther. It is quoted three times in the New Testament,[2] and it contains a vital, grand, everlasting truth. Righteousness was the supreme quest of the Hebrews, as wisdom was of the Greeks and power of the Romans. The Gentiles followed not after righteousness, but Israel followed after the law of righteousness.[3] The Hebrews exulted in the attainment of righteousness ; they were in an agony of penitence whenever they had broken the law and lost righteousness. Primarily "the ideas of right and wrong among the Hebrews are forensic ideas—that is, the Hebrew always thinks

[1] Tholuck.          [2] Rom. 4³, Gal. 3⁶, Jas. 2²³.          [3] Rom. 9³⁰, ³¹.

of the right and the wrong as if they were to be settled before a judge. Righteousness is to the Hebrew not so much a moral quality as a legal status."[1] He attains this status, however, not by good works, tithes, or sacrifices, but by faith in the LORD. "The requirement of faith runs through the entire Old Testament."[2] "In the Old as in the New Testament, faith is the subjective condition of salvation."[3] It is the prerequisite of all spiritual blessings—pardon, guidance, enrichment, help, discipline, communion. The words regarding Abram contain the essence of evangelical faith. When the typical believer was counted righteous by the divine Judge, the meaning is not that he was acquitted, for acquittal declares that a man has done no wrong, but that God accepted him in spite of his sins. The evangel of both Testaments is that righteousness is not achieved by deeds, but received as a gracious gift. Had Abram won God's favour by his extraordinary merits, he would have been no example to his posterity ; but he was accepted by God for his faith, which all could imitate. Here, as Ewald says, is "a sketch and model of genuine faith which could never be forgotten, but in all succeeding ages exerted a wonderful influence. The writer regards faith in its extreme importance as the chief and crowning excellence of a man's life in God." "Know ye therefore that they who are of faith are children of Abraham . . . are blessed with faithful Abraham."[4]

## GRACE
### Genesis 15:18

"The covenant of grace inwraps the unchangeable love and favour of God."—JOHN OWEN.

COVENANTING.—The religion of the Hebrews did not consist of mere instincts, feelings, and aspirations, but of definite objective

---

relations historically established between God and His people. The primary fact in their religion was not their rising to God in prayer and praise, but God's coming down to them in grace and mercy. The connection between the LORD and His people had a historical beginning ; it was based not on nature, but on grace ; and God's manifestation of His grace is from the earliest times described as the making of a covenant with the Hebrews. Such a covenant He is represented as entering into with Abram, the typical believer. Having for the third time received the promise of the possession of Canaan, Abram desired to see the promise in some way confirmed ($15^8$). Men naturally crave present and visible tokens of future and spiritual blessings. Before the diffusion of the art of writing, and the consequent use of written bonds, signs, and seals in the making of agreements, there were various means by which a man's promise was made stringently binding upon his conscience. In early times "it cost the most gigantic efforts to get men at all accustomed to respect truth and abhor perjury."[1] Of the solemn religious sanctions used for this purpose the most awful and impressive was the covenant. Victims were slain and divided, the pieces were laid on the ground with a space between them, and the persons forming an agreement then passed between the pieces, virtually or really imprecating on themselves the fate of the victims if they should break their word. They could not look at the blood of the slain beasts without an involuntary shudder, and it symbolised the death deserved by him who violated his promise. The covenant was thus "an intensified oath."[2] Abram made such a covenant with Mamre and his brothers ($14^{13}$), and with the king of Gerar ($21^{32}$) ; and the LORD is represented as confirming His promise to Abram by making a covenant with him. What men demanded from their treacherous fellow-men, that the true and faithful God deigned to offer His people. He acted just as suspected human promisers were required to act. Being directed to make the needful preparations for the rite, Abram waits all day beside the slain victims, warding

[1] Ewald.     [2] A. B. Davidson.

off unclean birds. At sunset he falls into a deep ecstatic sleep, a horror of great darkness descends upon his mind, and awful coming events cast their shadows before. Awaking in the darkness of night, he sees the covenant concluded. A smoke as of a furnace, and a flaming torch—the symbols of God's presence—move down the lane between the divided victims, the LORD thus binding Himself to perform His gracious promise. Abram does not pass between the pieces : it is not for him to make terms with the Almighty ; he is simply a witness and recipient of the covenant graciously made by God. The promise itself is then repeated to Abram in an ideal form, giving his posterity as a possession the whole region that stretches between the Nile and the Euphrates (15[18]).

GRACE.—An ordinary covenant, entered into by equals, was a security for mutual benefits and services to be rendered, an end of enmity and uncertainty, a basis of friendship and mutual confidence. But the covenant between God and man—between the Infinite and the finite, the Holy One and the sinner—was in every way unique. It could only originate with God, and could only be a covenant of pure mercy. Man could not make peace with God, or confer favours on God, or exact terms from God. But God could make peace with man, could bestow benefits on man, could lay down conditions for man. All this He does in the covenant. It is a divine institution or dispensation rather than a contract. It is all of grace. God stoops down to the weakness and want of His creatures, and makes Himself a debtor to them. He lays His love under bonds, freely pledging Himself to bestow His favours. This does not mean that He did not love men before He made a covenant with them : He loved them with an everlasting love. God is eternally Love. The covenant is not the beginning of His grace ; it is the declaration of His grace. It gives weak human nature a firm hold of the love of God. Embracing at first but a single promise (15[18]), it is gradually widened till it includes all divine favours, and the LORD stands pledged to bestow numberless, priceless, endless blessings. The covenant was the great and sacred charter of the Hebrews. It was the mould of their ideals, the spring of their enthusiasm, the argument of their prayers. They loved it ardently, they clung to it passionately. It gave them everlasting consolation and good hope through grace.

SYMPATHY.—Men who have been brooding over their own cheerless and lonely lot are startled out of their fantastic sadness by a vision of real suffering. The mystery of the world's pain, the tears that are in mortal things, steel the heart to brave and silent endurance of its own trials. Individual murmuring is hushed by the still sad music of humanity. "Brave men are perceivers of the terror of life, and have manned themselves to face it." [1]   God therefore made Abram a witness of the awful tragedy of Israel in Egypt. In a night-vision He unfolded to him the future of his own race, not concealing from him that for long dark ages they would be afflicted as bond-servants in a strange land, but consoling him with the promise that they would ultimately be avenged, and return to their own land with great substance ($15^{13-16}$). Abram is brought face to face with grander sufferings than his own, becomes one with other men by the enlarging power of sympathy, and learns God's way of disciplining His people for His service. As the vocation of the Hebrews was higher than that of any other nation, they were to be subjected to severer trials, to be trained by a stern and exceptional process. It was the dark periods of adversity, rather than the sunny times of prosperity, that made the Hebrews a people prepared to serve the LORD. Suffering had a chastening, softening, purifying, enlightening influence upon them. The memory of the terrible bondage and glorious deliverance at the beginning of their history kept the Hebrew consciousness ever alive to God's providential method of dealing with His

[1] Emerson.

people. His ways with them never changed ; and though they might shudder at the prospect of pain, they always saw in the end how sweet were the uses of adversity. "I have chosen thee in the furnace of affliction,"[1] said the LORD to His people. "It is good for me that I have been afflicted,"[2] was the response of a nation.

JUSTICE.—Abram learns that the conquest of Canaan must be delayed for a long time—four generations or centuries— because the iniquity of the Amorite is not yet full ($15^{16}$). The old civilisation of Canaan, sated with morbid vice, is to be dismissed, and the young Hebrew race, hungering for the higher truth and pressing toward a divine ideal, is rising into favour. God has ordained that the corrupt and decadent nations of the earth, as cumberers of the ground, shall make room for new and morally healthy races. When vice has sapped the vital strength of a people, they fall like a rotten tree. There is a profound truth in the saying that "the history of the world is the judgment of the world."[3] God wills it that in the struggle of nations for existence the morally strongest and purest shall survive. The destiny of a nation is the result of its character. When a people has filled up the cup of its iniquity, it must drink the cup of judgment. The conquest of Canaan was divinely decreed before it was carried out by men, and the Hebrews were the appointed executioners of the LORD'S sentence. As yet, however, the Amorites had not outlived their day of grace, and were not outlawed of God. He is not unjust to one nation in order to be indulgent to another ; He governs all nations for moral ends ; and not even for the sake of Abram's seed would He anticipate by an hour the stroke of vengeance on the wicked races of Canaan. "The LORD is righteous in all His ways, and gracious in all His works."[4]

LIGHT.—Symbols are mysteriously suggestive. They are like

[1] Isa. $48^{10}$.    [2] Ps. $119^{71}$.    [3] Schiller.    [4] Ps. $145^{17}$.

music, of which we can never say, It means just this one thing and nothing more. God was to be to His people "an awful guide in smoke and flame " ; [1] and at the making of the covenant of grace His presence is symbolised by a smoking furnace and a flaming torch appearing in the night ($15^{17}$). Abram receives the assurance of God's love, not in the full blaze of noonday, and not during his own happiest and sunniest mood, but in the darkness of midnight, and while his mind is oppressed with supernatural fear. Everything terrible is called in to heighten the awe and solemnity of the divine presence. The approach of the supernatural awakens a sensation of dread quite beyond the control of the will. The darkness, the silence, the solitude, the tension are all terrible to the covenanter. The still forms of the slain beasts around him are awful symbols of merited death. Then the LORD'S coming, the sudden transition from gloom to glory, the shining of a great light in the thick darkness as the sign and symbol of covenant love, produces a striking effect. All real knowledge is by contrast : light is known by darkness, and God's grace by man's sin. A great writer has said, "Mere light is too common a thing to make a strong impression on the mind, and without a strong impression nothing can be sublime. . . . Darkness is more productive of sublime ideas than light." [2] But it is the sudden change from the one to the other that causes the greatest surprise and delight. The first rays of dawn, following the deepest darkness, thrill our souls with joyful wonder. So God's love, symbolised by light, has always made the deepest impression upon those minds which have first been oppressed with "an horror of great darkness." At no time did God leave His covenant of love without the dread symbols and awful sanctions of His might and majesty. He would not let men abuse His love by forgetting that it was mercy ; and herein lay the strength of the Hebrews' religion, that in their relation to God there was a wonderful union of the deepest awe and reverence with the most intimate personal friendship and love. The

[1] Scott.                    [2] Burke.

*new* covenant was sealed amid darkness and earthquake.[1]  Even
in heaven, when the seer beheld the symbol of the covenant,
"there followed lightnings and voices and thunderings."[2]  Thus
God still

> "with majesty of darkness round
> Circles His throne."

If our modern religion is weak, it is because, having no great
fear of God's majesty and holiness, no horror of great darkness
on account of sin, we are not *surprised* at God's love.  In true
religion the love of God to men is an astonishing, amazing,
all but incredible thing.

> "Philosophers have measured mountains,
>     Fathomed the depths of seas, of states, of kings ;
>   Walked with a staff to heaven, and tracèd fountains :
>     But there are two vast spacious things
>   The which to measure it doth more behove ;
>     Yet few there be that sound them—Sin and Love."[3]

DOMINION.—Abram received the promise that his seed
should one day possess the whole region extending from the
Nile to the Euphrates ($15^{18}$).  Some scholars think that "the
river of Egypt" is the *Wady el Arish*, a torrent in the desert of
Sinai, dry during the greater part of the year.  But it would be
entirely out of harmony with the ideal character of the prophecy
to name "the great river" in the same breath with a desert
stream.  The river intended must be the peer of the Euphrates.

> "It flows through old hushed Egypt and its sands,
>   Like some grave mighty thought threading a dream."

Once in the history of the Hebrews was this glowing vision of
dominion realised.  "Solomon ruled over all the kingdoms
from the River unto the lands of the Philistines and unto the
border of Egypt."[4]  And though his wide possessions were lost,
and the glory of his kingdom dimmed, by his feeble successors,

[1] Matt. $27^{45, 51}$.    [2] Rev. $11^{19}$.    [3] George Herbert.    [4] 1 Kings $4^{21}$.

the ideal was never forgotten. On the contrary, the people of
God constantly widened their outlook, until at length they predicted the coming of a King who should have "dominion from
sea to sea, and from the river unto the ends of the earth,"—
an ideal with which they entwined the highest hopes that could
be conceived for humanity.[1]


## PATIENCE
### Genesis 16

" All things are best fulfilled in their due time,
And there is time for all things."—MILTON.

ENDURANCE.—"The LORD is good unto them that wait for
Him." [2]  He teaches all His servants to have patience till His
hour strikes : their times are in His hands, and He keeps none
of them waiting a moment beyond the right and appointed time.
For the drawing out of their faith and the exercise of their
patience, He may cross them in their desires and hopes, but His
delays are not refusals.  He knows "the time to have pity, yea,
the set time." [3]  The restless and the feverish lose the reward ;
the blessing is for those who endure.  Gen. 16 tells us of three
people who needed to acquire the grace of patience.  (1) One of
them, a slave-girl, more sinned against than sinning, was hard
beset in the tent of her jealous mistress, and at length, exasperated
beyond endurance, fled into the wilderness (16[1-6]).  The angel of
the LORD found her by a fountain, gently rebuked her waywardness, charged her to return and submit herself to her mistress,
and promised that great blessings would be found in the way of
patient obedience.  Duty might seem to her an irksome bondage,
vexatious restraints might be put upon her liberty, and it is not
so easy to be in subjection to the froward as to the good and
gentle.[4]  But in the dark day let her wait for the dawning of a
brighter.  True patience, the endurance of evil for the LORD'S

[1] Ps. 72.          [2] Lam. 3[25].          [3] Ps. 102[13].          [4] 1 Pet. 2[18].

sake, never misses its reward. "Fret not thyself, . . . be still before the LORD, and wait patiently for Him."[1] (2) Hagar's master and mistress, having long expected a promised blessing which was to complete their lives and make them thoroughly happy, became impatient of delay, and tried to snatch the boon in another than God's way. He punished them in His own way. Having waited ten years and grown impatient, they were required to wait other fifteen ; and having grasped the coveted blessing before the time, they found that it was not what they expected. Instead of bettering themselves by expediency and policy, they only brought elements of discord and confusion into their lives. "Do not thou hasten above the Most High : for thy haste is vain to be above Him."[2] Better to wait long, meekly, silently, in solitude, weariness, and darkness, than to anticipate God by a single movement of rash haste.

> " Endurance is the crowning quality,
> And patience all the passion of the saints."[3]

COUNSEL.—Abram and Sarah were knit together by a love which knew no alteration. Through a long lifetime they were true helpmates and soul-comrades. They were heirs together of the grace of life. Yet Abram was Sarah's tempter, and Sarah was Abram's tempter. Sarah erred by following the counsel of Abram (12[13]), and Abram erred by hearkening to the voice of Sarah (16[2]). "Walk softly, lest, without knowing it, your love should make you sin."[4] We are easily seduced through our affections, and we need to beware of our bosom friends, and they of us. The subtlest allurements come from the lips of a lover. The mistaken kindness of a real friend, who wishes to give us a pleasure or spare us a pain, may be as fraught with danger as the malicious counsel of a false friend, who seeks to lure us to our destruction. The masterpiece of the spirit of evil is to set a friend to take us off from holy self-denial. It may

---

[1] Ps. 37[1.7].   [2] 2 Esdr. 4[34].
[3] J. R. Lowell.   [4] George Macdonald.

be no repellent fiend, but a winsome friend, who makes the worse appear the better reason. It was no enemy, but the choicest and best of friendly comrades and counsellors, who persuaded Hopeful to turn into Bypath Meadow. Peter, as well as Satan, tempted the Lord to lower His ideal, and had to be answered in the same words, "Get thee behind me, Satan." The gentlest and most tender-hearted have need of a note of austerity in their speech. Some Hebrew of wide experience has left this appallingly stern precept : "If thy brother, the son of thy mother, or thy son, or thy daughter, or the wife of thy bosom, or thy friend who is as thine own life, entice thee secretly . . . thou shalt not consent unto him, nor hearken unto him ; neither shall thine eye pity him, neither shalt thou spare, neither shalt thou conceal him."[1] It has been well said that "they seem to take away the sun from the world who withdraw friendship from life,"[2] and human love is God's best earthly blessing to man. But Abram had only one perfectly wise and faithful Friend, and we have but one Friend and Lover of our souls of whom we can always be absolutely sure that He will "lead us not into temptation, but deliver us from evil."

VIRTUE.—Sarah's portrait is firmly and distinctly drawn by a master-hand. She is of the high heroic type of womanhood. She is far from being a puppet or plaything to her lord, as an Eastern wife too often is. In many features she resembles the wise man's ideal of a "virtuous woman," given at the end of the Book of Proverbs. "Virtue" used to denote mind-force or strength of character. Sarah took a full share in all the serious concerns of her husband's life, cherished the same faith (16[2]), and bore all the real hardships of her lot with cheerful patience. St. Peter says that all women who "do well and are not put to fear by any terror" are daughters of Sarah.[3] But it was Sarah's fault and misfortune that she could not bear the petty grievances of her lot. She was easily stung and irritated by her inferiors.

[1] Deut. 13[6-8].　　　　[2] Cicero.　　　　[3] 1 Pet. 3[6].

She could not endure the insolence of a maid; she let Hagar's
foolish pride and contempt rankle in her breast; and when
her heart was so hot with jealousy that she gave up the control
of her temper, her husband had to bow his head beneath the
blast, and her maid to flee into the wilderness. She lacked one
of the loveliest traits of woman's ideal—the law of kindness was
not on her tongue.[1] "This is the peculiarity of ill-temper, that
it is the vice of the virtuous. It is often the one blot on an
otherwise noble character. You know men who would be nearly
perfect, and women who would be entirely perfect, but for an
easily-ruffled, quick-tempered, and touchy disposition. . . . Generally, too, it is the weak who are the sufferers; for temper is the
prerogative of superiors; and inferiors, down to the bottom of
the scale, have not only to bear the brunt of the scorn, but to
sink their own judgment and spend their lives in ministering to
what they know to be caprice."[2] St. Peter praises in woman
"the ornament of a meek and quiet spirit."[3]

> " Her voice was ever soft,
> Gentle and low, an excellent thing in woman."[4]

LOVE.—The law of monogamy is not found formally enunciated
in the Hebrew Scriptures, yet the love of one for one is unques-
tionably a Hebrew ideal. "They twain shall be one flesh" ($2^{24}$),
is a very ancient divine precept, contained in the earliest
stratum of Genesis. "The marriage of one man and one woman
is to form the fundamental indissoluble relationship before
which all other ties, even the most sacred, must give way."[5]
Almost every specimen of polygamy given in the Bible is so
thoroughly bad that no one can doubt its radical wrongness even
in its mildest form. Abram's relation to Hagar was not contrary
to the customs of primitive nations, but Abram's standard of
action was the will of God and not the ways of men. He
entered into that relation at the instance of his wife, not in

[1] Prov. $31^{26}$.    [2] H. Drummond.    [3] 1 Pet. $3^4$.
[4] Shakespeare.    [5] Schultz.

obedience to God, as whatsoever is not of faith is sin. The
practice of the majority, the current of opinion, the spirit of the
age, the laxer notions of society, are poor substitutes for the
counsel of God. The Mosaic law tolerated polygamy for the
hardness of men's hearts, but never sanctioned it ; and all the
beautiful delineations of wifehood contained in the books of
Wisdom and Prophecy presuppose monogamy as the ideal.
Nearly all the happiness described in Genesis springs from right
relations between men and women, nearly all the misery from
wrong relations. Pure love bestows incomparable happiness,
impure love creates piteous tragedies. True religion, which is
the foundation of the highest and holiest manhood and womanhood, is the best friend of the home and the best guardian
of its sanctities. Love refined, purified, and consecrated by
faith is necessarily opposed to polygamy. Abram, Sarah, and
Hagar had all to suffer for the error in which they were all
involved. The avengers of injured love are envy, hatred, malice,
and all uncharitableness. Concerted sin is punished by mutual
recrimination. Nothing is so hard to bear as love changed to
hatred. Sarah had brought Hagar up with her from Egypt to
be her lady's-maid, had preferred her to all the girls of the
camp, and made her the companion of her solitude. They lived
happily together till the shadow of sin fell between them, and
then each became to the other an instrument of torture. Polygamy also makes men callous. Abram allowed Hagar to be
hardly dealt with (16[6]), and remained silent and inactive while
she was being driven from his house at the time when she most
required kindness. "These devices, which produced such ir-
regularities and heart-burnings in the families of the patriarchs,
are equally mischievous at the present day. The whole system
is productive of evil, and that only, to the individual, the family,
and the community."[1] Polygamy is the profanation of marriage
and the degradation of woman. True religion emancipates
woman, raises her to spiritual equality with man, and restores

[1] *Land and Book.*

marriage to its proper dignity and purity. The Hebrew ideal of wedded life—the entire self-surrender and mutual delight of two souls—is expressed in the exquisite idyll of the Song of Songs : " My beloved is mine, and I am his." [1]

SELF-KNOWLEDGE.—One of the invariable effects of sin is that it blunts our sensibility and dims our perception of truth and righteousness. It blinds us to our own faults ; it makes us special pleaders for ourselves. Having committed a mistake and begun to suffer for it, Sarah first persuaded herself that she had done no wrong ; then she looked round for an accomplice on whom she might cast all the blame ; after that it was but a step to call God Himself to see and judge if she was not an innocent and injured woman (16[5]). Happily kind Heaven did not take her at her word. Sarah was too proud to admit her error. " In general, pride is at the bottom of all great mistakes." [2] An honest, unreserved acknowledgment of sin is the rarest and most difficult thing in the world. Human nature always bids us accuse others to screen ourselves. Apologies for sin are as ancient as human history. Adam shifted the blame from himself to his wife ; Sarah shifted the blame from herself to her husband. There is always a convenient scapegoat on whom we can lay our hands and say, " My wrong be upon thee " (16[5]). We excuse, or extenuate, or altogether deny our sin ; self-love, self-trust, self-pity will not let us see anything against ourselves. While the spirit of evil has possession of us, lashing us to do his will, we do not hesitate to incriminate our dearest friend, sacrificing our love to our pride. Or we lay the burden of guilt upon God by blaming our position, our constitution, our fate, our stars— anything but the right thing. When a sinner comes to himself, he blames nobody but himself ; his prayer is, " Have mercy upon me, O God, according to Thy loving-kindness," [3] or, " God be merciful to me the sinner." [4] The Hebrews regarded self-knowledge as so difficult that only God could enable them to

[1] Song of Songs 2[16].    [2] Ruskin.    [3] Ps. 51[1].    [4] Luke 18[13].

acquire it. "Search me, O LORD, and know my heart,"—so
each was taught to pray,—"try me, and know my thoughts: and
see if there be any wicked way in me, and lead me in the way
everlasting." [1] Happily we know, better than the Hebrews
knew, that there is one Substitute who permits us to say to
Him, not in bitter anger, but in penitent faith and adoring
gratitude, " My wrong be upon Thee."

## COMPASSION
### Genesis 16:7, 10, 13

" The heart of the Eternal
Is most wonderfully kind."—FABER.

VISION.—When Hagar was alone in the silent desert, weary
and sad and despairing, thinking there was no eye to pity her,
no heart to feel for her, no hand to guide her, no friend to
take her part, "the angel of the LORD found her by a fountain
of water in the wilderness" (16[7]). " It has been disputed
whether the angel of the LORD be one of the angels or the
LORD Himself in self-manifestation. The manner in which
He speaks leaves little room to doubt that the latter view is
the right one : the angel of the LORD is a theophany, a self-
manifestation of God. In Gen. 16[10] the angel of the LORD says
to Hagar, 'I will greatly multiply thy seed,' and in Gen 21[18]
the angel of God called to Hagar out of heaven, 'Lift up the
lad, and I will make him a great nation.' The angel identifies
himself with God, and claims to exercise the prerogatives of God.
Those to whom the angel appears identify him with God : in
Gen 16[13] Hagar called the name of the LORD who had spoken
unto her, 'Thou art a God that seest (all-seeing)'; in Gen. 18
the angel is called the LORD." [2] " Though the angel dis-
tinguishes himself from God, and speaks of Him in the third
person, as when he says to Hagar, 'Jahveh hath heard thy

[1] Ps. 139[23, 24].                    [2] A. B. Davidson.

affliction' (18¹⁴), yet his appearance and speech are equivalent to the appearance and speech of Jahveh."[1]  "God, working at a particular spot, and at a definite point of time, is called the angel of God."[2]  It was not in the stir of the Hebrew camp, but in the silence of the wilderness, that the LORD found Hagar. She had been for years in Abram's household, had daily seen her master offer sacrifice, and heard him call upon the name of the LORD.  Religion was one of the proprieties of Hebrew camp-life, a solemn and awful ceremonial which had only a distant relation to herself.  But God makes a silence in her heart that she may hear Him speak.  In the desert He meets her with words of tender rebuke, wise counsel, and gracious promise (16⁷⁻¹²).  He reveals to Hagar the greatest secret in the world, that God cares for Hagar.  For the first time in her life she realises that the LORD sees her, hears her, thinks of her, feels for her.  She receives a revelation of the divine pity ; she finds God a refuge and strength, a very present help in trouble.  All that she had heard of God in the camp at Mamre flashes back into her mind, and she wonders that here in the desert God has seen her and she has looked after God (16¹³).  To *look after* God was to recognise Him by the traces of His working.[3] Hagar is allowed to see something of God, and to realise that God sees everything in her.  All true heart-religion begins with this, "He looked to me, I looked on Him."  It is the mutual recognition of the Divine Spirit and the human spirit.  There is one faith of hearsay and another of vision : " I had heard of Thee with the hearing of the ear : but now mine eye seeth Thee."[4] Hagar's experience was recorded in the name she gave the desert fountain beside which her God met her ; " Beer-lahai-roi " means "the well of the living One who seeth me."  God's ways and means of winning His people to Himself never undergo any essential change.  He still makes a silence and a solitude around us that we may hear Him speak to our hearts.  Having robbed us of human comfort and hope, He favours and enriches

[1] Schultz.　　　[2] Hitzig.　　　[3] Schultz.　　　[4] Job 42⁵.

us with a revelation of His love. His method is exquisitely described by one of the great Hebrew prophets : " Behold, I will allure her, and bring her into the wilderness, and speak comfortably unto her (*Heb.* to her heart). And I will give her the valley of Achor (Trouble) for a door of hope." [1]

SELF-EXAMINATION.—Self-scrutiny is often the most unpleasant, and always the most difficult, of moral actions. But it is also the most important and salutary ; for, as the wisest of the Greeks said, "an unexamined life is not worth living." Because self-examination is both so essential and so difficult, God Himself asks us questions which set us about undertaking this task. "The righteous God trieth the hearts and reins " ; [2] His word is "quick to discern the thoughts and intents of the heart." [3] If the Searcher of hearts puts questions, it is for the benefit, not of the Questioner, but of the questioned. When He found Hagar in the desert, He asked her, " Hagar, Sarai's maid, whence comest thou ? and whither goest thou ?" He who knew her name and her mistress' name, knew everything else. He questioned her that she might know herself. She was drifting on in a course which she had now for the first time paused to consider, and a pointed and searching question would make her tell herself in plain words just what she was doing. God calls her to review her past and forecast her future. His questions, whence ? whither ? seem on the surface very easy to answer, yet they pierce far into the heart of things. They are questions about life, conduct, character, and destiny. Hagar answered the first question very simply, " I flee from the face of my mistress, Sarai " (16[8]). But she began to realise that she was also turning her back upon the best home, the purest life, the finest opportunity that she could find anywhere in the world. She was fleeing from goodness, and hope, and happiness, and grace. She was going out of the light, and whither ? But she does not attempt to answer the second question, and her silence

[1] Hos. 2[14, 15].　　[2] Ps. 7[9].　　[3] Heb. 4[12].

is expressive. She knows what is behind her, but she knows not what is before her. She has come to the wilderness of want and hunger and thirst ; will she go farther, to the land of darkness and cruelty and sin ? The thought is too terrible. Instinct itself makes us " rather bear those ills we have than fly to others that we know not of." God's searching questions, whence ? whither ? imply that for Hagar and for every one there is a right way, and that our great business is to know it and keep to it with full purpose of heart and will. If we have erred from God's way, He says to us, " Return " (16⁹). At the same time He persuades and enables us to do it. His presence searched and humbled and changed Hagar, till, submissive to God, she was willing to submit herself to her mistress. Before the LORD found her, and while she felt nothing but her own bitter wrongs, it would have been the hardest thing in the world for her to acknowledge her fault to her mistress. After she saw the LORD, and felt her heart suffused with His wonderful love, she was ready to return and say, " I have sinned, forgive me."

FREEDOM.—God has designed that each of the nations of the earth shall have its distinctive aims, spirit, and ideals. Nature, climate, and environment make it impossible that they should all be alike. Nations as well as individuals have a distinctive character stamped upon them. Ishmael the Arab was never intended to be a Hebrew, any more than the Celt is meant to be a Saxon, or the Hindoo an Englishman. To Hagar it was foretold regarding her son, " He shall be as a wild ass among men (*Heb.* a wild-ass man) ; his hand shall be against every man, and every man's hand against him ; and he shall dwell in the presence of all his brethren " (16¹²). The prophecy is spoken, " not of Ishmael's person, but of his progeny. It is applicable only to the whole nation." [1] Ishmael's destiny may not seem very attractive, especially the first part of the threefold prophecy. But it should be remembered that the wild ass of the desert is

[1] Calvin.

quite different in character—as well as in his Eastern names—
from his stupid second-cousin, and our estimate of him should
not be prejudiced by his connections.   The Arabian wild ass is
as expressive and appropriate a national emblem as the British
lion.   The author of Job knew and admired the wild beasts of
the field, and there are few finer pieces of nature-poetry than his
description of this beautiful untameable creature of God.[1]

> " Who hath let the wild ass go free?
> And who hath loosened his bonds?
> God hath made the wilderness his home,
> And the barren steppes his dwelling.
> He scorns the multitude of the city,
> And has no heed of the driver's cry.
> He ranges the hills as his pasture,
> And searches out every green thing."

*There* is Ishmael the Arab, the wild-ass man, limned to the
life : his unrestrained love of freedom ; his scorn of city crowds ;
his hardy, frugal, unconquerable spirit ; his home the illimitable
desert; his heart in the green oasis.  There are few nobler types of
manhood than the ideal Arab, and the time to favour Ishmael will
come.   Unsubdued by arms, Arabia's desert ranger may be won
by love.   In a beautiful description of the Messiah's reign it is
said, "They that dwell in the wilderness shall bow before Him." [2]

OBSERVANCE. — Hagar's simple confession of faith, "Thou,
God, seest me" ($16^{13}$), contains an unwelcome and alarming
thought for the bad, a grateful and comforting truth for the
good.   Max Müller says he once heard a child exclaim, "Oh,
I wish there were at least *one* room in the house where God
could not see me"; and adds, that the words reminded him of
the Psalmist's "Whither shall I go from Thy spirit? or whither
shall I flee from Thy presence?" [3]   Hagar fled into the wilderness, but God was there ; and God sees every one in the dark,
in the crowd, in solitude, everywhere, and always.

[1] Job $39^{5-8}$.          [2] Ps. $72^9$.          [3] Ps. $139^7$.

> "Among the deepest shades of night,
>   Can there be one who sees my way?
> Yes,—God is like a shining light,
>   That turns the darkness into day."

This is one of the primary beliefs which transformed the Hebrews into the people of God. " The eyes of the LORD," they said, " are in every place, keeping watch upon the evil and the good" ;[1] " His eyes behold, His eyelids try, the children of men."[2] The faith in God's oversight gives an awful depth and meaning to life and duty. It signifies that God fixes His attention upon us, perceives our motives, scans our thoughts, weighs our actions, and is " acquainted with all our ways."[3] It differs totally from idolatry, whose gods are blind ; from atheism, which has no God ; from deism, whose God is too exalted to take notice of man ; and from agnosticism, to which God is unknowable. Among those who believingly say, " Thou, God, seest me," there are some who say it tremblingly, some who say it rejoicingly. God's omniscience is an appalling thought to transgressors ; they dread to think that nothing screens them from God's all-seeing eye ; they tremble when they hear of One "unto whom all hearts are open, all desires known, and from whom no secrets are hid." But to all who love and trust the LORD, the belief in His gracious oversight is the creed of creeds. Their only fear is lest God should *overlook* them, lest they should have to say, " My way is hid from the LORD."[4] " Thou, God, seest me," brought intense comfort and cheerful hope to Hagar at the fountain in the desert. Mr. Barrie has told us that it was his mother's favourite text. She had a little son who meant, when he grew up, to be a minister and preach his first sermon from this text ; but when he was six years old a cart went over him, and his mother carried him home in her arms lifeless. After he had been " twenty years dead," she would say, " That day he was coffined, for all the minister prayed, I found it hard to say, 'Thou, God, seest me.' It's the text I

[1] Prov. 15³.        [2] Ps. 11⁴.        [3] Ps. 139³.        [4] Isa. 40²⁷.

like best noo, though, and . . . I turn't up, often, often in my Bible. I read from the beginnin' o' the chapter, but when I come to ' Thou, God, seest me,' I stop . . . I let the Book lie in my lap ; for aince a body's sure o' that, they're sure o' all."

MERCY.—"Abram called the name of his son, whom Hagar bare, Ishmael" (16$^{15}$). The name means " God heareth." "Samuel" is another combination of the same words. It is very important to note what God hears. The angel of the LORD said unto Hagar, "Thou shalt call his name Ishmael ; because the LORD hath heard thine affliction" (16$^{11}$). This is one of the tenderest sayings in the Bible. If the words express a general truth, it is a marvellous one. It was no articulate prayer, but the mute appeal of a lonely woman's distress, which moved God to give a gracious answer. Mere misery has a wonderful pathos when it speaks in the ear of mercy. Affliction is a voiceless prayer which God understands, and to Him its pathos is irresistible. He attends not to words, but to wants. Eloquent prayers which are uttered without sincerity have no wings, and never leave the ground ; but the human distress which has no language, or no language but a cry, flies upwards and enters into the heart of the Eternal.

## POWER
### Genesis 17

" You have all the power of heaven at your back, and you *must* succeed."
HENRY DRUMMOND.

POWER.—God was about to call Abram to a higher level of service and a higher range of truth—to require of him a perfection which might seem unattainable, and to unfold to him a grace which might seem incredible. But He prefaces the call with the revelation, "I am El Shaddai—God Almighty, the Wielder of power, the All-sufficient" (17$^1$). After that nothing is impossible, nothing incredible. The august title reveals the infinite resources from which man can draw, the divine energy which ensures his success. Absolute reliance on God's almightiness is the condition of power. For every duty there is an appointed dynamic: "Thy God hath commanded thy strength." [1] The Almighty will not let His servants fail or be put to shame, else that is not His name. He links His power to His imperatives. What we can do in our own strength is one thing, what we are empowered to achieve by omnipotent grace is far different. The possibilities of life are to be measured, not by the ability of man, but by the power and will of God. Instead of desiring a lower ideal, we should pray for a higher energy. "Lord," said Augustine, "give what Thou commandest, and command what Thou wilt." "Attempt great things for God, expect great things from God," said Carey. "Who is sufficient for these things?" asked Paul, and presently answered, "Our sufficiency is of God." [2]

GODLINESS.—God sets before Abram two ideals. First, He requires him to walk before God ($17^1$). He is to be a model of the consecrated life to all his descendants. The Hebrews had a dislike for abstract terms. Their profoundest thoughts on religion were vivid pictures. They did not speak of cultivating godliness, or of deepening spiritual life, but of walking before God. To live in the realised presence of God, to order their thoughts and acts so as to harmonise with His character, to rejoice in His company, to look up to Him with a smile of loving recognition in the work and warfare of life—this was to walk before God. It was the Psalmist's ideal to set the LORD always before him,[3] to walk in the light of His countenance;[4] Micah's, to walk humbly with his God.[5] It was Milton's ideal to live ever in the Taskmaster's eye; Brother Lawrence's, to practise the presence of God. "God and the angels are

---

[1] Ps. $68^{28}$.      [2] 2 Cor. $2^{16}$ $3^5$.      [3] Ps. $16^8$.
[4] Ps. $89^{15}$.      [5] Mic. $6^8$.

spectators," said Bacon. It is the thought of God's presence which makes men serious, devout, earnest, trustful, consecrated, holy. Agnostics preach an independent morality : they would have men to do their duty without a thought of God, who, they say, is in any case unknowable. But common men find, and history proves, that the morality which goes without God soon grows limp and tired, while the righteousness which stays itself on God has an unquenchable ardour and energy. " They that wait on the LORD shall renew their strength ; they shall run and not be weary ; they shall walk and not faint."[1] God is the indispensable moral dynamic, and walking before God is the highest ethics. The everlasting goodness is after all godliness— a living before, with, in, for, and like God.

PERFECTION.—The other ideal which God presents to Abram is perfection (17¹). The LORD shows Himself "strong in the behalf of them whose heart is perfect toward Him."[2] The Psalmist calls himself perfect.[3] God called Job a perfect man,[4] and the reader of the Hebrew Scriptures is bidden mark the perfect man for imitation.[5] Here it is evident that we need a definition. " Perfect " means true-hearted and whole-hearted in the service of God. The Hebrew Scriptures speak of many men as perfect, while they call none sinless. The man who walked with a perfect heart[6] was the man of integrity or sincerity, who saw that the LORD'S service was an integer, not a fraction of life. God could not be satisfied with a partial love, a divided allegiance. No true lover offers less than a whole-hearted affection, nor can he be content with less. Where there is a right to all, partial love is a mockery and an insult. The divine Lover of our souls gives to us, and asks of us, a perfect love. " Thou shalt love the LORD thy God with all thy heart, and with all thy soul, and with all thy might."[7] Perfection, in the Hebrew sense, was a passionate, whole - souled love of

---

[1] Isa. 40³¹.    [2] 2 Chron. 16⁹.    [3] Ps. 18²³.    [4] Job 1¹.
[5] Ps. 37³⁷.    [6] Ps. 101².    [7] Deut. 6⁵.

God. Partial loyalty was disloyalty ; partial obedience was disobedience. The perfect life was simple, because it had one
ruling motive—the love of God, and one chief end—the glory of
God. The divided life was difficult, because it had mixed
motives and heterogeneous ends. Perfection was what we
express by such terms as full allegiance, absolute surrender,
complete consecration. It was what Bunyan expressed by saying that Emmanuel would not give the least corner of Mansoul
to Diabolus to dwell in ; He would have all to Himself. It
was what Henry Drummond meant when he said, " Don't
be an amphibian, half in one world, half in another." It was
what Mr. Moody meant when he said, " Be out and out."
But the very men whom God called, and who sometimes called
themselves, perfect, were the last to say or imagine that they
were sinless. The best of men feel themselves the greatest
sinners. It was " a perfect man " who said, " I abhor myself,
and repent in dust and ashes." [1] The Hebrews called no man
on earth sinless : " Who can say I have made my heart clean,
I am pure from my sin ? " [2] The perfect adjustment of the
will or devotion of the heart is a very different thing from
the perfect attainment of the ideal. In the latter sense no
man was perfect. " I have seen an end of all perfection," said
the Psalmist, " but Thy commandment is exceeding broad." [3]
" Not as though I had already attained, or were already
perfect," said St. Paul ; " but I press on." [4] One sinless life has
been lived on earth, and no second. " There's nobody perfect,"
said Rabbi Duncan ; " that's the believer's bed of thorns, that's
the hypocrite's couch of ease."

WORSHIP.—Abram had an awe-inspiring sense of a mysterious
presence, and fell on his face before God ($17^3$). Another time
he " bowed himself to the earth " ($18^2$) ; another, he " stood
before the LORD " in an act of intercession ($18^{22}$). The Hebrews
had no fixed rules as to attitudes in devotion. The posture

[1] Job $42^6$.    [2] Prov. $20^9$.    [3] Ps. $119^{96}$.    [4] Phil. $3^{12}$.

which the worshipper assumed varied with his mood of feeling. Some men stood as they prayed—Abraham, Phinehas, Solomon (so the penitent publican); some knelt in prayer—Solomon, Daniel (so Jesus, Peter, Stephen, Paul); some fell on their faces —Abram, Moses, David, Job, Elijah (and so Jesus); some prayed in a sitting posture—David and perhaps Nehemiah; some prayed with the hands lifted up and spread forth—Moses, David, Solomon. Gestures were natural signs of devotional feeling, and powerful aids to it. Faber says that reverential attitudes are half the battle of vocal prayer. It is natural and befitting to stretch out the hands in supplication; to bow the head in reverence; to bend the knees in petition; to cover the face, close the eyes, or prostrate the whole body, before the majesty of God; to lie "in dust and ashes" before Him under a sense of guilt. Man, penetrated with the mystery of sin, cannot endure without agony the blinding light of God's holiness. Even Moses the servant of God exceedingly feared and quaked in the presence of God;[1] Isaiah felt undone when his eyes saw the King, the LORD of hosts;[2] Daniel had no strength left, and fell with his face toward the ground, when he beheld the great vision;[3] John, when he saw the Son of man, fell at His feet as one dead.[4] This humiliation of the soul is what prepares it to receive a revelation. "Can a man, to this hour, get guidance by any other method than intrinsically by that same—devout prostration of the earnest struggling soul before the Highest?"[5]

SOVEREIGNTY.—God renews His covenant with Abram ($17^4$), and connects seven promises with it: that Abram shall be the father of a multitude of nations, that kings shall be among his posterity, that the LORD will be a God to him and his seed, that the land shall be given to them as an everlasting possession, that circumcision shall be the sign of the covenant, that Abraham shall have an heir by Sarah, and that the covenant shall be

[1] Heb. $12^{21}$.    [2] Isa. $6^5$.    [3] Dan. $10^{8.9}$.
[4] Rev. $1^{17}$.    [5] Carlyle.

established with Isaac. The third provision—that the LORD will be the God of Abraham and his seed (17⁷·⁸)—is the all-embracing covenant-promise. It means that God will be to His people all that God can be—that He will exercise His power, wisdom, faithfulness, and grace on their behalf, and never cease working for their happiness. All His attributes are pledged for their welfare. His power will be their protection, His wisdom their guidance, His faithfulness their security, His grace their salvation. It is a promise as large and unlimited as language can express. No words can sum up all that the LORD will be to His people. The "shalls" and "wills" of the covenant—twenty of the former and fifteen of the latter in this chapter—express the fixed purpose of God. They are absolute and infallible. There is no "if" in the covenant of grace. God speaks in imperial language. Man is free, yet God has a plan for humanity which He will carry out. He is "great in counsel, and mighty in work."[1] The covenant is not to be annulled by the sins and shortcomings of any particular generation. It is impossible for the unbelief of man to make the promises of none effect. God has absolute control over the course of history as over the forces of nature. Man's sin does not thwart His purpose any more than His purpose interferes with human freedom. He is the LORD, and changes not.[2] "If we are faithless, He abideth faithful; He cannot deny Himself."[3] "The gifts and calling of God are without repentance."[4]

FATHERHOOD.—A Hebrew proper name was significant. It was a condensed creed, or story, or prophecy. Abram (High Father) and Ishmael (God heareth) are creeds; Isaac (laughter) and Jacob (supplanter) are stories; Abraham (father of a multitude) is a prophecy. "Abram" does not describe the man who bore the name, as if "High Father" were equivalent to Patriarch; "it is rather the recognition of God as a Father by him who is so named." So at least Delitzsch thought; and if his

---

[1] Jer. 32¹⁹.     [2] Mal. 3⁶.     [3] 2 Tim. 2¹³.     [4] Rom. 11²⁹.

view is correct, the name contains an indication of the early groping of men's minds after the truth of the Fatherhood of God. The Hebrew word for father is AB, and the divine Fatherhood is the alphabet of the Christian religion. Though this doctrine never had anything like the same prominence among the Hebrews, still there are clear enough indications of it in their writings; and certainly the filial consciousness, the childlike spirit of trust, is not wanting in the Old Testament. The LORD says to His people, "Thou shalt call Me, My Father," [1] "for I am a Father to Israel." [2] And Israel responds, "Thou, O LORD, art our Father," "Thou art my Father." [3] "Like as a father," says the Psalmist, "pitieth his children, so the LORD pitieth them that fear Him." [4] As applied to God, the word "Father" has lost all physical associations, and is used to denote the loving relation to Himself in which God has placed His people. It is only through the divine Son, however, that men are learning to acknowledge and rejoice in the universal Fatherhood of God.

NATIONALITY. — The LORD said unto Abraham, "I will establish My covenant between Me and thy seed after thee. . . . And as for thee, thou shalt keep My covenant, thou and thy seed after thee" ($17^{7.9}$). He makes His covenant with the people or nation. The ideal of a covenanted nation was the heart of the Hebrew religion and the life-blood of Hebrew history. The Hebrews had the unalterable conviction that God had entered into a covenant with their race, and that they had solemnly bound themselves to be His people and to serve Him. The covenant ideal was at once the consecration and the inspiration of the people. There was the spirit of duty and service and self-surrender in it ; there was the spirit of power and freedom and invincibility in it. It is well known that the ideal of a nation in covenant with God has had an extraordinary fascination for the people of Scotland. Of its value and power one of the greatest

[1] Jer. $3^{19}$.　　[2] Jer. $31^{8}$.　　[3] Isa. $63^{16}$.　　[4] Ps. $103^{13}$.

of living Scotsmen has spoken thus : "A thought has played a large part in Scottish story. . . . Side by side with the intense type of personal piety there was, in Reformation and later days, an equally clear perception of the duty, not of a Church, but of a nation to its God. . . . When our typical form of individual piety is taken, as it ought always to be taken, along with the old desire to make the collective life of a community subserve the ends of righteousness, to make the nation an instrument of doing God's will on earth, our hereditary ideal of religion—I at least will not hesitate to avow it—is the grandest, the most catholic, the broadest which any Church or land has ever endeavoured to embody throughout the nineteen Christian centuries. The thought of a covenanted nation was both great and true—a thought most difficult in virtue of its greatness to apply in adequate detail, but better fitted to raise men's daily practice out of selfishness and sin, and to make them fellow-workers with the risen Christ, than any separate thought in the history of the universal Church." [1]

CONSECRATION.—Circumcision was the appointed sign of the covenant ($17^{11}$). Sometimes the covenant itself was said to be in the flesh (v.$^{13}$), the thing signified being used for the sign. It is somewhat difficult for us to appreciate the sacred significance of this rite. Whatever it originally was,—and it may be traced to what were intellectually very crude conceptions,—it was invested by the Hebrews with profound spiritual meaning. It was the symbol of moral purity, of ethical circumcision—the cleansing of the heart from the pollution of sin : "The LORD shall circumcise thine heart, to love the LORD thy God with all thine heart." [2] Circumcision was the mark of entrance into the believing community with all its rights and duties. It consecrated a man to the worship and service of the LORD, and secured to him the blessings of the covenant. It was designed to be an avowal of faith, a testimony to faith, and an assistance to faith. St. Paul

[1] Principal William Millar, of Madras.          [2] Deut. $30^6$.

calls it "a seal of the righteousness of faith."¹ All male
Hebrew children were consecrated to God by this rite (17¹²). It
was the sign and seal of their privileges, signifying that the LORD
was their God in childhood as He would be in manhood. It was
the mark of the rights of slave children as well as of the freeborn
(17¹². ¹³). Bond and free alike were heirs of salvation. To the
pure all things are pure, and even the child Jesus was "circum-
cised on the eighth day, according to the commandment."² If
any man despised and neglected the sacrament, he declared
himself to have broken the covenant and denied the faith, and
that soul was cut off from his people (17¹⁴). As believers are
still in the same covenant of grace with Abram, as they are still
justified by faith, the promise is still unto them and to their
children.³ Now are the children holy.⁴ Their privileges have
never been withdrawn or curtailed. The children have not been
cast out of the covenant. Jesus did not rob them of their
charter. He simply replaced the sacrament of circumcision by
the sacrament of baptism, which equally seals and secures to
the children the same ancient covenant rights.

FAITH.—When Abram was promised a son in his own and
Sarah's old age, "he fell upon his face, and laughed" (17¹⁷).
Questions arose "in his heart," but never came to his lips. The
tidings seemed almost too good and too wonderful to be true ;
yet "looking unto the promise of God, he wavered not through
unbelief, but waxed strong through faith, giving glory to God,
being fully assured that what He had promised, He was able
also to perform."⁵ We read of believers who, on receiving
extraordinary tidings, "believed not for joy, and wondered."⁶
Abram laughed, and wondered, and for a moment questioned,
but did not disbelieve. Ten thousand difficulties do not make
one doubt. Behind all natural obstacles, behind all our questions, suggestions, and surmises, we see God, and faith triumphs.

¹ Rom. 4¹¹.　　² Luke 1⁵⁹.　　³ Acts 2³⁹.
⁴ 1 Cor. 7¹⁴.　　⁵ Rom. 4²⁰.　　⁶ Luke 24⁴¹.

There is no presumption in believing God. The Hebrews gave the quietus to many doubts with the reverent question, "Who is like unto Thee, O LORD, glorious in holiness, fearful in praises, doing wonders?" The principle underlying the narrative is of immense value. Reason makes its careful distinctions between the likely and the unlikely, and teaches that probability is the guide of life. Men raise their doubts into a system, and declare that miracles do not happen. Faith looks to God's almightiness, and concludes that the unexpected will happen. Unbelief laughs at miracles, and calls them impossibilities :

> " Faith laughs at impossibilities,
> And says, It shall be done."

LIFE.—The joyful promise of an heir suddenly brought a spasm of fear to Abram's heart. What if the birth of another son should bode ill to his firstborn ? Would the LORD withdraw His tender mercies and shut up His compassions from Hagar's child ? Would He abandon him to some cruel fate ? Abram uttered a passionate heart-cry for his son, "Oh, that Ishmael might live before Thee !" Fear made him an intercessor. Parental love and solicitude find their natural outlet in fervent prayer, and nothing reacts upon and increases parental affection so much as earnest intercession. Abram's prayer was ejaculatory, swift as an arrow of light or a glance of the mind. Every devout heart sends up many such winged words to heaven every day. The important matter is not how long one prays, but how intensely and earnestly. The longest prayer may have the shortest flight, the shortest prayer the longest. If one's prayer reaches heaven it is long enough. "Prayer is like lightning, and does not take time."[1] Abram prays for Ishmael, naming him in prayer, not describing him in a circular way, and stating distinctly the blessing he craves for him. Great love and great fear make definite prayers. The boon Abram seeks for his son is life before God. The LORD is He "in whose hand is the soul of every living

[1] Henry Drummond.

thing, and the breath of all mankind." [1] Abram knew that he had no grounds for anxiety about Ishmael's physical health. The archer boy was as robust a child as ever felt the wild joys of living. What the father desired was that his son should not be excluded from the sphere of God's love, that he should be cared for, guided, and blessed by God. In the Hebrew idea of life "there is always included the thought of blessedness, of fellowship with God. No one who does not rejoice before God in the light of life can be said to live. An existence without God, and without joy in Him, is not worthy of the name." [2] "Life in His favour lies," [3] and the thought of a beloved child missing the true life fills the sympathetic heart with a dread which speeds the soul's petitions up to the throne of God. The modern question, "Is life worth living?" was answered long ago. Life without God, the Hebrews believed, was certainly not worth living. But life before God, life irradiated by the light of His countenance, life embosomed in His love, is infinitely desirable, now and for ever.

## HOSPITALITY
### Genesis 18:1-15

"Among the guests there never cometh
One who can find such high and honoured place."—SPITTA.

SCRIPTURE.—The narrative contained in Gen. 18-19 is one of enthralling interest. It is an Epic of Mercy and Judgment. The divine acceptance of the righteous and reprobation of the wicked are the double theme of the piece. Good and evil, light and shade, are as vividly contrasted as in Michael Angelo's Last Judgment. Above, on the clear heights of Mamre, the friend of God, radiant in moral beauty, receives celestial visitants, and the presence of God makes a heaven on earth ; below, in the sunken cities of the Plain, flagitious vice and insatiable lust turn human

---

[1] Job 12[10].          [2] Schultz.          [3] Ps. 30[5].

life into a hell. Here, the children of light, the beauty of holiness, the rewards of righteousness ; yonder, " the city of dreadful night," the works of darkness, the wages of sin. The glory of saints and angels is intensified by contrast with the vileness of incarnate fiends. The style of the narrative is in keeping with the great ideas. Only in the Hebrew Scriptures can we find language so noble and simplicity so fearless. " The Bible," says one of the great masters of style, " should be read if it were for nothing but the grand language in which it is written, an education in itself."[1] "The excellence of Holy Scripture," says another of them, " does not arise from a laboured and far-fetched elocution, but from a surprising mixture of simplicity and majesty, which is a double character, so difficult to be united that it is seldom to be met with in compositions merely human."[2]

HOSPITALITY.—Heaven was far away and inaccessible to the Hebrews, but earth was not inaccessible to God. It was possible for God to reveal Himself, to visit the sons of man,[3] and what was possible became actual. This was the essential fact, and it was clothed in many forms by "the poetical, vivacious, and powerful phantasy of the people of Israel."[4] Sitting at the door of his tent in the slumberous Eastern noontide, Abraham sees three strangers draw near. He is unconscious of their supreme dignity, and for this reason the welcome he extends to them serves all the better as a pattern of hospitality. He runs to offer them obeisance. The ancient Hebrew "looked upon politeness not merely as a desirable outward formality, but as the indispensable expression of a good disposition."[5] Abraham begs the strangers to honour him by resting under his tree and accepting a morsel of meat. "A gentleman," says Newman, " makes light of favours when he is doing them ; he thinks he is receiving an honour when he is conferring a kindness."[6] The

[1] Tennyson.    [2] Newman.    [3] Ps. 84.
[4] A. B. Davidson.    [5] Gunkel.    [6] Newman.

morsel turns out to be an ample repast, "tender and good." Abraham has many servants at his beck, and Sarah many maids; but the master and mistress bestir themselves to prepare the meal with their own hands ; and when the table is spread under the green tree, Abraham stands to wait upon his guests (v.⁸). His lowliness of mind deems no office degrading which can be lovingly rendered. This is sweet, stately, noble hospitality. Times and manners change ; every age has its etiquette, and East differs from West ; but courtesy and loving-kindness are the same under all guises. True welcome never consisted in meats and drinks, but in the affection of the heart. Love can make a little gift excel. The sympathy which feels for others' need, the kindness which is happy in serving, the modesty which says little and does much, the open house and heart and mind—these are some of the elements of hospitality. But this grace cannot be analysed. " There is an emanation from the heart in genuine hospitality which cannot be described, but is immediately felt." [1] Abraham and Sarah found that the rewards of hospitality are spiritual. It brings a blessing to the giver as well as the receiver, and some who show love to strangers entertain angels unawares.[2] The hosts and hostesses of the Bible, generous and philanthropic souls who did not squander the gifts of God on sinful pleasures, nor hoard them for selfish ends, but delighted to spend them in doing good,—Abraham and Sarah, Rebekah and Abigail, the women of Sarepta and Shulem, and like them the sisters of Bethany, Lydia, and Prisca, and Gaius,—found that their kindness came back to them an hundredfold in the hallowing memories and heavenly influences which lingered in their homes, and in the joy of the diviner life to which they were called and stimulated by the messengers of God.

FAITH.—When it was announced to Abraham that he should have a son, Sarah was not present, Eastern etiquette requiring a lady of rank to remain in her private apartment during a visit of

---

[1] Washington Irving.      [2] Heb. 12².

male strangers. Nigh in her tent she sat, of all unseen, but hearing all. Through the intervening curtain she listened to the promise, and laughed at it with bitter incredulity. It sounded liker irony than truth, and awoke in her the spirit of doubt and denial. But when she heard the Guest rebuke her secret laughter, and expose the dissimulation into which she was then betrayed by fear, and ask in tones which seemed more than human if anything was too hard for God, she was shaken out of her doubt, and restored to the humility of faith. She received the great blessing, " because she judged Him faithful who had promised." [1] Incredulous laughter at divine things, the mockery of the unbelieving human heart, betrays one's natural disposition to limit the power of God, and to judge the future, not by faith, but by our own notions of what is reasonable and likely. Low and unworthy thoughts of God are at the bottom of all doubt as to His power to perform what He has promised. We glide into the dialect of infidelity, into bitter and arrogant questioning, because we forget that we have a great God and of great might, who gives splendidly and graciously after His own nature. " No word from God shall be void of power." [2] The language of faith is, " Thou art great, and doest wondrous things." [3] The whole Old Testament regards the miraculous as a matter of course. " No pious Hebrew ever doubts that when God wishes to give His servants special help, the necessary occurrences must take place, whether they be ordinary or extraordinary." [4] The greatest of men soon find their limitations ; but " is anything too hard for the LORD ? " (18[14]). Is " difficult " or " impossible " a word in His vocabulary ? One of the great prophets makes answer, " Ah, LORD God ! behold, Thou hast made the heaven and the earth by Thy great power and stretched-out arm, and there is nothing too hard for Thee." [5] Morally, some things are, of course, impossible for God. He " cannot lie," [6] He " cannot deny Himself," [7] He

---

[1] Heb. 11[11].     [2] Luke 1[37].     [3] Ps. 86[10].     [4] Schultz.
[5] Jer. 33[17].     [6] Heb. 6[18].     [7] 2 Tim. 2[13].

"cannot look on iniquity" without displeasure.[1]  But no miracle
of grace or power is too hard for Him to perform.  Omnipotence
knows no limits to its sphere of action.  This was what Job
believed : " I know that Thou canst do everything" ;[2] and what
Jesus taught : "With God all things are possible."[3]

WIFEHOOD. — Sarah  called  her  husband  "Adoni"—"My
Lord" (18[12]).  St. Peter, when writing about "the ornament
of a meek and quiet spirit," praises the holy women of the olden
time, who trusted in God and were in subjection to their
husbands, "as Sarah obeyed Abraham, calling him Lord."[4]
Sarah's use of this title of honour in reference to her husband
would in itself be an insufficient reason for making her a pattern
of wifehood, especially as some words of quite an opposite import
are recorded against her (16[5]).  But the apostle sees that the
dutiful word is weighted with all the love and loyalty of a lifetime.  When Abraham made the great venture of faith, renouncing hearth and home for conscience' sake ; when he lived
a nomad life among strangers, summering and wintering under
canvas, enduring trials and afflictions, she was always by his
side, lightening the way he travelled, doubling his joys and
dividing his sorrows, ordering the peace and comfort of his
house, cheering him to face all hardships with constancy of
mind, and sometimes in hours of temptation and danger putting
him to shame by her quiet-hearted heroism.  Nothing is finer
than the courage of a true and noble woman.  Sarah was a
Princess in name and in nature.  She understood her husband's
divine vocation, shared his religious aspiration, and never ceased
to be his true helpmate.  He could not but see in her "the
stately form of female fortitude, of perfect wifehood."[5]  Thus
she has her rightful place in the great Roll of Faith.[6]  The
strength of character and woman's love which carried her
through all her trials with a spirit unbroken and a fountain of

---

1 Hab. 1[13].          2 Job 42[2].          3 Matt. 19[26].
4 1 Pet. 3[6].          5 Tennyson.          6 Heb. 11[11].

laughter still in her heart, were not less worthy of praise than the faith which subdued kingdoms and wrought righteousness.

## EDUCATION
### Genesis 18:16-19

" I acknowledge the all-but omnipotence of early culture and nurture."
CARLYLE.

FRIENDSHIP.—The visit of friendship at Mamre over, the strangers turned their faces toward Sodom, Abraham escorting them on their way (18¹⁶). A work of inquisition and judgment was now about to begin. But the LORD first revealed His purpose to Abraham. There were two reasons for making him the man of His counsel : it was befitting that the Hebrew who was His friend should be made His confidant ; and it was necessary that the man who was chosen to be the head of a holy family, the founder of a great nation, the channel of blessing to the world, should know the principles of divine government. When Philo the Jew quotes Gen. 18¹⁷ in one of his books, the text runs, " Shall I hide from Abraham, *My friend*, that which I do ?" The Septuagint has " from Abraham, My servant." The words " My friend " may once have been in the Hebrew, and nowhere would they be more appropriate than in this passage. The relation of friendship was a strong reason why the LORD should confide His secrets to Abraham. In Isaiah He calls Israel " the seed of Abraham, My friend " ; [1] and St. James says [2] expressly that Abraham was called the friend of God. " El Khalil," " El Khalil Allah "—" the Friend," " the Friend of God " [3]—is the name which the Arabs habitually give their renowned ancestor. No prince, or noble, or hero ever had so honourable a title as " the friend of God." Abraham would never have dreamed of assuming it. As Dr. Whyte has said,

[1] Isa. 41⁸.    [2] Jas. 2²³.    [3] 2 Chron. 20⁷.

"Abraham would have protested against, and would have repudiated the name of friend with fear and shame." But while it was received with all humility, it must have filled his heart with unutterable joy. No man has any claim to God's friendship ; all men are by nature enemies to God. Friendship between God and man can be initiated, continued, perfected by God alone. God reveals His love to man, and, when man responds to the divine call, there is opened in his own renewed heart a fountain of love to God which becomes the master-passion of his soul, transforming his life, and making him great, wise, good, and noble enough for the LORD to call him, and for all men to call him, the friend of God. Abraham's friendship with God was once unique, it is now typical. Divine friendship is within the reach of every believer. It is the high ideal which our Lord set before all His disciples : "Ye are My friends, if ye do the things which I command you. No longer do I call you servants . . . but I have called you friends ; for all things that I heard from My Father I have made known unto you."[1]

FOREKNOWLEDGE. — Abram's election to service was the second reason for his being taken into God's counsel. Because he was chosen to be the founder of a holy nation, and a channel of blessing to humanity, God reveals to him the principles on which He rewards and punishes men. "Surely the LORD God will do nothing, but He revealeth His secret unto His servants the prophets."[2] "I have *known* Abraham," He says, "to the end that he may command his children and his household after him" (18[19] R.V.). This means, "I have taken knowledge of him in grace, I have befriended and chosen him." The same idea is found in Amos' words, "You only have I known of all the families of the earth."[3] We often ask the question, "Is God knowable to man?" That seems to be the fundamental question of religion. But there are more important preliminary questions, "Is man knowable to God?" and "Has God taken knowledge

[1] John 15[14, 15].        [2] Amos 3[7].        [3] Amos 3[2].

of man?" The Hebrews were certain that man could never by searching find out God,[1] but they were equally certain that God could and did take knowledge of man in such a way that man should have a real though imperfect knowledge of God. Every believer knows that God has known him; he is as sure of that as he is of anything. He would never have left the realm of spiritual darkness of his own accord; his salvation has been planned, provided, secured, and maintained, as it will be perfected, by God. He gives God all the praise. "Truly," said Luther, "our knowledge is more passive than active, *i.e.* it is rather being known than to know." One of Paul's self-corrections is full of significance, "But now that ye have come to know God, or rather to be known of God."[2] When a friend of Frederick Maurice said, "I have found God," Maurice interposed, "Or rather have been found by Him." Abram was chosen to be a spiritual leader of men, and his sense of divine foreknowledge was invaluable and indispensable to him. "He who is destined for a work of religious revolution must have a full conviction that God is acting directly, immediately, consciously, and therefore with irresistible power upon him and through him. He who is not predestined, who does not believe himself predestined, as the author of a great religious movement, but in whom God is not manifestly, sensibly, avowedly working out His pre-established design, will not be a saint or reformer."[3]

EDUCATION.—Abraham was chosen to be a blessing to the whole earth (18[18]); but his vocation was to begin to take effect in the simplest way. He was called to teach his own children and his household (18[19]), who again would hand down the truth to their children and their households. His being a blessing to the world depended on his being a blessing to his own home. The lamp of truth must first be lighted in one dark place. Saving knowledge is diffused over the earth, not like sunlight,

[1] Job 11[7].    [2] Gal. 4[9].    [3] Dean Milman.

but like torchlight, which is passed from hand to hand. Abraham is chosen "that he may command his children and his household after him, that they may keep the way of the LORD, to do justly and rightly" ($18^{19}$). This is the first Welfare of Youth scheme—God's own unalterable scheme. He makes the family the spiritual unit of society, and His educational code, addressed to every Hebrew parent, ran thus : "These words which I command thee this day shall be in thine heart, and thou shalt teach them diligently to thy children, and shalt talk of them when thou sittest in thine house, and when thou walkest by the way, and when thou liest down, and when thou risest up."[1] This divine method may be supplemented, but must never be supplanted. The responsibility of the religious training of the young can never be shifted from parents to strangers. "Train up a child in the way he should go" is addressed to a parent ; and no other work that God gives a man to do is so important, so sacred, so far-reaching in its influence. The parent is the child's first and best teacher, whose duties can never be adequately done by a substitute. No one can lodge a great moral or religious truth in the opening mind of a child as a father or mother can. No person has the same opportunities, the same motives, the same obligations, the same power as the parents have. Neither the Church nor the State can subvert the order of nature. The words and ways, the ideal and spirit of the parents do more to shape the character of their children than all other influences combined. It was the home that made the Hebrews the people of God and the most influential nation in the history of mankind. "It is from the nursery," said Tholuck, "that the world is governed." "Believe me," a Prime Minister has said, "the roots of empire are in the home. It is in the family we build the commonwealth."[2] The home-school has been called the great factor of national success ; it is certainly the fountain of a nation's purest and noblest life. "All other causes," says Sir John Gorst, "have a comparatively small effect upon national

[1] Deut. $6^7$.     [2] Rosebery.

character, which is in the main the product for good or evil of powerful causes which operate, not in the school, but in the home." Progress in secular education is no compensation for the loss of domestic religion. God will not let us change His methods with impunity. One quarter of an hour daily devoted to earnest family worship does infinitely more for the formation of character than all the long hours given to secular knowledge. "*Pro aris et focis*"—"For altar and hearth"—is still the most sacred of battle-cries. Church, school, and home are three abiding institutions ; but the greatest of these is home. "Blessed is the son who has studied with his father, and the father who has instructed his son." [1]

AUTHORITY.—It was the LORD'S purpose that Abraham— here as usual the ideal Hebrew—should command his children and his household after him (18[19]). "Command" is a strong word, but not too strong to express the authority which God delegates to parents, and for which they are to give account to God. Only a strong government can be true and tender. Human nature is such that a lax discipline, which tolerates sin or treats it lightly, which allows a false freedom, which humours the child and gratifies his appetites and his vanity, is essentially weak and cruel. The Hebrews teach us that "the laws of the family have a religious character, and are to be regarded with holy awe." [2]  It is the parent's right and duty, not to make laws for his household, but rather to exact obedience to divine laws : "As for me and my home, we will serve the LORD." Parental authority is here based on faith ; and if the children lose their reverence for their parents, the first reason is that the parents have lost their reverence for God. When authority is not arbitrary but moral, it secures the blessings of order and peace and happiness ; and reverence for parents becomes reverence for all that is just and true and pure and good. Nothing is so wholesome and bracing to one's character as to grow up under

[1] Talmud.                    [2] Schultz.

strong and wise and holy laws. Discipline, it has been said, is
so important that it may almost be called salvation. Where
strong and true love exercises a spell which makes the lightest
word a law—where "all's law and yet all's love"—obedience is
a spirit and not a form, and there is true liberty in exact proportion to obedience. The failure to assert authority is the
betrayal of a solemn trust, which endangers the best interests
of a household. It was a good and devout Hebrew's condemnation that "his sons made themselves vile, and he restrained them
not,"[1] that he honoured them above God.[2] Soft, easy, indulgent
as he was, Eli plagued himself and his house by his kindness to
his children's sin. There is the rigour of true love in these words
written by the mother of two of the best men that have ever
lived : "In order to form the minds of children, the first thing
is to conquer their will and bring them to an obedient temper.
This is the only strong and rational foundation of a religious
education, without which precept and example will be ineffectual.
As self-will is the root of all sin and misery, so whatever
cherishes this in children ensures their after wretchedness and
irreligion ; whatever checks and mortifies it promotes their
future happiness and piety."[3] Some parents delay the religious
discipline of their children under the impression that serious
thoughts are not to be encouraged in the young ; others do it
on the principle that every one should be left to decide for
himself in matters of religion. "Thewall," says Coleridge,
"thought it unfair to influence a child's mind by inculcating
any opinions before it should have come to years of discretion,
and be able to choose for itself. I showed him my garden, and
told him it was my botanical garden. 'How so,' said he, 'it is
covered with weeds.' 'Oh,' I replied, '*that* is only because it
has not yet come to its age of discretion. The weeds, you see,
have taken the liberty to grow, and I thought it unfair in me to
prejudice the soil towards roses and strawberries.'"

[1] I Sam. 3¹³.                    [2] I Sam. 2²⁹.
[3] Susannah Wesley.

GUIDANCE.—Every believer was to teach his children and his household to keep the way of the LORD (18¹⁹). Here is another instance of the Hebrew love of simple and concrete terms. "The way of the LORD" was the whole course of moral and religious thought and action which the people of God were to pursue—the ideal life which. God set before His servants. He did not leave them to find out their own way. "O LORD," said the prophet, "I know that the way of man is not in himself: it is not in man that walketh to direct his steps."[1] But as God has given the stars their orbits, the earth its path, the rivers their courses, so He has given man his way. This is not merely the way of life which God prescribes for man and approves of in man; it is the LORD'S own way revealed to man. There is a moral law universal in its operation and binding upon all moral beings, binding even upon God. This law is the expression of God's perfect character; and though no man fully conforms to it, it is the true law of every man's life and happiness. As there are not two or many gods, but one God, so there are not two or many ways of life, but one way. To learn it is the best education and noblest science which man can receive. This way is perfect, and permanent, and free— every man enjoys the right of way. "And a highway shall be there, and it shall be called the way of holiness; the unclean shall not pass over it; but it shall be for His people: the wayfaring men, though simple, shall not err therein."[2] It is called the way of understanding, the way of truth, the way of righteousness, the way of holiness, the way of wisdom, the way of peace, the way of good men, the right way, the highway, the perfect way, the way everlasting. God sent many prophets to teach men His way, and at length One who could say, "I am the Way."

CHARACTER. — Abraham followed the divine method of instruction with the best results. He did not give his children

[1] Jer. 10²³.  [2] Isa. 35⁸.

and his household what we now usually understand by education. Among the Hebrews reading and writing were long the
accomplishments of the few. The very words are not found in
Genesis. Yet the young Hebrews received, in happy circumstances, a noble education for head and heart, body and soul.
Abraham taught them by word and example to *know* the way
of the LORD—true religion, and to *do* justice and judgment—
true morality ($18^{19}$). He showed them how to walk before God,
to trust in Him for righteousness, to pray to Him for guidance.
He required them to be faithful in their service, simple in their
habits, pure in their lives. He instructed them to be peaceful
and generous and brotherly. At the same time he trained them
to be strong and brave and manly, to fight, when occasion
required, for a good cause, and to be submissive to God's will,
if need be, even unto death. They learned the lessons to good
purpose. Isaac was consecrated to God in spirit from his childhood; Hagar believed in the all-seeing God; God was even
with the lad Ishmael ($21^{20}$); the steward Eliezer had a
perfectly childlike trust in his master's God; and Abram's
home-born trained men ($14^{14}$) were the bravest of the brave,
going into battle with their master like Cromwell's Puritans or
Havelock's Saints. The highest education is not the storing of
the memory with knowledge, but the cultivation of manly and
womanly character.

## INTERCESSION
### Genesis 18:23-32

"What are men . . .
If, knowing God, they lift not hands of prayer,
Both for themselves and those whom they call friend?"

TENNYSON.

JUDGMENT.—Viewed from the heights above Mamre, the guilty
cities lay still and peaceful in the lovely Circle of Jordan. Even

in the hush of evening no audible voices came up the slopes to where "Abraham stood yet before the LORD" (18$^{22}$). But from the cities a great mysterious cry ascended to God the Judge and Avenger (18$^{20. 21}$). There are loud testimonies to all human wrongs. Sin, once committed, seems over and done ; sinners promise themselves impunity, and earthly judges sleep ; but the cry of violated purity—as of yore the cry of an innocent brother's blood,[1] and in later ages the cry of labourers' hire kept back by fraud [2]—fills earth and heaven, eloquently appealing to God to punish the guilty.

> " My conscience hath a thousand several tongues,
> And every tongue brings in a several tale." [3]

This idea of crime demanding retribution pervaded the ancient world ; it was exhibited with terrific power in Greek tragic poetry. Hearing the cry of the cities, God purposed to "go down and see" their actual condition (18$^{21}$). This is a vividly human way of expressing and visualising the fact that God acts according to the strict laws of justice, that His judgments are pre-ceded by a full and impartial inquiry, that He condemns no man without a trial. " He is gracious and merciful, slow to anger, and of great kindness."[4] Vengeance is called His strange work.[5] Still He vindicates His character as the Judge of all the earth, who will by no means clear the guilty. All His judgments have a merciful purpose. His severity has love at its core as its motive. It condemns the wicked in mercy to the rest of mankind. It prevents the torrent of sin from rushing over the world. It seeks the purity of the race when it removes those families which have become horribly depraved. "When Thy judgments are in the earth, the inhabitants of the world learn righteousness."[6]

INTERCESSION.—Abraham stood on the heights overlooking the valley of the Jordan—according to tradition at the spot now

---

[1] Gen. 4$^{10}$.    [2] Jas. 5$^{4}$.    [3] Shakespeare.
[4] Joel 2$^{13}$.    [5] Isa. 28$^{21}$.    [6] Isa. 26$^{9}$.

called *Kepher Barucha*—and made intercession for Sodom. He sought to avert from the cities of the Plain the judgment which was threatened. The LORD listened graciously to his prayer. He loves intercessory prayer, for the less of self there is in our petitions, the more of love, and therefore the more of God. No man ever receives a divine blessing without having poured upon him the spirit of prayer for others. Every true believer's soul is consumed with holy desires for the good of men. He grasps the mighty promises and attributes of God, and turns them all into arguments. When a man comes out of himself, and becomes an intense pleader for others, the LORD is near to answer him. There is much in Abraham's intercession to admire and imitate.
(1) He prayed with *charity*. He assumed that there were at least fifty righteous men in Sodom. He could not believe that the whole populace was debased. Since the wisest may err in their opinions of their fellow-men, we ought always to begin with the judgment of charity, which hopes and believes all things. Brotherly love is the secret and strength of intercession. The believer's detachment from the world does not mean indifference to the world. He loves the world because God loves it. Separation from sin and sympathy with sinners are equal and not opposite. As Abram had once saved Lot and Sodom by the sword, it was natural that he should now seek to save them by intercession. Prayer and good deeds constantly react on one another. Do a man a kindness, and you will be disposed to pray for him ; pray for him, and you will be kind to him. While Abram's pleading was generous and large-hearted, it turned out that he was mistaken in his charitable judgment ; for instead of fifty righteous men being in Sodom, there was only one. Still his mistake was nobler than that of the great prophet who thought there was but one faithful man left in Israel, when there were seven thousand.
(2) He prayed with *jealousy* for God's glory. He believed in the rectitude of the Judge (18$^{25}$), and feared that God's name would be compromised if Sodom were destroyed. The Hebrews held that both the righteous and the wicked shall be recompensed in

the earth.[1]   They could not believe in the present failure of
justice, and as yet they did not know of the future recompense
for the immense wrongs of the world.   Rightly or wrongly,
Abraham supposed that God's honour demanded a certain
course, and in any case his zeal for the divine glory is admirable.
He was sensitive to everything that touched the divine name.
He would not sacrifice a ray of God's glory.   God's character
was dearer to him than his own, and his chief desire was that it
should be vindicated in the world.   Men pray best when God's
cause and honour lie near their own hearts.   "Glorify Thy
name," "hallowed be Thy name," should always be the first and
most urgent of all our petitions.   (3) He prayed with *humility*.
He whom others called the friend of God, the father of the
faithful, called himself "but dust and ashes" (18[27]).   The higher
he rose in God's favour, the lower he sank in his own esteem.
He was nothing, God was all.   "Humility does not consist in
abasing ourselves lower than we are.   But as all virtue is founded
in truth, so humility is founded in a true and just sense of our
own weakness, misery, and sin."[2]   Growth in humility is progress towards truth.   Abraham's fellowship with God, his partaking of the divine nature, his sublime calling and destiny, did
not prevent him from remembering that his native home was in
the dust.   The nearer he got to God, the more he was conscious
of his unworthiness to be there.   "If we think we are something,
we have only to turn our eyes to God, and immediately we
acknowledge that we are nothing."[3]   (4) He prayed with
*reverence*.   He twice confessed his fear that he was guilty of
overboldness in having "taken upon him to speak to the LORD"
(18[27, 31]); and twice prayed God not to be angry with him for
persisting in speaking (18[30, 32]).   He felt he was too audacious
in appearing to expostulate with God.   He feared that his
earnestness bordered on presumption.   He hardly realised his
right to speak at all.   Nearness to God increases one's awe of
His majesty.   Perfect love casts out fear, but deepens and

[1] Prov. 11[31].          [2] William Law.          [3] Calvin.

intensifies reverence. (5) He prayed with *importunity*. He renewed his request time after time,—six times in all,—asking a greater thing each time. He pressed and urged his suit. He "stood yet before the LORD" (18²²), he "spake yet again" (v.²⁹); he would "speak yet but this once" (v.³²). Again and again he used almost the same language, as men do when their hearts are deeply stirred. True prayer is earnest, intense, fervent, importunate. God gives men what they seek with their whole heart. He cannot endure lukewarm petitions. If we pray without fervour, we as good as ask a refusal. It is the ardent, persistent suppliant whom God rewards. The boldest words of a loving heart are not irreverent in His ear. Luther sometimes prayed in this audacious strain : "Lord, I will have my will of Thee at this time, for I know that my will is Thy will." As he would take no denial, God did not deny him, and people looking at him as he passed would say, "There is the man who can get what he likes from God." (6) Abraham prayed with *success*. "The fervent prayer of a righteous man is strong in its working."[1] The prayers of the Hebrews were all based on the assumption that prayer moves the will of God. The modern theory that prayer is useful to ourselves, but cannot be operative upon God, is neither Hebrew nor Christian. It is true that Abraham's intercession did not avert the doom of Sodom itself. The depraved inhabitants of the Jordan Valley were worthy of death. But "it came to pass, when God destroyed the cities of the Plain, that God remembered Abraham, and sent Lot out of the midst of the overthrow" (19²⁹). Thus God made Abraham "a second time the deliverer of Lot from ruin, strongly marking the contrast between the two, in that the weak brother owed his safety to the intercession of him who, enjoying God's favour, was content to be without earthly portion."[2]

RIGHTEOUSNESS.—"Shall not," asked Abraham, "the Judge of all the earth do right?" It was the glory of the Hebrew religion

[1] Jas. 5¹⁶.                    [2] Newman.

that this question admitted of only one answer. The Hebrews believed in a righteous order of the world under the sovereign rule of a righteous God. The Hebrew conscience has been called the keenest religious instrument of the ancient world, and it made religion ethical through and through. (1) The grandest possession of the Hebrews was the character of their God. They had a noble passion for righteousness, and exalted it to the supreme place among human interests ; but they had no abstract righteousness, no independent morality. They derived their ideas and their practice of righteousness from God ; they had and knew no other justice than God's. The LORD their God was the personal source, sanction, standard, and ideal of righteousness. He was not merely the impersonation of ethics, but the Creator of universal law ; and to suppose God swerving from justice was to suppose the spring and pattern of morality becoming immoral, which was unthinkable. We moderns are in the habit of saying that there is *something* above ourselves which makes for righteousness, or that the soul of the world is just. The Hebrews teach us rather to say, "Righteous art *Thou*, O LORD, and upright are Thy judgments" ;[1] "the LORD our God is righteous."[2] (2) The Hebrews attained the idea of a righteous order and judgment of the world. There is justice in heaven, and it is extended to earth ; God rules the world in righteousness. "Verily, there is a God that judgeth in the earth."[3] The essential feature of His rule is its morality. His government is not despotic ; for absolute power in His hands cannot err or act unjustly. The righteousness of God is "the mighty rock on which the moral order of the universe is founded. . . . It is the pledge that justice will triumph in the world."[4] Should the Judge of all the earth once act unjustly, this moral order would be turned into chaos, which is again unthinkable. "If the foundations be destroyed, what can the righteous do?"[5] Confidence in the absolute rectitude of God and the righteous government of the world made the Hebrews,

---

[1] Ps. 119[137].  [2] Dan. 9[14].  [3] Ps. 58[11].
[4] Schultz.  [5] Ps. 11[3].

despite all their faults, morally the strongest race of antiquity. The Greeks and Romans wanted the divine ideal and sanction of virtue. They could never count on righteousness being done in heaven or on earth. They were tormented by fear of the fickleness and injustice of the gods—privileged despots who took a malignant delight in levelling down human greatness. Their best men were morally not inferior, but superior to the gods. Hence their faiths have been completely dissolved, while the Hebrew faith, having a God of absolute righteousness, is everlasting.

INFLUENCE.—"And the LORD said, If I find in Sodom fifty righteous men, then I will spare all the place for their sake. . . . I will not destroy Sodom for ten's sake" ($18^{26.\ 32}$). The whole Circle and its cities would have been saved had there been ten righteous men in Sodom. The presence of one imperfectly righteous man was for a time sufficient to prevent the stroke of justice from falling ; the LORD could not do anything to Sodom till Lot had reached a place of safety ($19^{22}$). Righteous men have always been the saviours of society, the salt of the earth. A pure and upright character is a common and public good. The lives of true men are fountains overflowing with blessing for their fellow-men. When Jerusalem was threatened with ruin, one of the great prophets cried in God's name, "Run ye to and fro through the streets of Jerusalem, and seek in her squares, if ye can find a man, if there be any that doeth justly and seeketh truth, and I will pardon her."[1] A city's best defence is not its walls and battlements, but its upright and God-fearing citizens. "It is a mighty encouragement that He who saves by many or by few has invested human agency with the power of so wide an operation, insomuch that one man has by his single voice decided the fate of nations. Ten righteous persons would have saved Sodom."[2]

[1] Jer. $5^1$.　　　　　　　　[2] Chalmers.

## MERCY
### Genesis 19:1-14

" In mercy and justice both
Through heaven and earth,—so shall My glory excel ;
But mercy first and last shall brightest shine."—MILTON.

PURITY.—The Book of Genesis was written, not only with the design of commending virtue as lovely, but for the purpose of branding sin as hateful. The authors sought by the pen, as the prophets by the living voice, to arouse the public conscience, to create a hatred of the levity and frivolity of heathen races. Gen. 19 presents a terrible picture of the condition into which men fall when, abandoning moral restraints, they refuse to have God in their thoughts, and He therefore gives them up to a reprobate mind. The companion picture is St. Paul's awful description of the pagan world as it was in his time.[1] It has been said that if virtue were once embodied, and came down among men, all men would worship her. But the facts are against this beautiful theory. When the angels of God visited the Circle of Jordan, their presence only roused the brute and the demon in men. When perfect virtue was at length embodied on earth, it was crucified. The heart must be cleansed by divine grace before it can love the light and reverence the ideal. Progress in civilisation has been progress towards moral purity. Plato despaired of exterminating vice ; he called the thought of doing so " a romantic aspiration." The Hebrews did not despair. They succeeded, and their success made them the greatest benefactors of the human race.

GAIN.—Lot's choice of a home in Sodom was dictated by lust of gain and pleasure rather than by regard for the will of God. When he went down from Bethel to the well-watered

[1] Rom. I.

Plain of Jordan, he never dreamed of losses. He was grasping his earthly ideal, he was coming into his kingdom. He had a vision of princely wealth and civic honour and domestic felicity, crowned in the distant future with a serene old age. But when he entered Sodom, he left peace for ever behind him. His life became a vexation of spirit. He was out of his element, alone and friendless, hated as an intruder, mocked as a blunderer. He lost the holy and helpful influence of his best friend ; he lost his property, first in war, then in fire ; he lost his kindred and his wife ; and it was of the LORD'S goodness that he did not lose his life in the general conflagration. His soul, too, was beggared. He retained goodness enough to make him thoroughly unhappy amid the carnivals of sin ; but he lost a righteous man's clearness of vision, sensibility of honour, purity of heart. " Lot chose the Plain of Jordan because it was well-watered, but his soul was all but withered there." [1] The story of Lot's unwise choice and its unhappy issues is an old commentary upon our Lord's saying, " He that loveth his life shall lose it " ; [2] while Abram's blessedness is an illustration of the beautiful words—

> " Happy is the man that findeth Wisdom,
> For . . . her gain is better than fine gold.
> She is more precious than rubies :
> And none of thy delights are to be compared with her.
> Length of days is in her right hand,
> And in her left hand riches and honour.
> Her ways are ways of pleasantness,
> And all her paths are peace." [3]

CHARITY.—Lot was to be rescued from Sodom, not merely because he had Abraham for an intercessor, but because he was himself a servant of God, "a righteous man." He had begun well, renouncing heathenism, embracing a spiritual religion, and linking his fortunes to those of a strong man of faith. Even in Sodom he was not without good qualities.

[1] M'Cheyne.　　　[2] John 12$^{25}$.　　　[3] Prov. 3$^{13\text{-}17}$.

His righteous soul was daily vexed with the lawless deeds which he saw around him.[1] He practised the sacred rites of hospitality when everybody else was shamefully violating them (19[1-3]). His house was the only place in Sodom where strangers were safe. The messengers of God accepted his kindness. He exposed himself to the violence of a raging mob in order to shield his guests (v.[6]). The worst thing which the citizens could allege against him was that, being a stranger, he had set himself up as a censor (v.[9]). He retained the instincts of faith and obedience to God. He believed the warnings of coming judgment, earnestly but vainly endeavoured to rescue his kinsmen (v.[14]), was thankful for divine grace and mercy (v.[19]), and cried to God in his distress (v.[20]). St. Peter reviewed the facts of Lot's life, and, with a restored backslider's tenderness to a broken man, recorded the judgment of charity, that Lot was a righteous man. It was unfortunate that, like many another man who is justified by faith, Lot gave himself scarcely a chance to become nobler in character.

ZEAL. — Lot's moral righteousness lacked the quality of passion. The revellers of Sodom beset his house like a swarm of demons let loose from hell. Burning words of holy indignation were urgently needed. But Lot parleyed with the criminals. He called them his brothers. He begged for peace at any price, and was willing to sacrifice the honour of his daughters. But while Lot's sensibility was so blunted that he sordidly bargained with the licentious crew, the sacred writer's heart has a glow of consuming indignation against sin—a glow which he communicates to the reader. Anger is not always wrong, and peace is sometimes far from right. The lack of moral indignation is the lack of manhood. He who is not angry at sin is not in love with virtue. While there is an anger which is holy love and pity aflame, there is a kind of prudence which is one of the deadly sins. The continuous

---

[1] 2 Pet. 2[8].

enjoyment of worldly ease sensualises the mind till the grossest vices are but mildly rebuked or silently tolerated. "A gentle reproof encourages sin and makes it seem as slight as the censure implies. To reprove sin mildly is to patronise it." [1] The man who barters his ideals for a false peace, whose working principle in hours of danger is "anything for a quiet life," flatters himself that in a troublesome world he gives proof of an amiable and conciliating disposition; but what he really proves is that the Spirit of God is departing from him. Every heart which God indwells has an intense love of purity. Moderation in morals is treason against God. "No heart is pure which is not passionate; no virtue is safe which is not enthusiastic." [2]

MERCY.—Lot and his family were to be rescued from the wicked and doomed city, but they had to be saved almost against their will. Even when they knew their danger, they lingered in Sodom (19[16]), hesitating, doubting, wavering. There is a critical state of mind in which a man knows his duty, and feels that he ought to do it without delay, but something pulls him back and keeps him from doing what is right. The angels who were sent on a mission of mercy to Lot and his family gave an example of true kindness which is worthy of imitation. Being hospitably entertained in the house of Lot, and receiving conclusive evidence of the city's abandonment to sin, they delivered their message to those whom it concerned. They began by directing (19[12]), proceeded to warning (v.[13]), advanced to commanding (v.[15]), and ended by fairly compelling (v.[16]) Lot and his family to quit the City of Destruction. There is a gradation in the methods by which angels and ministers of grace fulfil their sacred obligations to souls in danger. They may enlighten the mind, alarm the conscience, move the heart, and at last, when all else fails, grasp the lingerers by the hand with the holy vehemence of love, lead them forth from the place of danger, and set them in the way of safety. An exquisite parenthesis

[1] Robert Hall.    [2] *Ecce Homo.*

in the narrative implies that this last method is the one which
answers the tenderness of divine pity and fulfils the purpose
of divine love. "While Lot lingered, the men laid hold upon
his hand, and upon the hand of his wife, and upon the hand
of his two daughters—*the LORD being merciful unto him*—and
they brought him forth, and set him beyond the city" (v.[16]).

> " Thus while they waver, surely long ago
>      They had provoked the withering blast,
>   But that the merciful Avengers know
>      Their frailty well, and hold them fast.
>   ' Haste, for thy life escape, nor look behind '—
>      Ever in thrilling sounds like these
>   They check the wandering eye, severely kind,
>      Nor let the sinner lose his soul at ease." [1]

Holy love has an urgency which will brook no denial. It
is severely kind. It snatches brands from the burning. Its
apparent violence is the proof of real love. " Compel them," [2]
are words of One who was all love. Unhappily it always remains
possible that the utmost endeavours of mercy may prove unsuccessful. The human soul retains its freedom, and may in the
end chose destruction instead of salvation. After the heralds of
mercy had done all that men or angels could do, one member of
the rescued family was a pillar of salt when the sun rose upon the
earth (v.[26]). " If thou," said a great prophet, " warn the wicked
of his way to turn from it ; and he turn not from his way, he shall
die in his iniquity ; but thou hast delivered thy soul." [3]

## JUDGMENT
### Genesis 19:15-29

" Infinite love, yet also infinite rigour of law."—CARLYLE.

PRAYER.—When the angels had led forth Lot from Sodom,
the LORD directed him to escape to the mountain—the mountain
range of Moab is meant—lest he should be consumed (19[17]).

---

[1] John Keble.       [2] Luke 14[28].       [3] Ezek. 33[9].

But Lot's imagination conjured up all kinds of danger in the mountain region. "The morbid fear of the hills, which fills any human mind after long stay in places of luxury and sin, is strangely marked in Lot's complaining reply, 'I cannot escape to the mountains, lest some evil take me.'"[1] His heart was still in the Plain, and he pleaded for permission to turn aside to the little town of Zoar and live there ($19^{19. 20}$). Lot's prayer teaches us how *not* to pray. The substance of all true prayer is, "Not my will, but Thine, be done." Lot prayed in effect, "Not Thy will, but mine, be done." With the waywardness of unreason, he ventured to differ from God, he dictated to God, he argued with God, he begged God to change His mind. He set aside an express divine commandment, and tried to wrest a blessing from God; whereas humility always pays, "Deny me this, O LORD, if it be not for Thy glory and my good." His prayer was the fretting and chafing of an unhumbled spirit. Whenever Abraham received a divine injunction, he said not a word, but simply and implicitly obeyed ($12^4$ $22^3$). When Lot learns the divine will, he grows loquacious; instead of obeying, he gives many reasons for disobeying—reasons which are merely the murmurs of his restless self-will. Augustine used to pray, "Lord, deliver me from that evil man, myself." It is significant that Lot's selfish prayer was granted (v.$^{21}$). He was punished for his wilfulness by getting his way. He quickly discovered the misery of a wrong prayer answered. He was permitted to eat of the fruit of his doings until he loathed them. He had not been long in the city of his choice before he changed his mind, and "went up and dwelt in the mountain" after all (v.$^{30}$). But it was not the same. A tardy submission does not win the reward of a prompt unquestioning obedience. St. Bernard says there are three bad kinds of prayer—timid prayers, tepid prayers, and temerarious prayers. Lot's prayers were temerarious—rash, inconsiderate, wilful, daring without reason. The language of humble faith is, "I delight to do Thy will, O my God."[2]

[1] Ruskin.          [2] Ps. $40^8$.

"Oh let Thy secret will
  All Thy delight in me fulfil!
Let me not think an action mine own way,
  But as Thy love shall sway,
Resigning up the rudder to Thy skill!"[1]

MORALITY.—The effects of Lot's sojourn in Sodom at length became apparent. He had deliberately chosen to dwell "in the tents of sin," and the grace of God does not make even a righteous man invulnerable to the deteriorating influences of an illegitimate calling or a dishonourable situation. Neither good habits, nor prudence, nor self-respect saves him from the slow infection of a poisonous moral atmosphere. The friendship of the world inevitably lowers the temperature of the soul, and lukewarmness never kills the germs of temptation. One of the great prophets says, "Behold, this was the iniquity of Sodom : pride, fulness of bread, and prosperous ease was in her."[2] Luxury is the mother of licence. An easy accommodation to evil and a lowering of the moral ideal are the natural results of an overestimate of the comforts of civilisation. The man who makes pleasure his chief good, will, in the common course of things, mildly rebuke sin, tolerate it, connive at it, succumb to it, and finally be overwhelmed by it. When Lot went up out of Zoar, after his act of disobedience had put him out of harmony with God, the good no longer predominated in his character. The man's moral fibre was gone, and nothing remained but a shuffling, cringing, sensuous egoist. Having long lingered on the confines of the kingdom of evil—"the borderland dim 'twixt vice and virtue"[3]—he at last fell into foul sin, and his name was covered with infamy. "We allow temptation to come and go at pleasure, and one day the soul wakes up to find itself possessed with all manner of evil. . . . There is no such thing as an unrelated sin in any life. The great fall which suddenly stains the reputation of a public name, and which the world's charity glosses over as merely a sudden slip, is never the first of a series but the

---

[1] George Herbert.        [2] Ezek. 16⁴⁹.        [3] Arnold.

last." [1]  When Lot fell, his lamp went out in obscure darkness.
Better, we are apt to say, had the good angels left him to perish
in Sodom ; he would have gone to heaven with a cleaner record,
and we should have been spared one of the most ghastly stories
in the Bible ($19^{30\text{-}38}$).  His life—like every backslider's—was a
series of contradictions.  He was the friend of the faithful Abram,
and the citizen of Sodom ; he was the host of angels, and the
kinsman of scoffers ; he was "that righteous man," and an in-
cestuous drunkard.  But no one who knows the gracious power
of God will deny that his manhood might be restored.  He
might again be as he had been, and feel as he had felt.  The
tears of repentance might flow in the withered waste of his life.
The prophet Amos was thinking of Lot when he coined his
terrific simile of "a brand plucked out of the burning." [2]  And
St. Paul may have been alluding to him when he spoke of the
man who "himself shall be saved, yet so as through fire." [3]

TEMPERANCE.—Sometimes the Bible seems a stern book.  It
is as stern and as tender as nature and grace.  One of the ways
in which it commends virtue is to paint vice in its naked
ugliness ; and here it tells the frightful, humbling truth about
strong drink.  The story of Lot's fall gives expression to the
repugnance which the Hebrews felt against the drinking customs
of the nations on the other side of the Jordan, Lot being the
father of the people of Moab-Ammon.  It was written for the
purpose of creating an intense aversion to the degrading vice of
drunkenness.  Lot would never have fallen into gross sin if he
had not first been sodden with wine—if his reason, conscience,
and manhood had not been drowned in drink.  Innumerable
crimes are the work of senseless drunkards, who are covered
with shame when they return to reason and realise their guilt.
They "mortgage miserable morrows for nights of madness." [4]
"O God!" cried Cassio, "that men should put an enemy in

---

[1] Henry Drummond.      . [2] Amos $4^{11}$.
[3] I Cor. $3^{15}$.      [4] Charles Lamb.

their mouths to steal away their brains! that we should with joy, pleasance, revel, and applause, transform ourselves into beasts! . . . O thou invisible spirit of wine! if thou hast no name to know thee by, let us call thee devil."[1]  The praises of wine have often been sung, but the true story of strong drink is a record of misery, brutality, vice, crime.  Chaucer said long ago—

> " A lecherous thing is wine . . .
> For drunkenness is very sepulture
> Of manne's wit and his discretion."

There is a connection of the vices, one sin facilitating and provoking worse sins.  Strong drink undermines the foundations of the moral life, so that a sot is an easy prey to the worst and vilest passions.  The most ghastly evils of civilisation could never exist unless they were propagated and supported by strong drink, which breaks down all the restraints of reason, prudence, affection, and religion.  Carlyle rightly described strong drink as "the most authentic incarnation of the infernal principle yet discovered."  Charles Lamb called it "wet damnation."  Drunkenness was the shame of heathen Moab, and it is the shame of Christian Britain.  " It has been said that greater calamities are inflicted on mankind by intemperance than by the three great historical scourges, war, pestilence, and famine.  This is true for us, and it is the measure of our discredit and disgrace."[2]  Immense power for good or evil always lies in the hands of the women of a nation.  The mothers of Moab-Ammon made themselves odious by exerting their influence to encourage the use of strong drink.  On the other hand, the women of Britain have it in their power to achieve the honour of delivering their country from the vice of intemperance, which one of the noblest of womankind, Queen Victoria, characterised as " so great a curse."

KINSHIP. — It was Lot's duty to shelter his family from danger and sin, but his worldly choice left them exposed to the fiercest temptation, and it was no wonder if they fell before

[1] Shakespeare.          [2] Gladstone.

it. Our Lord bids us "remember Lot's wife." The painful things of the Bible are to be kept in memory ; they are written for our admonition ; they are absolutely necessary as beacons to warn us of danger. Lot's whole family was deeply infected with the evil of the fascinating, fatal Circle. Only the strongest minds can fortify themselves against the influence of a bad environment. (1) Lot's *sons-in-law* are types of the happy-go-lucky fellows who trip merrily through life, counting earnestness folly. When Lot went out at night to warn them of judgment to come, he seemed unto them "as one that mocked" (19¹⁴). God's word was to them an idle tale or a fool's jest. "They might see my fears," Lot would say afterwards like Pilgrim, "in my countenance, in my tears, and also in my apprehension of the judgment that did hang over our heads ; but all was not sufficient to prevail with them to come with me." Listening to their father's lecture with amusement and scorn, growing merrier as he grows more earnest, heedless of warning, reckless of danger, thoughtless to the last, they were suddenly overwhelmed by the fire-shower of ruin. (2) Lot's *wife* left Sodom unwillingly ; her treasure and her heart were still there ; and it was for a love-look that she forfeited her life. The backward glance revealed her character. She turned with a sigh of regret, a fierce spirit of disobedience, a defiance of divine counsel, a passionate desire—all that was in the retrospect. As she stood to gaze at the splendid home of her luxury, she was caught on the margin of the fire-shower, the sulphurous smoke enveloped and stifled her, the saline matter encrusted her, and she was transformed into a pillar of salt. Lingering, longing, looking, she was lost. Jesus bids us remember her as a type of those whose attachment to earthly things is their ruin—who, in the day of trial, perish with the perishing goods from which they cannot separate themselves.

> "Once gain the mountain-top, and thou art free ;
> Till then, who rest, presume ; who turn to look, are lost." [1]

---

[1] John Keble.

(3) Lot's *daughters* are among the most pitiful figures in the Bible. The consequences of an evil choice often fall most heavily upon those who least deserve them. Lot was bound by every motive of religion and love to care for and protect his daughters, to shield them from sorrow, sin, and shame. But he gave them a home and an upbringing in Sodom, and they could not live in that noxious atmosphere without being tainted. When they were rescued from the guilty city, their lovers were burned and their mother was a salt pillar. They had no home but a mountain cave. They were saved from the wicked city, but not from its wickedness. Womanly grace and delicacy they had none. The daughters of the friend of Abraham were unclean savages. They fell into abysmal depths of sin, and we are glad when the kindly darkness covers them from our sight. So swift and sure is the descent from the highest to the lowest when temptations are strong and the restraints of godly fear are withdrawn.

RETRIBUTION.—Milton represents Satan as saying, "Evil, be thou my good." There are men who practically say the same—men of earthly, sensual, devilish minds, who glory in their shame and abandon themselves to the fascination of vice. Such men are abhorred of the LORD, whose hatred of sin and purpose to exterminate it are as strong and unwavering as His love of purity and holiness. God pities weakness and infirmity, but not sin. He "is angry with the wicked every day."[1] God is love; but love is not all sentiment, pity, and tears. "It is love that burns ; it is love that judges ; it is love that damns. No other love would be worth having."[2] When men make evil their good, God's Spirit ceases to strive with them.[3] He bids "leave them alone," as Hosea says.[4] He "gives them up," as Paul thrice has it.[5] He suffers them to "eat of the fruit of their own way and be filled with their

---

[1] Ps. 7[11].    [2] Joseph Parker.    [3] Gen. 6[3].
[4] Hos. 4[17].    [5] Rom. 1[24. 26. 28].

own devices." [1]   He holds His hand, and lets sin do its own sad work in their souls.   That is the first retribution of sin.   Unclean passion is the most speedily self-punishing and ruinous of all sins.   It desolates brain and heart and life.   It ruins the grace and health of the body ; it ruins the tone and temper of the mind ; it ruins the taste and capacity for pure pleasures ; it ruins the reputation ; it ruins the soul.

NATURE.—When God sent His angels of death to destroy Sodom and her sister cities ($19^{13}$), natural agencies were no doubt employed in the overthrow.   The words, "the LORD rained brimstone and fire out of heaven" ($19^{24}$) are to be compared with such words as, "God gave us rain from heaven." [2] In both cases heaven is the atmosphere.   The elements, fire and water, ascend before they descend.   Milton speaks of "that bituminous lake where Sodom fell," and bitumen affords the means of solving a difficult problem.   Had the sacred historian viewed the catastrophe as a man of science, he might have written thus : "Now around and underneath the Sea of Salt were bituminous and sulphur springs, by which reservoirs of petroleum and gas were formed far beneath the surface of the earth ; and these being suddenly discharged, either by their own pressure or by the shock of an earthquake, the gas escaped with explosive force and carried far into the air the ignited petroleum, which fell back in burning rain ; and the inrushing draught of air produced a vortex which carried the fiery element upward to a still greater height, and distributed it still more widely ; and it fell on four cities and consumed their inhabitants, and covered the Circle of Jordan with a thick crust of salt unto this day."   There have been explosions of this kind in the petroleum regions of Canada, and the similarity of the geology of these districts to that of the Dead Sea suggested to Sir William Dawson the theory above summarised. [3]   At the same time, as this man

[1] Prov. $2^{31}$.                    [2] Acts $14^{17}$.
[3] The destruction of St. Pierre by a whirlwind of fire (8th May 1902)

of science himself say, "the scientific account does not detract from the providential character of the catastrophe." God is the Lord of Nature. He is able, by the secret yet mighty power of His will, to control the unconscious elements and make them minister to the highest interests of His kingdom. The laws of nature have been called the hands of God, and His hands are not tied. Though the tempest of fire did not come from another world, it was none the less the red hail of the LORD's judgment. "He turneth a fruitful land into a salt desert for the wickedness of them that dwell therein." [1]

JUDGMENT.—When Abraham rose up early in the morning and returned to the heights above Hebron to see how his prayers had sped, an appalling spectacle met his view. The sacred writer may well interject a "Behold!" in his brief description of the sublimely awful scene, at which Abraham gazes transfixed. "The scene has value not merely as an event, but for the *thoughts* which Abraham must have had : still the writer does not describe them ; he gives us merely the outward facts, and we ourselves have to add the chief thing." [2] The hurricane of vengeance has fallen on the guilty cities, crime is punished, righteousness is vindicated, the haunts of infamy are destroyed, the plague-spots are burned from off the face of the earth. Fire has ended the rout and riot, and signalised the divine abhorrence of sensuality. Purity has triumphed. Abraham "looked toward Sodom and Gomorrah, and toward all the land of the plain, and, lo, the smoke of the land went up as the smoke of a furnace" ($19^{27. 28}$). There is no relief, no softening, to the stern and terrible picture, which makes the same impression upon the mind as the reading of the whole of Dante's *Inferno*. On the face of nature God wrote once for all, in letters of fire, for all the world to read, "Vengeance is Mine, I will repay."

presents, from a purely physical point of view, a still more awful parallel to the overthrow of the cities of the Plain.

[1] Ps. $107^{33}$.          [2] Gunkel.

## INTEGRITY
### Genesis 20

"Dare to be true! Nothing can need a lie!
A fault, which needs it most, grows two thereby!"—HERBERT.

HONOUR.—The story in Gen. 20 is regarded by many scholars as a replica of Gen. 12¹⁰⁻²⁰. The scene is laid in Gerar instead of Egypt, but the principal features of the narrative are the same. The writer of the earlier story uses the divine name *Jahveh*, the LORD, and is therefore often called by scholars the Jahvist; the writer of the later narrative uses the name *Elohim*, God, and is called the Elohist. The two traditions are inserted in appropriate places. If the incidents are regarded as separate occurrences in one and the same life, the lesson is the familiar one, that good men may, after a long interval, lapse into the very sins which darkened their former days. No man ever gets so clean away from evil as to be beyond the reach of danger. There are surprises of sin in holy lives. The prophet's words, "Thy first father sinned,"[1] may refer to Abraham. The heroes of the Bible are not immaculate; they are never called, like the classical heroes, divine; they are in themselves frail human beings, made good and noble only by the power of divine grace. Sarah, whose beauty fascinated kings, is again represented as too willingly giving her consent to her husband's unworthy stratagem. "The soul's armour is never well set to the heart unless a woman's hand has set it, and it is only when she braces it loosely that the honour of manhood fails." The love of man and woman is not ideal unless their love of truth is even greater than their love for one another.

"I could not love thee, dear, so much,
Loved I not honour more."[2]

INTEGRITY.—Abraham erred whenever he began to ask him-

[1] Isa. 43²⁷.       [2] Lovelace.

self the questions, "What is now the safe and expedient course for me? What is politic in the circumstances? What will make for my present advantage?" He never erred when he asked himself, "What is God's will? What is His thought, His ideal, His plan for me?" In Gerar as in Egypt he was actuated by the fear of man, which "bringeth a snare."[1] Fear is the indication of a weakening of faith. A strong faith transcends all fear. Chrysostom once said in reply to a threatening message from an empress, "Go, tell her I fear nothing *but sin.*" Abraham endeavoured to excuse the untruth he told Abimelech, king of Gerar, by saying he was afraid there was no religion in the place ($20^{11}$). But there was more of the fear of God—more genuine religion and integrity—in Gerar than he expected. Abimelech, heathen though he was, had instincts of reverence and kindness. He spoke and acted with true kingliness and dignity. He esteemed and practised the virtues of truth, justice, and humanity. His conscience—God's voice in his soul—was a witness for honour and uprightness; he received the divine warning with meekness; he shrank with horror from the sin of adultery; he earnestly pleaded before God his integrity and innocence; he deprecated the punishment of a righteous nation; he rebuked the servant of the LORD for "deeds that ought not to be done"; he accepted with magnanimity the offender's feeble apology; and he went so far as to make an honourable amend for a quite involuntary error. His piety is surprising; his generosity, courtesy, and self-restraint are admirable. In whatever unexpected quarter such noble qualities are found, their source is God; they are rays of the light which lighteth every man that cometh into the world. "All good desires, all holy counsels, all just works" proceed from God. "The figure of Abimelech, like that of Melchizedek, shows an unmistakable superiority to national limitations."[2] "In every nation," the sacred writer seems to say, "he that feareth God and worketh righteousness is accepted of Him."[3]

[1] Prov. $29^{25}$.          [2] Schultz.          [3] Acts $10^{35}$.

TRUTH.—When Abraham departed from the truth, he was under the impression that Divine Providence needed the aid of human cunning. But God may always be trusted to carry out His plans without requiring any man to deviate an inch from the line of truth and honesty. Abraham was convicted of violating a code of honour which is elementary and universal. The law of truth is part of the moral endowment of the rudest savage ; all the stronger are the reasons why the servants of God should set a strict watch by the door of their lips. Men have a right to be indignant, as Abimelech was, when they find that those who suspect them of irreligion are themselves not perfectly straight. Nothing commends true religion to "them that are without" like "walking honestly."[1] "I would rather," said Cromwell, "miscarry in justice to the believer than to the unbeliever." It is the part of a Jesuit to dissemble, to palter in a double sense, to speak with mental reservations, to lie for the glory of God. The higher life conjoined with the lower standard of truth is the scorn of the world. "My soul," says Montaigne, "naturally abominates lying, and hates the very thought of it. For my own part I have this vice in so great horror, that I am not sure I could prevail with my conscience to secure myself from the most manifest and extreme danger by an impudent and solemn lie." Abimelech's reproof gained in severity by being temperate in expression : "Thou hast done deeds unto me that ought not to be done" (20⁹). The words of the heathen king were the verdict of God. Untruthfulness is not only evil in itself, but has remote issues. It propagates itself. A bad man's example has little influence over good men. But the bad example of a good man, eminent in station and established in reputation, has an enormous power for evil. For all that the prophets could do, lying remained an ugly characteristic of the Hebrew race, and Hebrew subtlety is a byword to the present day. It is un-English to lie. Macaulay said that "English valour and English intelligence have done less to extend and preserve our Oriental empire than

[1] 1 Thess. 4¹².

English veracity." "As for the truth, it endureth and is always strong ; it liveth and conquereth for evermore." [1]

SINCERITY.—Though Abraham was convicted of a grave offence, yet he was a prophet of God (20⁷), and his prayer for Abimelech and his household was heard (v.¹⁷). His errors did not prove him to be either a hypocrite or a recreant to his ideal. Righteousness was still the characteristic, the habit, the law of his life. God makes imperfect men His prophets, and answers their prayers, else His work could never be done in the world. The best of men have memories which fill them with regret and shame. Men are not to be judged by the presence or absence of faults, but by the *direction* of their lives. The believer's bent is toward truth and goodness ; he loves the LORD in sincerity ; he habitually faces the light, not the darkness ; he has "breast and back as either should be" ; and in spite of many stumbles and bruises he is pressing upwards toward a divine ideal.

## LAUGHTER
### Genesis 21:6

"And one laughed, and another laughed, and they all laughed together."
BUNYAN.

PRAISE.—The greatest joy is the rebound from sorrow. If hope deferred makes the heart sick, the desire accomplished is sweet to the soul.[2] It was every Hebrew woman's ambition to be the mother of good and great men. Sarah had resigned herself to the belief that it was not God's will to give her the holy joy of motherhood. She laughed a bitter laugh at the promise, which sounded like a mockery to her lonely heart. But when the child of promise was born, she laughed in pure ecstasy. A new light was in her eyes, a light from heaven ; a new tone in her voice, a music from heaven. She praised God

[1] 1 Esdr. 4³⁸.     [2] Prov. 13¹².¹⁹.

the Giver of her heart's desire ; and her motherhood doxology is
recorded—

"God hath prepared laughter[1] for me ;
Everyone that heareth shall laugh with me."

Her joy was at once natural and spiritual. It was hallowed and
deepened by the knowledge that God was the Author of her
happiness. As she folded her child to her bosom, she knew
that both mother and child were wrapped round with the love
of God. All the world had suddenly grown brighter to her, and
she saw her joy reflected in every face. The natural response
to a miracle of love is a song of praise ; and Sarah's simple
words breathed the same pure joy and devout gratitude which
afterward found much grander expression in the magnificats of
two other Hebrew mothers. "My heart exulteth in the LORD,"
sang the mother of Samuel. "My spirit rejoiceth in God my
Saviour," said the mother of Jesus. These three holy women
mused on the mystery of Love till the fire burned in their hearts,
and they caught for once the inspiration of poetry and praised
the LORD for His gifts to them and to the world.

LAUGHTER.—Laughter, like sunshine and music and love, is
prepared for us by God (21[6]). It is not one of man's "many
inventions." "Laughter," wrote John Brown, the good physician,
"like all else, is a gift from the Supreme Giver, to be used and
not abused." It has been said that we must have touched a
graver side of life before we can take in the fact that Heaven is
not opposed to laughter. At any rate the deep sad undertone of
the world makes the high clear notes of heavenly joy the more
thrilling. The heart-easing mirth which is prepared by God—
happy laughter which readily blends with grateful tears—is the
natural and inevitable expression of the soul's dawning sense of
God's all-encompassing love. It was another woman who sang—

"I smiled to think God's greatness flowed around our incompleteness,
Round our restlessness His rest."[2]

--------

[1] R.V. margin.  [2] E. B. Browning.

Incomparably fine is the language in which a Hebrew poet has expressed the ecstatic feelings that accompany the sudden cessation of a long and wearing sorrow—

> "When the LORD brought home again the captives of Zion,
>   We were like them that dream;
>   Then was our mouth filled with laughter,
>   And our tongue with melody." [1]

Our Lord Himself has made laughter the symbol of all spiritual gladness: "Blessed are they that mourn: for they shall laugh;" [2] and Luther, with his wonderful note of childlike genius, declares that the whole evangel of the grace of God is "*Nichts anders als Lachen und Frolocken*"—"nothing but laughter and joy." There are always abundant causes for sweet and jubilant laughter in the surprising loving-kindnesses of the LORD; spiritual life flourishes best in the warm atmosphere of joyful feeling; and whenever God's people begin to let their religion grow too decorous, too restrained, too cold, God ordains that "a little child shall lead them" back to the truth.

JOY.—"Blessed be childhood," said Amiel; "it brings down something of heaven into the midst of our rough earthliness." Isaac's weaning—which would take place when he was two or three years of age [3]—was made the occasion of a great feast ($21^8$). In Genesis there are many feasts and no fasts. The voice of rejoicing was in the tents of the righteous. The Hebrew religion not only permitted but appointed many festivals, when the people of God came before Him with gladness and mirth. Every feast had a religious character. Men drew nigh to God on the footing of sacrifice, then they ate and drank with the consciousness of His blessing. "Ye shall rejoice before the LORD your God;" [4] "thou shalt rejoice, thou and thy household;" [5] "thou shalt rejoice in thy feast," [6] are the directions for

---

[1] Ps. $126^{1,2}$.      [2] Luke $6^{21}$.      [3] 2 Macc. $7^{27}$.
[4] Deut. $12^{12}$.      [5] Deut. $14^{26}$.      [6] Deut. $16^{14}$.

such occasions, reiterated times without number. "They saw
God and did eat and drink,"[1] "they did eat and drink before
the LORD with great gladness,"[2] are accounts of festivals. Every
happy and important occasion in Hebrew domestic life was
celebrated with sacrifice and feast. The rejoicing was always
before the LORD. Innocent mirth was no offence to Him. The
wise patriarch, with his grand sunny nature, was minded to give
his children and his household an idea of life as essentially bright
and joyous because God was so near and so good. A little child's
memory of such festive days observed for *his* sake fills his heart
with trust and gladness, and binds him for ever to his home.
The ideal Hebrew saint himself retained the child-heart. He
was no ascetic of pale countenance and wasted form practising
self-inflicted austerities and pleasing God by renouncing pleasure.
The Hebrew race were a robust and happy breed of men, whose
natural enjoyment of life was not diminished but immeasurably
enhanced by the assurance of God's favour. Their faith made
them a strong and manful people, who did not question the innocence of happiness, and were not unduly cast down by sorrow.
"The joy of the LORD," they said, "is your strength."[3] Their
strenuous earnestness did not damp their happiness, but only
made it intenser and purer. "There is an endless variety of
phrase for the thought that the pious exult in God, delight in
Him, as at a gladsome thanksgiving festival."[4] The patriarchs
were rarely if ever morbid, and never sick except with old age.
We do well enough to follow the practice of calling them
saints, though the word "holy" is not found in Genesis. But it
is beyond question that their piety was healthy and joyous and
human ; their lives were spent, not in celibacy, but in the
midst of little children ; not in fastings and vigils, but in the
free and full enjoyment of life ; not in cloistered shades, but in
God's greenest fields, and under His bluest skies. Their
optimism finds abundant expression in their sacred poetry—

---

[1] Ex. 24$^{11}$.   [2] 1 Chron. 29$^{22}$.
[3] Neh. 8$^{10}$.   [4] Schultz.

"Let all those that trust in Thee rejoice,
Let them ever shout for joy ;
Let them also that love Thy name be joyful in Thee." [1]


## TEARS
### Genesis 21:11-17

" The wise God will have it so : some must pipe and some must weep."
BUNYAN.

BIRTHRIGHTS.—Gen. 21 is like a day that dawns in brightness, darkens at noon, and ends in clear shining after rain.
Laughter and tears, ecstasy and agony, meet in a chapter
and in a day's experience. One person's joy is too often
another's sorrow. Isaac, the innocent, happy, prattling child,
could not know that his feast was gall and wormwood to
his brother. Ishmael never till that day felt so keenly, or
resented so bitterly, his birth's invidious bar. Brought up as
presumptive and undisputed heir of Abraham's possessions, he
suddenly found himself a nobody. It was hard for a lad of
fifteen to be superseded by a child, to be ousted from what he
counted his birthright, and to have all his prospects in life
darkened. Under these conditions the worse side of Ishmael's
character displayed itself. Sullen, moody, and mischievous,
full of envy and bitterness against the little child who had
already the power to make such a mighty stir in the camp, he
became the killjoy of the feast. Sarah's watchful eye fell upon
him mocking and teasing her son—*Isaac-ing* him—turning the
beloved name into a jest. It was not innocent mirth, but un-
mannerly rudeness and wanton cruelty. " He that was born
after the flesh persecuted him who was born after the spirit." [2]
The jealous mother's smouldering wrath was quickly rekindled,
with the result that she demanded the instant expulsion of the
bondwoman and her son. Abraham was deeply grieved, but

[1] Ps. 5[11].     [2] Gal. 4[29].

God showed him that the rough measure required by his wife would prove in the end the best thing for his son. Sarah meant no good to Ishmael, but God would turn evil to good. Ejection might be too severe a punishment for a piece of boyish insolence ; but it was well that Ishmael should early be cast upon his own resources, and obliged to strike out a path for himself in the world. A youth with hot Egyptian blood in his veins was never meant for the monotonous life of a Hebrew shepherd.

> "The pastoral scene, its quiet joy,
> They only chafe the archer boy."

Ishmael's birthright was his bow. His hero was Nimrod, who "was a mighty hunter before the LORD." He needed the free adventurous life of sport and war to nurture his manly strength, to buffet him into the healthy hardness which is required by men who are to mould the destinies of the world. Self-reliance is so important a trait of character that scarcely any price is too high to pay for it. Ishmael in his father's camp was an idle and mischievous boy, whose masterpiece was profane jesting. Ishmael cast adrift on the world, spurred by adversity to put forth all his native vigour, becomes a man of heroic spirit,—"a noble of nature," as Dr. Chalmers finely describes him,—fit to be the founder of a great nation. God has designed the desert for Ishmael, and Ishmael for the desert. Let its free air once penetrate his blood, and he will never leave it till the end of life, nor his descendants till the end of time. God has a plan for every life. There is no youth but has received special talents which require a special field for their exercise. To bind a lad to an uncongenial occupation, to put a check upon the natural outflow of his vital energies, to tame and subdue a high heart, is to spoil a life. Our happiness consists in finding our destined sphere of service, and providence often leads us in strange ways in order that we may discover it. Many an "unwanted" boy, like Ishmael, who has had a rough and cold beginning, has turned out an exceptionally brave and noble man. Early losses are transmuted by a divine alchemy into permanent gains. "Reverses, difficulties, trials, are often God's best blessings. The man compelled to labour gains energy, strength of character, the development of all that is within him. Can you call that loss?"[1]

AFFECTION. — Abraham's fatherly love encompassed his wayward and wilful son. His affection shines in bright contrast to Sarah's step-motherly dislike. The expulsion demanded "was very grievous in Abraham's sight on account of his son" (21[11]). Grief is love bereaved of its object. The father's heart had for many years been bound up in his only son; he loved him still; and fondest love makes sorest parting. Calvin takes Abraham to task for his love of the bondwoman's son and unwillingness to him cast out. "It may truly seem absurd," he writes, "that the servant of God should thus be carried away by a blind impulse; but God deprives him of his judgment, not only to humble him, but also to testify to all ages that the dispensing of His grace depends upon His own will alone." Even Homer nods. The patriarch's blind impulse, his warm natural affection, his father's heart, guided him better than the commentator's cool judgment. Under all conditions a father's love to his child is lawful and imperative. God is always in nature, not always in theology. Nothing in Abraham's story becomes him better than his warm love and clinging affection for his son, and his keen distress at parting from him.

TEARS.—Gen. 21 contains a whole group of exquisite and pathetic traits of maternal love. One mother is seen bending radiant with smiles over her newborn babe, another sobbing with breaking heart beside her dying son. Sarah, crooning her cradle song in her quiet tent, reaches the acme of earthly happiness; Hagar, laying her swooning boy under a desert bush, averting her face from the pallor of death, and raising

[1] F. W. Robertson.

her impotent cry in the pitiless desert, touches the nadir of human sorrow. But God is near them both, the one in her joy, the other in her sorrow. Their maternal love is a ray from the glowing heart of infinite love. " Can a woman forget the child she bare ? " It is all but incredible. Hagar would gladly give " a mother's free and final sacrifice " to save her son. The sensitiveness of a mother to suffering which she cannot relieve, is the most touching thing in the world. But there is a divine meaning in tears as well as in joy. God does not mock the immense mother-love which has brooded and planned and toiled so long for a child. Only, He answers prayer in His own way ; and he endures the pain of seeing His children weep, because sorrow has saving and healing virtues. Abraham prayed that his son might live before God ($17^{18}$). God answers the prayer by bringing Ishmael within an inch of the grave. Many who have been at the gate of death, and have looked through it into eternity, come back to confess that " by these things men live, and wholly therein is the life of the spirit." [1] It was good that Hagar's son should know his frailty and mortality before he received the gifts of power and fortune which were in store for him. Prosperity would be disastrous to almost every man if he were not prepared for it by adversity. " Take out of your character all the fine qualities which came into it through sorrow, and you would be turned into a crude and selfish creature." [2]

> '' But who can so forecast the years,
>    And find in loss a gain to match ;
>    Or reach a hand through time to catch
> The far-off interest of tears ? '' [3]

COMPASSION.—" When the poor and needy seek water, and there is none, and their tongue faileth for thirst, I the LORD will hear them, I the God of Israel will not forsake them." [4] " God heard the voice of the lad " Ishmael ($21^{17}$). It is not said that the boy uttered an articulate prayer for help. It is

[1] Isa. $38^{16}$.    [2] Joseph Parker.    [3] Tennyson.    [4] Isa. $41^{17}$.

rather implied that the only voice which God heard was that of Ishmael's dying sobs and groans. As He once heard the mother's affliction, so He now hears the son's anguish. He was near them in the desert, and very compassionate. Hagar's son was not called Ishmael—God hears—in vain. Sceptics question the utility, indeed assert the futility, of prayer.

> "And yon inverted bowl we call the sky,
>   Whereunder crawling cooped we live and die,
>     Lift not your hands to *It* for help—for It
> As impotently moves as you or I." [1]

But the Hebrews have given us a better and a truer creed. The living God heard the cry of the outcast Arab in the desert of rocks and sand ; He hears the street "Arab" in the wilderness of great cities ; and He cares for all the waifs and strays of humanity. The cry of the children "who are weeping in the playtime of their brothers," moves the kind heart of the Eternal. There is no impassable gulf between His greatness and their littleness. The Ancient of days is the Friend and Guardian of childhood. Above the songs of angels and the music of the spheres, God hears a child's cry. "The tradition of God's listening to the voice of weeping Ishmael was so touching to the ancient hearers because it told of His compassion for a *child* : this God, they said, will also regard the weeping of our children ! " [2] The most beautiful saying to be found in the Talmud is, "When the gates of prayer are shut in heaven, those of tears are open."

VISION.—Ishmael was fainting, panting, dying of thirst in the lonely desert. His cries of pain were growing fainter ; the tides of life were fast ebbing from his heart. His mother was wringing her hands in the anguish of despair, oblivious of everything but her child's distress. Resentment, weariness, and grief had blinded her. She had cast aside her shrivelled water-skin, "the

[1] Omar Khayyam.          [2] Gunkel.

last drop drained, the sweetest and the last, drained at her darling's lips."

> " The scrip is emptied and the flagon dry,
> And nothing left them but the leave to die.
> To die—and one so young and one so true,
> And both so beautiful and brave to view." [1]

Yet all the time a desert well was brimming and bubbling beside them. " God opened Hagar's eyes, and she saw a fountain of water " (21[19]). There it was—

> " Into the sunshine,
> Into the light,
> Leaping and flashing
> From morning to night." [2]

It was but a moment's work for Hagar to snatch up her water-skin, dip it in the living stream, put it to her child's parched lips, and moisten his burning brow. His thirst was slaked, his fever allayed, his spirit came again, his life was saved. To have died of thirst beside a fountain of water would have been a doubly horrible fate. " Hear, O LORD my God ; give light to mine eyes, lest I sleep the sleep of death." In a world which is full of divine blessings, the greatest of all boons is open eyes to see them. Hagar's desert well is a symbol of present but unperceived blessings. Till God opens our eyes we are like those mariners who, having lost their course and been becalmed off the mouth of the Amazon, were dying of thirst, imagining there was no drop of water to drink, while all around them for hundreds of miles there was nothing but fresh water. We thirst where streams of living water flow. Our souls are parched and fevered and faint at the very " wells of salvation." For lack of vision we despair because there is no God, or no God who can be known, whilst—

" Closer is He than breathing, and nearer than hands and feet." [3]

---

[1] Edwin Arnold.      [2] Lowell.      [3] Tennyson.

We are like one who wept inconsolably for her Lord, till her eyes were opened, and He was before her;[1] like the travellers who mourned the loss of their Master, till "their eyes were opened, and they knew Him."[2] Wordsworth tells how his sister Dorothy "couched his eyes" to see the beauty of the world. "The light of the eyes rejoiceth the heart,"[3] and every one needs some divine or human voice to say to him, "Ephphatha"—"Be opened." Then, and not till then, do we know of a certainty that God, the great Fountain of blessing, is, as Rebecca sang, "present still, though now unseen."[4]

## ASPIRATION
### Genesis 21:22, 31

" Thou who canst think as well as feel,
Mount from the earth! Aspire! Aspire!"—WORDSWORTH.

CHARACTER.—Abraham's grand and commanding character won the admiration of the princes of Canaan and Gerar, among whom he lived as a stranger and sojourner. They came to pay court to him, and to seek alliances with him. "When a man's ways please the Lord, He maketh even his enemies to be at peace with him."[5] "In nothing," says Ewald, "is the memory of the reality and grandeur of Abraham's far-reaching life more clearly preserved than this, that powerful men even in foreign countries were compelled to confess that God was with him, and eagerly sought his friendship and blessing." King Abimelech came to renew his acquaintance with him. He and Phicol his captain paid him a fine tribute when they said, "God is with thee in all that thou doest" (21[22]). They were so impressed by his character that they could not help thinking he must have a wonderful God. They might have but a vague notion of the

[1] John 20[16].  [2] Luke 24[31].  [3] Prov. 15[3].
[4] *Ivanhoe*.  [5] Prov. 16[7].

real springs, motives, and aspirations of his life; they judged him chiefly by his outward bearing, conduct, and success. Still they could not fail to see an intimate connection between his faith and his life, and they had the sense and candour to give the praise to his God. A believer in the living and true God can have no higher ambition than this, to bring glory to God by his noble conduct and character. .The best defence and recommendation of the faith is the life of a servant of God which constrains the world to say, " God is with thee."

TRUTH. — Abraham consented to make an alliance with Abimelech, and the name of the well at which they met and covenanted was called Beer-sheba, the Well of the Oath, " because there they sware both of them " (21^{31}). At the same time they settled an old dispute about the possession of this well, which Abimelech's servants had, without their master's knowledge, " violently taken away " (v.^{25}). Curious rites were employed to ratify the treaty and to put the future possession of the well beyond dispute. The Hebrew word for " to swear " means literally " to bind oneself by seven things." The parties to an agreement invoked or touched seven sacred objects as witnesses of their declaration. " If from some special causes—for example, in the ratification of a treaty—it was desired to make the oath still more impressive, seven gifts were also taken, and the person more interested in the safe keeping of the treaty sought by the presentation of these to bind the other party more firmly to himself and to the oath, just as might be done by any acceptable gift." [1] The ceremonial varied, but the significance of the oath was always the same. It changed a promise made to man into a promise made to God. The person swearing invoked the vengeance of God on himself if he should fail to fulfil his engagement. Grievous dishonour was done to God when a man sware with the secret intention of violating his oath. To perjure oneself—to deceive by false oaths—was an awful defiance of

[1] Ewald.

God. The oaths taken by Abraham and Abimelech had something of a public nature. But even "private oaths, used soberly, sacredly, and reverently, on necessary occasions, it were perilous to condemn, supported as they are by reason and example." [1] In ordinary conversation, however, the Perfecter of our faith has forbidden all swearing : our yea is to be yea, and our nay nay. "Execrations, being manifestly insulting to God, are unworthy of being classed among oaths. God's name is vulgarised and vilified when it is used in oaths which, though true, are superfluous." [1] If a man is known to be truthful, his oath is unnecessary, his word being as good as his bond ; and if a man is known to be untruthful, his rash and passionate oath makes no impression on others, and is an aggravation of his own sin.

ASPIRATION.—"Abraham planted a tamarisk tree (R.V.) in Beersheba, and called there on the name of the LORD, the everlasting God" (21[33]). When the old Semites worshipped by a fountain of water, or under green trees, or on a high hill, they regarded the spot as the sacred dwelling of a deity. The fountain refreshed them, the forest thrilled them, the mountaintop awed them ; they cast their gifts into the well, hung their presents on the trees, and anointed the mountain rocks with blood or with oil. "To the primitive man all the forces of nature were divine : either for propitiation or for admiration, many things, and in a sense all things, demanded worship from him." [2] The wonder was right, the worship wrong. Devout men of a later and more enlightened age, entirely free from idolatry and superstition, might still worship in the same sacred spots, simply because they loved to dwell close to the heart of nature, and

> " The still retreat, the silent shade
> With prayer and praise agree."

Thus Abraham worshipped God at the well and grove of Beersheba, and there, in the midst of his ordinary life, he was con-

[1] Calvin.                                    [2] Carlyle.

tinually overawed by voices and visions from another world. He lived a life of pastoral activity. Rising early in the morning, going forth to his labour until the evening, striking and pitching tents, rearing and tending flocks and herds, digging wells and planting trees, training and overseeing serfs—that might have seemed to be the nomad flock - master's whole life. It was certainly an important part of his life. The Hebrews were entirely free from the Greek and Roman scorn of practical business and vulgar toil ; and they never dreamed that religion required them to renounce the ordinary activities. of the world. Abraham entered into business, mixed with men, cultivated social relations, handled money (23[16]). He was interested in all kinds of people—in his herdmen, his shepherds, his craftsmen, his soldiers, his neighbours, his allies. He fulfilled all the duties and obligations which devolve upon a practical man of the world. Yet this constituted but the minor half of his life. All the time that he lived in the world and seemed to be engrossed in its affairs, he was detached from it all, and aspired above it all ; his faith continually drew him to elevating communion with the Eternal ; and his sacred tamarisk-tree, pointing upward, reminded him that the monotonous lives and ways of men need to be connected with the blue heavens. His vision of eternal things was preternaturally keen, and the window of his soul that looked heavenward was never shut. Earth was his work-field ; but he belonged to, and had business with, another world—a spirit-world. He knew that far above the green valley of Beersheba, alive by day with the bleating of flocks and the hum of human voices, peaceful at night with folds closed and tents hushed, was the LORD, the Everlasting God, keeping watch and ward over the little lives of men. On this God he continually called (21[33]). His real business and highest happiness in the world were to have communion with his Divine Friend and to be morally like Him. His preoccupation with the world's affairs never detained him from fulfilling his high vocation to consecrate himself to the holy service of the Eternal. This became every believing Hebrew's lofty and inflexible ideal of life.

FAITH.—It was a great and ennobling thing for a man to worship the Everlasting God (21³³), to have his own existence linked in a sense to the boundless ages of the past and the future. This gave his life a spacious background, a far horizon, an outlook upon the infinite. It was the Hebrew's supreme aspiration to know God and rejoice ; and to this end the inspiration of the Almighty gave him understanding.[1] Every advance in knowledge was at once a revelation and a discovery, and every new divine Name was the recognition of another aspect of the divine nature. Abraham, the typical Hebrew, already knew God as *Jahveh*, the LORD, the God of Revelation (12⁸) ; as *El Elyon*, God Most High (14²²) ; as *El Shaddai*, God Almighty (17¹). To the thoughts of God's grace, elevation, and power he now adds the sublime thought of God's eternity. His conceptions of God were important, not only in themselves, but because they determined his thoughts of the world and of his own duties and relations in it. He necessarily became more and more like the Being whom he loved and worshipped. His faith made him the great, reverent, just, humane, valiant man he was. Nothing could be more erroneous than the common idea that it does not matter what a man believes. The fortunes of the Hebrews invariably followed their faith. Their conceptions of God were the vital principles which shaped their destinies ; and faith is the root of every nation's greatness. " The history of a nation becomes fruitful, soul-elevating, as soon as it believes. . . . This is what I mean by a whole 'nation of heroes' ; a believing nation. . . . Scepticism is not intellectual only ; it is moral also ; a chronic atrophy and disease of the whole soul. . . . You lay your finger on the heart of the world's maladies, when you call it a sceptical world." [2] Right conceptions of God always liberate, expand, and purify men's minds ; wrong conceptions

[1] Job 32⁸.            [2] Carlyle.

narrow, darken, and defile them. "The truth shall make you free,"[1] "consecrate them in the truth,"[2] are divine words ; and Jesus' own manhood was nourished on Old Testament ideals. It was the mission of the Hebrews to give the world a true theology—grand, noble, just, radiant thoughts of God, such as all nations need and will one day welcome ; and their claim to our reverence and gratitude rests on the fact that they fulfilled their high task incomparably well. The Greeks gave us art, the Romans gave us law, the Hebrews gave us faith. Multitudes of men have not yet entered into their heritage ; but God's purpose of grace embraces mankind ; and "the earth shall be filled with the knowledge of the glory of the LORD, as the waters cover the sea."[3]

## DISCIPLINE
### Genesis 22:1-3

" Pain is the deepest thing we have in our nature, and union through pain has always seemed more real and more holy than any other."

A. H. HALLAM.

STYLE. — The narrative of the offering up of Isaac is of surpassing interest as a tradition, and it embodies many of the great ideas which dominated the minds and hearts of the Hebrews. Like most of the narratives in Genesis it is written in a purely objective, calmly historical style. Much of the pathos of the perfect tale lies in its reticence. Tenderness, passion, and emotion are understood rather than expressed. From first to last not a word is said of the feelings of the father and the son. When "Abraham rose early in the morning," after receiving the divine command to offer up his son, there was under his calm exterior a world of trouble—a mind bewildered and amazed, a heart wrung with anguish, a will divided by the con-

[1] John 8³².     [2] John 17¹⁷.     [3] Hab. 2¹⁴ ; Isa. 11⁹.

flicting claims of love and duty. But of this we are told nothing.
What the narrative says is that Abraham rose up early in the
morning, saddled his ass, and clave the wood. The historian's
complete silence regarding the storm of feeling which swept
through the patriarch's mind is more moving than any words
could have been. A great narrator rarely attempts the minute
delineation of feeling. He increases his power by reserve, and
expresses more than he seems actually to say. He knows
how to enlist the reflective imagination and sympathy of his
hearer or reader, and to create an atmosphere in which the
commonest words tingle with emotion. Thought is much swifter
than language ; and the imagination, stirred by sympathy, fills
up a bare outline instantaneously. The power to produce the
deepest impression by the simplest means, whereby the half
says more than the whole, is the highest kind of art. The
story of Isaac has all the elements of fateful tragedy, yet it
is pervaded by an atmosphere of spiritual peace which was
peculiarly Hebrew in the ancient world, being the reflection
of a perfect trust in God. It has the repose without which
no work of art can be great ;[1] yet the writer can scarcely have
had a thought of art. His style was himself, and his own
characteristics were the product of his faith.

PERFECTING. — "After all these things God did tempt
Abraham" (22[1]). "All these things" were the trials—numerous,
varied, and severe, yet comparatively minor — by which his
faith had been already proved and disciplined, and which
brought him unto this last. The supreme test of his submission to the divine will was to be the complement of all his
spiritual experiences. When he was full of years, and might
have flattered himself that he had entered on a period of perfect
peace, the LORD subjected his faith to the fiercest trial of all.
But thanks to the preliminary and preparatory work of his
lifetime, his character had ripened into such strength, that he

[1] Ruskin.

was now able to bear the severest test to which man could be subjected, and fit to graduate in the school of suffering. God understands how to time and grade men's trials. He works by weight and measure. He sends "afflictions sorted, anguish of all sizes." [1] He knows our strength or frailty, and does not lay too heavy burdens on young shoulders. "God is faithful, who will not suffer you to be tempted above that ye are able; but will with the temptation make also the way of escape, that ye may be able to endure it." [2] "He adjusts our trials to our strength by the care of His providence, and our strength to our trials by the power of His grace." [3] Temptations are not accidents in a man's life; each of them is part of a plan, a step in the progress to a higher life. Abraham's life was a long succession of trials, each of which increased his faith and displayed it in some new aspect. "The obedience of faith," says Delitzsch, "drew him into a strange land; by the humility of faith he gave way to his nephew Lot; strong in faith he fought four kings of the heathen; firm in faith he rested in the word of promise; bold in faith he entreated the preservation of Sodom; joyful in faith he received the child of promise; with the loyalty of faith he expelled Hagar and Ishmael; with the gratitude of faith he planted a tamarisk to the Everlasting God. Now his faith was to be put to the severest test, to prove itself victorious, and to be rewarded accordingly."

PROBATION.—The Authorised Version says, "God did tempt Abraham." The Revised Version has "God did prove Abraham." The temptation was appointed by God's holy will; but God tempts only in a beneficent way. He never allures a man into moral evil — never deceives his judgment, or seduces his affections, or perverts his will. He brings men into temptation for the purpose of testing their latent capabilities, exercising and strengthening their graces, and proving the sincerity of

[1] G. Herbert.    [2] I Cor. 10[13].    [3] Matthew Henry.

their faith in Himself. Our enemies tempt us for the purpose of bringing out the evil that is in our hearts; God tries us to bring out the good. He desires nothing except our perfecting. " There is no way to self-knowledge but through trial," said Augustine. "Temptation," said Luther, " is the best school into which a Christian can enter." Trial is a sacred privilege of all the sons of God. It is a man's temptations that make his life profitable to himself and interesting to others. All that is best in us is developed by struggle. Battles make the soldier, storms the seaman, conflicts the hero, and temptations the saint. "Talent is formed in solitude, character in the stream of the world." [1] More is required than mere seclusion from evil to make us truly good; there is needed the contact of evil, the struggle with evil, the victory over evil. An untried, undisciplined life were flat, stale, and unprofitable. Brave spirits learn to welcome the storm and stress of temptation, knowing that, while God loves innocence, He prizes still more highly the strength of character which comes from the formed habit of resistance to evil. Untried innocence is not so grandly beautiful as tempted but untainted virtue. " Count it all joy when ye fall into manifold temptations. . . . Blessed is the man that endureth temptations." [2]

DISCIPLINE. — Abraham was commanded to take his only and well-beloved son and offer him for a burnt-offering ($22^2$). Isaac was the son of his old age, his heir, his pride, his hope, the delight and laughter of his life. Isaac was also the hope of the world, the visible pledge of the promises, to whose person God had annexed the assurance of blessing to mankind. The command to sacrifice this tenderly loved son— to lay him on the altar, slay him, and burn his body—struck like a knife through the father's own heart. The narrator does not attempt to describe his grief; as the ancient painter who had to represent the Greek hero preparing to sacrifice his

[1] Goethe.　　　　[2] Jas. $1^{2. 12}$.

own fair daughter, put a veil on his face, to signify that it was impossible to depict such a degree of sorrow. The human mind is bewildered when in the course of nature the hand of death strikes down the young and good, whom the world seems to need the most. But for a father to be commanded to take the life of a beloved son with his own hand, to plunge the knife into the dearest heart in the world, was enough to make reason reel on its throne. Nevertheless, God does all things well, and it is better to be purified through suffering than to be spared pain. Sooner than disobey God and lose His blessing, wise men cry, " Come suffering to the uttermost." " O Lord, give us more grace, and never mind the trials," was Whitefield's brave petition ; and one of the gayest and gravest spirits of our time, expert in the lore of pain, prayed thus to the Celestial Surgeon—

> " Lord, Thy most pointed pleasure take,
> And stab my spirit broad awake ;
> Or, Lord, if still obdurate I,
> Seize Thou, before that spirit die,
> A piercing pain, a killing sin,
> And to my dead heart run it in." [1]

SACRIFICE.—The practice of human sacrifice, which was widespread in ancient nations, and exercised a strange fascination over the Hebrews, was a perversion of two great truths : that God deserves the best that man can offer Him, and that man needs an atonement for his sin. (1) It is man's duty to dedicate himself and his property to God the Giver. "The best to God" is the heart of all true religion. A living sacrifice, holy and acceptable, is His reasonable service.[2] This sacred truth was perverted into the horrible error that to sacrifice a precious life was to destroy it ; to devote an innocent child to God was to slay him on the altar,—as if one could gratify God with massacre and murder. That Hebrew parents had once the power of life and death over their children is proved by Jephthah's sacrifice of his daughter, and by the cruel practice of offering

---

[1] R. L. Stevenson.          [2] Rom. 12[1].

children to Moloch. (2) Deep down in the human heart there is the craving for atonement. That we need to be reconciled unto God is as certain as that we sin. This fact was distorted into the terrible, barbarous, detestable idea that God could be appeased—made merciful—by the offering of human blood ; and that the greater joy the sacrificer had in his possession, the greater pleasure the offended God had in its destruction. Men were slow to agree with the prophet who asked, " Shall I give my firstborn for my trangression, the fruit of my body for the sin of my soul?" [1] The Hebrew conscience needed to be enlightened on this subject. God's people had to learn that He would neither require nor accept human sacrifice at their hands. Abraham was accustomed to witness this awful rite. He knew that in Chaldea and Canaan the sacrifice of the firstborn was counted the highest act of worship. He saw other parents offer their children to their gods, and the question would force itself upon his mind, " Couldst thou do as much for the true God as they for their false gods? Wilt thou give as much for love as they for fear?" The command to offer up Isaac would connect itself with such natural self-questioning. It was in accordance with the spirit of the times. While it would lacerate a father's heart, it would not violate his conscience. God, to whom all human sacrifice was abhorrent, gave the command as a test of Abraham's faith, with the unexpressed purpose of preventing the completion of the sacrifice. He gives many experimental, educative commands ; He addresses trials to the human heart with the intention of filling it with greater blessing when the trials have been endured. " God's design was to disentangle the true idea of sacrifice from the false—to emphasise the truth that human life ought to be consecrated to God, and to condemn and reject the hideous distortion of this truth which had arisen in heathenism." [2] Abraham's experience would establish a precedent for the guidance of all God's people, and transform the bloody sacrifice

[1] Mic. 6[7].                          [2] Oehler.

of the firstborn into a bloodless and holy consecration. "After the greatest pains and dangers, the hero victoriously attains the higher truth and blessedness, which, as soon as they have once been reached by one man, must become the common possession of all who behold this model." [1]

FAITH.—God promised to Abraham, "I will establish My covenant with Isaac for an everlasting covenant for his seed after him" ($17^{19}$). But now He commands him, "Take thy son, and offer him for a burnt-offering" ($22^2$). The command seems to cancel the promise. If Abraham's hopes are wrapped up in Isaac, they cannot be fulfilled when he is dead. The promises will be buried with the child of promise. On this passage Chrysostom says, "God seems to contradict God"; Calvin, "God in a sense assumes a double character"; Delitzsch, "the God who requires Abraham to sacrifice his only son after the manner of the Canaanites is only apparently the true God." The apparent inconsistencies of God's Providence are the trial of man's faith. "Sometimes He condescends to look mutable and fickle. He shows His face and then He hides it. He puzzles us as to His will. He lets half words fall into our heart. He sends us what look like leadings, and are not so. He lets us think He has contradicted Himself, who is eternal truth, unchangeable simplicity." [2] When He promises a lifetime of love, and quickly makes the heart desolate; when He shatters the hopes He has built; when He quenches the light He has kindled, His character seems to be at stake. "One while He is the most indulgent of fathers, another while the least forbearing of masters; now the most patient of teachers, and again the sharpest of critics; here the most gracious of sovereigns, there the most exacting of despots." [2] "Providence is a daily mystery, and often a daily torment, even to the most reverently studious minds." [3] But here comes the opportunity of faith. To believe when

[1] Ewald.      [2] Faber.      [3] Joseph Parker.

we cannot see ; to trust God where we cannot trace Him ; to be willing that He should have His way and vindicate His reputation in His own time—that is faith. Come whatever may, God has given us sufficient grounds for believing that He is infinitely good ; that suffering is not the contradiction of love, but one of its methods ; that " He causes suffering for reasons of the highest, purest, and kindest import, such as when understood must be absolutely satisfactory to the sufferers themselves " ; [1] that there is no pang or pain or sorrow which He does not feel with a sympathy infinitely greater than we can understand ; and that in spite of the apparently monstrous contradictions of life there is a harmony in His Providence like the music of the spheres. The children of faithful Abraham do not challenge God to give an account of His matters, but trust Him when He frowns as when He smiles, believing that He has in His hand the solution of every mystery, and that He will be His own interpreter. " Heroism feels and never reasons, and therefore is always right." [2] The highest moments in a man's life are those in which the action of the believing heart supersedes all other action.

DILIGENCE.—When " Abraham rose early in the morning " ($22^3$), there was but one thought in his mind—the doing of God's will. His early rising for the same purpose is mentioned in two other places ($19^{27}$ $21^{14}$). It was habitual. We read that many servants of God—Jacob, Moses, Joshua, David, Job, and others— rose up early. We do not read of any of His servants who rose up late. The early hours were regarded as the best. The Psalmist " prevented the dawning of the morning." [3] " Awake up, my glory, I myself will awake right early." [4] Jesus, "rising up a great while before day . . . prayed." [5] There is a charm about the first moments of the day which should not be broken by the intrusion of common things ; it is a time too sacred for

---

[1] George Macdonald.     [2] Emerson.     [3] Ps. $119^{147}$.
[4] Ps. $57^8$.     [5] Mk. $1^{35}$.

anything but communion with God. "When I awake, I am still with thee." [1] "Knowest thou not, O man," said Ambrose, "that thou owes the daily first - fruits of thy heart and voice to God." God's presence at the beginning consecrates the whole day for zealous and faithful service. To do a thing *rising up early* was a Hebrew synonym for doing it earnestly, strenuously, thoroughly. God was frequently said to do things *rising up early*.[2] This means that the Hebrews had a working God, ever intent on the fulfilment of His great designs ; that He who needed nothing yet worked, because all His creatures needed Him. Men are called to be diligent fellow-workers with God, and nothing mars their service more than indolence. "He that chooses to enlarge the slothful indulgence of sleep, rather than be early at his devotions to God, chooses the dullest refreshment of the body, before the highest, noblest refreshment of the soul ; he chooses that state which is a reproach to mere animals, rather than that exercise which is the glory of angels. . . . This is the right way of judging the crime of wasting a great part of your time in bed." [3] The time is precious because it is so short. The morning cometh, and also the night ; and soon the long night cometh, in which no man can work.

OBEDIENCE.—Abraham "went unto the place of which God had told him" (22³). God required him to go to the mount of sacrifice and offer up his dearest possession, and he did not shirk the awful task. (1) He obeyed *in faith*. He at once acknowledged the authority of the supreme Lawgiver. He might have expostulated, pleaded, objected, cried out in despair ; but he was absolutely silent. He did not charge God foolishly. God's will was painful, but without abatement he would carry it through. This is true religion, "to obey, no matter how you feel." When a brave and faithful man knows God's requirements, he does not reason or reply ; he gives himself no time for

[1] Ps. 139¹⁸.　　[2] Eleven times in Jeremiah.　　[3] William Law.

reflection; he knows that first thoughts are best; he makes haste, and delays not to keep God's commandments. Abraham had schooled himself to go anywhere and do anything at the divine bidding. He obeyed in no resentful spirit. He believed that God had a wise plan for him, and he would not change the purpose of unerring love.

> " All is right that seems most wrong,
> If it be God's sweet will." [1]

He did not defer obedience till he should understand God's secret counsels. He knew that God desired, not his comprehension, but his confidence. Commands are simple, positive, practical; reasons are difficult, abstruse, metaphysical. Duties are man's, reasons and results are God's. (2) Abraham obeyed *in love*. His obedience was possible only because his heart was aglow. Strength of will depends on depth of feeling. The heart fired with love is equal to any task, and much as Abraham loved his son he loved God more. Love made him one in will with God. In a sense his own will merged and lost itself in God's will. But he was not on that account willless and merely passive. On the contrary, the will that is yielded to God is far more active than the will which obeys the lower and selfish inclinations. When the will receives a new and right direction, it receives a new and supernatural power. Love energises it for obedience, duty, and sacrifice even to the uttermost. Abraham's life is thus designed to be a perfect illustration of two things : the believer's personal, conscious, unquestioning, unreserved surrender of himself to God ; and God's personal, conscious, and constant possession, mastery, and use of the believer for His own high ends. The ideal presented to us is the figure of a man who is in action a hero because he is in faith a little child.

[1] Faber.

## SACRIFICE
### Genesis 22:6-18

" Thou hast been as one,
In suffering all, that sufferest nothing."—SHAKESPEARE.

FORTITUDE. — From the camp at Beersheba Abraham journeyed to the land of Moriah (22²), to the mount of the LORD (v.¹⁴)—the holy hill on which the Temple was afterwards built. He was to be additionally tried by the great distance he had to travel before he came to the place of sacrifice. The deed was to be done, not on the impulse of the moment, but after days of reflection. During the journey no word or look betrayed his secret ; he controlled his emotion and went quietly forward, seeming to perform the most difficult task without an effort. Nothing relaxed the tension of his purpose. Even his son's naïve and infinitely pathetic question, " Where is the lamb ? " left him outwardly unmoved. He retained complete mastery over his feelings. This was the calmness, not of stoical apathy, but of implicit trust in God. The Stoic sullenly submits to the inevitable, acts as if he had no feelings, triumphs over pain by sheer power of will. The believer wins his victory over suffering, not by denying pain, defying fate, affecting insensibility, but by confiding in a God of love whose will is always wise and good. The Stoic submits because all is law, the believer because all is love. "A man's mind will be bright and calm even at the moment he is going to fearful misery, if he does but know that his suffering is his duty, and that his trial is his heavenly Father's will." ¹ God is honoured, not by the stern and stubborn spirit which submits to an irrevocable decree, but by the meek faith which accepts His good pleasure, and in the hour of greatest darkness clings to Him as a Friend. Confidence in Him is the secret of perfect peace—" peace subsisting at the heart of endless

¹ Charles Kingsley.

agitation," like the calm at the centre of a whirlwind. The believer's "heart is fixed, trusting in the LORD . . . he shall not be afraid." [1] "Acquaint thyself with Him, and be at peace." [2]

PROPHECY.—When Abraham came to the land of Moriah, and began to prepare for the dread sacrifice, he left his servants behind, telling them that he and Isaac would go to worship on the mount and come again ($22^5$). A German scholar [3] says that Abraham here makes "an untrue statement," which he compares with Gen. $12^{30}$ and $20^{12}$. But that is taking a superficial view of the matter. The promise, "we will come again," was not an attempt to deceive ; it was the expression, if not of an assured confidence, at least of a trembling hope, that God would intervene to make Isaac's safe return possible. The answer to Isaac's question about the lamb for the burnt-offering is of the same kind. Never renouncing hope, the father cries out, as if involuntarily, yet by a true prophetic impulse, "God will provide Himself the lamb" ($22^8$). It is a heart-cry of faith, an expression of heroic confidence in God, bursting from a believer's lips before the light bursts upon his soul. In the appalling darkness he never loses his conviction that God is with him, God is his Friend, God is providing. "True believers are never left without such a presence and support of the Spirit of God as keeps them from sinking into utter despair." [4] Everything is bearable but one—to be without God.

> "It is better to walk in the dark with God than to walk alone in the light ;
> It is better to walk in the dark by faith than to walk alone by sight."

Faith resting on the omnipotent love of God has a prophetic power ; and when the worst comes to the worst, hope is still the highest reason. "By faith Abraham offered up Isaac . . . accounting that God was able to raise him up even from the

[1] Ps. $112^7$.  [2] Job $22^{21}$.  [3] Knobel.  [4] Larger Catechism,

dead." [1]  St. Paul says that those who are of the faith of Abraham believe in a God "who quickeneth the dead, and calleth the things that are not as though they were." [2]  The believer who stays himself on God—*El Shaddai*, the All-sufficient—will unhesitatingly prophesy a happy issue out of all the ills that flesh is heir to.

SONSHIP.—Nowhere in the Bible is there a more winsome picture of filial reverence, obedience, and love than is found in the story of the offering of Isaac.    Nothing finer could be conceived than the tender colloquy between the father and son as "they went both of them together" to the place of sacrifice. The gravity of age and experience, and the simplicity and innocence of youth, are knit together by the tie of holy love. The father and son could not be more different in nature or more united in affection.    Abraham's love for his son was divinely recognised $(22^2)$; no trait of his character was more marked than his paternal affection ; and this constituted the crux of his trial.    Isaac was worthy of his father's love.    All the most beautiful traits of filial devotion are seen in his character— responsiveness to strong and tender love, recognition of the claims of age and wisdom, openness of mind and wondering eagerness to learn, and obedience even unto death.    " The glory of children are their fathers." [3]    Abraham and Isaac " went both of them together" in their walk with God, in their faith and obedience.    Abraham's obedience was active, Isaac's passive, both perfect.    Isaac's age at the time of his great renunciation is not stated ; but he was old enough to walk from Beersheba to Moriah, and to carry uphill the wood for the burnt-offering $(22^{3\text{-}6})$.    He was old enough to understand God's will ; and when the hour of trial suddenly came, it found him ready to die.    Life is sweet to everybody, especially delicious to the young ; and few youths have ever had brighter prospects than Isaac.    It is appalling to think of being cut off in early manhood,

[1] Heb. $11^{19}$.        [2] Rom. $4^{17}$.        [3] Prov. $17^6$.

when one's lifework and enterprises are scarely begun. Isaac might, had he so pleased, have resisted his father's will, and asserted his right to live and enjoy life. But he meekly allowed himself to be bound on the altar, and lay unresisting till the sacrificial knife was raised to slay him. In its great gallery of portraits the Bible has nothing finer than this thoughtful, reverent, believing, obedient boy, so gentle and beautiful and innocent, yet in the grasp of God's grace so calm, so sub-missive, so strong to endure. Unless piety had struck its roots in him when he was a child, and grown with his growth and strengthened with his strength, he could never have endured this fiery trial. To find another instance of a Son voluntarily surrendering His life and laying Himself upon the altar at a Father's bidding, we have to go from Moriah to Calvary.

SACRIFICE. — "By faith Abraham, being tried, offered up Isaac."[1] The deed was virtually done when he raised his hand to slay his son. In spirit and intention he had offered up the life that was dearer to him than his own. He had endured all the pain of parting and the bitterness of death. He had given infallible evidence that he loved God sincerely and supremely. His faith was tried and approved. "Was not Abraham our father justified by works, in that he offered up Isaac his son upon the altar?"[2] More than this could not be required of him. The spirit of the act, the all-surrendering faith, was acceptable to God ; the deed itself, a human sacrifice, was abhorrent to Him. He could not allow the projected offering to be completed. He permits trial no further than moral perfecting requires. There was no effusion of blood. The angel of God arrested the uplifted hand (22[12]), and the father received back his son as from the dead.[3] The eternally valid and imperishable meaning of sacrifice — the surrender of the will to God—was clearly illustrated. The immolation of human life was reprobated. At

[1] Heb. 11[17].     [2] Jas. 2[21].     [3] Heb. 11[19].

the same time there was ideally instituted—by the offering of a sheep instead of a man ($22^{13}$)—that kind of sacrifice which was destined to keep alive in Hebrew hearts the sense of sin and of the need of atonement, until "one full, perfect, and sufficient sacrifice, oblation, and satisfaction" should be made for the sin of the whole world.

SYMPATHY.—The Angel of the LORD—*i.e.* God in self-manifestation—said to Abraham, "*Now I know* that thou fearest God, seeing thou hast not withheld thy son, thine only son, from Me" ($22^{12}$). This is one of the many instances in which God is represented as speaking in a human fashion, as if He were not omniscient. When the cry of Sodom came up to heaven, the LORD said, "I will go down and see . . . and *I will know.*" To Abraham He said, "*If I find* in Sodom fifty righteous men, I will spare it." The Infinite voluntarily approximates the ways and thoughts of finite beings. He is above all limitations, and to Him nothing is ever unknown. "I am God," He said, "and there is none like Me, declaring the end from the beginning."[1] But if He were to speak to men in terms of His foreknowledge absolute, they would "find no end, in wandering mazes lost."[2] The All-wise in His intercourse with men is represented as like a human father conversing with his children. He speaks very simply, that He may be understood. Every teacher knows that he must sympathise with his pupils' ignorance, else they will never understand his knowledge. He must condescend to their condition, place himself alongside of them, study their limitations, take into account their inexperience. He has to bridge over the gulf that separates his mind from theirs. Unless he can express his ideas, not in his own language, but in theirs, their ears might as well be closed, and all his wisdom will be lost upon them. That is the principle on which the Divine Teacher of the human race acted in His Revelation. He made His meaning intelligible by translating His great thoughts into

[1] Isa. $46^{10}$.    [2] Milton.

simple forms of speech. He spake to men in the language of earth, that they might learn the laws of Heaven.

REVERENCE.—Having done his duty under great temptation and at great sacrifice, proving that the LORD was the supreme object of his love, Abraham was commended and accepted for his *fear of God* (22¹²). This fear is a very different thing from the natural, slavish, tormenting fear which it displaces. It is a grace in which God delights. It is a holy fear begotten in hearts renewed and reconciled to God. It resembles the fear of a loving child who would not in anything offend his parents. It is the fear of grieving the Spirit, and incurring the displeasure, of a God of love. It implies a quick sensibility to discover sin and an intense shrinking from its contact. "To fear God and to love Him with the whole heart and soul are feelings indissolubly connected."[1] "Among the children of God," says Ruskin, "there is always that fearful and bowed apprehension of His majesty, and that sacred dread of all offence to Him, which is called the fear of God." It is an abiding characteristic of the believer's life. He never ceases to be penetrated by a subduing sense of religious awe, to be moved by a holy dread of wounding the love of God and violating the law of righteousness. Every step in holiness is measured by the increase in this fear, and the best men are the most full of it. But holy fear is consistent with intense delight in God ; and "happy is the man that feareth alway." The profoundest reverence is compatible with the most trusting confidence. The fear of the LORD is the beginning of wisdom ;[2] to fear God and keep His commandments is the whole duty of man ;[3] all God's servants are devoted to His fear ;[4] and holiness is perfected in the fear of God,[5] which is akin to the holy reverence that befits even the angels of God in heaven.

PROVIDENCE.—After his trial was over, Abraham gave a new

[1] Schultz.    [2] Prov. 1⁷.    [3] Eccles. 12¹³.    [4] Ps. 119³⁸.    [5] 2 Cor. 7¹.

name to Mount Moriah which made it a memorial of God's providence. He called it *Jahveh-jireh*, "the LORD will see or provide." This was the thought which fortified his mind during the whole ordeal. He could not see, and had not wisdom to conjecture, how the trial would end, but he was confident that God would provide. Though he was at his own wits' end, he knew that God would not be baffled. His extreme necessity threw him back on the thought of the variety and fulness of the resources of his God. When God is regarded as exercising foresight, care, and direction for and over His creatures, He is often called—though not in the Bible—by the beautiful name of *Providence*. When we are fulfilling His behests, we may transfer all the pressure of forethought to Him. The whole responsibility of the issues of our conduct rests upon Him whom we obey. Our difficulties are His as well as ours, and we have no need to carry His anxieties and cares. "Roll thy burden on the LORD, and He shall sustain thee; He shall never suffer the righteous to be moved." [1] By renaming the spot where God was a Providence to him, Abraham made it easier to all future generations in Canaan to trust in God. He left "footprints on the sands of time" which would give heart to other tried and tempted men. Canaan was by this process gradually to be filled with sacred names, memories, and associations which would make it a Holy Land.

REVELATION.—Abraham's experience of God's goodness on Moriah also gave rise to a Hebrew proverb, which may be translated in two ways: "In the mount of the LORD it shall be seen," or "In the mount the LORD appeareth" (22[14]). One man's happy experience was generalised for the encouragement of benighted souls in all ages. Painful trials bring men into great darkness, but to all earnest and obedient servants of God there come times of surprising insight —moments on the mount—in which they suddenly see the

[1] Ps. 55[22].

hidden things of God so clearly that they can only call the experience a revelation.

> "God be praised that to believing souls
> Gives light in darkness, comfort in despair." [1]

Moriah became the mount of vision to many Hebrews. Asaph found the sanctuary on God's holy hill the place of solved problems.[2] Beautiful prospects are to be had from Mount Clear. But it is especially on the mount of sacrifice that "the LORD appeareth." His best revelations come to the soul which has been cleansed by the last agony of self-denial. To the man who lays his most cherished possessions on the altar He shows all the riches of His grace. Selfishness necessarily shuts us out from all communion with a God of love ; but let His people deny themselves, and a celestial light will surprise them— "God in His glory shall appear."

> "No cloud across the sun
> But passes at the last, and gives us back
> The face of God once more." [3]

ASSURANCE.—Abraham was confirmed in the grace of God at a time when he had proved his fidelity and loyalty by obeying to the uttermost. All who follow him in the path of real sacrifice have the same deliverance from misgivings, doubts, and fears. Full assurance is the reward of perfect obedience. We rise to confidence, not when we are painfully examining ourselves, and searching for evidences, but when we are earnestly doing the will of God in the face of difficulties and temptations. To make men's assurance doubly sure, the LORD bound Himself to them with an oath ($22^{16}$). "When He made promise to Abraham, since He could swear by none greater, He sware by Himself." [4] He pledged His word by His own person and nature, "that by two immutable things, in which it is impossible for God to lie, we might have strong consolation." The phrase, "in blessing I will bless thee" (v.[17]),

---

[1] Shakespeare.    [2] Ps. $73^{16}$.    [3] Kingsley.    [4] Heb. $6^{18}$.

is the Hebrew way of saying, "I will verily, richly, abundantly bless thee." God would shower blessings on Abraham as the rewards of obedience. Six times the promise had already been given.[1] This is the seventh and last time; and as the final victory of Abraham's faith was the most glorious, so the last promise is the most splendid. This was "a point of unprecedented lustre in the Old Testament. The form as well as the contents of the promise is exuberant. For the victor of Moriah is higher than the victor of Dan."[2] The divine mind which conceives and utters the promise ($22^{16-18}$) seems to burn and glow. Supreme sacrifice is crowned with rapturous blessing. God has purposes so gracious and promises so generous that the grandest similes are required to express them. Abraham's seed shall be as the stars of heaven and as the sand upon the seashore; they shall be victorious over all their enemies; and in them shall all the families of the earth be blessed. The friend of God has done well, and his obedience wins the most emphatic testimony of God's approbation. "Surely," He said, "I will bless thee . . . because thou hast obeyed My voice." No Hebrew could ever hear or read the story without learning that the spirit of obedience gives more joy to God than anything else on earth. "For Thou delightest not in sacrifice, else would I give it; Thou hast no pleasure in burnt-offering."[3] "Behold, to obey is better than sacrifice."[4]

## PILGRIMAGE
### Genesis 23

"They were strangers to the world, neighbours and familiar friends to God."—THOMAS À KEMPIS.

SORROW.—Sarah died in Hebron in the land of Canaan, and Abraham came to mourn for her and to weep for her ($23^2$).

---

[1] Gen. $12^{1-3}$ $12^7$ $13^{14-16}$ $15^{18}$ $17^8$ $18^{10}$.　　　[2] Delitzsch.
[3] Ps. $51^{16}$.　　　[4] 1 Sam. $15^{22}$.

Reverently he bowed before her, and gave way for a time to the rush of sorrow. She had been the companion of his youth, and the partner of all his fortunes. They had toiled, planned, hoped, suffered, rejoiced together during a long life. Now she was silent in death, and Abraham shed natural tears in which there was no bitterness or remorse. The unspoken memories of a lifetime were in those tears. The strong man's heart was true and tender, and he was not unmanned, but more truly man, for weeping. True religion neither eradicates nor reproves sorrow, but tempers and hallows it, and binds up the broken heart. The Hebrews were not ashamed of their emotions, and did not take pride in repressing them. It is no part of heroism to affect insensibility to suffering. The strongest manhood has its roots in tender feeling. The ideal man's emotional nature is as quick, powerful, urgent, undeniable as his intellect is lofty and his will unbending. The patriarchs are all represented as men of tender feeling. "Abraham came to weep." "Jacob lifted up his voice and wept." "Joseph fell upon his father's face and wept." But genuine sorrow does not parade or indulge itself. It was in the stillness of the death-chamber that Abraham wept. When he "rose up from before his dead" and went to purchase a grave, the Hittites saw no tears. Among them he spoke only of burying his dead out of his sight, the strong man using cold words to shield himself from his own surging emotion. Isaac's grief for his mother was no less keen than his father's. For three years his gentle heart continued to mourn its loss.[1] The woman who inspired an affection so tender and lasting in the two men who knew her best, her husband and her son, needed no other praise.

PILGRIMAGE.—The presence of death drew from Abraham the pathetic confession, "I am a stranger and a sojourner with you" ($23^4$). When he was reminded of the uncertainty of his tenure of all earthly things, he was more heartsick and homesick than ever he had felt before. He had never been able to say in

[1] Gen. $23^1$ $24^{67}$ $25^{20}$.

Canaan, " I am at home." He left his one home in Chaldea, and never found another. Wherever he went he built an altar to God, but never a house for himself. He was encamped in many places, but naturalised and domesticated in none. He roamed hither and thither without forming a deep-rooted attachment for any one locality. He saw no spot of earth in which he felt disposed to settle down and live out his life. If he paused for a time in any green valley, and established friendly relations with the natives, they found some morning on awaking that he had folded his tents and silently passed away. He was always an outlander. In Canaan, in Egypt, in Gerar—wherever he went, he sought in vain for a place of rest, till he came to the conclusion that he must always be a stranger and sojourner in the earth. The thought of life as a pilgrimage sank deep into the Hebrew mind ; and even after the Children of Israel had conquered Canaan, and were wanderers no more, but settled owners of the soil, they were still but strangers and pilgrims with God.[1] They lived their life on earth in fellowship with God, without thinking much about a life to come. They had not our Christian knowledge of the future ; but they had our faith in the goodness of God. They were like little children who are sure of their father's love, but are not able to conceive the future, and do not trouble themselves about it. Still it is impossible to doubt that *some* idea of another state of existence underlies their habitual description of life as a pilgrimage. " For," as the writer of the Epistle to the Hebrews urges, "they that say such things make it manifest that they are seeking after a country of their own."[2]

COURTESY.—Those who have witnessed bargain-making in the East say that Gen. 23 depicts it to a nicety. The seller opens the transaction by assuring you, with an expressive *salaam*, that everything he has is yours, and bidding you take just what you want. You return the salutation, and protest against such kindness ; he continues to urge you to oblige him

[1] Ps. 39[12], 1 Chron. 29[15].　　　　[2] Heb. 11[14].

by taking whatever you desire. That is etiquette, meaning no more than, " I am at your service, command me." When you at length get nearer business, and he condescends to name a price, which he does in an offhand way as a matter of no importance, it is sure to be six times the real value ; "but what," he asks, "is that between thee and me?" With much manœuvring, and a leisurely disregard of time, the negotiation then proceeds, till the seller is brought to reasonable terms and a bargain is struck. The author of *The Land and the Book* regards the courtesy of the Hittites in this light. It was mere palaver ; the generous phrases were idle compliments ; the noble offer "meant nothing whatever," as Abraham knew quite well, but "as he was in no mood to chaffer with the owner, whatever the price might be, he proceeded forthwith to weigh out the money." Dr. Thomson may be right, but most readers of the narrative will prefer another view : that the sons of Heth, impressed by Abraham's noble character, touched by his lonely sorrow, and moved by his pathetic appeal, sincerely desired to pay him a tribute of respect ; in all good faith offered him the gift of a field and a sepulchre ; and only when they saw his resolution to decline a present and his desire to pay for the ground at its full market value, consented to bargain with him and to convey the property to him with all legal ceremony. On this theory the story is designed to teach a lesson of genuine reverence for true greatness. It seems more natural to read the narrative in this light than to compare the manners of a simple primitive age with the inanities of the modern bazaars. "Courtesy is not a falsehood or a grimace. 'Bending before men' is a recognition that there does dwell in that presence of our Brother something divine."[1]

SENTIMENT.—Abraham's anxiety about the possession of a sepulchre may seem to have been a matter of sentiment rather than of reason. But sentiment plays a great and important part in human affairs, and no sentiment is more sacred or potent than

[1] Carlyle.

that which is connected with the ashes of our beloved dead. The last resting-place of a household is holy ground, and it is a proverb that the graves of the dead mark the homes of the living. "Our father's sepulchres are here . . . how should we love another land so well?" Reason concurred with sentiment in Abraham's decision that he and his people must be separate from the heathen in death as well as in life. Events proved how wisely he was guided in the matter. In later ages the holy sepulchre of Machpelah was the magnet which drew the hearts of the Hebrews back from distant lands. At the present day scarcely any shrine is more devoutly hallowed or more jealously guarded than the cave which Abraham purchased as a burying-place for his wife. Dr. Thomson calls it "the most interesting of all spots on the face of the earth." It is at present in the possession of the Turks, and for many centuries not more than half a dozen "unbelievers"—our King and Dean Stanley being two of them—have seen so much as the outer enclosure built over the cave. No Christian eyes ever see the actual tomb. What it may contain is a mystery which future events will disclose.

BUSINESS.—The account of the transference of the property which Abraham bought of the sons of Heth at the gates of Hebron reads like a legal document ($23^{17. 18}$). The conveyance was carried out with scrupulous care. The purchase was completed, the bargain attested, the title "made sure." The man of faith was as attentive to business as to devotion, and sought the glory of God in both. It is extremely misleading to draw a sharp line of demarcation between sacred and secular duties. All duties are duties to God. We are in the habit of saying that religion is religion and business is business, as if they were to be kept separate and conducted on different principles ; but a believer's life is too full of God to allow such a cleavage. A man can only have one character. "True religion, which is to obey God, mixes itself up with all the cares and business of this mortal life, this work-day world."[1] All secular things—business, art, science, politics, war, labour, pleasure—instead of being detached from religion, have such intimate relations with it that they are, or may be, and ought to be, essentially religious. There is not the lowliest task which may not be undertaken with prayer and performed to the glory of God, and so made sacred. Religion is not satisfied with a limited sphere ; it controls the whole domain of life ; and the servant of God who carries his religious principles into all human affairs cannot but be the ideal man of business.

NOBILITY.—Abraham was not excelled in politeness, chivalry, high-breeding by the children of Heth. Touched by their generous kindness, he twice " rose up and bowed himself before the people of the land " (23[7. 12]). " There is something pleasing in the courteousness of the Hittites to Abraham ; and inexpressibly affecting are the noble, graceful, and dignified returns of his obeisance."[2] No one suggests that *his* courtesy was unreal. Had there been a Hebrew word for " gentleman " he would have borne it without abuse ; he was the personification of the gentle and manly virtues. The Hittites, searching for a word to characterise him, found one which hit the mark. They called him a " prince of God" (23[6]). He was a dweller in tents, with no claim to high or long descent ; yet he was princely in his whole bearing, address, and character. "Abraham," says Charles Kingsley, " was a prince in manners and a prince in heart." The Hittites partly divined his secret. His personality was grandly impressive to them. He rose in uncrowned sovereignty above them all, the strongest, noblest, gentlest man ; and they saw that he was a prince of God's own making. He owed his power and charm, not so much to natural endowment, as to the transforming and ennobling influence of divine grace. Great aspirations and ideals created his great character. He kept company with God till he became a partaker of the divine nature. Beginning as a man of God, he ended as a

[1] Kingsley.        [2] Chalmers.

prince of God. True religion develops the highest kind of manhood. Under its influence a common man becomes princely in soul, unconsciously regnant among his fellow-men, and does the most common things in a noble, gentle, royal spirit. Being to God what the wax is to the seal, he is stamped with the image of God.

> " Self-reverence, self-knowledge, self-control,
> These three alone lead life to sovereign power."

## LOVE
### Genesis 24

> " For all love greatens and glorifies,
> Till God's aglow to the loving eyes
> In what was mere earth before."—BROWNING.

IDYLLIC.—Gen. 24 is one of the sweetest idylls ever penned. It is interesting as a picture of the primitive manners and customs of a great race. It is charming as a revelation of the beauty of common things and the dignity of homely life. It is delightful as a study of human characters—the wise and venerable master, the shrewd and faithful steward, the careful and covetous guardian brother, the lissome and winsome maiden, the pious and pensive bridegroom. It is impressive as a delineation of the manner in which Providence brings the counsels of good and devout men to a happy issue. The whole tale is warm and throbbing with humanity, rich in colour and incident, affording bright glimpses of a sunny and natural, sweet and believing life in the far past. We prize it not only for what is said, but for the manner in which it is said. The style of the narrative may well be called perfect. Its homely ease is the consummation of unconscious art. The Hebrews had their ideals of beautiful form in writing, and inspiration made them all the more skilful in fitting aptest

words to things. It would have been strange if they had been
blind to the fascination of literary form or deaf to the music
of words. We cannot, however, as Newman observes, imagine
great minds "accustomed to aim at diction for its own sake."
We must rather think of them as "being inspired with their
subject, and pouring forth beautiful words because they have
beautiful thoughts." The Hebrew traditions, refined and sifted
by frequent repetition, became perfect in point of form. Nothing
could exceed the dignity, elevation, and beauty of this tale of
Isaac and Rebekah, which satisfies alike the religious, the moral,
and the æsthetic sense. The chapter is a casket of gems, which
one is afraid to touch. To paraphrase Scripture is always to
court humiliation. It is like gilding refined gold, or painting the
lily. The great authors of the Bible have "the charm of an incom-
municable simplicity."[1] To see the beauty, to feel the charm, to
catch the secret of their writing—all so closely allied with noble
living and thinking—were to have the highest culture.

MARRIAGE.—Abraham made his steward swear that he would
not take a daughter of the Canaanites as a wife for his son Isaac
(24³), and the solemnity of his words indicates the great importance of the injunction. There are many evidences that Abraham
lived on amicable terms with his heathen neighbours. He made
leagues with them, fought side by side with them, transacted
business with them, and treated them with princely courtesy.
Nevertheless he lived in a world of ideas to which they were
complete strangers. He never forgot that he was divided from
them by the barrier of religion. He saw that a marriage connection with a princely heathen family would be no real benefit,
but rather a deadly injury, to true religion ; it would mean an
alliance between the young Faith and the old Paganism ; and it
would defeat the purpose for which God called the Hebrews to
be a separate people in the world. A true marriage was, in the
beautiful Hebrew phrase, "a covenant of God,"[2] that is, a sacred

[1] Newman.     [2] Prov. 2¹⁷.

promise mutually given in the presence of God as Witness.[1]  God
would not suffer any of His people to form a sacred alliance with
His enemies ; He could not witness it without displeasure ; He
could not give it His benediction.  The "holy seed" must not
"mingle themselves with the peoples of the lands."[2]  It was not
mere pride of race, it was the sense of a divine calling, that
made the Hebrews shun alliances by marriage with surrounding
tribes.  There was an inexorable rigour as well as a divine
pitifulness in true religion.  Holiness was intolerant of sin.  It did
not confound charity with indifference.  While it was far removed
from contempt of any men, it necessarily created antagonisms.
Those who love God will never seek a love which is incon-
sistent with their supreme affection.  The distinction between
the children of God and the children of the world is ancient and
vital.  Paul was simply echoing Abraham's words when he said,
"Be not unequally yoked with unbelievers : for what communion
hath light with darkness ?"[3]  A true marriage implies an affinity
of heart and mind, an identity of aim and purpose, a community
of faith and worship.  It is a union of souls ; and God will not
"to the marriage of true minds admit impediment."  The narrative teaches that holy wedlock is a sacred contract in the making
of which God is consulted, which God approves and blesses,
which none but God can break, and He by death.

FIDELITY. — "It is required in stewards that a man be
found faithful."[4]  Abraham's steward perfectly fulfilled this requirement.  His name is not mentioned in Gen. 24, but he is
naturally regarded as the same servant who in Gen. 15 is called
Eliezer.  His ideal is his master, from whom he has received his
knowledge of the true God, and whom in return he serves with
a self-forgetfulness as beautiful as it is rare.  He prays to the
God of his master on behalf of his master ($24^{12}$) ; he gives thanks
to the God of his master for kindness to his master (v.$^{27}$) ; when
he becomes eloquent it is in the praise of his master ; and his

[1] Mal. $2^{14}$.  [2] Ezra $9^{2.3}$.  [3] 2 Cor. $6^{14}$.  [4] 1 Cor. $4^2$.

favourite expression, "my master," occurs eighteen times in one chapter. He finds in the words a sweet savour and holy gladness. So reverent, so chivalrous is he that he all but worships his master. He and George Herbert are of one mind—

> "How sweetly doth 'my Master' sound! 'my Master!'
> As ambergris leaves a rich scent
> Unto the taster,
> So doth these words a sweet content,
> An oriental fragrancy, 'my Master.'"

For himself Eliezer has never a name or title but "Abraham's servant." He does not call himself the elder or ruler of Abraham's house (v.[2]), and he never breathes the fact that he was once the heir-elect of Abraham's whole fortune (15[2]). The interests of Isaac, his younger "master" (v.[65]), so absorb his attention, that at the end of a long journey he refuses to touch food till he has told his errand and despatched his business. And when his mission is crowned with success, he desires nothing so much as to return without delay and announce the good tidings to his master (v.[56]). His master's happiness is all the reward he seeks. In this man self is dead. He is not his own, he is his master's, he is God's, and not a trace of egoism remains in his character. The goods of his master are in his hand (v.[10]), the cause of his master is in his heart, the God of his master is above him, and he is perfectly content. His watchwords are kindness and truth (or love and faith). Kindness is what he prays to God for (vv.[12, 14]); kindness and truth are what he thanks God for (v.[27]); kindness and truth[1] are what he asks from his master's relatives (v.[49]). Leal love and faithfulness are evidently his own characteristics. Shrewd and practical as he is, he has the guileless simplicity of a child. No Hebrew servant could have been more ready than he to say, "I love my master, I love his house, I love his service, I will not go free, I will serve him for ever."[2] At the end he could wish nothing

---

[1] "Deal kindly and truly" is lit. "show kindness and truth."
[2] See Ex. 21[5, 6].

better than to hear his Divine Master say, ' Well done, good and
faithful servant"; and for a place of reward there was nothing
like "Abraham's bosom."

> "O good old man! how well in thee appears
> The constant service of the antique world,
> When service sweat for honour, not for meed." [1]

WOMANHOOD. — The narrative gives a lifelike picture of a
Hebrew maiden. The salient features of her character are
sketched in the fewest and aptest words. (1) Reference is made
to Rebekah's *beauty*. She "was very fair to look upon" ($24^{16}$).
The Bible always speaks quite naturally of the charm of personal
grace. Sarah, Rebekah, and Rachel were all lovely women.
Sarah is portrayed in the beauty and power of ripened womanhood. Rebekah is radiant with the loveliness of early youth ;
she has the freshness of springtime and the prime ; her
presence is bright and exhilarating as sunshine. Beauty in its
essence is the form of the true and the good. Milton speaks
of the "human face divine." All pure eyes are keenly
susceptible to beauty, as it is a revelation of the beauty of
the God in whose image we are made, and a prophecy of the
glory of the children of God. " All partial beauty is the pledge
of beauty in its plenitude." But because in itself "favour is
deceitful and beauty vain," [2] the narrative passes lightly from the
comeliness of face and form to the loveliness of perfect deeds,
without which the spell of physical beauty soon becomes powerless. The finest beauty is a radiation from character. " There
is no beautifier of complexion, or form, or behaviour, like the
wish to scatter joy and not pain around us." [3]   (2) Reference is
made to Rebekah's *industry*. She was coming to draw water
when Eliezer first saw her. In Hebrew homes high-born girls
were taught to prefer work to idleness. The Hebrews believed
that beauty was never so attractive as when it was combined with
active usefulness. Rebekah belonged to a wealthy family, and

[1] Shakespeare.       [2] Prov. $31^{30}$.       [3] Emerson.

had maids of her own to wait upon her (v.$^{61}$); yet she busied herself with household tasks, "deeming it," as Dr. Guthrie says, "no more dishonour to bake bread than to eat it, to draw water than to drink it, to make a dress than to wear it." If we admire her jewellery, we must not forget her earthenware. The artist's eye overlooks her ring and bracelets, and rests with delight upon her pitcher, the work of the hands of the potter, which she carries gracefully poised on her shoulder. She has the spirit of service by which woman is the queen of the beautiful realm called home. (3) Rebekah enjoys *liberty*. She appears in public alone and unveiled. She converses freely with a man, a complete stranger. We see

> " Her household motions light and free,
>   And steps of virgin liberty."

Nowhere is the influence of true religion more apparent than in its effect upon the position of woman. Eastern women have always been morally and intellectually degraded. They are regarded without respect or chivalrous sentiment. They have not the qualities which would fit them to be the companions, friends, and advisers of men. Nothing is expected of them but extreme ignorance and frivolity. Man's licence everywhere ends in woman's bondage. But among the Hebrews true religion emancipated woman, and won for her a high position, a commanding influence, a chivalrous regard. Man's virtue and woman's liberty go hand in hand. To the present day nothing but pure and undefiled religion gives woman safety and freedom. "Show me ten square miles," said Lowell, "outside of Christianity, where the life of man and the purity of woman are safe, and I will give up Christianity." (4) The story refers to Rebekah's *chastity*. She guarded a love that was virginal and pure. She was undefiled for the undefiled. Her innocence was her strength : "she that has that is clad in complete steel." [1]

[1] Milton.

Matthew Arnold chooses her as his ideal of stainless maiden-
hood —

> "What girl
> Now reads in her bosom as clear
> As Rebekah read, when she sate
> At eve by the palm-shaded well?
> Who guards in her breast
> As deep, as pellucid, a spring
> Of feeling, as tranquil, as sure?"

(5) The story lingers over Rebekah's *courtesy* to a stranger and
*kindness* to animals. These were the qualities by which Eliezer
hoped to discover Isaac's destined bride. He asked God to
send him, not the loveliest girl in Haran,—though Rebekah was
no doubt that girl,—but the kindest. When she comes to the
well, she finds an unknown traveller resting there, who begs a
little water to drink. She lowers her pitcher, puts it to his lips,
and bids him drink. Her word for "drink" is different from
his: he asks a little water "to sip"; she bids him "drink
abundantly." But she goes further; unasked, she finds out ways
of doing deeds of kindness. A glance at the kneeling camels
tells her that they too are thirsty, and she volunteers to draw
water for them till they have done drinking (v.19). This is no
easy task, for a camel drinks enough at a time to last three
days, and the well is down a flight of steps; but Rebekah is as
good as her word. Gliding down with the empty pitcher and
returning with it filled, repeating the action times without
number, glowing the while with the healthy exertion, she never
pauses till the last of the ten thirsty beasts has raised his head
content. While Eliezer looks on in silent admiration (v.21), she
is unconscious of having done anything remarkable. The
beauty of such actions as hers lies in the fact that the doer of
them sees nothing to admire. They are little nothings —
"nameless unremembered acts of kindness and of love." But
some day they fix one's destiny. Trivial things both make and
reveal character. "Trifles!" said a very great man, "perfection

is made out of trifles, and perfection is not a trifle." [1] Rebekah was never more lovely than when she was completing her self-imposed task at the well. Kindness in the heart is light in the eyes, music in the voice, grace in the motions. The first element of vital beauty, as Ruskin says, is " the kindness and unselfish fulness of heart which receives the utmost amount of pleasure from the happiness of all things." (6) The story refers to Rebekah's *hospitality*. She would be no true daughter of an Eastern chieftain if she did not remember that a stranger must never look in vain for shelter and rest and food. Without consulting anybody she invites Eliezer and his men to enter her brother's house. The fare she first offers and the right she assumes to offer it indicate her practical and independent habit of mind. " We have," she assures Eliezer, " straw and provender and room to lodge in." This beautiful, high-spirited maiden, throbbing with fulness of life, gifted with the charm of perfect freedom, nimble intelligence, and eager vivacity, hasting (v.[18]), running (v.[28]), leaping down from her camel (v.[64]), yet always quiet and self-possessed, saying the right word and doing the right deed, naturally captivates all hearts. Eliezer wonders at her (v.[21]), all her friends bless her (v.[60]), Isaac loves her (v.[67]). Sincere and ardent, she reaches right conclusions as by instinct, has no affectations, and wastes no time or words. Oriental custom has always given a father the right to dispose of his daughter's hand as he sees fit. But to a maiden of Rebekah's spirit this would have been intolerable. The narrative shows that among the ancient Hebrews " regard was had to the personal inclinations and wishes of the young people." [2] Asked if she would go with Eliezer, Rebekah answers with prompt decision, " I will go," which in her own Hebrew is one short word. We naturally ask what made her so willing to leave her father's house, to go on a long and venturous journey, to become a pilgrim in a strange land. Some will suggest the spirit of romance ; others will see the glint of the stranger's gold. But

[1] Michael Angelo.  [2] Benzinger.

it was Eliezer's prayer. When Rebekah stood at the well, and heard this traveller from a far country thanking and praising God, in the twinkling of an eye she looked into the clear depths of a guileless soul, felt the thrill of awe which always passes through a pure young heart in the presence of a saint, and after that she was ready to put her life in his hand and follow him to the ends of the earth.

PROVIDENCE.—While Eliezer was shrewd and cautious in fulfilling the delicate commission with which he was charged, he ascribed all his success in finding a bride for his young master, not to his own intelligence, but to God's guiding hand. Before he set out for Syria of the Two Rivers, the difficulties which naturally presented themselves to his mind were overcome by his master's assurance that the LORD would send His angel with him (v.[7]). When he came to Haran he sought divine guidance. "O LORD, the God of my master Abraham," he said, "send me, I pray Thee, good speed this day" (v.[12]). He had no doubt that God intervened in human affairs to make a plain path for the feet of devout men. He confidently sought to learn God's will; he knew that he would not ask in vain; and when his petition was answered to the letter, he became eloquent as he told, with delightful epic repetitions, how the LORD had prospered his way ($24^{35-49}$). He was certain that it was not his own sagacity, but God's providence, that led him to success. He was not wise enough to find a way for himself; he would have despaired of his own judgment and foresight; but he believed in a God who beset him behind and before, and laid His hand upon him. This does not mean that he expected God to lead him independently of the exercise of his own faculties. He used his reason, experience, and common sense. God's influence did not suspend, but intensified and quickened his mental energies. At the same time God's providence controlled both his movements and those of others whom he was destined to meet. Everybody knows that there is an element

in earthly affairs which is beyond all human foresight and skill.
"Shallow men believe in luck," says Emerson. They enlarge
on happy accidents and undesigned coincidences. Or they
talk of a blind irresistible power which they call fate. But
others, far wiser, say "there's a divinity which shapes our ends,
rough-hew them how we will."[1] "In what unbelief regards as
chance, faith sees an act of God."[2] Our times are in the hands
of One who superintends the issues of the moral life, and
watches over all the fortunes of His children.

> "Great works, the secret and sublime, forsooth,
> Let others prize ! . . . what are these at best,—beside
> God helping, God directing everywhere?"[3]

Eliezer clung to his master's belief that the LORD would send
His guiding angel with him. That was entirely a matter of
faith. Eliezer has no visible supernatural guide at his side
in his journey. "The angel of the LORD is perhaps a
poetical and realistic conception of the special providence of
God."[4] In any case Eliezer—who is a type of every believer
—did not doubt that God was guiding him and working with
and for him; and if he did not say in so many words that
a true marriage—like that of Isaac and Rebekah—is made in
heaven, that was exactly what he meant.

FAREWELL.—Rebekah has to forget her own people and her
father's house.[5] A friendly discussion arises as to the time of
her departure for the new country. Laban's household and
Eliezer take opposite sides (24[54. 55]). Rebekah's mother and
brother naturally wish that she should "wait a few days, at
least ten." Faithful Eliezer, however, is inexorable. In his
eagerness to announce at home how the LORD has prospered
his journey, he begs leave to depart with Rebekah without
delay, that he may go to his master (v.[56]). Rebekah settles

---

[1] Shakespeare.      [2] Schultz.      [3] Browning.
[4] A. B. Davidson.   [5] Ps. 45[10].

the matter to his satisfaction, and the preparations for departure have to be hurried through. Rebekah's maidens are to go with her, and Deborah her nurse—the busy *bee* of the household, as her name signifies—cannot be left behind. Deborah will be her lifelong friend, and see her children's children (35[8]). The parting with kindred is pathetic. In moments of farewell bursting hearts seek relief in the utterance of boundless good wishes ; such ideals as good people chance to cherish must find expression ; everybody craves from Heaven something infinite for the loved one who will be seen no more. Language is taxed for hyperboles, and yet scarcely a tithe is said of what is felt and meant. The conquest of the world is not too good for Rebekah. "Our sister," cry the daughters of Haran as they wave their last adieus, "be thou the mother of thousands of ten thousands" ; "and," shout the warlike youths, "let thy seed possess the gates of them that hate thee" (v.[60]). Next to the favour of God, the blessing of beloved friends is the sweetest thing in the world. With this hearty God-speed ringing in her ears and making music in her heart, Rebekah, bidding adieu for ever to the home of her youth, and wrapped in a dream of hope and wonder, rides away with her train of maidens into the strange wide world.

MEDITATION.—The scene suddenly changes to "the land of the south," where Isaac is meditating in the field at the eventide (v.[63]). The son of a strong man of action is often a quiet man of thought, and Isaac is seen at his best in meditation. This is the attitude in which we naturally portray him. His life was spent in still retirement ; he was a gentle presence, a gracious influence, rather than an active force in the life of the world. It was not in him to summon a council of war, to head a midnight charge, to silence a king with a word. It was not his fault that he was not cast in heroic mould. He had the constitutional delicacy of a child of old age, the gentleness of an only son tenderly mothered, the shyness of a boy who has never known brothers and sisters, the passiveness of a youth who has the misfortune never to learn the meaning of hardship, and the air of abstraction from the world which is natural to one who has been laid on the altar and has in a sense come back from the dead. All his days his gentle spirit was in love with solitude. He lived remote from the haunts of men, on the very edge of the wilderness, by Hagar's quiet well. Let him be among green fields and beside still waters, and he was content. But quiet, reserved, unobtrusive, unambitious as he was, Isaac had a joy all his own. No happiness is more real than that of the meditative spirit which reaps "the harvest of the quiet eye." The calm brooding soul has depths of thought and secret experience which are unfathomable to restless minds. Our English Bible says, "Isaac went out to meditate at the eventide." Luther's Bible (and our margin) has "he went out to pray." The word has both meanings, and in that sentence Isaac's character is enshrined. He needed no oratory but the green fields, no incense but the falling dew, no dim religious light but nature's holy twilight, no candles but the lamps of heaven. There he had whole-hearted undisturbed fellowship with God. "I meditate on all Thy doings; I muse on the work of Thy hands; I stretch forth my hands unto Thee."[1] Isaac did not altogether, or perhaps at all, belie the happy name of *Laughter* which his fond parents gave him. In his reverential musing there was a radiance of heaven-born joy.

> "Alway his downcast eye
>   Was laughing silently,
>   As if he found some jubilee in thinking;
>   For his one thought was God,
>   In that one thought he abode,
>   For ever in that thought more deeply sinking."[2]

Isaac as well as Abraham is a true Hebrew type. His character ranks as a great creation. Walking in the fields at eventide,

[1] Ps. 143⁵.          [2] Faber.

praying, musing, adoring, Isaac lives for ever in the imagination of mankind. The nation which cherished such an ideal was destined to be pre-eminent in the best things, and to have the task of teaching a restless and noisy world the secret of peace, leading it back to the green fields and the still dews.

LOVE.—The closing scene is depicted in few words, but it belongs to the great literature of the world. God had prepared another joy for Isaac. As he came from "the well of the living God that seeth me," his meditation was cut short. He was suddenly in the charmed realm of romance. A fair picture painted itself in the setting sun. Isaac "lifted up his eyes, and saw, and, behold, there were camels coming." The dumb creatures again play their part in the story. Rebekah's kindness to them had won her a husband ; they fetch her across the desert to her future home ; and in the golden twilight the approaching cavalcade makes an imperishable image in Isaac's heart. Rebekah leaps lightly down from her camel and glides into his life. They twain were destined for one another. Each was the counterpart and fulfilment of the other. "The happiness and perfection of both depends on each asking and receiving from the other what the other only can give." [1]

> " He is the half part of a blessed man,
> Left to be finished by such as she ;
> And she a fair divided excellence
> Whose fulness of perfection lies in him." [2]

"Each fulfils defect in each"—the passive, pensive, patient Isaac ; the ardent, active, eager Rebekah. *L'allegra* weds *il penseroso*. The providence of God, the sanction of parents, the approval of friends, community of faith, manly virtues, maidenly graces, conspire to bless their union ; Heaven's gift of love makes them one ; and they are faithful unto death. Nothing could more clearly indicate the essential greatness of the Hebrew race than the fact that such pure and lofty ideals

[1] Ruskin.  [2] Shakespeare.

were conceived and realised. "The fair type of matrimony presented in the story of Isaac and Rebekah does no more than represent with little alteration marriage as it really existed in the majority of families in the best days of the nation. . . . And here we may clearly see the mighty working of an elevated religion." [1]

COMFORT.—There are volumes in the simple words, "And Isaac brought Rebekah into his mother's tent, and took Rebekah, and she became his wife : and Isaac was comforted after his mother's death" (v.[67]). Isaac's chief characteristic is a fine sensibility. He is keenly alive both to the joys and the sorrows of life. His spirit is like a sensitive plant, which responds to the touch of the softest light. He is from first to last essentially and unalterably a lover ; for him to live is to love. And love is the secret of all that is best and strongest in him. His emotions are tremulously intense, and it is his happiness that his love is from the first directed to the right objects. Love misdirected is the sum of misery. Isaac is a lover of God, a lover of nature, a lover of home, and his spiritual love keeps his other affections pure. Like a delicate musical instrument, he answers every touch and breath of love. He so loves God that he is willing to lay down his life at His command. He so loves nature that a summer evening stirs him to high and reverent ecstasy. He so loves his mother that when she is taken from him time brings him no surcease of sorrow ; he loves her all the more that he sees her in the light of memory ; in his rich and deep nature love burns long and fervently ; and after three years his grief is still fresh and keen. He is not comforted till he feels the transforming power of a new and altogether different affection—a love strong as death, which many waters cannot quench, neither can the floods drown.[2]

HARMONIES.—Nothing could be more beautiful than the way in which nature, religion, and love are blended in the story of

[1] Ewald.　　　　　　[2] Song of Sol. 8[6. 7.]

Isaac and Rebekah. God inspires the author to hallow and glorify love. *Nature* helps him to realise it. The magnificence of sunset and the stillness of twilight form a fit environment for it. The great things of the world, of which love is the greatest, have a natural affinity. "The lover sees no resemblance except to summer evenings and diamond mornings, rainbows and the song of birds." [1]

> "Your love? That's high as you shall go ;
> For it is true as Gospel text,
> Not noble then is never so,
> Either in this world or the next."

*Religion* does still more to make love what God designed it to be. The author surrounds Isaac with an atmosphere of meditation and prayer before he introduces him to his bride. Isaac will love Rebekah the more purely and chivalrously because he already loves God so well. His love will be a light to lead him, not away from, but nearer to God. "That man knows little either of love or of religion who imagines they ought to be kept apart. Of what sort is either if it is unfit to approach the other? Has God decreed, created a love which must separate from Himself? Is Love then divided? Or shall not the heart created lift up the heart to the Heart creating?" [2]

> "Thrice blest whose lives are faithful prayers,
> Whose loves in higher love endure." [3]

## HEAVEN
### Genesis 25:7-10

> "On the earth the broken arcs ; in the heaven, a perfect round."
> BROWNING.

OLD AGE.—Abraham was old, and well stricken in years (24[1]). But of his old age three things are said which redeem it from sadness and make it beautiful, noble, venerable. (I) It

[1] Emerson.     [2] George Macdonald.     [3] Tennyson.

was "a good old age" (25[8]), such as only a good man could have. The Hebrews regarded life as visibly and ideally complete when it was full of days, riches, and honour. They believed that righteousness lengthened life and glorified it at the end. "The hoary head is a crown of glory ; it shall be found in the way of righteousness."[1] Age being a sign of divine favour, the good man's days were long in the land, while the wicked man was cut off by a premature and miserable death.

> "What man is he that desireth life,
> And loveth many days that he may *see good*?
> Keep thy tongue from evil,
> And thy lips from speaking guile ;
> Depart from evil, and *do good*."[2]

The heathen made pathetic attempts to render age endurable and even desirable ; but in the ideal old age of the Hebrews one discerns a grandeur, a meekness, and a mellowness which are unique. Advancing life was made good by increasing brightness and honour—"Thy age shall be clearer than the noonday ; thou shalt shine forth, and be as the morning"[3] by increasing fruitfulness—"They shall still bring forth fruit in old age ; they shall be full of sap and green"[4] by the continual presence of God—"Even to old age I am He ; and even to hoar hairs will I carry you."[5] "At evening-time there shall be light."[6] The memory of an active past, the sense of victory over trials, the silent waiting for the great change, made the sunset of life tranquil and beautiful. As even the lovely springtime of the year has not the charm of mellow autumn, so no beauty of youth can rival the features of old age which have been purified by time and trial and sorrow. Browning begins his finest poem with the words—

> "Grow old along with me,
> The best is yet to be,
> The last of life for which the first was planned."

---

[1] Prov. 16[31].   [2] Ps. 34[12-14].   [3] Job 11[17].
[4] Ps. 92[14].   [5] Isa. 46[4].   [6] Zech. 14[7].

And Arnold speaks of the "solemn peace" of the evening of life—

> "As the stars come out, and the night-wind
> Brings up the stream
> Murmurs and scents of the infinite sea."

(2) Abraham was "full of years," or "satisfied with life" ($25^8$). He had seen, felt, laboured, loved, suffered enough ; he knew all the contents of time ; earth had no more to offer him ; and so the years brought him a sense of completeness. Ripened by divine grace, satisfied but not sated, enjoying life to the last, yet willing to let it go—that is how we picture an aged servant of God. He will be—

> " With ease gathered, not harshly plucked, for death mature." [1]

(3) The LORD had blessed him in all things ($24^1$). To one who looked back upon the joys and sorrows, sins and sufferings of a long life, that was a splendid conclusion of the whole matter. Through God's loving-kindness he had found good in everything. He was rich, and riches were not a curse to him ; he suffered, and trial was a blessing to him ; he sinned, and by God's wonderful grace he got good out of evil. Every aged believer can say, as he reviews the past—

> "I have seen God's hand through a lifetime, and all is for best." [2]

REUNION.—When Abraham died, " Isaac and Ishmael, his sons, buried him in the cave of Machpelah " ($25^9$). This is the only transaction in which the brothers are ever mentioned together. They had never met since the day on which Ishmael, a lad of some fifteen years of age, was banished from home as a scapegrace for mocking his infant half-brother. Now they are both bearded men, and they stand side by side at the entrance of a rock-hewn sepulchre, and bear into its shadows the lifeless form of their father. The heroic huntsman from the steppes of Arabia and the gentle shepherd from the pasture-

[1] Milton.                    [2] Browning.

lands of the South vie with each other in paying the last honours to the beloved dead. They are both dutiful sons. Neither of them can ever forget how much their father loved them ; neither of them ever cease to revere his name and memory. Death brings estranged brothers together to drink the cup of a common sorrow ; they look at each other with tear-dimmed eyes ; they see, in the light of eternity, how paltry are all causes of earthly strife ; and they cannot return to their homes with hard hearts. When all other means of reconciliation fail, death makes kindred and brethren kind. The last enemy is a friend ; the great divider is a mighty reconciler.

IMMORTALITY.—When Abraham died, he " was gathered to his fathers" ($25^8$), as God had promised, "in peace" ($15^{15}$). The phrase "gathered to his fathers" cannot mean that his body was laid to rest where the dust and ashes of his ancestors reposed. He died far away from the home of his fathers, and was interred in a new sepulchre, where only the remains of Sarah had been buried. The statement that he "was gathered to his fathers" is quite different from the preceding one, that he "gave up the ghost" ($25^8$), and from the succeeding one, that " Isaac and Ishmael buried him in the cave of Machpelah" ($25^9$). The gathering place was not in Chaldea, but in the unseen world. The words imply a certain doctrine of another life, though what that was it is not easy to say. The old Shemitic idea was that all the dead, good and bad alike, went to the spectral realm of Sheol, " the congregation of shades," "the land of darkness and forgetfulness," " the house appointed for all living," where men were but feeble, flaccid semblances of their former selves, life was a pale image of the activities of the upper world, and fellowship with God was for ever at an end. But this cheerless prospect could not satisfy men who believed in a living, personal, gracious God ; and it was here that inspired idealism achieved its most splendid results. " For all that appears, the idea that any human person could become extinguished or be annihilated never recurred to the prophets and saints of the Old Testament."[1] On the contrary, men of faith were enabled to apprehend and proclaim the truth that their communion with God would never cease ;[2] that they would overleap Sheol ;[3] that they would see God's face and be satisfied ;[4] that they would dwell in the house of the LORD for ever ;[5] that, though their flesh and heart failed, God would be the strength of their heart, and their portion for ever.[6] How far this was believed by the writers of Genesis we can hardly know. But the argument for immortality, with special reference to the patriarchs, has been stated by the highest Authority. The words, "I am the God of Abraham, and the God of Isaac, and the God of Jacob," contain the doctrine of immortality, since "God is not the God of the dead, but of the living."[7] "As soon as the expressions 'communion with God' and 'life' begin to be at all synonymous, the foundation is laid of a true religious assurance of immortality, even although the doctrine itself is not yet consciously held."[8] Men who have lived in covenant and fellowship with God cannot dissolve into a handful of dust and cease to be. The desires which God has implanted in their hearts will be satisfied ; their ideals are prophecies of their possessions. The Almighty will not forsake His friends. He does not call, and justify, and sanctify men, and then extinguish them. Machpelah does not hold the patriarchs. The Syrian stars look down on their sepulchre ; *they* look down on the Syrian stars.

HEAVEN.—An exiled patriot has said, "Love and reverence above everything the ideal. The ideal is superior to every country, superior to humanity ; it is the country of the spirit, the city of the soul."[9] When Abraham left Chaldea, he was allured

---

[1] A. B. Davidson.  [2] Ps. 73$^{23. 24}$.  [3] Ps. 49$^{15}$.
[4] Ps. 17$^{15}$, Job 19$^{26}$.  [5] Ps. 23$^{6}$.  [6] Ps. 73$^{26}$.
[7] Matt. 22$^{32}$.  [8] Schultz.  [9] Kossuth.

by the hope of finding a country of his own ; and when he entered Canaan, the land was promised him for a possession ($12^7$). But his hope was never literally fulfilled. "In the land of promise he sojourned as in a strange country." [1] He obtained no inheritance there, "no, not so much as to set his foot on." [2] Still he was not disappointed, and never complained of being deceived. His ideals were unrealised, but not shattered. He knew that all his expectations would be fulfilled in some grander way than he had ever imagined. His hope was unquenchable, and he never supposed that the unattained was unattainable. He so identified himself with the future of his people, that he rejoiced in it as if it were his own. He and all his children "saw the promises and greeted them from afar." [3] Many things in the future were mysterious to him ; but all the ideals of the Hebrews were prophetic of Christ, and to cherish them was to have a certain vision of the Fulfiller. "Abraham," said Jesus, "rejoiced to see My day, and he saw it and was glad." [4] For himself Abraham continued to cherish the ardent desire for a country. This was not the Chaldean's longing for the well-watered plains of Shinar. Had he pleased, he could easily have recrossed the Euphrates and ceased to be a Hebrew.[5] His sense of exile ever increased, but his *Heimweh* was not for the country from which he came out. Nor was it any longer the mere desire to possess the land of Canaan, where he knew that he must always be a stranger and sojourner ($23^4$). Even in Canaan he suffered the pain of an unfulfilled ideal ; his reach always exceeded his grasp ; he had in his heart a divine discontent ; he was conscious of "moving about in worlds not realised." Herein was his greatness ; for it is not what a man achieves, but what he believes and strives for, that makes him noble and great. The writer of the Epistle to the Hebrews interprets the thoughts of the people of God. "Now they desire a better country, that is, a heavenly." [6] "By faith Abraham

[1] Heb. $11^8$.  [2] Acts $7^5$.  [3] Heb. $11^{13}$.
[4] John $8^{56}$.  [5] Heb. $11^{15}$.  [6] Heb. $11^{16}$.

sojourned in the land of promise as in a land not his own, dwelling in tents, . . . for he looked for the city which hath foundations, whose Builder and Maker is God." [1]   The man who was a pattern to all the Hebrew race lived believing, hoping, aspiring, but unsatisfied.   When at length his exile and pilgrimage were ended, his hope was fulfilled, his ideal realised, in the presence of God. [2]

> " All we have willed or hoped or dreamed of good, shall exist;
> Not the semblance, but itself . . .
> When eternity confirms the conception of an hour." [3]

---

[1] Heb. 11⁹.          [2] Compare Ps. 16¹⁰⋅¹¹.          [3] Browning.

# HEBREW IDEALS
# in GENESIS
## Part Two

### BIRTHRIGHT
### Genesis 25:12-34

'We barter life for pottage, sell true bliss . . .
Then wash with fruitless tears our faded crown.'—KEBLE.

HISTORY.—The second half of the Patriarchal Story contains 'the generations' of Ishmael ($25^{12}$), of Isaac ($25^{19}$), of Esau ($36^{1.\ 9}$), and of Jacob ($37^2$). The generations were the family history of these men. They might be short or long. In the case of Ishmael they are compressed into half a dozen verses ; and in the case of Esau they are little more than a genealogical tree. The sons of Ishmael and Esau, Arabs and Edomites, did little to further the providential purpose of God—the education and salvation of the human race. Their history, if expanded, might have interested antiquarians, but would scarcely have benefited mankind in general. Ishmael, as we read, had villages and encampments, princes and nations ($25^{16}$), but—at least not till a much later time —neither seers nor poets nor saints. Edom was rich enough in dukes and kings ($36^{15.\ 31}$), but they contributed nothing to the world's real wealth. The sons of Ishmael and Edom lived their eager lives and went their way, and their simple generations have the pathetic brevity of an inscription on a tombstone. But the generations of Isaac and Jacob are written on a different scale; for among the descendants of Isaac and Jacob are found those leaders of men whose inspired words and heroic deeds have largely shaped the destinies of our race. Israel's appointed task was to conceive those ideals which are still the creative principles of the moral and religious life of nations. His history is the richest part of our spiritual heritage.

PRAYER.—The children of Isaac and Rebekah are regarded as children of prayer, born a score of years after their parents' marriage, given because they are asked. 'Isaac entreated the Lord . . . and the Lord was entreated of him" (25²¹). The word used here for prayer ('athar, from which comes our attar of roses) is a very interesting one. It had at first a purely physical sense; it suggested to the mind a cloud of fragrant smoke rising up from earth to heaven. The offering of incense—originally the smoke of sacrifice and later aromatic perfumes—was associated, almost identified, ·ith prayer. It was a silent, anthropomorphic form of propitiation. The ascending cloud was either the vehicle or the symbol of petition. In the growth and progress of Hebrew worship the physical always receded as the spiritual advanced. Enlightened minds learned to separate realities from signs. The name preserved the original idea; prayer was still set forth before God as incense,[1] and the golden bowls of incense were called the prayers of the saints.[2] But as soon as God was known as a spiritual Being, prayer was understood as a spiritual act—man's utterance of the longings of his heart to God, who heard and answered his cry.

ORACLES.—When Rebekah was about to become a mother, her thoughts turned to God. 'She went to inquire of the LORD' (25²²). She did what any devout Hebrew was in the habit of doing in time of anxiety—she goes to a holy place where

---

[1] Ps. 141².          [2] Rev. 5⁸.

a seer gave counsel and comfort in God's name. 'Beforetime in Israel, when a man went to inquire of God, thus he spake, Come, and let us go to the seer : for he that is now called a prophet was beforetime called a seer.'[1] Other ancient peoples besides the Hebrews had shrines where oracular responses were given to troubled minds, but often given in words of studied ambiguity. Such an institution as that of prophecy—speaking for God—was liable to abuse anywhere. Its benefits depended on the character of the persons by whom the responses were given. There were lying prophets among the Hebrews ; but there were also true men who, guided by the Spirit of God, delivered messages which were in accordance with the Divine mind. This was indeed the unique thing among the Hebrews, that there arose a wonderful succession of seers and prophets who were really called and qualified to speak to the perplexed in the name of the true and living God—men to whom 'were committed the oracles of God.'[2]

SOVEREIGNTY.—We are told that Jacob was predestined to be greater, and to have a greater name, than Esau. The prediction refers not to individuals but to nations. 'The one people shall be stronger than the other people' (25[23]). 'The children being not yet born, neither having done anything good or bad, . . . it was said to Rebekah, The elder shall serve the younger.'[3] Esau as a person never served Jacob as a person, but the descendants of Esau served the descendants of Jacob. The relative position of the two nations was in accordance with the will of God. That God has a hand in the affairs of this world ; that there is 'a Divinity that shapes our ends' ; that God does His pleasure in the army of heaven and among the inhabitants of the earth,[4] were facts early and indelibly impressed upon the minds of the Hebrews. While these were high mysteries to them, they were also practical and priceless truths. 'The purpose of God according to election'[3] was seen running all through

[1] 1 Sam. 9[9].     [2] Rom. 3[2].     [3] Rom. 9[11].     [4] Dan. 4[35].

human life. He who makes one star differ from another in glory makes one man excel another in natural endowments. Some who bear His image have more strength, beauty, talent, power than others. Some are predestined to a higher and a harder service than others. One son has the stronger arm, another the larger brain. God divides 'to every man severally even as He will.'[1] The Hebrew belief in Divine sovereignty is entirely different from fatalism. Those who hold it hold also that every man's will is left absolutely free ; that God is good unto all ; that He condemns no man to be, still less to remain, a sinner ; and that to all who faithfully serve Him, whether with greater or lesser talents, He gives rewards which are infinitely satisfying.

CHARACTER.—Children of the same family, twins as well as others, often have the most diverse, apparently antipathetic, temperaments. Esau and Jacob were contrasts from the first, and as they grew up the differences between them became more and more marked. Esau was a high-spirited, careless, roving lad ; impatient of control ; swift to take offence, but frank and ready to forgive ; surging with strong passions and quick emotions ; always swayed by the impulse of the passing moment. He followed his natural bent when he became 'a cunning hunter, a man of the field' ($25^{27}$). He loved the thrill, the dash, the sensation of the chase, and the keen-scented air of the mountain, the forest, the desert. Excitement, adventure, danger, escapades of every kind, the view-halloo and the death-cry, were life to him. His joy was to start off at sunrise and return at night laden with the spoils of a noble hunt. To scour the fields for the prey, to lure it into his net, or transfix it with arrow or spear, was legitimate 'cunning.' He liked the sport for its own sake, but it added to his pleasure that he was able to give a haunch of savoury venison to his aged father. So much did he live in the open air, that the old man said his very garments had a smell of the hunting.

[1] I Cor. $12^{11}$.

fields (27²⁷). The Hebrews were never lacking in admiration of physical strength, agility, daring ; and the sportsman had an undisputed place in a land abounding with the wild creatures of the chase. Ruddy, shaggy, brawny, fearless and impetuous, Esau was an ideal huntsman. But there was a serious flaw in his character. So much did he enjoy the warm, sensuous, earthy side of things, that he had no thought of the awakening of the soul. He was a 'profane person,'[1] not in the sense of taking God's name in vain,—there is no suggestion of that,—but in the sense of never feeling and recognising God's claims upon him at all.

Young Jacob's disposition and habits are entirely different. Quiet, wary, home-loving, he is evidently called by nature to the peaceful occupations of the pastoral life. He is quite content to follow slow-moving flocks from field to field and well to well. He never, if he can help it, strays far from the tent and the pasture-ground. Timid and diffident, he shrinks from too close contact with his rough, impulsive brother, and runs away rather than stand up face to face with him if by chance they come to a serious difference. Clever and ambitious, and well aware that he is not able to match strength with strength, he does not scruple to do it with cunning—a cunning of a very different kind from Esau's. Keenly alive to his own interest, and not above taking a mean advantage of another's weakness, he lets this subtle, secretive, slippery characteristic grow until he becomes a master of intrigue. But he has redeeming qualities. Chaste and temperate, he can deny himself a present gratification for the sake of a future good. He knows how to labour and to wait. And he is awed by the thought that there is another world above this one. Things unseen and spiritual are very real to him. The purposes and promises of God captivate his imagination. Visions beckon and voices call him to a life of fellowship with God. He reverently feels that he ought to walk by faith rather than by sight.

[1] Heb. 12¹⁰.

AFFECTION.—Some minds are attracted to one another by affinity, others by contrast. 'Isaac loved Esau,' who was his opposite ; and 'Rebekah loved Jacob,' who was her image ($25^{28}$). In spirit and manner of life Esau presented the most striking unlikeness to his father. The one was at home in strenuous action, the other in quiet meditation. Isaac was not more gentle, placid, retiring than Esau was fierce, bold, intrepid. Yet Isaac was irresistibly drawn to the hot, impulsive youth, seeing in him all that he missed in himself. He listened with delight to the huntsman's tales of adventure. The breathless pursuit, the hazardous encounter, the hairbreadth escapes stirred his imagination. He felt that his son's noble stature and restless energy were prophetic of future greatness.

Jacob, on the other hand, was Rebekah's favourite. Mother and son were drawn to each other by strong affinities. She saw in his patience, his self-control, his spiritual leanings, the promise of great and good things. She hoped much from his mother-wit —the cleverness he inherited from herself. She was the readiest of teachers, he the aptest of pupils. In many ways he was happy, in some not so happy, in having such a mother, who fostered in his mind the love of high things, and stirred him to act a great, if not always a noble, part. Her influence over her son in the formative years of his life was incalculable. Mothers have shaped the characters of the men who have moulded the destinies of nations. A true 'mother in Israel' was always greatly revered, and a nation's ideal of motherhood is the measure of its greatness. In modern times Napoleon said of his country, 'What France needs for her regeneration is mothers.' It is the world's need. Tennyson, depicting a young man's home privileges, says :

> ' Happy he
> With such a mother ! faith in womanhood
> Beats with his blood, and trust in all things high
> Comes easy to him, and though he trip and fall
> He shall not blind his soul with clay.'

FEAR.—The story of Esau selling his birthright is one of the most striking and impressive tales in the Bible. The narrator's sympathy makes the figures of a bygone age live before our eyes to-day. He knows both how to tell a story in simple dramatic language, and when to stop and let the reader's imagination do the rest. The old-world tale has a moral for every conscience. It not only stirs our hearts to pity for another's fall, but arouses us to a sense of the possibilities of disaster in our own lives. Every thoughtful reader feels that he may become another Esau ; and wholesome fear is one of the principal elements in moral education. The facts are stated without comment, but each of us seems to hear a chorus saying, ' *Mutato nomine, de te fabula narratur* : Change only the name, and *you* are the person of whom the story is told.'

BIRTHRIGHT.—Esau, in virtue of being a few minutes older than Jacob, was Isaac's natural heir. He had the rights of primogeniture, and believed that no man could wrest them from him. If ever he parted with them, it could only be by an act of his own free will. We see that he was highly favoured. For one thing, the eldest son of Hebrew parents received a double portion of his father's property to enable him to maintain the family honour and dignity.[1] For another thing, Esau's birthright meant more than an ordinary firstborn son's privilege. He was in a unique position, which afforded him brilliant prospects and golden opportunities. He was born to an inheritance which all the world's wealth would not buy. To be in the patriarchal succession with Abraham and Isaac, to be the recipient of great and precious promises, to be the founder of a holy nation, to be the minister of a covenant by which all the families of the earth were to be blessed,—this was within his reach. But his eyes had never been opened to the worth of spiritual possessions. He spoke of 'this birthright' with frank contempt. A thing so high and ideal aroused no enthusiasm in his mind. On the other hand, he had never learned to curb his violent passions.

[1] Deut. 21¹⁷.

One day when he returned home after an unsuccessful hunt he was proved to be the slave of appetite. Faint and famished, he was tempted to sell his birthright for a mess of pottage—a steaming dish of lentil soup. The idea did not shock him, partly because he had long despised his birthright, and partly because the pangs of hunger make him utterly reckless. At any cost his voracious appetite [1] must be appeased. If his brother covets his birthright, let him have it, and much good may it do him! Let the future take care of itself. Birthright or no birthright, Esau must have his supper. And with a fine heady recklessness, an exultant sense of doing a thing worthy of his manhood, an exhilarating consciousness of escaping from the meshes of spiritual bondage, Esau barters his birthright. We see that he will regret his bargain, but not yet. His hunger is keen, the lentils are delicious, and with a light heart he eats and drinks and goes his way ($25^{34}$). He does not know that in despising his birthright he is despising God. He has come to one of those critical moments in life which are fatal to us all if we have no guide to conduct except desire. He is illustrating 'that inexorable law of human souls, that we are preparing ourselves for sudden deeds by the reiterated choice of good or evil that gradually determines character.' [2]

FAITH.—If Esau sold his birthright, so may we sell ours. Heirs of all the ages, who cannot exaggerate the grandeur of our privileges, we may forfeit our highest good. 'All the ability of the present, all the contributions of the past, all the hopes of the future' [3] are ours, and we may lose our title to them. Every man who lives below his true self, who prefers pleasure to duty, who lets the clamorous wants of the body drown the voice of the soul, who is too impatient to wait for God, sells his birthright. For a mess of savoury red pottage Esau's birthright was sold. For a handful of glittering red earth, for a glass of sparkling

---

[1] 'Feed me' ($25^{30}$) means 'let me devour'—like a wild beast.
[2] George Eliot.　　　　　　　　　　[3] Emerson.

red wine, for a strip of bright red ribbon, for a kiss of smiling red lips, many birthrights have been sold. 'I saw, moreover, in my dream,' said Pilgrim, 'Passion seemed to be much discontent, but Patience was very quiet. . . . Passion will have all now, this year, that is to say, in this world ; so are the men of this world : they must have all their good things now, they cannot stay for their portion of good. That proverb, "A bird in the hand is worth two in the bush," is of more authority with them than are all the Divine testimonies of the good world to come.' Indifference to the high and sacred things of life, 'the malady of not wanting,' the refusal to sacrifice a solid-seeming reality for a visionary ideal, is the explanation of many moral tragedies.

> ' The world is too much with us ; late and soon,
> Getting and spending, we lay waste our powers :
> We have given our hearts away, a sordid boon !' [1]

'With the generality of men, ingenuity, strength, and skill do but imply that the soul must first of all be banished from their life, that every impulse that lies too deep must be carefully brushed aside.' [2] Only Faith saves us from this fatal error,— faith which realises the sacredness of life, grasps the promises of God, and constrains us to hold fast our fellowship with Him as our chief good.

RESPONSIBILITY.—At a later time, when it dawned upon Esau that he had made an ill bargain, he bitterly complained of the conduct of his selfish, designing brother. Jacob, he said, had overreached him—had taken away his birthright (27[36]). And certainly Esau had just cause of complaint. With a bitter jest he said his brother was rightly called Jacob—supplanter [3] (v.[36]). It is cruel to drive a hard bargain with a faint and hungry man, all the more if he is a brother. When a buyer knows the

---

[1] Wordsworth.          [2] Maeterlinck.
[3] Compare Cromwell's shrewd characterisation of a well-known historical figure as 'Sharp of that ilk.'

true value of a thing which the seller despises, it is mean to take advantage of the other's ignorance. Jacob's conduct was unbrotherly and ungenerous. But this is only a part of the truth. Jacob did not injure Esau half so much as Esau wronged himself. It is impossible to absolve a man from the responsibility of his actions. Esau rejected his own true good. If he was punished, it was not for a solitary act of rashness committed in a moment of overmastering impulse. The selling of his birthright simply gathered up his whole past life into a single definite act, and embodied his character. It was not Jacob's plotting that was his undoing, but his own passion. 'He took away my birthright,' Esau bitterly cried. But, in truth, Esau himself, with his own hand,

> ' Like the base Judean, threw a pearl away
> Richer than all his tribe.'

TRAGEDY. — Sometimes 'the story of Jacob and Esau has been read as reflecting the historical relations of the peoples Israel and Edom, and their respective characters. If so, the historian who depicted his own people as crafty, unscrupulous, and godly, and their bitterest enemy as the careless, noble, natural man, was a humorous satirist of the highest rank. Historically the satire must be judged less than just to his own people, and more than partial to Edom.'[1] But neither Esau nor Jacob can be regarded as a mere epitome of racial characteristics. A really creative literary power does not produce types but persons, who may or may not be afterwards seen to be the representatives of a class or people. The tragic hero of the Bible, like the tragic hero of the great dramatists, has so many good qualities that he at once wins our sympathy, and so much greatness, that we are vividly conscious of the possibilities of human nature. No one ever reads the story of Esau with the feeling that this man is a poor creature. At first every reader

[1] A. B. Davidson.

greatly prefers him to his brother. It is Esau's native nobility that compels us to realise the worth of that which he misses. He is the kind of man of whom we are in the habit of charitably saying that he is nobody's enemy but his own. But, in truth, he is God's enemy, because he wastes the splendid manhood which God has given him. Passionate, impatient, impulsive, incapable of looking before him, refusing to estimate the worth of anything which does not immediately appeal to his senses, preferring the animal to the spiritual, he is rightly called a 'profane person.' 'Alas! while the body is so broad and brawny, must the soul lie blinded, dwarfed, stupefied, almost annihilated?'[1]

# MEEKNESS
## Genesis 26

' Strong
In the endurance which outwearies wrong,
With meek persistence baffling brutal force,
And trusting God against the universe.'—WHITTIER.

VERACITY.—The story of Isaac's sojourn in Gerar, and his attempt to deceive the king of the land (26[1-11]), is almost identical with an earlier narrative regarding his father (20[1-18]). There are some differences of language which indicate a difference of origin. For example, the Divine name in the earlier story is Elohim, in the later Jahveh. There is no lack of verisimilitude in the conduct ascribed to Isaac, whose life, for better or worse, was modelled on his father's example. His action in this instance is anything but heroic. He fears to acknowledge his wife. When Abimelech asks him in astonishment how he could call her his sister, he has nothing better to say than this: 'Because I said, lest I die for her.' No one will call that a

[1] Carlyle.

gallant speech. Isaac merely tries to excuse himself; of course he does not attempt to justify himself. He has done wrong and knows it. Conscience calls us to suffer when we cannot avoid suffering without sin. Some moralists have tried to defend the falsehood that is prompted by love. But such a classical instance as that of Jeanie Deans refusing to speak an untruth even to save her sister's life, will always commend itself to the moral sense. In any case, nothing can be said for the lie of base and selfish fear. Isaac could not even plead, as Abraham had feebly done, that his wife *was* his sister. He lied outright, and Abimelech reproved him with the stern accents of moral indignation. It must be admitted that there is a great deal of lying and prevarication in Genesis. But there is always some touch in the narrative which commends the true and condemns the false. The God of the Hebrews is 'the God of things as they are.' 'Veracity and the kindred virtues are essentially and immutably good, and it is impossible and inconceivable that they should ever be vices and their opposites virtues.'[1] 'They who tamper with veracity tamper with the vital forces of human progress.'[2]

GREATNESS.—Isaac figures better in the scenes which follow (26[12-33]). When we read that 'the man waxed great, and grew more and more, until he became very great' (v.[13]), we perceive that the reference is to material greatness. Isaac is great as a landowner, a sheep-master, a well-digger, a householder. Greatness is not predicated of him in the sense in which it was ascribed to Abraham (18[18]) and to Joseph (39[9]). He did not become great, as they did, in the eager pursuit of a missing good, in the conflict with evil, in the bracing necessity of thinking and acting for himself. He was to a large extent what his surroundings made him. We see in him the familiar type of the great man's son, who is overshadowed by his father's greatness. His position was made too easy, his path in life too smooth. Everything was found for him. His parents planned for him,

[1] Lecky.  [2] J. Morley.

Eliezer wooed for him, Esau hunted for him, and the land almost of its own accord yielded its increase for him. The result of all this kindness was that he was lacking in the qualities of a strong manhood. He could never be actively great, original, daring. But there is room in the world for many types of excellence. Enough that Isaac was from the first absolutely pure-minded, that he was meek and peaceful, that he cherished his father's lofty ideals, and that 'the LORD blessed him' (v.12). It was left to him to excel in the passive virtues, and in this respect he is almost matchless among the men of the Old Testament. He cultivated a gentleness which after all made him morally great.

LIBERTY.—Isaac paid the penalty of success in being envied (v.14), in having his rights disputed (v.20), and his servants molested (v.20). He could not but feel that his jealous neighbours hated him (v.27), and wished to be quit of him (vv.16. 27). They were painfully conscious of his superior power, and fully expected him to use it to their hurt (v.16). But, in truth, they had nothing to fear. So far from exercising his power offensively, Isaac did not even use it defensively. No injury could provoke him to strife. When his neighbours coveted a well which his servants had dug, he quietly surrendered it to them. 'They contended with him' (v.20), but he would not contend with them. Even a well of living water, infinitely valuable as it is in the East, was less precious to him than human life. Other valleys were waiting to be pierced and yield up their treasure. A second spring was opened, then coveted, and then surrendered in the same way. Isaac 'removed from thence and opened another well' (v.22). It takes two to make a quarrel, and he would not strive nor let others strive. He was the least aggressive of men. His placid good humour found expression in the names which he gave his wells. He did not break his heart because he could not drink out of the wells of 'Contention' and 'Enmity'; he cheerfully resigned them to those who cared for them. He was happy if he was left in peace to drink the sweet waters of 'Liberty'

(Rehoboth). 'For now,' he said, 'the LORD hath made room
for us' (v.[22]). Doubtless there is a deep sigh of relief as well as
a cheerful note of gratitude in his words. Broad places, green
expanses, virgin solitudes, in which one can lead a restful,
sheltered life, are all that he asks for. He is the religious quietist
of that ancient time.

MEEKNESS.—The noblest kind of sacrifice is the self-denial of
those who have the clearest rights. Isaac was again and again
placed in circumstances in which others would have quickly
drawn the sword. The question arises whether he surrendered
too much for the sake of peace. If a man cannot waive his
rights without neglecting his duty, violating his conscience,
surrendering his religion, losing his self-respect, betraying the
rights of others, he is bound to resist. Otherwise he may yield,
and scarcely any price is too high to pay for peace. Isaac
was right. He is the first example in the Old Testament of the
Christian or New Testament type of excellence. After him, as
the Talmud says, 'we find in the Bible many instances of the
pleasure which meekness and humility in the creature afford the
Creator. The noblest of our ancestors were those who were
free from self-pride.' Nothing can be saner or sweeter than this
ancient tale, with its apparent moral for those who think that
the strongest thing is to retaliate, to assert every claim, to cede
no possible advantage. 'The grandest thing in having rights
is that, being our rights, we can give them up.'[1] 'Why do ye not
rather take wrong?'[2]

FRIENDSHIP.—In the end Isaac is no real loser, but a great
gainer, by his meekness. He disarms enmity by gentleness;
he overcomes evil with good. His patience wears out the malice
of his enemies. They begin to be ashamed of wronging one
who absolutely refuses to take offence. Laying aside their
jealousy, they at length come to seek an alliance with him.

[1] George Macdonald.          [2] I Cor. 6[7].

With some audacity they remind him that they have always lived at peace with him (v.²⁹). That is the language of diplomacy. Isaac might have something to say to it, but he forbears. He can afford to be magnanimous. It is enough that he has turned enemies into friends. That is better than to defeat them and have them as enemies still. Generosity has won the day. The policy, or rather the holy instinct, of self-sacrifice always justifies itself. Men whose hearts not so long ago burned with hatred sit down to a love-feast, and enter into a solemn covenant of peace and friendship (vv.³¹·³²). The cordial understanding between Hebrew and Philistine is assured. Grant that such alliances are not very deep-rooted, yet in a world of conflicting interests and passions everything which tends towards unity is welcome to all peace-loving men. If neighbours—men or nations—were rigidly to insist upon their rights, there might be endless war. But, happily, two things are true : mercy triumphs against justice, and the meek inherit the earth.

SONSHIP.—On the first night of Isaac's sojourn at Beersheba he had a vision. 'The LORD appeared to him, and said, I am the God of Abraham thy father ; fear not, for I am with thee, and will bless thee, and multiply thy seed for My servant Abraham's sake' (26²⁴). This is the first time the grand name, 'God of Abraham,' meets us in the Bible. It became very dear to the Hebrews ; it was used by Christ and His apostles ;[1] and it is sung in Christian hymns. The God who revealed Himself to Abraham, who was his Friend, who shaped his career and destiny, could manifest Himself under no sweeter name than this to Abraham's son. 'God of our fathers!' and 'My father's God!' can never cease to be peculiarly heart-stirring invocations. That the Being whom we are called to worship was the God of our forefathers, and made them such men as we know them to have been ; that He was the God of our own father, whom we dutifully regard as the best man in the world,

[1] Matt. 22³², Acts 3¹³.

—these are strong reasons why He should also be our God, or why
we should at least think a thousand times before we change our
religion.  It is the sorest of all trials for a young man to have to
condemn his father's misbelief or unbelief by his own faith.  Thrice
happy are those sons and daughters whose personal religion is
inextricably interwoven with their filial reverence and love.

MARRIAGE.—Esau married two daughters of Heth, called
Judith and Basemath, and 'they were a grief of mind' to his
parents ($26^{35}$), who saw that such an alliance must tend to
subvert the purpose for which God sought to make the Hebrews
a separate people.  Esau loved, as he did everything else,
impulsively and passionately, and the joyous recklessness with
which love overleaps all barriers seems at first sight rather an
admirable thing.  Yet is it so good?  Some barriers are
artificial things, mere devices of men, conventions of society or
whims of individuals, and no harm, but rather much good, is
done when love merrily breaks them down.  But other barriers
are sacred, being made by God, awful laws by which His love
guards us from sin and sorrow; and those who hastily break
them do great wrong to society and their own souls.  Esau
disregarded the instruction of his father, and forsook the law
of his mother, and brought upon them 'bitterness of spirit.'[1]
There is no suggestion that he was ever deliberately unkind to
his parents.  In his own way he tried hard to please them.  But
when a son goes out into the world and plays the fool, that is
the unkindest cut of all.  A physical blow would cause far less
pain.  There may be no outward change in the parents' attitude
—no doors closed, no upbraiding words, no privileges withheld;
but there is an inward, incessant, almost insufferable heartache.
'A wounded spirit who can bear?'[2]  In later times a strict
law was imposed upon the Hebrews against inter-marriages
with the Canaanites.  'Neither shalt thou make marriages
with them; thy daughter shalt thou not give unto his son, nor

[1] Gen. $26^{35}$ margin.         [2] Prov. $18^{14}$.

his daughter shalt thou take unto thy son.'[1]  That was not a hard law ; it was an ordinance of love by which the Hebrews were preserved from racial absorption and spiritual death.

## BLESSING
### Genesis 27

'No great system has ever yet flourished which did not present an ideal of happiness as well as an ideal of duty.'—LECKY,

READINESS.—' Isaac was old, and his eyes were dim, so that he could not see' (27[1]).  He was suffering from no specific ailment—nothing but the incurable disease of old age.  His pulse was slow and feeble, his blood thin and cold.  He was at a time of life when one does not look far forward ; at any moment the silver cord might be loosed and the golden bowl broken ; and he did not wish death to come and find him unready.  No obligation is more imperative than that of preparing for a future which we shall never see.  Through the warnings of nature, if not through the death-sentence of the physician, God says to each man in turn, ' Set thine house in order, for thou must die and not live.'  And the happiness of future generations may depend to no small extent upon the dying man's last will and testament.

OLD AGE.—Isaac's last stage of all can scarcely be compared in grandeur and dignity with the latter end of Abraham and Jacob.  It is, of course, far from being contemptible.  Even in the physical helplessness of second childhood his mental vision is clear and strong.  He is not that saddest of all figures in the world—an old man without faith.  But he does not command the high veneration of his own people as the other patriarchs

[1] Deut. 7[3].

do. His sickbed is surrounded with tender devotion, and his every want lovingly supplied ; but his kindred do not hesitate on occasion to take advantage of his infirmities and deceive him for their own selfish ends. Nor does his eagerness for venison, his frequent mention of the savoury meat which his soul loves, make a favourable impression upon our minds. The love of delicate fare, which he has allowed to grow upon him (25²⁸), is an infirmity which is apt to beset the indolent. There needs a more strenuous youth and a more active manhood than Isaac's to prepare for a morally grand old age.

MOTHER-LOVE.—Rebekah's words and ways are always full of interest. She is a fascinating woman, with a clever, eager, inventive mind ; with a genius for laying plans and overcoming difficulties ; accustomed to give orders and to be obeyed ; ready to make any sacrifices for those whom she loves ; but impatient of opposition, and vexed beyond measure and weary of life itself when she has to deal with things beyond her comprehension, or simply to submit to the inevitable. It is impossible to question the strength of her mother-love. When her son expresses his fear of bringing a curse upon himself, she quickly answers, ' Upon me be the curse, my son' (v.¹³). We tremble at the audacity of her wild words. She is reckless of personal consequences if so be she can secure a coveted distinction for her son. He is dearer to her than her own soul. It is no mean advantage that she desires for him ; it is a covenant blessing, a heritage of spiritual promises ; and she believes it is God's will that he should obtain this privilege (25²³). But neither a high purpose nor a great love ever consecrates the use of dishonourable means ; and Rebekah, with all her charm, must be numbered among those mothers who love not wisely but too well.

OBEDIENCE.—Rebekah was, no doubt, right in judging that her younger son had qualities which made him fitter to receive his father's blessing and inherit the covenant promises than her elder son. But she was not right in tempting the one to deceive the other. She had an unlimited influence over her favourite son, and she exercised it to the utmost. 'My son,' she said, 'obey my voice according to all that which I command thee ; . . . only obey my voice' (vv. $^{8. \ 18}$). She not only prompted and persuaded, she commanded him. We remember that Abraham commanded his children to keep the way of the LORD, to do justice and judgment ($18^{19}$). Rebekah commands her son to cheat. Temptation is never so strong as when it is suggested by one who loves us. A mother's affection, enlisted on the side of evil, has power to break down almost any scruples. Jacob obeys his mother, knowing well that he is doing wrong,—that he will rightly be regarded as 'a deceiver,' and likely bring upon himself 'a curse and not a blessing' (v.$^{12}$). He obeys, and his obedience is the beginning of all his sorrows. There are exceptions to the moral law that a son should obey his parents. Disobedience for conscience' sake may be his clear and imperative duty. Parental authority, being delegated by God, must be exercised in accordance with His laws. We must obey God rather than—our parents. The secret tragedy in many a son's life turns on his knowledge of the fact that his parents wish him to do one thing and God another. Reverence, gratitude, and love pull him the one way, reverence, gratitude, and love pull him the other way. But conscience makes its voice heard, and conscience must be the guide of our lives. 'Children, obey your parents *in the Lord*.'[1]

TRUTH.—Having once entered on a course of untruthfulness, Jacob pursues it to the end with astonishing coolness. He begins with the acted lie (v.$^{15}$), and follows it up with the lie direct (v.$^{19}$), the lie impious (v.$^{20}$), and the lie persistent (v.$^{24}$). He talks of 'my venison' (v.$^{19}$), though he probably never killed a gazelle in his life, and he says that the LORD has given him good-speed in his hunting (v.$^{20}$), though he knows that the LORD

[1] Eph. $6^1$.

has had nothing to do with it. Worst of all, he stoops down and kisses his father with the lips which have just uttered these lies. There is something appalling in the audacity with which he braves it out. Luther, trying to put himself in Jacob's place, cries out in wonder, 'For my part, I should have dropped the dish and run.' Are we to suppose that the writing which preserves this ancient tradition, the Book which was a mirror of morals and manners to the young Hebrews, approved of clever and successful lying? Quite the contrary. Whenever truth is referred to in this Book, it is regarded as an indispensable attribute of God, and a virtue loved by all good men ($24^{27. 49}$ $32^{10}$ $42^{16}$); and whenever any man is guilty of untruthfulness, there is something in the narrative that condemns his conduct. We are not asked to admire Jacob as a supplanter. 'The writer perceives very well that his action can be described by no gentler term than that of cheating.'[1] Jacob had to become a very different man, chastened by the suffering which his untruthfulness entailed upon him, before he won by faith the prize which he sought to capture by fraud.

BLESSING.—The Blessing of Isaac, as may be seen in the Revised Version, is a little poem. The aged patriarch, kindled for an hour into prophetic ecstasy, and speaking as the oracle of God, bequeaths his benediction to his younger son, and through him to the great nation which is to spring from him. Using language at once rhythmic in its flow and poetic in its ideas, he promises his son a field which the LORD has blessed (i.e. the goodly land of Canaan), the dew of heaven, the fatness of the earth, abundance of corn and wine, the homage of other nations (called Israel's 'brethren,' the Hebrews and kindred races being regarded as children of a common mother), and concludes by invoking a curse upon all who curse his son (Israel as a people rather than an individual), and a blessing upon all who bless him (vv.$^{27-29}$). The words aptly describe the land of Israel and its

[1] Oort.

people in the palmy days of fruitfulness and power. No one
would dream of calling the Holy Land as it is to-day a field
which the LORD hath blessed. Great tracts of it strike thoughtful
travellers as lying under a curse.[1] What began best has ended
worst, and what was once blest has proved accursed. The
beauty and bloom are gone. The foot of the Turk has blighted
everything which it has touched. But the real end is not yet ;
and under some juster and kindlier régime the fatness and
fragrance may return. There is still some virtue in the patriarch's
benediction, 'God give thee of the dew of heaven.'

CANAAN.—It has sometimes been remarked, not without
surprise, that the Blessing of Isaac 'seems confined to secular
matters, and is such as any man of ordinary wealth and power
might have pronounced on his favourite son with a view to the
increase of these.'[2] The things promised are the fragrance of
the field, the dew of heaven, the fatness of the earth, abundance
of corn and wine, and peaceful habitations. One is led to ask
whether the ideal of the charming little poem is not simply an
earthly Paradise. Have not the poets of other lands depicted
similar scenes ?—

> ' Hills all rich with blossomed trees,
> And fields which promise corn and wine,
> And scattered cities crowning these,
> Whose far white walls along them shine.'[3]

But the truth is, that to the Hebrew believer and thinker nothing
is secular ; fields and dew, corn and wine and oil, are all
sacred, because they are the gifts of God. While the servant of
God seemed to find his 'good,' his 'life,' his 'blessing' in those
things which we regard as mundane,—a peaceful heritage, fruitful
fields, children's children, the love of friends, the victory over
enemies,—it was not these desirable things in themselves which
constituted his chief good. It was these things with the favour

[1] Kelman.    [2] Chalmers.    [3] Byron.

of God. The ideal was, after all, a spiritual one. It is significant that the Blessing of Esau fails in the essential thing. God's name is not found in it. Good things were promised to Esau ; he obtains all that he can appreciate ; and his sons enjoy it for many centuries. Even to-day the Land of Edom is in some parts very fruitful. 'Goodly streams flow through the valleys, which are filled with trees and flowers ; while on the uplands to the east pasture - lands and cornfields may everywhere be seen.'[1] But for all that the Land of Edom has never been regarded as 'a field which the LORD hath blessed.' It did not enjoy the loving-kindness which is better than life, the consciousness of the Divine Presence, which is the blessing of blessings.

SENSIBILITY.—It is no wonder if Isaac is greatly agitated when he finds that he has unwittingly blessed his younger instead of his elder son. He trembles 'with an exceeding great trembling' (v.[38]). He asks in amazement what this thing can mean. Does it merely signify that there has been a conflict of human wits and wills, in which he has been worsted? He sees that there is far more in it than this. It is borne in upon him that man is playing only a minor part in this matter, and that the hand of God is in it. He suddenly realises, with a flush of shame, that he has been trying to thwart the will of God. Of course he has been trying in vain. God's will has been done after all. And then, by a swift transition, the finer side of Isaac's character appears. Weak in action, he is strong in endurance. As soon as he sees that he has simply been used to carry out the purpose of God, the feeble wilfulness of the man who has been bent on having his own way passes into the complete self-abnegation of one who is determined that God's shall be done. No one would call Isaac self-assertive, but he asserts God's will with emphasis. To the frenzied entreaties of his elder son he turns a deaf ear. Once sure of his ground, nothing can

[1] Palmer.

induce him to leave it. What he has spoken he has spoken. His soft and pliant nature, as if suddenly steeled by the touch of God, has become inflexible. Knowing God's will and his own duty, he will cleave to both without a shadow of turning. We see how wholesome is that 'exceeding great trembling,' which makes the spirit of man so wonderfully susceptible to divine impressions. Every good man has often trembled in this way, and the oftener the better ; for it is in the hour of shuddering amazement that sin is discarded. 'Serve the LORD with fear, and rejoice with trembling.'[1]

DESTINY.—Esau did not despise the blessing as he had despised the birthright. He was confident of receiving it. He knew that though he had sometimes grieved his father's heart ($26^{35}$) he had never lost his love, and he never doubted his father's intention to bless him. He was overjoyed when the expected day at length came. He 'went to the field to hunt for venison and to bring it' ($v.^5$), and he 'came in from his hunting' with the expectant thrill which precedes the realisation of a long-cherished hope. Then came the poignant moment of disillusionment, when it flashed upon him that he had been tricked and befooled, and that the blessing was gone beyond recall. Hot tears of passion leaped to his eyes, and he cried with an exceeding great and bitter cry. Wave after wave of uncontrollable grief swept over his soul ($vv.^{34.\ 39}$), while he mingled loud reproaches of his unbrotherly brother with plaintive appeals to his father's pity. Every reader profoundly sympathises with him in his tragic sorrow, in which 'there is a deep pathos which is scarcely surpassed elsewhere even in the Bible, the most pathetic of all books.'[2] But his regrets were vain. An apostle says that 'he found no place for repentance,' which means that there was no means of undoing what he had done. 'We know that when he afterwards desired to inherit the blessing he was rejected, though he sought it diligently with

[1] Ps. $2^{11}$, Phil. $2^{12}$.              [2] Lightfoot.

tears.'[1]  Whatever the future might have in store for him the
past at least was irrevocable

> ' The moving finger writes ; and, having writ,
> Moves on : nor all thy piety nor wit
>    Shall lure it back to cancel half a line,
> Nor all thy tears wash out a word of it.'[2]

Esau's exceeding loud and bitter cry sounds the needful note of
alarm in a world in which so much evil is wrought for want of
thought as well as want of will.  He lost the coveted blessing
because he despised the birthright.  'It is in those acts called
trivialities that the seeds of joy are for ever wasted, until men and
women look round with haggard faces at the devastation their own
waste has made, and say, The earth bears no harvest of sweetness.'[3]

RESTRAINT.—Esau was a man of simple nature and elemental
passions.  His anger, while it lasted, was dark and fierce, and
during the mad fit it was wise to keep out of his way.  'Being
wrought,' he was 'perplexed in the extreme,'[4] like another man of
simple, heroic character.  His impetuosity made him dangerous.
But he was not a man who nursed his wrath.  No one would call
him sullenly vindictive.  If ever he declared that he would do
something desperate to an enemy, and did not do it at once, he
invariably forgot that he meant to do it at all (vv.[41, 45]).  He
was as changeful in his hatred as in his love.  He lived in the
passing moment ; his blood quickly boiled and quickly cooled ;
and he was as easily led into good as into evil.  He was terribly
provoked when his brother stole his father's blessing, and 'comforted himself' with the thought of killing him when his father
was gone.  The days of mourning were near at hand, and then
he would have his revenge—indeed he would.  Meantime he felt
constrained to delay.  The thought of his gentle father stayed his
hand.  He could not break that loving heart.  But the delay

1 Heb. 12[17].                          2 Omar Khayyam.
3 George Eliot.                          4 Othello.

settled the matter. For such a man as Esau, a revenge post-
poned was a revenge abandoned. Moreover, Isaac's end was
not yet; he was to have a long peaceful evening of life, and
his quiet presence would always act like a charm to restrain his
son's wild passionate nature and to foster in him feelings of kindly
natural affection

MARRIAGE.—It would not have been like Rebekah if she had
not quickly seen what possibilities of good there were in her
younger son's enforced flight from home. It would give him the
opportunity of visiting her kindred and seeking a wife. Esau
had blundered by marrying into two heathen families. His
wives had tried Rebekah's spirit beyond endurance. They were
a grief of mind to her (26³⁵), and she was weary of her life
because of the daughters of Heth (27⁴⁶). Her secret dread was
that Jacob might follow Esau's example, and marry women 'such
as these' (v.⁴⁶). If Jacob should take a wife of the daughters of
Heth,—wearily she repeats the words, 'daughters of Heth,'—will
his mother's life be worth living? (v.⁴⁶). One of our English
romancers has borrowed the idea which was such a nightmare
to Rebekah, and made 'A Daughter of Heth' the title of a
thrilling tale. He has given us the picture of a charming and
pure-minded, if a very wilful and unconventional young girl—a
most admirable 'heathen,' whom Rebekah would have loved with
all her heart. But the daughters of Heth who vexed Rebekah's
eager spirit and who 'pleased not Isaac' (28⁸), and of whom
Esau himself soon tired (v.⁹), was evidently very different from
Black's heroine. The heathen of real life and history present a
striking contrast to the 'noble heathen' of fiction. Heathenism
has never yet elevated and purified the ideal of womanhood.
The Old Testament gives us many glimpses of the life of heathen
women in Canaan; and if the picture appals us, we can imagine
how the reality appalled Rebekah. The very existence of the
Hebrews as a separate, clean, holy nation depended upon the for-
bidding of intermarriages with 'the heathen who knew not God.'

WOMANHOOD.—Rebekah said to Jacob when he was leaving home, 'Tarry with Laban a few days, until thy brother's anger be turned away ; then will I send and fetch thee from thence' (vv.⁴⁴· ⁴⁵). It was a well-laid scheme, but the result was different from the anticipation. Rebekah hoped that the absence of her favourite son, for which she herself was responsible, would last but a few days. But days lengthened into months, and the months wore into years. Seven years, which seemed to Jacob 'but a few days,' because they were full of love, were to his mother very real years, because she was yearning for love. And when the seven years were doubled and almost tripled, and her beloved son was still absent, she drooped and faded out of life. Retribution came to the too clever mother as well as to the too clever son. When they were parting, they said to one another that it was 'for a few days.' It was for ever.—The picture of Rebekah in Genesis is one of the most humanly interesting in the whole gallery of Bible portraits. Radiant in spirit, swift in action, pure and loving in heart, she lacks the grace of patience. Her eager mind is always moving her to ask questions, and she quits the scene with one of them—unanswered—on her lips (27⁴⁶). They are questions about the mystery of suffering, such as a woman can scarcely avoid asking. One of them is prompted by the pains of motherhood : 'If it be so, why am I thus ?' another by the dread of bereavement : 'Why should I be robbed of you both in one day ?' and a third by the greater dread of seeing her sons turn out prodigals : 'What good shall my life do me ?' These questions have leaped to many a mother's lips since Rebekah first asked them. Even now the answers may be far from certain, for the Bible is human enough to leave some mysteries unsolved. And we like to think of Rebekah, not as a perplexed questioner of the meaning of life, puzzling over

'The reason o' the cause an' the wherefore o' the why,
Wi' mony anither riddle brings the tear into my e'e,'

but as a happy young maiden gliding up and down the steps of the well at Haran, drawing water for the camels till they have done drinking.

## BETHEL
### Genesis 28

' As angels in some brighter dreams
Call to the soul when man doth sleep;
So some strange thoughts transcend our wonted themes,
And into glory peep.'—VAUGHAN.

DISCIPLINE.—Jacob's departure from home is sudden and furtive. He is a fugitive from justice, glad to get away alive. He goes alone and afoot. One would expect to see Isaac's son attended on a journey by a cavalcade of camels bearing costly presents for his friends. But he has nothing but the staff which he carries in his hand. His thoughts are naturally gloomy enough. He is stepping into the dark unknown, facing the world without a friend. He spends his first night away from home on a bare hillside, where he has neither tent for shelter, fire for warmth, nor pillow for rest. The days of the years of his wanderings— which made him afterwards call his whole life a pilgrimage (47$^9$) —are begun. God's discipline is becoming more stringent; poverty, hardship, weariness, and pain will teach him many lessons which he could never have learned in days of wealth and ease. His flight from home makes an epoch in his life.

FAITH.—Jacob has many faults, which are neither concealed by the writers of the Bible nor readily forgiven by the charity of its readers. But if we are to do him justice we must admit that his was the mind which received the revelation of Bethel, one of the most majestic and beautiful visions of the spiritual world ever given to men. God cannot divulge His secrets unless there is a mind capable of appreciating them. His light is for the seeing eye, His truth for the hearing ear A divine revelation becomes effective only in the thoughts and convictions of a mind susceptible of impressions from the world of spirits. Jacob, the typical Hebrew, has such a receptive mind. He has that imagination which, possessed and used by God, becomes the instrument of faith, the means of realising things hoped for and proving things not seen ; that imagination which has been called 'the most truth-bringing of mental powers.'[1] We shall never understand the Hebrew unless we know how he can pass at a bound from the hardness of materialism to the tenderness and elevation of mysticism. He is sensitively alive to spiritual influences ; the bent of his mind is Godward ; and when we imagine him sunk in the depths of earthliness, we are startled to find him rapt into communion with heaven, wistfully longing to find what lies behind the veil of sense, and confessing that man's sole happiness is to know and to do the will of God.

NATURE.—It is well known that Nature influences the mind and makes it peculiarly susceptible of spiritual impressions. If we must not make too much of what she can do, neither should we make too little. Jacob's vision was a mountain vision. God appeared to him upon the heights. The spot which became most sacred to him in all the world was the summit of Bethel. The æsthetic love of mountains may be a taste of advanced civilisation, a passion of the modern mind ; but the religious love of mountains is a primitive natural instinct of the soul. Canaan is a land of mountains. Jacob and other Hebrews lifted up their eyes unto the hills, and ascended their summits, because they discovered that God was nearer them there. They felt it easier to realise His presence there. Jacob found God on Bethel, and the time came when almost every mountain of that land had its sacred legend and shrine. The greatest prophets were mountain prophets ; the holiest temple was a mountain sanctuary ; and Jesus was in the succession when He preached, prayed, and was transfigured on mountains. If it is true that Bethel and many

[1] Dean Church.

another shrine had sooner or later to be desecrated, that was simply 'lest one good custom should corrupt the world.' The mountains had done their work, had whispered their secret. True religion can never cease to be a matter of spiritual elevation. Our whole outlook changes, our minds expand, our spirits rise as we ascend, and things invisible and incredible on the lower levels of life become self-evident on the heights.

Jacob's vision was also a night vision. The mystery of twilight increases the sensitiveness of the mind to spiritual things. Jacob saw the slopes of Bethel, which rise tier above tier like a gigantic staircase, receive 'the incomparable pomp of eve.' He saw the sun sink in splendour beyond the Great Sea. Some say that this is the psychological moment for a revelation.

> 'For sometimes when adown the western sky
>   A fiery sunset lingers,
> Its golden gates swing inward noiselessly,
>   Unlocked by unseen fingers.
> And while they stand a moment half ajar,
>   Gleams from the inner glory
> Stream brightly through the azure vault afar
>   And half reveal the story.'

But Jacob's vision comes later. Restless day is succeeded by quiet night. The wanderer lies down to rest; the stars are above him in their purity, calm, and glory ; the fever, the anguish, the excitement of the day subside ; sleep, the 'balm of hurt minds,' works its miracle ; and God reveals Himself 'in dreams, in visions of the night.'

> 'There is in stillness oft a magic power
> To calm the breast, when struggling passions lower ;
> Touched by its influence in the soul arise
> Diviner feelings, kindred with the skies.' [1]

REVELATION.—'Dreams are among the mysteries of the mind of man.' [2] It is well known that mathematicians have solved problems in dreams. Coleridge composed one of his finest poems in a dream. Stevenson conceived one of his thrilling romances

[1] Newman.  [2] Emerson.

in a dream.  Bunyan calls his great allegory a dream.  Who has not often occasion to say, 'I had a dream which was not all a dream'?  It is legitimate for any man to say :

> ' Yet in my dreams I'd be
> Nearer, my God, to Thee.'

There is no reason to doubt that God has often used men's dreams, not only to throw into brilliant and beautiful forms the thoughts and aspirations of the day, but also to bring forgotten and unimagined truths to light.  It is probable that Jacob's dream was 'woven out of the materials that, all day long, had been fermenting in his mind.'[1]  His ladder or staircase might be suggested either by a broad shaft of quivering light shot down from a summer cloud, or by the terraced mountain-slope bathed in the crimson of the setting sun.  Be that as it may, the mystic ladder of his dream, on which angels ascended and descended, and at the top of which stood the LORD, was the medium of a divine revelation.  Presenting heavenly truths to his mind in a splendid symbolism, it made the faith of his fathers, the belief in which he had been nurtured, for the first time vividly real and impressive to his own soul.  It is a crisis in any man's spiritual history when he can say, 'I had heard of Thee by the hearing of the ear, but now mine eye seeth Thee.'[2]  As a disclosure of the spiritual world, Jacob's vision makes life on earth far more wonderful than he has imagined it to be.  It shows him radiances and splendours hitherto unseen, stirs in his heart emotions hitherto unfelt, shapes in his will resolutions hitherto unformed.  The dream will fade, the symbols vanish, the voices fall silent.  But the facts will remain : God in His heaven, loving and caring for men, sending forth His ministering spirits, and Himself speaking to the souls of men.  These are no mere dreams but great realities, and the uniform result of the act of faith which accepts them is the shifting of the centre of life and all its interests from earth to heaven.

[1] A. B. Davidson.                    [2] Job 42⁵.

IDEALS.—The truths figured by Jacob's vision, the elementary facts of the Hebrew faith, have now happily become commonplaces, like sunbeams, rainbows, and other astonishing facts. The ordinary things both of nature and grace are the most wonderful of all. 1. The *Heaven* of the Hebrews was another and vaster order of things, beyond this scene of good and evil, as real to them as if they could see and feel and touch it, divine in origin, glorious in nature, eternal in duration ; in which God was supreme ; in which higher beings than man found blessedness in doing God's will ; and to which man was essentially and vitally related in consequence of his creation in the image of God, so that there was from the first the possibility, as by grace there came to be the reality, of communion between Heaven and earth. Heaven was the perfect or ideal world from which all good things came to men, and whose eternal laws were to be obeyed by men. Between Heaven, God's imperial palace or temple among the stars, and the world which He has given to the sons of men, there was a highway visible to the eye of faith, on which His messengers were ever speeding up and down on business relating to the welfare of men. 2. The *God* of the Hebrews was not an abstraction identical with nature or involved in nature, nor an absentee God careless of the affairs of earth, but a personal, gracious, loving, and lovable God, whose delights were with the children of men, who ordered their lives, whose presence made human life safe and delightful, whose goodness made it impossible for Him to break His promises or disappoint the sanguine hopes which men entertained of Him. 3. *Man's* place in the system of things was also made clear, and no part of the ancient Hebrew faith was more important than the belief about man. Created by God and for God, man came to himself only when he was taken into fellowship with God. He was a creature of this earth, dust returning to dust ; yet he was allied to the heavenly and divine, breathing the breath of God ; and the one thing which saved life in this world from being small and contemptible, which gave real worth and dignity to the passing things of time, was the belief that the Eternal cared for man, took account of his doings, sent His messengers to minister to him, and called him to become His servant and even His friend. Are not these divinely inspired ideas of God and man, of heaven and earth, as necessary to-day as they were three thousand years ago? They are the Hebrew legacy to mankind.

ENCOURAGEMENT.—At Bethel, Jacob is promised a great and glorious future. The divine promises to his seed precede the promises to himself. His offspring are destined to inherit the land of Canaan, to become as the dust of the earth, and to spread abroad in every direction until in them all the families of the earth are blessed (vv.[13, 14]). Explain it as we will, it is certain that a whole nation came to cherish this faith. One of the smallest races of the world was so confident of its own future blessedness that it believed in the future blessedness of mankind. Its national hope expanded into a universal hope. It expected the whole earth first to covet and then to share its felicity! 'There is,' as Dean Church says, 'something perfectly overwhelming to mere human judgment in the audacity with which this people claim for their faith, for their God, the inheritance of all nations, the spiritual future of all mankind.' But their bold, imperial thinking has been amply justified. Their faith is winning the world's assent and devotion. Their ideal is at length being swiftly realised by the world-wide triumph of modern missions.— Then there are divine promises for Jacob himself (v.[15]). Three painful feelings oppressed him when he lay down on the moorland of Bethel. He was lonely, he was fearful, he was forsaken. And his God, coming nearer him in his dreams, promises him three things—fellowship, protection, and guidance. 'I am with thee, and will keep thee . . . I will not leave thee.' It is ignorance of the future that begets anxiety about the future. Jacob has a God who not only foresees but foreordains his future, and who, to free him from care, gives him prophecies and promises which assure him that all shall be well. Graciously binding Himself

to do certain things for him, He gives him the right to expect
them, and so to face the future without fear.

REVERENCE.—When a new day is dawning over the hills of
Gilead, Jacob rises from sleep and stands amazed. He realises
that he is on consecrated ground. 'Surely God is in this place,
and I knew it not' (v.$^{16}$). He repeats the words, 'this place . . .
this place . . . this . . . this' (v.$^{17}$). He lay down on it, feeling
only the cold night-dew falling about him, conscious only of the
darkness without and within. Now he knows that he is in the
presence of God. 'How dreadful is this place!'

> 'What if Thy form we cannot see,
> We know and feel that Thou art here.

Has God, then, come to alarm, rebuke, condemn the wayfarer?
Is Jacob afraid of being crushed by a God of wrath? On the
contrary, he has received nothing but assurances of God's loving-
kindness, and promises of His watchful care. He has heard no
word of upbraiding or threatening. Yet he feels how awful it
is to be near God, how dreadful to have a heavenly search-
light flashed into his soul. He is penetrated with holy fear,
abashed by the pure splendour of the Divine. That does not
mean that he wishes for a moment to escape from God. He
would not for a world have spent this night anywhere but just
where he has spent it; and he would not for a ransom be anywhere now but just where he is. This spot will always be in his
memory the dearest on earth, this night better than a thousand.
But while he rejoices he trembles. No sinful man can be in
the presence of God without fear. That sense of awe—we may
feel it alone on a bare moorland under the stars, or in a great
temple among a multitude of worshippers, or in an upper room
where two or three friends are gathered together. But when
it comes to us there is no mistaking it, for that reverential
feeling is different from any other emotion that ever visits the
human heart.

BETHEL.—'This place,' said Jacob, as he stood at Bethel in the morning light, 'is none other than the House of God, and this is the Gate of Heaven.' What kind of a place is Bethel to look at? It is no green oasis with murmuring brooks and rustling leaves and soft refreshing shades inviting travellers to rest. Bethel is a bare moorland, gashed and scarred, strewn with tumbled rocks, where no one would voluntarily spend a night. Yet to Jacob—and to many another after him—it was like the Presence-Chamber of the Most High. 'Faith inverts the vulgar order of things, and brings the mind to call that apparent which it uses to call real, and that real which it uses to call visionary.'[1] The other expression which Jacob applies to Bethel—the Gate of Heaven—is equally wonderful. 'What strange sights a little faith helps us to see! How it transforms the complexion of the world, how it pierces the veil that is hung across the face of things, and sees marvellous things behind! Till God opens our eyes, we see little. We come into the universe of God like the lower creatures—born blind. A miracle of healing must pass upon us. The Lord must put His fingers on our eyes before we can see anything of the true depths even of our common life and its relations; and, much more, of the inner life. Nay, we do not know God Himself till our eyes are opened to see Him. This wanderer thought the land of promise a weary, God-abandoned spot; God opened his eyes, and he found himself lying at the gate of heaven.'[2] This is the right answer to Hazlitt's familiar and plaintive objection. He says, 'In the days of Jacob there was a ladder between heaven and earth; but now the heavens have gone further off, and they have become astronomical.' The open eye of faith can see God even more clearly in Newton's than in Jacob's sky. The astronomical heavens are profoundly theological.

CONSECRATION.—Jacob's eye rests on the stone on which his head has lain during this never-to-be-forgotten night. He sets

[1] Emerson.　　　　　[2] A. B. Davidson.

it up for a pillar, and pours oil on the top of it (v.[18]). What is his thought as he performs this act? How does he regard the stone? Some scholars believe that he thinks of it as the actual abode of the God (or rather the god) who has appeared to him in his dream. But that is not how the story is meant to be read. Genesis was not written for the purpose of encouraging fetichism. That there was such a thing as stone-worship among the primitive Semites is certain enough. ' Stones which had divine honours paid to them as being gods in corporeal form, or stones animated by a god, are of frequent occurrence among heathen peoples, not only in Canaan and among the Syrians and Arabs, but elsewhere in the East and in the West.'[1] But with fetichism the Bible has nothing to do except to get rid of it. It was the distinctive glory of the Hebrew faith, that it had power to throw off all kinds of superstition. The stone which Jacob sets up for a pillar is a simple memorial of a theophany. Whenever he comes this way again it will stir his soul to fresh devotion and gratitude. There is in the heart of man an insane passion for relic-worship, and Jacob's stone did not escape this foolish adoration. But the Hebrews were brilliant iconoclasts ; therein lay their power. As soon as any sacred thing was seen to be mischievous, it was forthwith destroyed. Jacob's sacred pillar was destroyed, and though Bethel had been to Jacob the House of God and the Gate of Heaven, the holy ground was desecrated, and accursed by God's truest servants.[2] God's worship was removed to other places uncontaminated by man's odious ritualism.

COVENANTING.—The LORD having covenanted to be with Jacob, to keep him, to guide him, and never to leave him (v.[15]), Jacob in turn solemnly covenants to serve the LORD. If God will —as he knows that He will—be with him, and keep him, and give him bread and raiment, and bring him home in peace, and be his God, he will establish His worship at Bethel, and give Him tithes of all that he possesses (vv.[20-22]). What is the spirit in

[1] Dillmann.                    [2] Amos 5[5] etc.

which Jacob makes this covenant? It is sometimes said that
he carries a mercenary spirit even into his prayers; that he
carefully guards himself against an incautious and hasty pledge;
that he makes his faith contingent on the divine bounty; that
his vow is a cool prudential calculation; that he receives absolute
promises but returns only conditional ones; that, in short, his
covenant is 'an iniquitous attempt to bargain with the Most
High.' 'Instead of being content with the glorious covenant
which God had just given him, and taking God at His word,
and thanking God for what He has done, he gets up and puts
that "if" in. He wanted to make a bargain right there with the
LORD.'[1] But this is hardly the way in which 'the great
transaction is done.' The 'if' is logical, not theological. Jacob
repeats the divine promises, not with shrewd suspicion, but
with unquestioning acceptance. God's love and power are
undoubted; His word is sure; and if the wayfarer puts
bread and raiment among the promises, he may be forgiven.
'Then' in v.[21] is misleading, being too strong for the original.
The spirit of the whole passage is reproduced almost to perfection in Doddridge's hymn, 'O God of Bethel,' a paraphrase
of Jacob's words which is universally regarded as one of the
most heart-moving poems in our language:

> 'Through each perplexing path of life
>     Our wandering footsteps guide;
> Give us each day our daily bread,
>     And raiment fit provide.
>
> O spread Thy covering wings around,
>     Till all our wanderings cease,
> And at our Father's loved abode
>     Our souls arrive in peace.
>
> Such blessings from Thy gracious hand
>     Our humble prayers implore;
> And Thou shalt be our chosen God,
>     And portion evermore.'

---

[1] D. L. Moody.

# LOVE
## Genesis 29:1-30

' No man could be a bad man who loved as Jacob loved Rachel.'
COLERIDGE.

HOPE.—From Bethel 'Jacob went on his journey' (29[1]). He 'lifted up his feet,' as the livelier Hebrew has it. He went forward with a new buoyancy in his step and a higher courage in his heart. He was animated by the hope which always thrills the soul when it is fresh from real communion with God. There are spiritual experiences after which ' we become physically nimble and lightsome ; we tread on air ; life is no longer irksome, and we think it will never be so.'[1] It is a rapture to face the unknown future, if God has promised to be with us and guide us. As the Hebrew prophet says : 'They that wait upon the LORD shall renew their strength ; they shall mount up with wings as eagles ; they shall run and not be weary ; they shall walk and not faint.'[2]

IDYLLIC.—From bare mountains touched with a radiance from heaven and visited by angels, Jacob comes down to green pastures bathed in the light of common day and peopled by ordinary men and women. Yet in the simple life of the plains there is enough to move the heart and lift a man above himself. The story of the dawn of Faith is followed by the tale of the coming of Love. There is the same literary power and beauty in both narratives, but the change of tone and atmosphere is at once apparent. It is the difference between a solemn nocturne and a bright pastoral symphony. 'The land of the Children of the East' might be Arcadia, the classic country of peace and innocence and love, and the dialogue of the shepherds reads like

---

[1] Emerson.                    [2] Isa. 40[31].

a bit of Theocritus or Virgil. The scene comes vividly before
our minds. The panting flocks lying round the well's mouth,
the high sun beating down on the plains, the shepherds half
dozing in the languorous heat ; the entrance of a stranger who
arouses them to animated conversation, and finds to his joy
that he has come among friends ; the approach of a shepherdess
whom he finds to be his own cousin ; his chiding of the lazy
shepherds, whom he tries to dismiss that he may have the
happiness of meeting his cousin alone, but whom he finds too
clever or too stupid to take a hint ; the meeting of Hebrew
man and Syrian maid ; his sudden access of strength, wherewith
he heaves the huge well-stone from its place and waters her
flock ; his kiss of love and sudden uncontrollable burst of
weeping,—all this is depicted, with simple dramatic charm, by
a writer who has an eye to see, and the skill to make others
see, the idyllic beauty of common life.

WOMANHOOD.—What lovely pictures of maidenly grace and
freedom we find in the Old Testament stories ! Rachel is the
younger daughter of a Syrian flock-master. She is 'beautiful
in form and face' (v.[17]). She keeps her father's sheep (v.[9]).
She brings them to the watering (v.[6]). We see a gentle
shepherdess leading and feeding her flock ; now alone, now
moving freely and fearlessly among the shepherds ; unveiled,
and unashamed to let the sun dye her cheeks or any human
eyes look in hers. She has grown up in the light of day. She
has absorbed the elements. She runs (v.[12]), like another child of
the open air—

> ' sportive as the fawn,
> That wild with glee upon the lawn
> Or up the mountain springs.' [1]

Love comes to her, as it came to Rebekah, at the well, while
she is busied with the common tasks of her daily life. We
picture her with her crook in her hand, and her sheep behind

[1] Wordsworth.

her ; herself a free, graceful creature, destined to be the mother of one of the best and noblest of men. In Eastern lands at the present day, woman knows little or nothing of freedom. It is a sin for any stranger ever to see her, speak to her, or even to ask for her. Servile submission is her highest duty. In her home she is as much a captive as a linnet in a cage ; and if ever she is allowed to go out, she must veil her face and be silent. What she needs, what she unconsciously sighs for, is the religion which brings deliverance to the captive and gives every woman a woman's share in life's happiness. True faith and freedom have always gone together.

LOVE.—Henceforth the names of Jacob and Rachel are linked together. At first the course of their love runs smooth, and nothing in Jacob's after-life should blind us to the idyllic beauty of this earlier time. Whatever his faults might be, he had at least lived a clean and wholesome life. He had a pure heart to offer the maiden whom he loved, and the years in which he wooed her were the golden time of his life. The essence of a hundred love-tales is contained in the simple words, 'And Jacob served seven years for Rachel ; and they seemed unto him but a few days, for the love he had to her' (v.[20]). This is first love, radiant with the promise of hope, strong with the concentrated energy of 'all thoughts, all passions, all delights.' It is the love of one for one, pure, unselfish ; sweetheart love in its grace and charm ; heaven-kindled love with a magic power to change all sacrifice into joy. The music of a voice, the sound of a foot-fall, suffices to make hard tasks light. 'Love is a great thing, a blessing very good, the only thing which makes all burdens light, bearing evenly what is uneven, carrying a weight without feeling it, turning all bitterness into a sweet savour. It makes light of toil, would do more than it can, and pleads no impossibility, but is strong for anything.'[1] 'The best life is that in which one does and bears everything because of some great

[1] Thomas à Kempis.

and strong feeling, so that this and that in one's circumstances does not signify.'[1]   As Ferdinand, carrying his logs, exclaims :

> ' This my task
> Would be as heavy to me as odious ; but
> The mistress whom I serve quickens what's dead,
> And makes my labours pleasures.'[2]

RETRIBUTION.—Rachel was to be Jacob's helpmeet, comrade, and friend ; the sharer of his aspirations, hopes, and joys ; his fellow-traveller to the land of promise ; the angel of his earthly pilgrimage.   For this was a Hebrew, as it is now an English ideal :

> ' To lead sweet lives in purest chastity,
> To love one maiden only, cleave to her,
> To worship her by years of noblest deeds
> Until thou win her.'[3]

But the idyll of pure love ends in an act of base treachery. Laban and Leah play the part of conspirators against Jacob and Rachel.   Laban's excuse for his conduct is the lamest ever offered.   The information which he gives his nephew about the customs of Syria (v.$^{26}$) comes seven years too late (v.$^{19}$).   Delitzsch says in his *Genesis* that the custom of not marrying the younger daughter before the elder is still 'stubbornly adhered to in India and in the old imperial towns of Germany.'   It is well to circulate the information, that if any of Jacob's sons go to India or the old imperial German towns, they may be forewarned and forearmed.   In Haran, Jacob was kept all the time in the dark, and a base advantage taken of his ignorance.   'Wherefore,' he asks one of the conspirators, 'hast thou beguiled me?'   Guile is seen to be a mean and cruel sin. But we turn back a few pages in the narrative, and we hear Isaac saying to Esau, 'Thy brother came with guile, and hath taken away thy blessing' (27$^{35}$).   The beguiler is beguiled.   God's balance is true.   Sooner or later He gives measure for measure. The deceiver is deceived that he may learn to loathe deception.

[1] George Eliot.          [2] *The Tempest.*          [3] Tennyson.

The culprit changed into a judge sees all the baseness of his sin. 'The LORD will punish Jacob according to his ways ; according to his doing will He recompense him.'[1]

> 'The tissues of the life to be
>     We weave with colours of our own ;
> And in the field of destiny
>     We reap as we have sown.'[2]

## MEMORY
### Genesis 29:31-31:55

> ' I am sad, and fain
> Would give you all to be but where I was.'
>                                    BROWNING.

MONOGAMY.—Jacob found himself drawn, first by a cunning conspiracy, and then by his own too easy consent, into a marriage with two sisters. This unhappy relationship afterwards became very repellent to the Hebrews. 'Thou shalt not,' said their lawgiver, 'take a woman to her sister, to be a rival to her, beside the other in her lifetime.'[3] Jacob's double marriage was therefore regarded not as an example, but as a warning. A plurality of wives was never more than tolerated among the Hebrews. It might be endured for the hardness of men's hearts, but no one ever dreamed of commending it as well-pleasing to God. It was never supposed to be the divine ideal. 'There is a great difference between deeming a state permissible and proposing it as a condition of sanctity.'[4] The same writer[5] who tells the story of Jacob's marriage wrote also the memorable words, 'Therefore shall a man leave his father and his mother, and shall cleave unto his wife ; and they shall be one flesh' ($2^{24}$). 'We may regard monogamy either in the light of an intuitive moral

[1] Hos. $12^2$.    [2] Whittier.    [3] Lev. $18^{18}$.    [4] Lecky.    [5] The Jahvist.

sentiment, or in the light of the interests of society.'[1] Genesis
explicitly and implicitly advocates the construction of the family
on the basis of monogamy. The lifelong union of one man with
one woman—seen in the cases of Isaac and Rebekah, Joseph
and Asenath—is the normal and dominant type.

CHILDHOOD.—Jacob's home in Haran could not have much joy.
It contained too many elements of friction and disquiet. Rachael
and Leah might be happy enough together as sisters, but not as
the wives of one husband. No man ever gave his heart to two
women. Jacob's marriage with Leah was, and could not but be,
loveless. One wife was much loved and the other unloved ; the
unloved was a mother, and the much loved childless ; and other
elements made the situation still more complicated. 'Wherever
there is polygamy women in general show themselves addicted to
the petty forms of vanity, jealousy, spitefulness, and ambition.'[1]
Yet gleams of joy come to this Syrian home. Every child born
into it is regarded as a gift of God. Almost every name is a
thanksgiving for divine goodness, or a prayer for further blessing.
'The LORD hath looked upon my affliction' (Reuben) ; 'the
LORD hath heard' (Simeon) ; 'I will praise the LORD' (Judah),
are some of Leah's thoughts. 'God is my judge' (Dan) ; 'the
LORD add to me another son' (Joseph), are thoughts of Rachel.
Other names are self-congratulatory. 'Fortunate !' (Gad), and
'Happy am I : for the daughters shall call me happy!' (Asher)
are exclamations of Leah. Such names give us a glimpse into
an ordinary Hebrew household at the time when a fresh young
life comes 'out of the infinite into here.' Mother-love watching
an infant's slumbers is perfect love, and the earthly home to
which God's blessings are felt to come is not without its broken
lights of paradise. 'It is when children are born into the world
that the pious feelings of parents are most strongly evoked and
expressed. So the names of most children are compounded of
the Divine name. . . . The story of the naming of Jacob's

[1] Lecky.

children in Padanaram is full of indications how closely men and women felt Jehovah to be bound up with their history."[1]

LABOUR.—Joy in labour has ceased under the sun when a man no longer works for love, but only for pay. From his wedding-day onwards Jacob serves Laban with a deep resentment in his breast. He feels that he has been cruelly wronged ; he regards his uncle and master—now his father-in-law—as his enemy, whose purpose is to thwart him in every possible way. And Jacob retaliates. To defeat his kinsman and enrich himself at his expense becomes the chief end of his action. At the game of beggar my neighbour two can play. So the stress and toil and ambition of Jacob's life in Haran are henceforth utterly selfish. He knows how to make the feebler of the flock Laban's and the stronger his own, how to make white sheep drop black-spotted lambs and black goats have white-spotted kids, and how to turn every apparent loss into real gain. Success crowns his efforts, and the wily Hebrew can laugh in his sleeve at the domineering Syrian lord. 'The man increased exceedingly, and had large flocks, and manservants and maid-servants, and camels and asses' (v.[43]). But while the end is certainly reached, the means trouble every reader of the story. Many things are recorded in the Bible regarding the servants of God which are not endorsed. Probably no one has ever expressed a whole-hearted approval of Jacob's methods except Shylock, who says with a glow of admiring enthusiasm :

'That was the way to thrive, and he was bless'd.'

The universal conscience rather answers, 'No, better not to thrive at all than thrive in that way.' 'We must not suppose that at the time when the Book of Genesis was written the Hebrews had so little idea of honesty as not to disapprove of Jacob's conduct towards Laban.'[2] When we observe that in the heat of the long contest, in the daily presence of the enemy,

[1] A. B. Davidson.          [2] Oort.

Jacob's words become bitter, his spirit loses its calm, and time no longer swiftly glides as it did when his heart was ruled by love, we cannot but infer that in the midst of his worldly success he has fallen far below his ideal.

BETHEL.—The situation gradually became intolerable to everybody. Laban's frown was habitual (31²). His sons were loud and bitter in their complaints on the one side (v.¹), his daughters on the other (v.¹⁵). And Jacob grew sick at heart in the midst of it all. A crisis had to come, and it came through the resurrection of the divine ideal in his soul. Once and again, awake and asleep, he heard the God of Bethel calling him back to the land of his fathers and to his kindred (vv.³· ¹³). It was the voice of God in his own heart and conscience ; it was memory bringing the past to mind, and imagination making the distant near ; it was the divine discontent of a spirit that refuses to be for ever sunk in worldliness ; it was whatever was most sacred in his experience of life—kindred and fatherland, the holy mountain, the pillar, the anointing oil, the solemn vow (vv.³· ¹³)—crowding into his troubled mind ; it was the God of his father (v.⁵), 'the God of Bethel' (v.¹³), 'the God of Abraham and the Fear of Isaac' taking possession of his soul and saying, 'Return !' Into the midst of what is sordid and selfish, feverish and false, there come memories of another and a higher life, which the soul has once tasted and can never wholly forget. Heart-hunger for the old faith and home of one's youth, whetted by weariness and satiety in the midst of worldly success, has been many a man's salvation.

FATHERHOOD.—Laban never tells his daughters that he loves them, till they are leaving him for ever. Rachel and Leah have long thirsted for an affection which they have never received. At last they despair of ever receiving it. Though they are placed in a position in which mutual jealousy seems inevitable, yet their father's unfatherly treatment draws them together and makes them speak with one voice (v.¹⁴). The word father, which should be one of the sweetest in any language. is uttered by them with an accent of bitterness. They complain that they have no portion or inheritance in their father's house (v.[14]) ; they are counted by him strangers ; he has sold them as chattels, and devoured their money (v.[15]). So complete is their estrangement from their father, that they consent to steal away from home without saying a word of farewell. When they are carrying out their purpose, Laban follows and overtakes the fugitives, and shows himself the kindest father alive. They need not have fled away from him secretly : had he known they were leaving, he would have given them a send-off with mirth and with songs, with tabret and with harp, with the fond kiss of love (vv.[27, 28]). He adjures his son-in-law never to afflict his daughters, never to be unfaithful to them (v.[50]). Seven times he repeats the gracious words 'my daughters.' When he rises up early in the morning, kisses them, gives them his blessing, and then turns his face homewards (v.[55]), his heart is wrung with genuine grief. It is beautiful ; the only pity is that it comes so late. A little of the mirth and song, a touch of the tabret and the harp, an occasional kiss of love, a tender utterance of the words ' my daughter '—indeed a tithe of this farewell effusiveness, would have made all the difference in the world to those whose hearts were starving for a little natural affection. During all the long years Laban is a 'stranger' to his daughters, and only for one brief day of parting, a 'father.' 'There's the respect which makes calamity of so long life.'

> ' O the little more, and how much it is !
> O the little less, and what worlds away ! '

VINDICATION.—Jacob as a servant impeaches Laban as a master (vv.[36-42]). Being righteously angry, he speaks in a lofty tone. After a long silence he unburdens his mind. He has been twenty years in Laban's employment, and he has had hard work, poor wages, heavy losses, plain fare, and little sleep. He has endured the scorching sun by day and the biting frost by night. He has been patient and uncomplaining in the service of a hard

and grudging master, who at the end of it all would think nothing
of sending him away empty. God in heaven alone knows how
he has toiled and suffered, and it would have gone ill indeed
with him but for His presence and protection. It is an eloquent
speech, finely phrased, with an accent of personal feeling
vibrating through it. 'The speech of Jacob has, by reason of
the strong emotion and self-conscious elevation expressed in
it, both rhythmic movement and poetic form.'[1] 'Indignation
makes good verses,'[2] and a sharp sense of wrong makes telling
speeches. Jacob's words have the ring of sincerity : it is always
touching to hear a patient and long-suffering man tell in simple
language what he has come through ; and if ever a man deserved
to be humiliated, it was Laban. Yet every reader feels that
there is another side of the matter. Jacob's suffering is not
unmerited. It is only to Laban that he can throw down the
challenge, 'What is my tresspass? what is my sin, that thou hast
so hotly pursued after me?' Let him put these questions to God,
and the torrent of his eloquence will freeze on his lips. 'If *Thou*,
LORD, shouldest mark iniquities, O LORD, who shall stand?'[3]

FAITH.—The religion of Laban the Syrian is not quite easy
to understand. He acknowledges that 'the LORD' has blessed
him for Jacob's sake, having 'divined' it (30[27]). Receiving in
a night vision a warning that he must not injure Jacob, he feels
that it has come from 'the God of Isaac' (31[29]). Making a
covenant with Jacob, he invokes 'the LORD' to watch and
witness between them (vv.[49, 50]) ; and again he calls upon 'the
God of Abraham, the God of Nahor, and the God of their father'
to judge between them (v.[53]). Laban believes that this God,
under a variety of names, blesses, warns, watches, witnesses,
judges ; his belief affects him alike in waking and in sleeping
hours ; and he is in some ways a better man for it. But he
always speaks of this God as other people's God, never as 'my
God.' It is to him a derived and impersonal faith. On the other

[1] Delitzsch.　　　[2] Horace.　　　[3] Ps. 130[3].

hand, he contends with fierce energy for what he calls 'my gods';
he is intensely excited over the loss of them; he thinks that the
good fortune of his house somehow depends upon them. These
gods are teraphim,—little carved or graven images,—and have
their place among the other 'household stuff' (v.[37]). Some
Syrians would say, 'We do not worship these things; they are
only symbols of the true God, and aids to our worship of Him.'
So a few philosophical people have reasoned in all ages; but the
vast majority of people do not reason; and when teraphim
are kissed and adored and treasured as 'gods,' the spiritual
worship of the living and unseen God goes into the background
or is entirely discarded. Jacob and the other patriarchs use no
teraphim; they worship the Invisible alone; and the victory
which the Hebrews win for mankind is a victory of spiritual faith.

WATCHING.—As Laban and Jacob stand together on Mount
Gilead, the better elements of the two men's characters come
into view. The sense of the presence of God overawes them,
the thought of final parting solemnises them, and some touches
of nature finally make them once more kin. Arguing and
reasoning alone would never have reconciled them; but God
is above them, little children are around them, and they relent.
Angry recriminations cease, and they speak in softer tones.
'Now then,' is the proposal which comes from Laban, 'let
us make a covenant, I and thou' (v.[44]). They pledge themselves not to harm one another; they erect memorials of their
covenant; Laban gives the 'heap of witness' a Syrian and
Jacob a Hebrew name. Before they offer sacrifice and eat
bread together, before they kiss and part in peace, they agree,
at Laban's suggestion, to call their mount of reconciliation
'Mizpah.' They will think of it in future as God's 'Watch-
tower.' It will remind them that the LORD is watching when
they are absent from one another (v.[49]); and if either of them
shall violate the solemn covenant, it will utter its solemn protest.
Pointing to the skies, and visible from every side, it will silently

warn them that God, watching over Hebrew and Syrian alike, slumbers not nor sleeps. 'No man,' said Laban, 'is with us ; see, God is witness between me and thee' (v.⁵⁰). We can forgive much to Laban for that great thought and that beautiful name. There were many other Mizpahs in Israel in later times —common watch-towers where sentinels nightly stood on guard. But Laban's Mizpah makes us think of the high God on *His* watch-tower of the heavens. No friendship is so fast as that which is consecrated by a common faith. The breach of a covenant made in God's sight is only one point removed from atheism. It is our fidelity to God, our sense of responsibility to Him, that keeps us faithful in all our relationships to our fellow-men.


# WRESTLING
## Genesis 32-33:17

'Who never ate his bread in sorrow,
    Who never spent the darksome hours
   Weeping and watching for the morrow,
    He knows you not, ye heavenly Powers.—GOETHE.

PROTECTION.—Jacob was venturing back to Canaan after twenty years of exile. It was a perilous step to take, and his mind was not free from foreboding, nor his conscience from guilt. But he was not without a sense of divine encouragement and protection. He believed that he was returning in obedience to a divine summons, and when he lifted his eyes heavenwards, he somehow realised that the LORD of hosts was with him in His mighty power. 'He went on his way, and the angels of God met him' (32¹). 'Whether visible to an eye of sense, or, as would appear, only to the eye of faith, they *are* visible to this troubled man ; and, in a glow of confident joy, he calls the name of that place Mahanaim, two camps. One camp was the little

one down here . . . and the other was the great one up there.'[1]
Pilgrims passing the place in after days found a heartening
message in the very name of the place. The Hebrews believed
in the existence of spirits brighter, stronger, better, happier than
men ; messengers of One from whom all their glory was derived ;
benignant guardian angels, an armed host, charged to protect
God's servants in time of danger and cheer them on their way.
'The angel of the LORD encamps round about them that fear
Him, and delivers them.'[2]   Milton has given expression to this
belief in the words :

> ' Millions of spiritual creatures walk the earth
> Unseen, both when we wake and when we sleep.'

General Gordon's last letter from Khartoum, written just before
his betrayal and death, ends with the words, ' The angels of God
are with me—Mahanaim.'

TRUTH.—Jacob could not go to meet his brother with a bold
mien.   The old memory of a deceitful act on his part, followed
by a terrible threat on his brother's part, made him still afraid.
He could not go forward with the proud consciousness of rectitude.
He had not the open face of truth.   A sin on the conscience un-
nerves a man almost like a clot of blood on the brain.   Valour is
proverbially wedded to truth.   ' Sincerity, a great, deep, genuine
sincerity, is the first characteristic of all men in any way heroic.'[3]
' Truth is our only armour in all passages of life and death.'[4]

TRIAL.—Jacob sent messengers to 'my lord Esau' to find
grace in his sight.   How did Esau receive them?   The Talmud
hazards a guess.   It speaks of Esau thus : 'All the wrong which
Jacob had done him freshened in his memory, and his anger and
hate against his brother burned once more fiercely in his heart.
. . . And he answered with pride, "Twice he supplanted me

---

[1] A. Maclaren.        [2] Ps. 34[7].
[3] Carlyle.        [4] Emerson.

Therefore I come to meet him, and the vengeance for which I
have waited twenty years shall now be mine."' But this is unfair
to Esau. His mother, who knew him best, said that his anger
would soon turn away, and he would forget ($27^{44.\ 45}$). Esau was a
man of strong barbaric nature, with the virtues and the vices of a
heroic savage. If he was swept by stormy gusts of passion, he
was also melted into moods of tender pity. He oscillated between
the impulses of cruelty and of kindness. If he was terrible in
his anger, he was generous in his love. The uncertainty of
the envoys as to how he received their message intensifies
the dramatic interest of the story. They could only report
that Esau was coming to meet his brother with four hundred
men. Jacob's heart sank with terror. His imagination conjured
up a dreadful retribution. He and his whole family were in
instant peril of destruction. He saw Esau and his savage horde
smiting 'the mother with the children.' The situation was
horrible. But there is at least this benefit in a shock of mental
anguish, that it stirs a man to the depth of his nature, and
compels him to feel, think, and act from the very centre of his
being. It shows all that a man is and all that he is worth.

PRAYER.—At the core of Jacob's being there seem to be
always two things—a plan and a prayer. The one represents
his faith in himself, the other his faith in God. His fertility of
adroit adjustments is almost uncanny, and yet he seems in the
end to

> 'Grow willing, having tried all other ways,
> To try just God's.'

His first plan and prayer on this occasion are found in $32^{7\text{-}12}$.
He divides his people, his flocks, his herds, and his camels into
two companies, thinking that 'if Esau come to the one company
and smite it, then the company which is left shall escape.' But
the thought naturally brings him only cold comfort; in imagination he still sees a welter of blood; and the intolerable vision
brings him to his knees. He pours out his soul to God in prayer.

Among the ancient Hebrews 'prayer had no fixed form. So far as is known to us it was only the expression of real and strong feelings, such as gratitude, anxiety, and sorrow, and not a sacred form independent of special causes.'[1] Yet this heart-cry of a man in distress contains all the elements of a complete prayer. (1) In his solemn *invocation* he makes use of the names which give most glory to God and bring most comfort to his own heart : 'O God of my father Abraham, and God of my father Isaac, O LORD, who saidst unto me, Return unto thy country, and to thy kindred, and I will do thee good.' The divine attributes have to be realised before the troubled soul can recover any degree of confidence. Everything that God is known to be is a ray of hope in darkness, a source of strength in weakness. In the magnificent language of the Hebrew proverb, 'The name of the LORD is a strong tower ; the righteous runneth into it and is safe.'[2] (2) In his humble *confession* Jacob wrings his hands and cries, 'I am not worthy of the least of Thy mercies' ; which is the substance of every penitential utterance. He could make a strong enough self-defence, if occasion required it, before man $(31^{36})$, but he has no righteousness to plead before God. He never deserved God's mercies, and the miserable return he has made for them fills him with shame. He humbles, he condemns himself. With genuine pain in his heart and a break in his voice he mourns his unworthiness. 'For merit lives from man to man, but not from man, O LORD, to Thee.' (3) In his warm *thanksgiving* he is specific and detailed. He recalls the day on which he crossed this Jordan with no possession but the staff he had in his hand. He marvels at the contrast between what he was and what he has become. Can he be the same person ? He almost doubts his identity.

> ' When all Thy mercies, O my God,
>   My rising soul surveys,
> Transported with the view, I'm lost
>   In wonder, love, and praise.'[3]

---

[1] Schultz.     [2] Prov. 18$^{10}$.     [3] Addison.

He thanks God with a special emphasis for His truth (v.[10]). This man who has sometimes been so false remembers that his God has always been absolutely true. He has the divine ideal of truth in his own soul, as every other man has ; and he would despair if he imagined for a moment that God could ever be aught but faithful and true. (4) In his trembling *supplication* he prays for personal deliverance. He believes that his life is in imminent danger. He prays for the averting of a dreaded calamity. 'Deliver me, I pray Thee, from the hand of my brother, from the hand of Esau : for I fear him.' (5) In his tender *intercession* he pleads for the lives of 'the mother and the children.' His fear for them is proportionate to his love, and love and fear together make any man a strong and moving intercessor. (6) In his earnest *pleading* he entreats God to do all this for His own promises' sake. As at the beginning, so at the end of his prayer, he urges the plea : 'Thou saidst.' That is the element of hope in all prayer. In one way or another God has promised, and will be true. He can never go back on His word. To remind Him of His promises is to offer true prayer We get a grip for our hands out of 'Thou saidst'; we lay hold on the pledge of a faithful God.

POWER.—Fine as this prayer is, both in thought and in expression, it leaves something to be desired. It is a cry *de profundis*, but not out of the lowest depths of this man's complex nature. Having earnestly prayed for Divine deliverance, he rises from his knees and returns to his plans. Motives come surging up from the other side of his character. Ideas teem in his active brain. It is as natural for him to scheme as to breathe. His second device was more ingenious and effective than the first. He felt that the situation called for a sacrifice. He would send a princely gift from 'thy servant Jacob' to 'my lord Esau.' He would capture his brother with kindness. 'I will appease him with the present that goes before me, and afterward I will see his face ; peradventure he will accept me' (v.[20]). An offering of five hundred and eighty cattle of various kinds was despatched with 'a space betwixt drove and drove,' the messengers rehearsing their part ere they went. That seemed a good day's work, and Jacob might look forward with more confidence to the morrow. At anyrate, he felt that he had now done his best, and might as well go to rest. 'So the present passed over before him, and he lodged that night in the company' (v.²¹). But 'that night' (v.²²)—the repetition of the words at once arrests us—his eyes were to have no sleep ; that night he was to learn that there still remained something far greater and better for him to do ; that night Jacob was to become Israel, to have power with God and prevail, to discover a secret which was ere long to give his people the spiritual leadership among the nations of the earth.

WATCHNIGHT.—At nightfall Jacob was seized with an over-mastering desire for solitude. Long ago he was alone in a memorable night of peaceful sleep on the hill of heavenly vision (28¹¹), and now he was to be alone in a still more memorable watchnight of wrestling agony. The place was appropriate—he was on the banks of the twisting and moaning Jabbok. He rose and moved his camp across the rushing ford, and returned. He was left behind in the darkness. Then came the great spiritual experience of his life. 'That night' he did not simply commune with his own soul. He was 'wrestled with,' 'touched,' 'strained' ; he was questioned, renamed, and blessed. His experience is variously reported in mysterious language, as if one were trying to utter the unutterable. The narrator in Genesis says, 'There wrestled a Man with him until the breaking of the day' (v.²⁴). One of the prophets says, 'He had power with the Angel, and prevailed.'[1] Jacob says, 'I have seen God face to face' (v.³⁰). And the Unknown Himself says, 'Wherefore is it that thou askest after my name ?' Man, Angel, God, Nameless—here is a mystery which we cannot solve. If 'to the thoughtful mind that walks with Him, He half reveals His face,'[2] He also 'hides Himself most wonderfully.'[3] 'The secret things belong unto the LORD ; but the things which are

[1] Hos. 12⁴.        [2] Newman.        [3] Faber.

revealed belong unto us.'[1] Every spiritual experience is supernatural, and when divine facts have to be expressed in human
language, the instrument is not always adequate. One of the
Psalmists, for instance, says, 'Thou hast beset me behind and
before, and laid Thine hand upon me,' and adds, ' Such knowledge
is too wonderful for me ; it is too high, I cannot attain unto it.'[2]
But this much is certain—that Jacob's experience was not something unparalleled, and that many a man who tries to give expression to the deepest facts in his life has to use the language of
this narrative. The age of spiritual miracles never passes. Every
night God is changing some Jacob into an Israel. ' I have no
expectation that any man will read history aright, who thinks
that what was done in a remote age, by men whose names have
resounded far, has any deeper sense than what he is doing
to-day.'[3]

WRESTLING.—Till that night Jacob imagined that his an-
tagonist was Esau. On the previous day his prayer was :
'Deliver me from the hand of my brother, from the hand of
Esau : for I fear him, lest he come and smite me, the mother with
the children' ($32^{11}$). Now he forgets Esau, forgets mother and
children, loses all sense of personal danger at the hands of men,
and feels himself in the grasp of a superhuman Power, who
wrings from him the confession that he is a mean Trickster, and
lays him, quivering, convulsed, prostrate, at His feet. Jacob,
the most dogged, persistent, self-reliant of men, feels his strength
shrivel like a leaf at the touch of fire. And yet at this moment he
realises that God is not mercilessly, but mercifully, severe ; and
just when his faith in himself is extinguished, a new faith in God
suddenly shines forth inextinguishable. It dawns upon him that
the blessing which he has long sought will now be granted to him ;
and, with a new use of his old tenacity and strength of character,
he clings to God and claims His love ; and it is not refused.
Smitten and subdued, weeping and making supplication,[4]

[1] Deut. $29^{29}$.    [2] Ps. $139^{5, 6}$.    [3] Emerson.    [4] Hos. $12^4$.

'importunate in self-despair,' he obtains all that he asks—not as a supplanter but as a suppliant, not as Jacob but as Israel.

ISRAEL.—Among the Hebrews a new name was often given a man to indicate a change in his character. It marked a complete break with the past and the beginning of a new life. The name 'Israel' is an instance. In the morning after his night of wrestling, Jacob enters upon a higher life. 'The struggle perfects his character';[1] at least it tends in that direction. He has had power with God, and will prevail against men (v.[28] margin). The man of crafty and crooked dealing will now obtain the name and fame of a hero of faith. He is another man, humbled under the mighty hand of God ; another man, victorious and princely by his faith in God. He has become a partaker of the divine nature. Therefore he hears the divine word : 'Thy name shall no more be called Jacob, but Israel' (v.[28]). And what was true of this one man was to be true of a nation. 'It is the real spirit of Israel which is here glorified and set before the people as in a mirror.'[1] Israel's characteristics were not to be wealth and splendour, learning and genius, valour and enterprise. Athens became 'the mother of arts and eloquence,'[2] and it was 'thine, O Rome, to rule.'[3] But Israel had the highest, princeliest gift of all—power with God through faith and prayer. Weak and helpless, Israel clung to God, would not let Him go, and was blessed.

MYSTERY.—Jacob begged that he might know his Benefactor's name, but it was not conceded to him. 'Wherefore is it,' came the answer, 'that thou dost ask after my name?' Another Hebrew asked the same question, 'What is Thy name, that when Thy words come to pass we may do Thee honour?' and received almost the same answer, 'Wherefore askest thou after my name, seeing it is wonderful!'[4] God wraps Himself in mystery. He partly reveals and partly conceals Himself. His

[1] Dillmann.    [2] Milton.    [3] Virgil    [4] Judg. 13[17. 18].

purpose is to keep man, not in ignorance, but in lowly reverence.
Wonder is an element of worship. God is not angry with man
for his reverent curiosity ; He rather stimulates it to the utmost ;
but there are limits which He will not let it overstep. He says,
'Thus far shalt thou come, and no farther.' We have no
line with which to measure the Infinite. 'Who can by searching
find out God? who can find out the Almighty unto perfection?'

> No answer came back, not a word,
> To the patriarch there by the ford ;
> No answer has come through the ages
> To the poets, the saints, and the sages,
> Who have sought in the secrets of science
> The name and the nature of God
> But the answer that was and shall be,
> " My name! Nay, what is that to thee?"[1]

Yet God does reveal Himself. He is not the unknown and
unknowable. His revelations come to the heart and the
conscience ; they come in the experiences of life ; and they
come really rather than verbally. When God has wrestled
with Jacob and blessed him, Jacob knows God, although
His name is withheld. He knows His power and His grace ;
knows Him as the source of blessing ; knows how wonderful
and adorable He is. For the rest, mystery does not repel
men from God, it attracts them to Him ; and in view of the
infallible assurances of the soul we may reverently say even
of God, 'What's in a name?' If the Hebrews could do nothing
better, they could at least now call upon the 'God of Jacob.'
They could encourage one another by saying, 'The Name of the
God of Jacob defend thee.'[2] The contents of that designation,
the experiences which it recalled, were full of inspiration. 'Therefore, to whom turn I but to Thee, the ineffable Name?'[3]

DAWN.—Jacob's vigil at the Jabbok was a solemn night-scene.
But 'the sun rose upon him as he passed over Penuel' (v.[31]). It

[1] John Hay's *Israel.*   [2] Ps. 20[1].   [3] Browning.

was now full bright day within and without.'[1] 'Everything
assumed a smiling aspect.'[2] Touches like this are not put
into the picture by a happy chance. The narrator is an inspired
man of the order of Bunyan and Blake, who perceives the
deeper meaning of physical facts. When one has been toiling
upward through the night into the fellowship and favour of God,
the morning light has a radiance which it never had before.
There is an added splendour which comes from the soul that is
born to a new life. Then 'a pleasant thing it is for the eyes to
behold the sun.' Weeping endureth for a night ; but joy cometh
in the morning. The day dawns, and the shadows flee away. It
is recorded of Luther that the night before the most trying day
in his troubled life was 'a time of terrible depression, conflict,
despair, and prayer. Before the day broke the victory had been
won, and he felt in a great calm.'[3] 'O send out Thy light and
Thy truth : let them lead me. Why art thou cast down, O my
soul ? and why art thou disquieted within me ? hope thou in
God : for I shall yet praise Him, who is the health of my
countenance, and my God.'[4]

RECONCILIATION.—Jacob now goes to meet his brother without fear. The event shows, in truth, that there was small cause for
alarm. Esau's last uttered words, which hastened Jacob's flight
from Canaan, were fearful enough : 'The days of mourning for
my father are at hand ; then will I slay my brother Jacob' (27[41]).
But the fratricidal impulse was only momentary. While Jacob
remembered the dark threat, Esau himself forgot it. His
sudden blaze of anger, instead of smouldering down into a lifelong hatred, quite died out ; and on Jacob's return to Canaan,
'Esau ran to meet him, and embraced him, and fell upon his
neck, and kissed him : and they wept' (33[4]). Esau might be
reckless and impulsive, but he was not malevolent ; he was
quicker to forgive than to blame ; and when his heart was
touched, the strong man wept like a woman. The veil of

[1] Delitzsch.    [2] Dillmann    [3] Lindsay's *Luther*.    [4] Ps. 43[3, 5].

oblivion drops on a lifetime, leaving only the memory of home and mother-love and childhood. The springs of natural affection are perennial, time works its miracle of healing, and brothers mingle their tears of love. Genesis is a book of reconciliations. Families are for a time estranged, and one brother would not be sorry to see another dead. But absence makes the heart grow fonder, and evening brings all home.

ENOUGH.—It is remarkable that Esau speaks as one of those rarely fortunate men who can say, 'I have enough' ($33^9$), and Jacob as another (v.$^{11}$). Esau has to all appearance become the greater of the two. Surrounded by his four hundred men—'the folk that are with me,' as he says in his lordly style—he is a very striking figure. The hunter of stags has become a captain of soldiers. He has the physical prowess which commands the admiration of strong men. He is honoured as a mighty chieftain. He receives Jacob and his family almost like a king holding a court. Jacob 'bowed himself to the ground seven times. . . . Then the handmaids came near, they and their children, and they bowed themselves. And Leah and her children came near, and bowed themselves ; and after came Joseph near and Rachel, and they bowed themselves' (vv.$^{3. \ 6. \ 7}$). Jacob calls Esau 'my lord,' and himself 'thy servant.' Esau has obtained all that he ever wished—wives and children, wealth and honour and power. He has come into his kingdom ; he has realised his ideal ; what grudge can he bear against any man? Envy on his part is out of the question. In losing the birthright, what has he lost? A poet has tried to answer this question, and comes near the mark when he represents him as saying of his brother :

> 'He won the birthright—little won !
> He won, and yet I cannot see
> That what he won was loss to me.
> I am a prince, an army mine ;
> A kingdom grows around my sword ;
> The Hivites flee before my face ;
> I have my pleasure in the chase,

> Now hunting men, now hunting beasts . . .
> I live for what these eyes can see :
> This happy earth's enough for me!'

Jacob also says, 'I have enough' (v.[11]), but with a difference.
Words have shades of meaning which they derive from the men
who use them. The context often throws light on the text. Esau
says simply, 'I have enough ; my brother, let that thou hast
be thine.' Jacob says, 'Take, I pray thee, my gift ; because God
hath dealt graciously with me, and because I have enough.' The
one has enough, the other has enough by the grace of God. Some
may regard the *Dei gratiâ* as an empty formality. But to others
it is the matter of supreme importance. They count it as natural
to acknowledge an obligation to God as a debt to man. They
can never say, 'This happy earth's enough.' Nothing satisfies
them but the conviction that life itself and all the blessings of life
are the bountiful gifts of a gracious God. Lord Bacon's saying,
'Prosperity is the blessing of the Old Testament,' needs to be
qualified. Prosperity with the favour of God is the blessing of
the Old Testament. There are not a few noble instances in
which men declare with evident sincerity that the grace of God
without prosperity is enough for them. The feeling would be
expressed by the Welsh proverb, 'Without God, without anything ; with God, and enough.' Esau, with all his wealth, is not
a typical Old Testament saint. He founded a nation whose
portion was in this world, and it vanished. Jacob founded a nation
which said, 'The LORD is my portion,' and it lives for ever.

UNITY.—Esau and Jacob are now good friends, yet they do
not remain long in each other's company. The narrative
indicates with fine literary skill and quiet humour the diversity
of their temperaments. Jacob is, of course, too slow for
Esau. The elder brother soon becomes restless ; he hears the
call of the wild ; he wants to be up and scour the desert with
'the folk' who are with him. Mount Seir beckons him, the
scene of all the pursuits and pleasures that give zest to life.
If Jacob will come and visit him there, a royal welcome will

be accorded him ; and no better time than now. Esau will go
on ahead and make the pace, and let Jacob follow as fast
as he can (v.¹²). The well-meaning proposal is worthy of the
flying desert chieftain. But it takes Jacob's breath away. For,
happily or unhappily, he is no wild huntsman, and never drove
furiously in his life. It has ever been his wont to lead on softly.
His only pace is 'the pace of the cattle' and 'the pace of the
children.' The little ones are tender ; the flocks and kine have
sucklings ; and if they are overdriven for a day they must die.
Esau had not thought of that, and now it touches his kind heart
to think of the lambs and little ones. They are not safe ; Jacob
needs a bodyguard ; let him accept some of Esau's men—grand
fellows, who will keep them from all danger. But Jacob assures
him it is not necessary, while in his heart there is nothing he dreads
so much as those wild Idumeans. 'So Esau returned that day on
his way to Seir' (v.¹⁶). The brothers parted in peace, and it was
best so. The ties of nature are strong, and blood is proverbially
thicker than water ; but nature needs to be reinforced by something higher, if her work is to be lasting. It is only when brothers
see eye to eye on the great matters of faith, that their differences
of taste and temperament sink into insignificance. Like the radii
of a circle approaching a common centre, the nearer men come
to God the nearer they come to one another.


## PURITY
### Genesis 33:18-34:31

> ' Bear a lily in thy hand ;
> Gates of brass cannot withstand
> One touch of that magic wand.'—LONGFELLOW.

PEACE.—'Jacob came in peace to the city of Shechem,
which is in the land of Canaan' (33¹⁸). For the touch of ' peace'
we are indebted to the Revised Version. Jacob's days of
wrangling and strife, of fighting for his own hand and thwarting

the schemes of other men, are ended. At Gilead he has made a covenant of peace with Laban. At Peniel he has entered into the deep peace of God, and been reconciled to his brother. He next finds the people of Canaan peacefully disposed, and encamps among them in the quiet green valley of Shechem. Here he may at length taste the repose of a settled life. Having bought a 'parcel of ground'—a small estate—he builds an altar (vv.[19, 20]), and digs a well, destined to be one of the most sacred spots on earth, and to be known to the end of time as Jacob's Well. He may now abandon himself to the luxury of perfect rest. In Eastern lands, where strife is so common, peace is the all-inclusive blessing. To this day, when two people meet, the common salutation is, 'Peace be unto thee,' and the reponse, 'Unto thee be peace.' But peace may be purchased at too great a price. There is such a thing as 'a pestilent peace.' The rest which Jacob has found in the sweet vale of Shechem is fraught from the outset with elements of danger for his family. He encamps before the city (v.[18]). It is a heathen city, and the situation will not help his children to live the life of faith to which they are committed. The environment will not make it difficult for them to do evil and easy to do well. There is what is called good society at Shechem ; the palace sets an example of gaiety which is readily copied ; and the one thing believed to be worth living for under the shadows of Ebal and Gerizim is the pleasure of the senses. It is the pagan ideal all the world over. The 'best' society, even the society of princes, if it is not purged by the breath of God, is foul and corrupt society, in which peace is always treacherous, and mirth often ends in tragedy.

GIRLHOOD.—Jacob had an only daughter called Dinah. She was an innocent child when she came with her mother Leah from Haran to Canaan. The years of childhood quickly passed, and she was

> 'Standing with reluctant feet
> Where the brook and river meet,
> Womanhood and girlhood sweet,'

She might have been the guardian angel of her strong rough brothers, who loved her with a love that was quick to resent and strong to avenge even the shadow of an injury done to her. The might-have-beens of life are the saddest things in the world. Dinah had no talisman of faith or reverence or holy love powerful enough to save her from temptation, while there was something in her that seemed to court it. Eager and imaginative, thirsting for adventures, wistful to learn what raptures the world might have in store for her, 'she went out to see the daughters of the land,' who spent their butterfly life in flitting from pleasure to pleasure in those gardens of luxury. She was fascinated by the strange life to which she was introduced. New as it was, and liker a dream than a reality, she was at home in it. She found herself presented to a young prince, 'honoured above all the house of his father.' Something wild and lawless in her rose up to meet something wild and lawless in him. She listened to his wicked words, and fell. Honour, character, and peace gone, her sin must be expiated in a welter of blood. 'I adjure you,' cries a great lyric poet, 'I adjure you, O ye daughters of Jerusalem, that ye stir not up nor awaken love until he please.'[1] A moth fluttering round a flame, heedless of the singeing of its wings, darts feverishly into the heart of the fire, and quivers a little ere it dies. Why does its suicide so thrill our nerve of pity? Because there are so many human moths.

PURITY.—The word 'defiled,' which is thrice used in this narrative—a daughter, a sister defiled (vv.[5, 13, 27])—means desecrated. It is the same word which in a much later time made the beginning of the seventy-ninth Psalm so hard for a Hebrew to sing : 'O God, the heathen have entered Thy inheritance ; Thy holy temple have they defiled.' The dishonour of womanhood and the desecration of the Holy of Holies are regarded with the same feelings, and described by the same word. Which is the greater

[1] Song of Songs 2[7] 3[5] 8[4]

wrong?  We instinctively feel that a temple should always be
holy, and that God is somehow dishonoured when it is profaned,
though we know that the sacredness which we impute to it is no
more than a devout sentiment in our own minds, and that no
intrinsic sacredness can attach to stone walls.  But the human
body is really holy ; the breath which animates it is divine ;
every man and woman is a living temple of God.  In all ages
people have been using soft words for offences against the divine
laws of purity, and there are a score of euphemisms which need
not be set down here.  But the Book which makes shameful
things appear shameful, calling them by names which cannot be
uttered without a blush, is the best guardian of the honour and
peace of the home and the nation.

SILENCE.—When Jacob heard of his daughter's dishonour,
'he held his peace' (v.⁵).  Hamor, the prince's father, came to
commune with him (v.⁶), but Jacob was silent.  His sons came
home, and Hamor communed with them, and became quite
garrulous (vv.⁸⁻¹⁰) ; but Jacob was silent.  The prince came to
plead his own cause, and talked and talked (vv.¹¹· ¹²), 'and the
sons of Jacob answered Shechem and Hamor his father,' but
Jacob was silent.  His power of speech and action was gone.
His pride was humbled in the dust.  A flesh wound makes a
man cry aloud, but a vital wound stuns or paralyses him.  When
a man's eyes are dry and his lips unmoved, his heart may be
breaking.  There is no wrecker of the peace of homes like a gay
voluptuary.  And in this world there is a 'fatal doom by which
every crime is made to be the agony of many innocent persons as
well as of the single guilty one.'[1]

VIRTUE.—'The sons of Jacob were grieved, and they were
very wroth,' because Shechem the son of Hamor 'had wrought
folly in Israel, which thing ought not to be done' (v.⁷).  'Folly
in Israel' was not so much an intellectual term, denoting want

[1] Hawthorne.

of understanding, as a moral term, denoting lack of conscience. It was one of those proverbial expressions which reflected the proud moral self-consciousness of the Hebrew nation. Folly in Israel was the most reprehensible kind of folly, because it was the desecration of an ideal. Folly in Egypt, Moab, or Tyre might be comparatively venial, the peoples in those lands being lesser breeds without the law. 'Ought' has a meaning for every nation, but folly in Israel was guilt of the deepest dye, because sin is dark in proportion to the glory of the religion which it violates. The strongest light casts the deepest shadow. Israel should be before every people in the world for the honour and virtue of its men, the purity and modesty of its women. The shameless person who committed folly in Israel was a profligate who defiled what was sacred to the Lord.

NUPTIALS.—Hamor came to Jacob to ask the hand of Dinah for his son. He came in a very complacent mood, not as an offender anxious to make atonement, but as a king willing to condescend and be gracious. He was prepared to back up his son's suit with a proposal which was likely to commend it—a complex scheme of intemarriages, settlements, gifts of land, and co-operation in trade (vv.[9, 10]). Let Hebrew and Canaanite draw together and forget their little differences. What better opportunity is likely to occur than the present for a social and political union, which will be a real union of hearts. This quiet valley will soon be the home of a federated and happy people. Love has come to make them one. Shechem and Dinah are the representatives of two races. The young people have played their part better than they know. Their parents may congratulate themselves, and their tribes rejoice.—Then the prince himself comes on the scene. He leaves politics to his father. At present he has no mind for such things. Dinah is in the matrimonial market, and he wishes to buy her. 'What ye shall say to me I will give. Ask me never so much dowry and gift, and I will give according as ye shall say to me: but give me the damsel to be my wife' (vv.[11, 12]). The bribes and offers may be princely, but we see that all the sacredness has gone out of life. God's name is not found in this chapter (34), and how flat and stale everything becomes without Him ! Other Hebrew brides might have the joyous consciousness that God had ordered their steps and was smiling upon their nuptials ; but no one could imagine that He had any hand in Dinah's marriage, which, if it should ever take place, could only be of the earth, earthy.

LOVE.—But Dinah was never to be a prince's bride. Her brothers were too fiercely indignant to allow it. They were bent on taking a terrible revenge upon her lover. No doubt indignation against what is base and sinful is, in itself, a perfectly natural feeling. 'Anger is a sharp sword put into our hand by Nature herself ; and she does not intend that that sharp sword should rust in its scabbard'[1] 'In the silent grief of Jacob, the father, and the dark and fierce anger of his sons, we can observe the external securities which God has placed around the honour and innocence of woman.'[2] 'The thief—the mean, sneaking, pilfering thief—is a man of honour compared with him who steals a woman's virtue, and robs a household of its peace.'[3] But righteous indignation passes all too easily into unrighteous, and when men take law and justice into their own hands, and become both judges and executioners, the results are terrible. Revenge is at the best only 'a wild kind of justice,' and very easily becomes a sheer and barbarous injustice. The vendetta knows no distinction between the guilty and the innocent. How many wars have been waged, how many massacres have been perpetrated, to avenge the injury done to some frail woman ! It was a Hebrew girl's error that made blood to flow like water in the streets of Shechem. It was regarding one like her, in another land, that the question was asked :

> 'Was this the face that launched a thousand ships,
> And burned the topless towers of Ilium?'[4]

---

[1] Butler.    [2] Chalmers.    [3] Guthrie.    [4] Marlowe.

What do these and a thousand other instances teach us but that, as love is the greatest power in the world for good when it is pure and holy, so it is the greatest power for evil when it is impure and unholy? To violate its laws, to insult its spirit, is fatal, for 'the flashes thereof are flashes of fire, a very flame of the LORD.'

INFLUENCE.—The story of the foul treachery of Jacob's sons— their ostensible friendliness, their professed religious scruples, their proselytising zeal, all hiding a dastardly conspiracy—is one of the darkest tales in the Bible. Jacob speaks in the name of outraged humanity when he expresses to the ringleaders his horror of their crime. 'Ye have troubled me, and made me to stink among the inhabitants of the land' (v.[30]). If one thing on earth is more odious than another, it is villainy masked by hypocrisy. Beautiful flowers rank with poison, or 'whited sepulchres full of dead men's bones,' are what it suggests. Jacob saw to his dismay that a fatal misunderstanding would be created among the people of the land, which he would be powerless to remove. The Shechemites would say, 'Behold the man who builds altars and offers sacrifices to the LORD ; his hands are red with our best blood ; our curse be upon him and his altars !' A natural enough thing to say ; yet, in truth, it is not religion, but the lack of religion, that is the root of all earthly evils. When sin is committed under the cloak of religion, the offence is indeed 'rank, and smells to heaven.' But true religion is in its spirit fragrant as a June night, sweet as the breath of a dew-washed garden. 'Awake, O north wind, and come thou south ; blow upon my garden, that the spices thereof may flow out.'

## RESTORATION
### Genesis 35

' The errors cancelled, the dark shadows banished
In the glad light of a new world begun.'—G. MATHESON.

AWAKENING.—The thirty-fourth chapter of Genesis is God-less, the thirty-fifth is full of God. The former describes the Shechem life of the Hebrews, the latter their Bethel life. The contrast between a believer's and an unbeliever's life is scarcely more marked than the contrast between a half-hearted and a whole-hearted believer's life. There was a family altar even at Shechem (33²⁰), and nothing makes so surely for whatsoever things are pure and lovely as the worship of God. But the altar at Shechem somehow lost its influence over the worshippers, its power to restrain them from evil, to constrain them to goodness, to uplift and hallow their lives. The altar itself was profaned by their connivance at 'strange gods' (v.²), by the proximity of heathenism, by the incursions of worldliness. Foul things were done around it which it was powerless to prevent. The altar lost its glory and its terror, and young lives which needed the supernatural to subdue and tame them were consequently allowed to run wild. No children are further from God than those of half-hearted believers. On the surface everything seemed to be right enough in the vale of Shechem, but under the surface everything was going far wrong. The crisis had to come. One day that hollow Shechem life was shaken as by an earthquake. Dinah's fall was followed by her brothers' abominable crime, and in the shock of that calamity Jacob heard the voice of God.

RESTORATION. — This voice, sounding in the depths of the man's soul, comes with a clear and startling call, bidding him go back to Bethel and dwell there (v.¹). He no sooner realises the misery of the present than he remembers a happier past. His mind painfully contrasts the Then and the Now, the There and the Here. The brighter scenes which rush into his memory beget in him a bitter shame and an ardent longing. Bethel with its pure wind-swept spaces; Bethel with its awful divine presences; Bethel, the house of God and the gate of heaven; Bethel, to which his heart so wistfully turned in exile; Bethel, where divine promises were given which have all been kept; Bethel, where human vows were made which are still unpaid,—that is now the home of his soul. It is a full generation since he was there, but the long years have not unwoven the mystic ties which bind him to the sacred place. 'Back to Bethel,' 'Up to the House of God' become the watchwords which he gives his household (v.[1]). Realising at length how far he has declined, what can he do but acknowledge his error, turn backwards, toil upwards, and strive to recover his lost ideal? It may be hard to start afresh and struggle back into the right way, but it must be done though it should cost blood and tears. And it can be done by God's grace, for He pardons the penitent and gives them second chances. 'He restoreth my soul: He leadeth me in the paths of righteousness for His own name's sake.'

ICONOCLASM. — Jacob prepared himself and his family for Bethel by a grand act of purification. First he commanded them to put away the strange gods that were among them (v.[2]). He had too long tolerated, and they had too long loved, what God hated. They must not go into God's presence with unclean and divided hearts. Hebrew history, even at its beginning, is a record of the wars of the LORD against idolatry. He sought whole-hearted, not half-hearted, worshippers; He could not but be jealous of the reverence, love, and obedience of His people. It was all along imperative on those who wished to serve Him to put away their 'no-gods,' to break them in pieces or grind them to powder, to bury them, or burn them, or cast them to the moles and bats. Ear-rings were also voluntarily given up (v.[4]).

These were not mere ornaments, but charms or amulets. They were used to woo good fortune and ward off evil influences. They were regarded as foolish people still regard horse-shoes. Their use always indicated a lack of faith in God, whose providence alone orders human lives. As they fostered wild delusions in the brain, the best thing that could be done with them was to bury them deep out of sight. Whenever people return to God with contrite hearts, whenever there is the breath of a new spiritual life among them, all morally wrong practices are discarded as naturally as old clinging leaves fall at the first touch of the vital sap of spring.

PURITY.—The Hebrews were also commanded to prepare for Bethel by purifying themselves and changing their raiment (v.[2]). The God into whose presence they were going was a God of purity, who required that His worshippers should be pure. They must not profane His sanctuary by any conscious defilement either of the flesh or spirit. 'Who shall ascend into the hill of the LORD? And who shall stand in His holy place? He that hath clean hands and a pure heart.'[1] Cleanliness was a part of godliness. The craving for nearness to God was accompanied by the instinctive feeling that not a shadow of impurity should stain the worshipper who approached the pure and awful Presence. Faith in God was the highest sanction for both æsthetic and moral purity. To worship the LORD in the beauty of holiness was to come before Him not merely in linen garments of snowy white, but with a spirit that harmonised with His holiness. 'The earnestness with which Old Testament saints conceived of the holiness and majesty of Israel's God, and of man's natural unworthiness, is indicated by the various kinds of washings and purifications, which were very numerous, and were beyond a doubt in frequent use even in ancient Israel. . . . In every case the purpose was to bring into accord the majesty of God and the consecration of those who are His people.'[2]

[1] Ps. 24[3, 4].                [2] Schultz.

OBEDIENCE.—Nothing could be more radical than the moral reformation which Jacob requires his household to carry through ; yet it is effected with surprising readiness and ease. Whatever he asks is given, whatever he commands is done (v.⁴). His power and authority are now as apparent as his previous weakness and helplessness. When he spoke to his sons in his own name, they showed him very scant respect (34³¹) ; but when he speaks to them in the name of God, they freely and heartily follow him in everything. The secret of authority and obedience becomes evident. When a father, having heard the voice of God speaking to himself, feels that he is under obligation to God, and is not afraid to assert his will, his sons and daughters realise with an instinctive awe that he has the right to require of them whatever he thinks good, and that their obedience to him will be their own salvation. The parent who knows that he has a holy call, not to make laws for his household, but to see that God's eternal laws are respected, will rarely fail to receive an implicit obedience and a reverential love. It is when a father recedes from his position as God's delegate, and his commands are seen to be merely his own caprices, that he quickly and naturally becomes an object of contempt even to his own children.

SACRIFICE.—The erection of a new altar on holier ground was at this time the great thought which occupied Jacob's mind. He heard a divine voice calling him to go up and make an altar at Bethel (v.¹). He told his household of his purpose to make an altar at Bethel (v.³). And as soon as he came to Bethel with all the people that were with him, 'he built there an altar' (v.⁷). Nothing is said in Genesis about the theory or meaning of altars and sacrifices ; but the fact that altars were erected and sacrifices offered is everywhere made prominent. The patriarchs built no houses for themselves ; but wherever they pitched their moving tents they reared an altar to God. Four of Abraham's are mentioned, those at Shechem, Bethel, Hebron, and Moriah ;

one of Isaac's, at Beersheba; and two of Jacob's, at Shechem and Bethel. On these altars they offered their sacrifices; with the cloud of incense-smoke their thoughts and desires rose to God; and they trusted that He would accept their offerings, grant their petitions, and pardon their sins. We no longer offer sacrifices of that kind to God; but we have not outgrown, and never can outgrow, the feelings which prompted them. To the end of time the awakened conscience of man will always gravitate towards atonement of some kind as its one possible rest.

FIDELITY. — Three deaths occurred after Jacob's departure from Shechem. Deborah died at Bethel (v.⁸). She was the last link with a distant past. She was Rebekah's nurse (v.⁸); she attended Rebekah's wedding (24⁵⁹); and she lived to see Rebekah's children's children. She was honoured while she lived, and tears were shed for her when she died. The tree under which she was buried was called, in after times, Allonbakuth, the Oak of Weeping. Deborah is the faithful Hebrew maid-servant in Genesis, as Eleazar is the faithful man-servant. Instances of warm and lifelong sympathy between mistress and handmaid, as between master and servant, were of common occurrence in Hebrew homes. Among other ancient races it was extremely difficult, indeed hardly possible, to bridge over the gulf between the free and the servile classes. 'There is no fact more prominent in the Roman writers than the profound contempt with which they regarded slaves, not so much on account of their position, as on account of the character which that position had formed.'[1] But among the Hebrews the gulf was neither so wide nor so deep. There was no difference of colour to emphasise the class-distinction, and the religion of Israel both raised the status and refined the character of slaves. Because there were mistresses like Rebekah, there were maids like Deborah. The qualities which can expand and flourish in the servile condition—humility, obedience, gentleness, patience—won for many Hebrew servants

[1] Lecky.

esteem and affection in their lifetime, deep regret and fond remembrance when they were gone.

LOVE.—On the way from Bethel to Ephrath—*i.e.* Bethlehem—
Jacob suffered a far sorer loss. Rachel, the beloved of his heart,
was taken from him. The birth of her second son brought her
short life to an end. It is the first recorded instance of death in
childbirth. The writer of the narrative has the secret of that
naked simplicity of style in which alone the tale of an agony
too deep for passion, or tears, or earthly remedy can be told.
There are only five verses, and they contain but a bare record
of facts; yet this is 'one of the most beautifully touching
passages in sacred writ.'[1] Jacob's love for Rachel began with
tears of joy at the well of Haran. When she is so suddenly
snatched from him by the hand of death, the springs of his
emotion seem to be dried up. We do not read that he wept
for her as Abraham wept for Sarah (23²). His sorrow was too
deep for tears. His wound never healed. Long after, when he
was lying, far from his native land, in his gilded Egyptian
chamber, awaiting his own end, he recalled that journey to
Ephrath,—the halt by the way, the agonised suspense, the last
words, the awful stillness,—and with touching simplicity he said,
'She died to my sorrow.'[2] Rachel was not faultless, but he
remembered how she made the years pass like so many days,
and to him she was always the dearest and best of women.
She was Joseph's mother, and during the ten years in which
she had no other child she lavished all her love on him; he
learned nothing but good from her, and grew up to be one
of the best men the world has seen. This fragile, beautiful,
shortlived woman became to the Hebrews the type of suffering
motherhood—their *mater dolorosa*, mother of sorrows. Life is a
web of thin-spun texture, easily rent. Death sometimes takes
the mother from the child, sometimes the child from the mother.
In either case it is the mother who suffers. 'Rachel weeping for

---

[1] T. Chalmers.                    [2] Gen. 48⁷ R.V. m.

her children' became a proverb in Israel.   Jeremiah, most tender-hearted of prophets, heard her voice long after in Ramah,[1] as if her spirit still haunted the place ; and when the birth of Jesus was followed by the massacre of the innocents at Bethlehem, it was Rachel's cry of anguish that was once more heard on the hills of Ephrath.[2]   The pillar of Rachel's grave, set up by Jacob (v.[20]), became the monument of suffering motherhood, to which many another pilgrim, from whom God had taken away the desire of his eyes, turned aside to meditate on an irremediable sorrow with an unchangeable love.

> ' Deep as first love, and wild with all regret,
>   O death in life, the days that are no more.'

Fain would one know what the literal fact of death really meant to these Hebrews.   Was it simply the fading of beauty into ashes, of strength into dust ?   We are told here that it was a 'departure' (v.[18]).   Rachael's death was her passing.   At the stoppage of the fluttering pulse, and the glazing of the eye, the spirit took its flight somewhither.   'There is no death ; what seems so was transition.'   All else remained mystery, until at length a stronger faith asserted that death was a swift passing into the presence of God and the vision of His face.[3]

CONSOLATION.—Rachel had thought of a happy name for her child, as every mother does, before it was born.   But no one knows that name.   It was never spoken.   Another name took its place.   'Call him Benoni,' the dying mother said, almost with her last breath.   Benoni means 'son of my sorrow.'   It quivers with the infinite heart-ache of this mother of sorrows.   'Give me children, or else I die,' was her prayer (30[1]).   Her prayer was answered—and she died.   Benoni was a tenderly pathetic word, but to Jacob it was an impossible name for his child.   It would have cut him too near the quick every time he used it. He makes a brave effort to escape his grief.   What he sees is a

[1] Jer. 31[15].        [2] Matt. 2[18].        [3] Job 19[26, 27], Ps. 16[11] 49[15].

strong babe who has just come from the hand of God, a bringer
of joy who will not let others weep.

> 'Sorrow's self before thy smile
> Smiles and softens.'

He resolves that his child shall have a happy name after all to
go through the world with. He calls him Benjamin, 'son of my
right hand.' His people will have reason to thank him for that
name. No doubt there is an irony in human fate, but we need
not suppose that it is a bitter irony. This life which God has
given us is wonderfully sweet at the core. The child who began
his career by killing his mother, and grew up to be the 'ravening
wolf' of Jacob's family (49²⁷), became the ancestor of such splendid
types of manhood as King Saul and Saul of Tarsus.

REVERENCE.—Jacob went from Bethlehem to Mamre, where
his father was still living. Isaac had long before prepared himself for his end, but his placid temperament prolonged the
peaceful evening of his life, and he saw his son's sons ere he
died. 'One is pleased,' says one of the best writers on Genesis,
'to meet once more with good, mild, venerable Isaac. There
is no scripture character whom I love more to dwell upon,
or in whom I find more of that gentleness and repose in the
contemplation of which there is something inexpressibly sooth-
ing and delightful.'[1] 'Old and full of days,' Isaac was at
length 'gathered unto his people' in the unseen world, and
his two sons, brought together once more by the call of death,
laid his body in the field of Machpelah, beside the ashes
of his father and mother. Jacob used to speak of enjoying
the protection of 'the Fear of Isaac' (31⁴²), and he made a
covenant in the name of 'the Fear of his father Isaac' (31⁵³).
The archaic word translated 'Fear,' and thus applied to God,
indicates the profound reverence which was habitual to Isaac's
mind. His life was one of quiet and almost unbroken prosperity,

[1] Chalmers.

but his message to after ages might have been expressed in the words, 'The LORD of hosts, let Him be your Fear, and let Him be your Dread.'[1]   It was, of course, no slavish fear of God that he cherished.   It was that reverential awe, that sense of the seriousness of living daily in the presence of God, which really increases man's happiness a hundredfold by guarding him from everything hurtful and unholy.

> 'But present still, though now unseen,
>   When brightly shines the prosperous day,
> Be thoughts of Thee a cloudy screen
>   To temper the deceitful ray.'[2]

## DREAMS
### Genesis 37

> ' Dreamer devout, by vision led
> Beyond our guess or reach.'—KIPLING.

IDEALS.—' In order that the ideals of a race should acquire their full force, it is necessary that they should be represented or illustrated in some great personalities who by the splendour and beauty of their careers could fascinate the imagination of men.'[3]   Joseph is, by common consent, regarded as the fine flower of the ancient Hebrew race and religion.   His life-story, told with a natural grace that more than matches perfect art, was a precious heritage of the Hebrew people.   Long ere it was committed to writing, it must have done noble service as a tradition, firing the imaginations, touching the hearts, and bracing the wills of many generations of thoughtful and generous young men.   Only a great nation could create or cherish such an ideal, at once so princely and so popular.   The hero's chequered career throws him into an immense variety of situations, which give

[1] Is. 8¹³.        [2] Scott.        [3] Lecky.

free play to all his gifts and graces. Dreams and realities, dangers and deliverances, temptations and triumphs, toils and successes, undeserved ignominy and merited glory, are his portion. He owes much to nature. His physical charm is described in exactly the same words as his mother's;[1] and he is dowered with talents which make him a natural leader of men. But he derives still more of his power from his faith. It is the fear of the LORD that keeps his head steady and his heart sound amid all the trials of youth, the labours of manhood, the fascinations of worldly rank and power. Though his story has interwoven with it the airy and unsubstantial threads of dreams, its pattern is nothing but the common stuff of everyday life. As a tale of strong unwavering faith it fulfils its purpose by teaching us how our own lives may be transfigured by being lived in the light of God's countenance.

TRUTH.—Is the first thing that is told about Joseph to his credit or discredit? When he was seventeen years of age he was in the fields watching his father's flock with his half-brothers, Dan and Naphtali, Gad and Asher, and he 'brought an evil report of them to their father' (37[2]). He incurred the odium of being a tale-bearer. Because his brothers regarded him in that light, must we, too, so regard him? If a boy mischievously schemes to bring his comrades into disgrace, if he spies out their actions with the intention of peaching upon them, if he takes pleasure in lowering them in the eyes of a superior, he is of course a sneak, and deserves to be heartily detested. Malice is the meanest motive that can actuate any mind. 'The words of a tale-bearer are (to himself) dainty morsels,'[2] but the many ugly names — whisperer, backbiter, detractor — with which a meddlesome informer is branded show how offensive his conduct is to others. 'Thou shalt not go up and down as a tale-bearer among thy people.'[3] But must we not in justice regard Joseph

---

[1] Gen. 29[17] 39[6] 'beautiful' and 'comely' translating the same word
[2] Prov. 18[8].                                    [3] Lev. 19[16].

in another light? His conscience is tender and his heart pure; and when he is out all day with his brothers in the fields, he is startled and shocked at their abominable conduct. He hears them speak wicked words, and he learns how vile boys can be. They know very well that they are utterly wrong, and they demand of him that secrecy which is always congenial to vice. They scorn his scruples, his warnings, his entreaties. They threaten him with violence if he says a word about their excesses and follies to their father. If he does not hold his tongue between his teeth, they will make it the worse for him. Now, if he is to obey his conscience what is he to do? He must speak out, whatever the consequences may be. He will be a coward if he is silent. As it is rightly regarded as a crime to conceal the outbreak of a fever or a plague, so it is a sin not to do everything in one's power to stem the tide of sin. One of the headmasters of Harrow thus addresses his boys: 'You may be conscious of evil which exists in the school. You have found it out. Nobody else has found it out. You wish it were somebody else's duty, and not yours, to protest against it; but you, you are the only boy who can put it down. You shrink from speaking against it. It is a base feeling. You shrink from telling about it. It is an honourable feeling. What are you to do? My boys, speak out like a man. Say that it must not be, it shall not be; and that if it is not stopped, you will bring it to light. Never mind what happens to you. "If you perish you perish"; but the school is saved, or the house, and you have saved it.'[1]

LOVE.—We are told that 'Israel loved Joseph more than all his children' (v.[3]). He had twelve sons, and they had an equal need of his affection and an equal claim to it; but ten of them were impoverished because a favourite son received more than his share. Jacob did not love Joseph too well; that was impossible. His fault did not consist in loving one of his sons more, but

[1] Dr. Welldon.

in loving the others less. 'In the little world in which children
live there is nothing so finely perceived and so finely felt as
an injustice. It may be only small injustice that the child is
exposed to ; but the child is small and its world is small.'[1]
It was, no doubt, natural for Jacob to have a deep, fond love
for Rachel's son, and to decide to make him his heir. Nor
is it possible for a father to regard all his children with pre-
cisely the same kind of love. Some are brighter, more amiable,
more companionable than others, and give him more joy. Some
are unbelievers, and he regards them with a love of yearning
pity, with a great deep longing for their salvation. Others are
believers, and he regards them with a love of pure satisfaction
and delight. But he must never cease to hold the balance
evenly ; and if he loves one at the expense of the others the
results are inevitably evil. It is proverbial that a favourite has
no friend. Joseph's brothers saw that their father loved him
more than all the rest of them, and 'they hated him, and could
not speak peaceably to him.' Jacob did not see what harm his
partiality was doing, and made bad worse by presenting his son
with a splendid robe as a mark of distinction. This was not 'a
coat of many colours,' but a long, white, light robe of delicate and
beautiful texture, such as was worn by men of rank and wealth,
who did not require to soil themselves with manual labour. The
brothers had to wear clothes of a coarser stuff, and to be like
their work. 'Nowhere were distinctions of dress held in
higher estimation than in the ancient East ; a man's rank was
known by his dress.'[2] If this favouritism did not give a
tinge of self-consciousness to the handsome, gifted boy — we
are not told that it did—it was almost a miracle. It has been
finely said that 'there is no friendship so intimate as that
of a good father with a good child';[3] but if that intimacy
implies a forgetfulness or neglect of other natural ties, both
father and son are certain to find that nature does not
forgive.

[1] Dickens.　　　　　[2] Sayce.　　　　　[3] Dante.

DREAMS.—Joseph as a boy is a dreamer of dreams. There is, of course, something grotesque in his dreams. It is only in dreams that sheaves become animated ; only in dreams that the sun appears in company with the moon and stars ; only in dreams that a dear dead mother is seen in her old place within the family circle. And certainly many dreams must be dismissed as senseless and morbid. Yet great teachers [1] have exhorted their disciples to study their dreams on the ground that they reveal the latent tendencies of the mind. The dreams of happy childhood, bright visions of the future, wonders in the halls of fancy, projections of the soul's dim instincts and vague longings, are really prophetic. They are sent to beckon us the way we are to go. They are a divine inspiration to effort and hope. 'These hints, dropped as it were from sleep and night, let us use in broad day.' [2] It is God, the soul's Maker, who kindles those glowing hopes in it, and gives every child a dower of happy dreams. Out of some strange subconscious region of the mind they come stealing now into our sleeping, now into waking thoughts. If any youth misses them, the fault is not his Maker's. Joseph differs from other young men chiefly in cherishing his dreams ; and dreams believed in have a way of coming true. Joseph has an instinct for rule and power. A life of sweet repose and meditative calm, such as Isaac lived on the border of the wilderness, far from the noise of men, would have been no life for him. A certain high ambition is the motive force of his being, which he is powerless to resist. The cast of his mind is daring and aspiring ; he believes in his sheaf and his star ; he dreams of power and dominion. The thoughts that ferment in his youthful imagination will gradually clear themselves, and the dreamer would have the opportunity of proving himself a doer. He reminds us of Wordsworth's familiar saying, that 'the child is father to the man,' and of his Happy Warrior who all his life acts 'on the plan which pleased his childish thought.' Schiller's message to every

[1] *E.g.* Plato.　　　　　[2] Emerson.

young man is, 'Tell him to reverence the dreams of his youth.'

CONSCIENCE.—The ties of brotherhood should bind the members of a family together till their lives' end. But the strongest and most sacred ties may first be strained and then snapped. Home-life is not always gentle and peaceful and helpful. For lack of mutual forbearance, the spirit of give and take, self-suppression and kind good humour, the light of love burns low and is finally extinguished. This chapter contains the natural history of a crime committed by brothers against a brother. The root of the trouble was envy (v.[11]). Joseph's felt distinction, added to his father's foolish partiality, fretted and galled his brothers. His many apparent advantages—superior talents, nobler character, happier dreams, finer apparel— maddened them against him. 'Envy is acknowledged to be the most ungenerous, base, and wicked passion that can enter the breast of man.'[1] It looks at goodness with malevolence ; it cannot think of a brother's happiness without misery.

> 'Base envy withers at another's joy,
> And hates the excellence it cannot reach.'[2]

Joseph's brothers hated him (v.[4]), and their hatred went on increasing (v.[5]). They could not speak peaceably to him. Hot anger was in their hearts, dark frowns were on their brows, fierce words on their tongues. They nursed their sullen wrath till it could not but burst into a flame. The fateful opportunity came—sooner or later it always comes.

> 'The sight of means to do ill deeds
> Oft maketh ill deeds done!'[3]

Joseph visited his brothers in a lonely place, where there was no human eye to observe what they did. He was at last delivered into their hands. They sprang upon him like wild beasts

---

[1] William Law.    [2] Thomson.    [3] Shakespeare.

They would slay him, and see what would then become of his dreams. They stripped him of his princely robe, and flung him into a pit to die. Heedless of 'the distress of his soul' ($42^{21}$), they sat down to eat bread, fiercely exultant. It was their hour of triumph. They were avenged. The dreamer would no more come between them and happiness. Yet they had just enough of conscience left to keep them from being absolutely at their ease. After all, the dreamer was their brother. That might not be a reason for showing him any kindness, but it was a reason for being prudent about their own safety. Fratricide was perhaps too risky a business. The stain of a brother's blood has always been a nasty thing, and the remorse of Cain had better be avoided. But if conscience is afraid of blood, it will not be troubled at the thought of bondage. If capital punishment is too severe a penalty for dreaming, hard labour for life is not too much. So 'the patriarchs, moved by envy, sold Joseph into Egypt.' It was a crime which in later times became a capital offence. 'He that stealeth a man and selleth him . . . shall surely be put to death.'[1] Joseph's brethren did not at first realise the greatness of their sin. Their literal avoidance of blood sufficiently appeased their conscience for a time. But the day came when a voice said to them, 'His blood is required' ($42^{22}$), and they knew that the requirement was absolutely just. The fine distinction between scarlet sins and crimson sins is of unspeakably small account when an awakened conscience makes us cry out for the whiteness of snow.

TRUTH.—Wherever we find unkindness we are almost certain to find untruth. 'Kindness and truth' are wedded in Genesis ($24^{49}$ $47^{29}$); they naturally draw to each other everywhere; there is a pre-established harmony between them. The same is true of their opposites. Jacob's sons, having sold their young brother, made it next to impossible for themselves to speak the truth.

[1] Ex. $21^{16}$.

They had to concoct a story to account for his disappearance, and it was as audacious and cruel a falsehood as was ever uttered by human lips. They dabbled their brother's coat in goats' blood, brought it to their father, and asked him to say if he thought it was his son's or not. Naturally they avoid saying 'our brother's,' for brotherhood lives only with love and truth. But they give clear and circumstantial evidence of their innocence, and when they have seen their father's looks of anguish, they are surely satisfied at length. What more can they want? Their revenge is sweet and complete. Yet even the most cruel and callous men cannot help having a divine ideal of love and truth hidden in their souls. Their very lies are told in deference to a law of kindness which they instinctively honour. They would blush to appear to be what they have actually become. God made men so different, that evil never dares to be sincere. It always borrows the colours and wears the garb of innocence. It has a whole lifetime of hard labour in keeping up appearances. Hypocrisy is the tribute which all bad men have to pay to the ideal of goodness.

COMFORT.—When Jacob looks at the coat bedaubed with blood, a horror of great darkness falls upon his mind. Ghastly pictures rise before his imagination. The claws and teeth of some ferocious beast have drawn this life-blood from the veins of his darling son. Joseph is without doubt torn in pieces (v.[33]). His mangled body lies in some horrid lair. Jacob rends his garments. His anguish is pitiful. His hopes are crushed. The light of his life is gone out. He puts on sackcloth, and mourns for his son many days. 'He refuses to be comforted' (v.[35]). It is no wonder that his sons cannot comfort him. They deal him a staggering blow, and then bid him not be too much cast down. How can there be any ring of sincerity in their words of consolation? But we are disappointed to find that Jacob derives so little comfort from his faith in God. He does not realise that 'if a person weeps and mourns excessively for a lost

relative, his grief becomes a murmur against the will of God.'[1]
When the mind is overwhelmed with grief it does not reason
logically. Jacob sees nothing before him but a set grey life,
and then the dreariness of Sheol. He will follow his son into
the darkness. His faith in God is not so grandly steadfast as
that of Abraham, who believed that

> 'Even the hour that darkest seemeth
> Will His changeless goodness prove.'

Jacob looks too much at the gloomy face of death, too little at
the glorious face of God. Men of stronger faith have learned to
answer even such questions as, 'Is this thy son's coat?' without
rending their garments and refusing to be comforted. Richard
Cameron's head and hands were carried to his old father, Allan
Cameron. 'Do you know them?' asked the cruel men who
wished to add grief to the father's sorrow. And he took them
on his knee, and bent over them, and kissed them, and said, 'I
know them! I know them! They are my son's, my dear son's.'
And then, weeping and yet praising, he went on, 'It is the Lord!
Good is the will of the Lord, who cannot wrong me and mine,
but has made goodness and mercy to follow us all our days.'[2]

## VIRTUE
### Genesis 39:1-19

'True religion is the queen of the virtues and the destroyer of the vices.'
DANTE.

FELLOWSHIP.—It is a critical time in a young man's life when
he must leave the home in which he has breathed the atmosphere
of true religion, and go among strangers who have not the fear
of God before their eyes. He is tempted to take on the colour

[1] Talmud.          [2] *Men of the Covenant.*

of his surroundings, to do just as he finds others doing. But if he has faith for a safeguard, he will not be so soft and pliant. The consciousness of God's presence is the secret of victory. The story of Joseph's life in Egypt begins with the quiet statement that the LORD was with him (v.²). This is repeated three times in the chapter (vv.³, ²¹, ²³), and the reiteration indicates its importance. It was sometimes said among the Hebrews that Jahveh's presence was confined to the land of Canaan, to the streams and hills and groves of the country of their birth, while He left other territories to be ruled by other gods, so that when any of His people crossed the border they were beyond His reach and care. This was a popular notion which the writers of Genesis nowhere countenance. They say that the LORD was with Jacob in Syria and with Joseph in Egypt, and that in these lands the same God directed the minds of such men as Laban and Pharaoh. He was Joseph's Guardian in his exile. The God whom the Hebrew boy had learned to worship and trust in Canaan was with him, not as a mere memory or influence, but as a real Presence, in the land of Egypt and the house of bondage. Joseph was not a forgotten waif, uncared for by God. In the stately mansion of the captain of the guard, in the gloomy dungeon, and in the royal palace, he realised the nearness of God; and this was the secret of whatever was noble and beautiful in his character and career. The God of the Hebrews was not a shadowy Being, far remote and scarcely known, but a real present Help in time of need. We sometimes imagine that science has increased the difficulty of believing that God is actually with us in this world. Our growing knowledge of the vastness of God's universe makes us think of Him as far, far away. The God who was with Joseph does not seem to care for us. We fear that He has forsaken the earth where His guiding and guarding presence was once so vividly realised. But our fears are irrational. 'It is our power of imagination which is at fault, when it shocks us to bring Him from the throne of the universe to be the Father of the fatherless and the Guide of the wanderer. It is not reason. Why should He, who made and sees and upholds all things, *not* care for the least thing that His love and wisdom thought good to make?'[1]

WORK.—With the worst possible intentions, Joseph's brethren did him the best possible service. His successful career dated from the day on which they sold him as a slave. At first his soul was in great distress (42[21]), and no wonder ; for 'there is no despair so absolute as that which comes with the first moments of our first great sorrow, when we have not yet known what it is to have suffered and be healed, to have despaired and to have recovered hope.'[2] But the young mind, aided by health and hope, has a wonderful power of recovery from sorrow, and Joseph's bitter misfortune soon proved to be a real blessing. In Egypt he began the strenuous life. The dreamer became perforce a toiler. At home he was in danger of being pampered and spoiled, of thinking more of honour than of duty, of living a life that was merely ornamental. In Egypt he must earn his bread by the sweat of his brow. At first it was cruelly hard to have to work as the servant of a stranger who had bought him in the market like a beast of burden. He had to put a constraint on himself, to brush aside tears, and forget. But labour developed his character, drew out all his talents, and became ere long such a joyous necessity that he remained a strenuous worker to the end of his life. He did not forget his dreams, but he learned to combine the ideal with the practical. It is good that a young man should see visions,[3] but it is also 'good for a man that he bear the yoke in his youth.'[4]

STEWARDSHIP.—The story of Joseph's success in Potiphar's house was well worth telling. It is important to observe that there was nothing peculiar about his position as a servant. It

---

[1] Dean Church.  [2] George Eliot.
[3] Joel 2[28].  [4] Lam. 3[27].

was only a daily round of common tasks that he had to fulfil. But the presence of a man with an uncommon spirit redeems every situation from commonplaceness. The Divine Presence makes the difference in the man himself. As often as it is said that the LORD was with Joseph, it is added that he prospered. 'He was a prosperous man' (v.[2]), and 'the LORD made all that he did to prosper in his hand' (vv.[3, 23]). Being intelligent, industrious, and trustworthy, ready to forget himself and be absorbed in the interests of another, quick to learn the language, manners, and customs of Egypt, he won his master's favour, and was soon promoted to the highest position in Potiphar's house. As steward he had charge of the whole household, and his master had such faith in him that he asked him no questions (vv.[4, 6]). Joseph did not abuse his master's confidence. He was as conscientious as if his master's eye were always upon him, and as if he had to render a strict account of whatever he did. He was the best of servants, because he was always serving God as well as man. His faith created in him a keen sense of honour. His daily conduct was the practical expression among men of his sense of obligation to God. Such a servant has always been counted a treasure, and we are not surprised that 'the LORD blessed the Egyptian's house for Joseph's sake' (v.[5]).

VIRTUE.—The immortal story of Joseph's victory over temptation is one of those vivid tales which give the morality of the Hebrews the immense power of a personalised ideal. Mohammed calls it 'a most excellent story,' and spoils it in the retelling. It is told in Genesis with severe simplicity, yet it moves us like a drama of high and passionate thoughts, and whispers to us the secret of all pure and holy living. It was God's own will that Joseph should be tempted. 'The word of the LORD tried him.'[1] No one can live long in this world without being tempted, for it is full of gross and of subtle allurements. God

[1] Ps. 105[19].

often allows some fierce temptation to make a crisis in a young man's moral life. The trial will determine whether his past innocence has been the result of moral strength or of social seclusion. Many a man gets credit for goodness simply because he has not yet encountered a real temptation. Clearly, however, temptation is in itself no sin. 'It is only when a man sees temptation coming and goes out to meet it, welcomes it, plays with it, and invites it to be his guest, that it passes from temptation into sin. Until he has opened the door of his own accord and let it in, he has done no wrong. He has been a tempted man—not a sinful man.'[1] It is equally plain that the strongest temptation cannot justify us in sinning. When a guilty person pleads to God, as he is so apt to do, 'The woman gave me, and I did eat,' he is offering the meanest as well as the flimsiest of excuses. No outward temptation has power to seduce us unless we choose to allow it. What injures the soul is not the outward fiery solicitation, but the inner response. The power to say 'No' in the critical moments of life is a man's salvation. 'My son, if sinners entice thee, consent thou not.'[2] There is no sin except in the surrender of the will, and no real virtue except in the resistance of the soul.

TRIAL.—Joseph had a charm which was partly physical, partly spiritual. His beauty was his mother's gift. Rachel and her son were both 'beautiful in face and form' ($29^{17}$ $39^6$). He had the clear Hebrew complexion which was so wonderful in the eyes of the darker Egyptians. He had the magnetism and power of a richly endowed nature. He had graceful and winsome manners. He had the rarer gift of a beautiful soul, which communicates itself in an indescribable way to the light of the eyes, the tone of the voice, the touch of the hand. Apart from moral goodness and spiritual grace, physical beauty is apt to be a fatal gift, fatal to its possessor and to whoever casts eyes upon it—a curse, not a blessing. Young and beautiful, innocent

[1] Henry Drummond.        [2] Prov. $1^{10}$.

and untried. Joseph suddenly finds himself tempted to be impure. His mistress lets herself fall in love with him, and uses all her arts to seduce him, making her house a place of evil enchantments for the young Hebrew. One of our poets tells how his youthful hero is brought 'through the cave of Mammon and the tower of earthly bliss, that he might see and know and yet abstain.'[1] 'The righteous God trieth the hearts';[2] and 'blessed is the man that endureth temptation, for when he is approved he shall receive the crown of life.'[3]

VICTORY.—Three things kept Joseph pure—duty, honour, and faith. First, temptation assailed him when he was doing 'his work' (v.[11]). It found him where he should be and as he should be. He did not go a step out of his way to meet it, and when it came to him his mind was preoccupied. He was not taken off his guard. Intent on other and better things, he was safe. The temptation which comes to meet us, however great it may be, is not half so difficult to overcome as the temptation which we go to seek. We are strong so long as we are in our proper element, weak only when we are out of it. Faithful and honest work, which keeps head and heart and hand busy, is a perfect shield against temptation. The vacant, inquisitive, wandering mind is the thing to dread. 'Contamination taints the idler first.'[4] 'Every man's task is his life - preserver.'[5] Second, honour keeps Joseph right. He does not forget for a moment that he is a steward, to whom a high trust has been committed. An exceptionally kind master has raised him to greatness (v.[9]), has put all things in his hands, has confided in him implicitly. To abuse such a master's kindness, to return him evil for good, would be unspeakably mean ; it would be to deserve the name of traitor. A nice sense of what is right and just is a motive infinitely higher than the dread of consequences. Even if there were no punishment to fear, the loss

---

[1] Spenser.  [2] Ps. 7[9].  [3] Jas. 1[12].
[4] Clough.  [5] Emerson.

of self-respect would be to an honourable man an exquisite
torture.

> 'Say, what is honour? 'Tis the finest sense
> Of justice which the human mind can frame,
> Intent each lurking frailty to disclaim
> And guard the way of life from all offence
> Suffered or done.'[1]

Third, Joseph is saved by faith. God has given us many high
and pure motives to induce us to do the right—filial affection,
the memory of home, friendship, gratitude, self-respect, yet they
would not be sufficient to carry us safely through the strongest
and subtlest temptations of life unless they were transcended by
a still higher motive—the sense of responsibility to God Himself.
Our panoply would not be complete unless we had over all the
shield of faith. Joseph has a light from heaven flashed upon his
temptation, a strong, welcome, glorious light, in which he sees it
to be the hideous thing it is, and he stands aghast at it. He
does not say, 'this folly,' or 'this vice,' or 'this crime,' though
each of these words would be so far right. He goes both deeper
and higher; he shrinks from 'this great wickedness,' he
shudders at 'sin against God.' If he were to yield he would
be a fool, a voluptuary, a criminal. True; but, above all, he
would be a sinner against God. And that is what he will not,
he cannot, be. In the tempests and whirlwinds of passion it is
of small account to talk of injuring our own and other people's
souls; it is the fear of God that is our salvation.

SENSIBILITY.—A natural abhorrence rises in every young
mind at the first approach of temptation. We shrink from it as
a child from a toad. This instinctive repulsion should never be
weakened. It should always be painful to us to think, and still
more to speak, of vice. There are sins about which we should
never talk willingly or calmly. Nature protests against them by
mantling the innocent cheek with hot blushes at the mention of
them. 'It is a shame even to speak of those things.'[2] The first

---

[1] Wordsworth.                    [2] Eph. 5:12.

thing which all corrupters of youth try to do is to make vice seem beautiful, to array its foulness in fair colours, to conceal its real and hateful self. One of the outstanding merits of the Bible is that, like Ithuriel's spear, it makes shameful things appear shameful.

> 'For no falsehood can endure
> Touch of celestial temper, but returns
> Of force to its own likeness.'[1]

It is the Bible that makes the moral sense pure and strong—a light to guide, a voice to warn, a spirit to control. 'Keep thy conscience continually tender, and then it will check the first appearance of sinful passions, and will smart at the mere thought of sin.'[2] It is the Bible that keeps alive 'that sensibility of principle, that chastity of honour, which feels a stain like a wound.'[3]

PURITY.—The God whom Joseph worshipped was of purer eyes than to behold iniquity, and could not look upon sin. He was a righteous God, who loved righteousness. And when Joseph felt the hot breath of temptation in his face, he took refuge in God; he recollected the presence of God; he uttered the name of God.[4] He realised that to sin against a woman was to sin against God. Beyond the poor seductress' face he saw another Face, full of loveliness, which he dared not grieve or offend. It was not so much with Potiphar's wife or with Potiphar that he had to do, as with God. All human beings are made in God's image (1[26]); all human society is His creation; and to injure anything that is sacred to Him, is to strike at Himself. This was the thought which made sin an intolerable thing to the Hebrews. God's splendid purity—the terrible crystal[5]—shrivelled up all unholy lusts. 'Thou hast set our secret sins in the light of Thy Face.'

> 'The love which draws us nearer Thee
> Is hot with wrath to them.'[6]

FLIGHT.—Joseph 'fled forth' from the presence of his

[1] Milton.  [2] Richard Baxter.  [3] Burke.
[4] So Jesus in Matt. 4[4, 7, 10].  [5] Ezek. 1[22].  [6] Whittier.

temptress in shame and fear. He escaped as a bird from the snare of the fowler. All wise men counsel flight from allurement to sins of passion. It is fatal to dally with temptation, to deliberate when conscience is clear. When the young Greek was in the enchanted isle of Calypso, his mentor cried, 'Fly, Telemachus, fly!' The Hebrew spirit is still more Puritan, the Christian most of all. 'Flee youthful lusts.'[1] Some modern teachers, who have given up the Hebrew and Christian faith in a personal God, say that nature knows nothing of chastity,[2] and advise young men to take their licence in the field of time. Others encourage them to sin, that they may see life and gain a knowledge of the world—an astonishing means of self-improvement. 'Is any man,' Newman quietly asks, 'a better man for becoming a selfish beast?' To cast away the pearl of purity is at the same time to forfeit truth, faithfulness, love, justice, holiness—to make life poor indeed. No sin more swiftly and surely ruins the soul than unclean passion. One of the masters in Israel gives us a picture of what a young man becomes when he surrenders to the temptress:

> 'With her much fair speech she causes him to yield,
> With the flattery of her lips she forces him away.
> He goes after her straightway,
> As an ox goes to the slaughter . . .
> As a bird hastens to the snare,
> And knows not that it is for his life . . .
> Let not thy heart incline to her ways,
> Go not astray in her paths . . .
> Her house is the way to hell,
> Going down to the chambers of death."[3]

CONSCIENCE.—The temptress fawns and smiles and flatters one day, hisses and frowns and curses the next. Milton stated this fact in one awful sentence when he said that lust dwells hard by hate. Potiphar's wife, being immoral, was also malignant. Madam Wanton's languid, amorous eyes soon begin to blaze with dangerous fire, and her lascivious lips distil the

[1] 2 Tim. 2²².     [2] *E.g.* Renan.     [3] Prov. 7²¹⁻²⁷.

poison of asps. Her quick brain suggests a delicious revenge upon the Hebrew innocent. She will pose as a pure-minded wife whom he has tried to injure. She will not be sorry to see her husband — of whom she speaks with scant respect (v.$^{14}$) — beside himself with rage against his favourite servant, and hopes he will either smite off his head or at least give him prison fare for the rest of his life.

> ' Heaven has no rage like love to hatred turned,
>   Nor hell a fury like a woman scorned.'

Yet even Potiphar's wife is not without a conscience. She has a clear perception of the rightness of virtue and the wrongness of vice. She knows well enough that she is utterly wrong in tempting a man to sin, and that he would be equally wrong in tempting her. She knows that she is right in expressing a horror of vice, and demanding its punishment. Even when the reality of virtue is absent, the semblance is carefully displayed—a pathetic tribute which even the basest souls cannot help paying to the divine idea of purity which God has created in them.

MORALITY.—Thoughtful teachers in every age have confessed that moral teaching looks to religious teaching for its inspiration, its power, and its final justification. George Eliot says of one of her characters that his strength lay 'in his fervent belief in an Unseen Purity to which uncleanliness and lying were an abomination.' Now this was the strength of the Hebrew race as a whole—that they practically identified religion and morality. Among them a right faith was the inspiration of a right life ; creed was the mould of conduct and character ; the fear of the LORD created an atmosphere in which impure thoughts and unholy desires died a natural death. Among them the decadence of morality was never due to anything but a decadence of religion, and every ethical revival sprang from a religious revival. They had the highest conceivable sanction of virtue, because the God whom they adored, being Himself morally beautiful, was the Archetype of purity, righteousness, truth, and love. Among pagan races, theology was not less strikingly divorced from morality than among the Hebrews it was conjoined with it. Jupiter, the highest god of Greece, was notoriously adulterous. Krishna, the favourite god of the Hindoos, is the incarnation of abandoned immorality. But it is impossible to think of the God of the Hebrews as other than spotlessly pure ; and this is what makes their religion, as perfected by Christ, the absolute religion. Among all the grand ideals which the world has once won and can never afford to let slip, the transcendent one is the vision of a pure and holy God. All utilitarian sanctions of morality are shadows in comparison with that sanction which is appealed to in the young Hebrew's question, 'How can I do this great wickedness, and sin against God?'

# INSPIRATION
## Genesis 39:20-41:39

'God has a people whom He whispers in the ear.'—BROWNING.

SILENCE.—Joseph was the victim of a cruel calumny. A woman aspersed his good name, and her story was believed. If any shadows of suspicion crossed her husband's mind, he could not afford to regard them. Potiphar's wife must be above suspicion. He must assume that his Hebrew steward, whose coming had brought such prosperity to his house, had after all made moral shipwreck. Potiphar's wrath was kindled ($39^{19}$), and he took Joseph and 'put him into the prison, the place where the king's prisoners were bound' ($v.^{20}$). No trial was granted. Being a slave, Joseph was condemned unheard. The innocent had to suffer instead of the guilty. Bearing shame and scoffing, he stood condemned in her place. 'But the LORD was with Joseph,' and this made him content to suffer in silence. He was one of the first to find that God's presence almost changes a prison into a palace. To the very young injustice always seems strange ; it brings anguish to their souls (42²¹) ; they cannot reconcile themselves to it. But as they grow older it begins to appear customary and almost natural. We live in a tangled world, and while we try to do absolute justice to others, we must not despair if something less is done to us. Joseph was still well under thirty, but he had already learned the lesson. Amiel goes so far as to say that 'to hope for justice in this world is a sign of sickly sensibility. We must learn to do without it.'[1]  There are some whose wrongs so embitter them that they never smile again. There are others whose wrongs so madden them that their hands are raised to heaven in fierce upbraiding. But there is a nobler way. It has always been the mark of a hero to say, 'Blame I can bear, but not blame-worthiness.' To endure reproach and persecution, and let no murmur escape the lips and no bitterness enter the soul—that is true greatness, that is Godlikeness. 'The Lord was with Joseph' in prison, and the peace of his own spirit was the proof of it. 'A good man's glory is the witness his own quiet conscience bears. With a good conscience you have continual joy. It can bear much, and amid troubles is exceeding glad ; but the bad conscience is always restless and afraid. . . . Patience and lowliness in days of trouble are more pleasing to God than piety in days of prosperity.'[2]

> ' Oh, fear not in a world like this,
> And thou shalt know ere long,
> Know how sublime a thing it is
> To suffer and be strong.'[3]

BUOYANCY.—When Joseph was cast into prison he did not seek out a dark corner and weep. Sweet liberty was gone, but he did not for a moment give way to despair. We are told that his soul entered into the iron,[4] but not that the iron entered into his soul. Why should he be either lachrymose or callous? He

[1] Amiel.    [2] Thomas à Kemvis.    [3] Whittier.    [4] Ps. 107, R.V. m.

was without fear and without reproach; he had youth and heart's ease and hope to cheer him; and, like every healthy-minded person, he felt that the joys of life were far greater than its sorrows. He was no sooner in prison than he discovered how interesting a place a prison could be. He quickly adapted himself to his new surroundings, and the same qualities which won for him the stewardship in the house of the captain of the guard, raised him as high in Pharaoh's state prison. All the prisoners were committed to his charge, and the keeper trusted him absolutely (vv.[22, 23]). Joseph is the kind of youth who, as if by a law of nature, always seems to come out at the top. Submerge him, and he is soon on the crest of the wave again. His buoyancy seems almost miraculous; yet most of the qualities by which such a man rises and prospers in the world are perfectly imitable—brave-heartedness, honesty, patience, the love of hard work, the abiding sense of responsibility to God, the unshakable conviction that life means something intense and something good.

SYMPATHY.—Joseph spent some years of his life in the Egyptian king's prison. It was a good school for one who was destined to be a leader of men. He found himself among some of the highest of the king's subjects. He was rich in sympathy, and quickly forgot his own sorrows in helping others to bear theirs. He studied the faces of his fellow-prisoners; he inquired into their troubles; he listened to their tales; he became their confidant and counsellor. He learned many of the secrets of the human heart, and many of the ways of a king's court. He perceived—what his own case had already taught him—that a man might wear a felon's garb and chain without being a felon. He found that some who had worn purple and fine linen carried a heavy burden of woe. And he was able to help some of them. Besides being a dreamer, he possessed the gift of interpreting the dreams of others. He knew that the visions of the night often take shape from the hopes and fears of the daytime. He believed that promises and warnings were given to men in their sleep. He received impressions vividly, and he had the art—some men have it in a marked degree— of reading the mind's construction in the face. He was a discerner of spirits. His old master, the captain of the guard, committed to his charge two notable prisoners, the king's chief butler and chief baker. There had been an attempt at poisoning in the palace, and the one or the other was a traitor. Joseph had little difficulty in arriving at a conclusion ; he knew as by instinct which of the two was guilty and which innocent. His interpretation of their dreams did little more than put his verdict into words. He predicted that the butler would be restored to his butlership, and that the baker would be hanged.

LIBERTY.—Having interpreted the butler's dream, and fore- told his restoration, Joseph thought for once of himself, and asked a favour in return. 'Have me in remembrance when it shall be well with thee, and show kindness, I pray thee, unto me, and make mention of me unto Pharaoh, and bring me out of this house : for indeed I was stolen away out of the land of the Hebrews : and here also I have done nothing that they should put me into the dungeon'[1] ($40^{14, 15}$). These words, with their pathetic human touches, bring Joseph very near us. They give us a glimpse into his mind. He is perfectly simple and natural. Prison life is irksome enough to his brave, gentle spirit. He suffers like a captive bird, and when he sees a ray of hope he eagerly turns his face to the light. But while his petition is so simple in its pathos, so wistful in its plea for a little warmth of human kindness, it is also noble in its reticence. When he pleads his innocence, he breaks into no invectives against those who have wronged him. He stretches a point to avoid the remotest allusion to his brothers, saying he was stolen—not sold—into the land of Egypt ; and he says nothing of the lady of high degree in whose stead he is suffering. We see that if he is released he will not spend the rest of his life in wreaking

[1] Literally, 'the hole.'

vengeance upon his enemies. He only longs for liberty, the sweetest ingredient in the cup of earthly happiness. But his very calmness and moderation make our sympathy with him the intenser. Nothing kindles in generous hearts a warmer flame of mingled indignation and pity than the sad fate of an innocent person doomed by some miscarriage of justice to suffer long years of imprisonment as if he were guilty. If such things are hateful to man, how much more to God! 'He hath looked down from the height of His sanctuary, from heaven did the LORD behold the earth, to hear the sighing of the prisoner.'[1] It is His purpose 'to proclaim liberty to the captive, and the opening of the prison to them that are bound';[2] yet for His own high ends He has permitted some of the noblest men the world has ever seen to languish in the gloom of dungeons. But there is always this compensation, that He is with them in prison, and the sorrows of captivity make the joys of deliverance, when it at length comes, a hundred times sweeter to the soul.

MEMORY.—The chief butler could not but express his readiness to plead the cause of his innocent comrade in distress. Joseph should not lack a zealous friend at court. He might rest assured that everything would be done just as he desired. His hard case would be laid before the great king. All that judgment and tact and skill could do for him would be done. He need have no fear of forgetfulness, and little fear of any further miscarriage. The order for his release would soon be signed. Patience a little, and the prison door would be closing behind him, and his rescuer congratulating him on his happy deliverance. So the two men parted, confident of meeting again soon; and Joseph waited in hope. But the days became weeks, and the weeks stretched into months, and the months dragged on into years, 'yet did not the chief butler remember Joseph, but forgot him' (v.[23]). His forgetfulness was a sin of omission, but none the less grave on that account. Memory has a moral as well as a

1 Ps. 102[19, 20].　　　　2 Isa. 61[1].

mental aspect. Many people count it merely a misfortune to have what they call a bad, a weak, a defective memory. They think ' I forgot' a good and sufficient excuse. But a short memory is often another name for a cold and unfeeling heart. We never forget those whom we really love. If a woman forgets the child she bare, there is more to blame than a weak memory, there is a loveless, unmotherly nature. And if a prosperous man forgets the favours he received and the promises he gave in his days of adversity, the right name for his forgetfulness is ingratitude.

> 'Freeze, freeze, thou bitter sky,
> Thou dost not bite so nigh
>    As benefits forgot :
> Though thou the waters warp,
> Thy sting is not so sharp
>    As friend remembered not." [1]

SELF-JUDGMENT.—There is a law of association of ideas, whereby thoughts, words, and acts which occur together come to be so connected in the mind that, when one of them is afterwards suggested, a whole train of ideas is instantly set in motion. Some word or incident serves to rediscover great forgotten tracts of our past life, like a lightning flash illuminating a dark sky. A striking illustration is found in the narrative ($41^8$). Pharaoh has a troubled dream, about which all his courtiers soon come to hear, and among the rest his chief butler, to whose mind it recalls a dream which he dreamed, now years ago, at that terrible time, so strange to look back upon, when he was suspected of treason and cast into the king's prison, along with the poor chief baker who was the real criminal, and who also dreamed a troubled dream the very same night ; and neither of them could think next morning what their dreams meant, till a young Hebrew— At this point the chief butler's conscience smites him. He remembers his forgotten promise. He sees the innocent youth still languishing in prison. A word might have set him at liberty, and it has never been spoken. With a

[1] Shakespeare.

sharp pang of regret the butler condemns himself. He feels that
he is unworthy of the name of friend. He has undertaken to
show a kindness, and he has forgotten. We see that a promise
though forgotten is not effaced. It is doubtful if anything once
imprinted on the memory is ever really obliterated. There are
certainly whole trains of ideas lying silent, inactive, as it were
dead, in dim subconscious regions of the mind, yet ready to
spring to life again whenever the magnetic word shall be spoken.
And our own long-forgotten thoughts may be our judges.

MANHOOD.—The chief butler tells Pharaoh what he knows
about 'a young man, a Hebrew, servant to the captain of the
guard' (41¹²). The story at once arouses the interest of the
troubled king, whose savants—or sacred scribes (R.V. m.)—have
failed to give him any guidance in his perplexity; and Joseph
is suddenly ordered to appear before the greatest of earthly
monarchs. He comes without delay, and is conscious of being
tested, but he bears himself during the ordeal with quiet dignity
and self-possession. He is neither elated nor alarmed. He comes
as the bringer of 'an answer of peace' (v.¹⁶), and he is worthy
of the part which he plays, for there is peace in his own soul.
The first sentence he speaks in the king's presence contains the
name of God (v.¹⁶); over and over again he uses the sacred name
(vv.²⁵·²⁸·³²); and we do not need to guess the secret of his strength
and repose. He has never been more vividly conscious of God
than he is in this hour when he stands for the first time in a
king's court, and the mind's vision of God dims the lustre of all
created glory, so that no magnificence dazzles him, no power
overawes him. He speaks in the firm accents which proceed
from a lofty intellect and a pure heart. What he has all his life
been growing to, he now is. He has let himself be as clay in the
great Potter's hands, and has been so moulded that there is not
a weak line left in his character. We see in him the result of the
steady and commanding influence of the personality of God in
human life. He has reached the age of thirty with a clean

record ; and every temptation resisted, every ideal cherished, every victory won, has contributed something to his definite and marked individuality ; so that he now stands before the king, and before us, a pattern of pure and beautiful manhood.

INTERPRETATION.—If two men who speak different languages wish to converse with one another, they require to use an interpreter, who knows the languages of both. Is it possible that there may be interpreters, not only between man and man, but between God and man? Are there men who learn something of the mysterious symbolic language in which God speaks, and translate it to their fellow-men? It can scarcely be doubted that, in a wide sense of the term, there have been such interpreters in all ages. Joseph interprets the divine mind as mysteriously expressed to Pharaoh in dreams. At the present day anyone can accurately foretell what next year's harvest in Egypt will be like, but only by a miracle could one look fourteen years ahead. 'When, instead of the health-giving northern breezes, the deadly south-east wind blows day after day, it means that there is a rainless season in the south, and that next year's Nile will be low. Between the blasting east wind of Genesis and the low Niles, which brought famine with them, there was a close connection.'[1] Joseph predicts to Pharaoh what 'God is about to do' (vv.[25, 28]). 'The thing is established, and God will shortly bring it to pass' (v.[32]). To this interpreter every common phenomenon is also a divine act. It is God that sends rain from heaven and fruitful seasons. It is God that withholds the rain and visits the people of the earth with famine. Faith puts the emphasis upon the divine activity, science upon the natural agency. Both must be true. There were natural causes, unknown to Joseph, well known to us, for the years of plenty and the years of famine which he foretold to Pharaoh— the action of rain and snow, the rise and fall of mighty lakes, away in the heart of Africa. But he is right in tracing events to their supernatural cause. Nature

Sayce.

is not a godless mechanism. Her processes are controlled by reason. Her laws are but God's ways of working.

INSPIRATION.—Joseph's words and mien fill the Egyptian king with wonder. Pharaoh has never in all his life seen a man 'so discreet and wise,' not even among his oldest and most experienced counsellors. He has plenty of men around him who are learned in all the wisdom of the Egyptians, but this young Hebrew has something which lifts him above the wisest of them. To his servants Pharaoh speaks of him as 'a man in whom the Spirit of God is' (v.[38]); and to Joseph himself he says, 'God hath showed thee all this' (v.[39]). Joseph assents : he *is* a man in whom the Spirit of God is ; God *has* showed him all this. It is scarcely to be supposed that the Hebrews, still less that the Egyptians, already thought of the Spirit of God as a distinct Person. The Spirit or Breath of God is the divine energy working in the souls of men, illuminating, quickening, inspiring them, revealing to them the mind and will of God for the practical ordering of human life on earth. It will be seen that Joseph has all the unmistakable marks of inspiration. His childlike manner, his disparagement of his own talent, his almost absurd humility, combined with the splendid audacity which leaves no shadow of doubt or fear or modest hesitation about the message which he delivers, give him a kinship with all the great speakers for God. The pride of intellect and the energy of the Spirit are diametrically opposed. 'God lifts even the simple mind to understand more of the eternal truth than if a man had studied in the schools ten years.'[1] Ruskin has said : 'I believe the first test of a truly great man is his humility. I do not mean by humility doubt of his own power, or hesitation of speaking his opinions. . . . All great men not only know their business, but usually know that they know it ; and are not only right in their main opinions, but they usually know that they are right in them, only they do not think much of themselves on that account. . . .

[1] Thomas à Kempis.

They have a curious under-sense of powerlessness, feeling that the greatness is not *in* them, but *through* them, and that they could not do or be anything else than God made them.' 'Not unto us, O Lord, not unto us, but unto Thy name give glory.'[1] 'Not by might, nor by power, but by My Spirit, saith the Lord of hosts.'[2]

## HONOR
### Genesis 41:40-57

> ' Heaven doth with us as we with torches do,
> Not light them for themselves.'—SHAKESPEARE.

MERIT.—The men of history whose lives excite our deepest interest are those who have come through the fire of trial and triumphed through conflict. Joseph as a boy dreamed that he was destined to rule, but he came into his kingdom in ways which were not in his dreams. Milton praises the man

> ' whose worthy deeds
> Raise him to be the second in that realm
> Of Pharaoh.'

What were his merits? He was brave and patient in his thirteen years of rough apprenticeship ; he did his duty as in the sight of God ; and while he became deeply experienced in the ways of the world, he kept himself unspotted from its evil. He merited honour, and his reward came at length. He rose from a prison-cell to the seat next the throne. There is the very spirit of romance in the idea of the transformation of the dreamy Hebrew boy into the keen, bold Egyptian governor—the greatest statesman of his time. So others have risen : David rose from the sheep-cote to be the greatest king of his time, Elisha from the plough to be the greatest prophet of his time, Peter from the fishing-

[1] Ps. 115[1].　　　　　　　　[2] Zech. 4[6].

boat to be the greatest apostle of his time, Luther from the miner's hut to be the greatest reformer of his time, Bunyan from the tinker's kitchen to be the greatest seer of his time, Livingstone from the weaver's loom to be the greatest missionary of his time, Lincoln from the tanner's yard to be the greatest statesman of his time. 'The age of romance has not ceased ; it never ceases ; it does not, if we think of it, so much as very sensibly decline.'[1]    But the noblest of those whose names have been inscribed on the temple of fame have not sought for fame ; they have simply done the will of God and loved their fellow-men, and honour has been thrust upon them.    Joseph, whose public life began at thirty, might have stood for his portrait to one who depicted an ideal statesman :

> ' Dost thou look back on what hath been
>     As some divinely gifted man,
>     Whose life in low estate began
> And on a simple village green ;
>
> Who makes by force his merit known,
>     And lives to snatch the golden keys,
>     And mould a mighty state's decrees,
> And shape the whisper of a throne ;
>
> And moving up from higher to higher,
>     Becomes on fortune's crowning slope
>     The pillar of a people's hope,
> The centre of a world's desire.'[2]

MINISTRY.—Joseph is called to office as Pharaoh's Prime Minister.  The task is tremendous, the weight of responsibility great, and Joseph is only a young man.  But beyond the will of man he discerns the will of God, who is sending him to preserve life ($45^6$), and making him lord of all Egypt (v.$^9$).  Thrilled by the sense of a divine vocation, he can neither shrink back in alarm nor contemplate for a moment the possibility of failure. He who summons him to do His work will sustain him by His all-sufficient grace.  It is the consciousness of a high and holy calling, issuing in a constant sense of responsibility to God, that

[1] Carlyle.                    [2] Tennyson.

produces the noblest servants of any commonwealth. The statesman who owns his obligation to Heaven is not likely either to
abuse his power or to let his head be turned by the splendour
of his position. Some importance is attached in the narrative to
the fact that Pharaoh took off his signet ring from his hand and
put it upon Joseph's, arrayed him in vesture of fine linen, put
a gold chain about his neck, and made him ride in the second
royal chariot ($41^{42. 43}$). The value of insignia lies in what they
signify. The minister's seal and vesture, like the prophet's mantle,
the judge's ermine, the councillor's chain, cannot dignify mean
men, and mean men bring all insignia into contempt. Yet 'is not
a symbol ever, to him who has eyes for it, some dimmer or clearer
revelation of the Godlike?'[1]   If the insignia of an office are the
tokens of a people's admiration and love, they have their place
and worth. 'The ring and robe of Joseph,' says George Eliot,
'were no objects for a good man's ambition, but they were the
signs of that credit he won by his divinely inspired skill, and
which enabled him to act as a saviour to his brethren.'

WORK.—As Pharaoh's Prime Minister Joseph was exalted to
princely rank, had a majestic title—Zaphnathpaaneah—conferred
upon him, and wherever he went received the plaudits of the
multitude (vv.$^{43. 45}$). In his new position he met with new temptations, and overcame them. He gave himself, body and soul,
not to the pomps and shows, but to the duties and drudgeries,
of office. The ceremonials of the court and the genuflections of
the people were scarcely relevant to his divine mission. 'Joseph
went out from the presence of Pharaoh, and went throughout
all the land of Egypt' (v.$^{46}$). He had cities to visit, plans to
mature, proclamations to issue, agents to choose, wise men to
encourage, fools to restrain. While the earth was bringing forth
corn in handfuls, he saw in imagination a starving population
and heard the bitter cry for bread. He was at once a visionary
and a shrewd man of business. We see in him what has been well

[1] Carlyle.

called 'the most formidable combination of human qualities known in history—the combination of the religious mystic and the man of action.'[1]  Faith in God and sympathy with suffering men made him an earnest, incessant worker.  He did not subscribe to the opinion that idleness is the stamp of nobility. Though next the king in rank, he was the busiest person in the land.  To the man of happy temperament, labour is enjoyment, a sort of repose, a necessary condition; while inaction is an effort, a weariness, an impossible state.  In his youth Joseph saw himself the centre of a circle of envious brethren, whom he expected to bow down and serve him; in his manhood he finds himself the centre of a far wider circle of needy fellow-men, whom he toils with all his might to serve and to save.  One naturally asks the question, Was he, or was he not, ambitious?  What has been said of another Prime Minister will apply to him.  'If ambition means love of power or fame for the sake of glitter, decoration, or external renown, or even dominion and authority on their own account, I think he had none of it.  Ambition in a higher sense, the motion of a resolute and potent genius to use strength for the purpose of strength, to clear the path, dash obstacles aside, force good causes forward—such a quality as that is the very law of the being of a personality so vigorous, intrepid, confident, and capable as his.'[2]

LOVE.—Soon after Joseph was raised to power he married Asenath, the daughter of Potipherah, priest of On.  Her city, called by the Greeks the City of the Sun (Heliopolis), was the seat of the head of the official priests, who would hold much the same position in Egypt as the Archbishop of Canterbury in England, except that his office was hereditary.  'The priestly head of the State,' says Professor Sayce, 'stood next in rank to Pharaoh; and in marrying his daughter, therefore, Joseph was taken into the very heart of the royal circle.'  'The priests belonged to the great landed proprietors; they formed the highest

[1] Lord Rosebery.                    [2] Morley's *Gladstone*.

aristocracy ; they attended and controlled the kings ; they were proverbial for their scrupulousness in guarding the purity of their families.'[1] The religion of the Egyptians was certainly higher and purer than that of the native tribes of Canaan, with whom the Hebrews were forbidden to intermarry. We gather that Joseph's love did not lower him morally or spiritually. It did not incline him to become an Egyptian in belief or worship. He remained to the end true to the God of his fathers. He had that best preparation for an indissoluble covenant of love—a faith which refines and hallows the affections, a sense of the presence of God which ennobles all the relationships of life. He had a clean hand and a pure heart to give his bride. An Egyptian woman had once offered him an illegitimate love, which he rejected with loathing and horror. Had he sinned in the house of Potiphar he would never have rejoiced in the house of Potipherah. ' Canst thou reckon among the blessings which Heaven has bestowed on thee the love of faithful women ? Purify thy heart, and make it worthy of theirs. All the prizes of life are nothing compared with that one.'[2]

FORGETTING.—Joseph calls his firstborn son ' Manasseh.' ' God,' he says, ' hath made me forget all my toil and all my father's house' (v.[51]). The little child is received as God's gift, the token of His love. ' God thought of you, and so I am here,'[3] is what every babe says to understanding hearts. The name Manasseh is full of pathos, and tells its own tale. Joseph has been for many years homeless and friendless. Sensitive and emotional, as ready for smiles as for tears, dowered with an immense capacity for enjoyment, he has hid within his breast a wealth of affection unspent, of feeling repressed. His exile and bondage have not been easy to bear, and in Egypt he has been terribly alone, especially in crowds. Past him has streamed day by day a procession of human beings to whom he has been no more than the mire of the street. Can he ever forget that hard

[1] Kalisch.          [2] Thackeray.          [3] George Macdonald.

experience? God at length gives him a home and a helpmeet, happiness and hope; and at once all the unkindness of his father's house, the anguish of exile, the bitterness of long years of servile toil, begin to fade from his memory like an unpleasant dream. Love charms away his sorrow. Asenath and Manasseh teach him the secret of 'a sweet forgetting.' It will soon appear, of course, that he has not in any literal and absolute sense forgotten his home and his kindred. Does an exile ever really forget? 'If I forget thee, O Jerusalem, let my right hand forget her cunning.' Yet it may well be that 'a little warmth, a little light, of love's bestowing' has more virtue than all the waters of Lethe to efface from the soul the traces of trial and grief. 'Manasseh' meant toil and loneliness and weariness forgotten. There is a house in London called *Vergiss-Heimweh*,[1] where some Teuton has evidently found a happiness that has softened the poignancy of his regret for the old home in the Fatherland. It may be a little child's doing. Man as well as woman has a forgetting, though his is not so direct or profound as hers. 'A woman hath sorrow, but . . . she remembereth no more the anguish, for joy that a man is born into the world.'[2]

## CONSCIENCE
### Genesis 42

'Our acts our angels are, or good or ill,
Our fatal shadows that walk by us still.'—EMERSON.

RETRIBUTION.—There is a Nemesis, a divine Justice, which pursues, and sooner or later overtakes, all evil-doers; for while God is merciful, He is also righteous, and will by no means spare the guilty. The connection between sin and punishment is not always apparent, and men cheat themselves with the delusive

[1] Forget home-sickness.      [2] John 16²¹.

hope of escaping detection. 'Because sentence against an evil work is not executed speedily, therefore the heart of the sons of men is fully set in them to do evil.'[1] But 'be sure your sin will find you out.'[2] Joseph's brethren committed a crime in the fields of Dothan. Twenty years passed, and they tried to forget, and perhaps succeeded. But oblivion is not atonement. Time works many wonders, but neither time nor eternity makes a crime less heinous than it was at the moment of its commission. Troubles at length began to come to Joseph's brethren, each giving a painful tap to their memory. They suffered the pangs of hunger; they had to go abroad to seek bread; they found themselves thrown into an Egyptian prison. They had time to reflect, conscience began to do its work, and they said one to another, 'We are verily guilty concerning our brother' (v.[21]). As their troubles thickened 'their heart failed them,' and with trembling lips they said, 'What is this that God hath done unto us?' (v.[28]). They knew that they were at last coming face to face with their Judge, and that He would not spare them. The relation between sin and suffering, which is as certain as the laws of nature, can only be broken by God, and He does not break it until sinners have sincerely repented. Conscience, experience, and revelation join in saying, 'Whatsoever a man soweth, that shall he also reap.'[3] Wrong-doers congratulate themselves that they have not been observed, or that their sin has been forgotten, and that they are safe, until suddenly a train of circumstances, laid by the hand of God, reveals to their startled consciences the fact that nothing has been unobserved, nothing forgotten. 'Judgment for an evil thing is many times delayed some day or two, some century or two, but it is sure as life, it is sure as death! In the centre of the world-whirlwind verily now as in the oldest days dwells and speaks a God. The great heart of the world is Just.'[4]

TESTING.—When Joseph overheard his brothers saying, 'We

[1] Eccles. 8[11].      [2] Num. 32[23].      [3] Gal. 6[7].      [4] Carlyle.

are verily guilty' (v.²¹), he did not at once reveal himself to them and offer them forgiveness. Some readers blame him on this account. A foreign writer says, 'He is hard-hearted enough systematically and in cold blood to punish them for the suffering they inflicted on him,' and 'to put them to the torture,'[1] when he should have instantly fallen upon their necks and kissed them. If Joseph had been a weaker man he would have done as is here suggested. If his amiability had been untempered by principle, he would have done it. But Joseph's conscience was as sound as his heart was tender. He had serious work to do before he indulged in emotion. He avoided the sentiment which blurs the distinctions between good and evil. Forgiveness was not his only duty to his brothers. He had to test the reality of their repentance, to drive the arrow of conviction deeper into their hearts, keeping his own lips sealed till the right moment came for divulging to them his secret. He could endure the pain of seeing them suffer, in the hope that suffering would bring them to a better mind. Providence was making him their judge, as nature had made him their brother, and he loved them with that exacting love which has often been an erring brother's salvation. He would rejoice to have them reconciled to himself, but still more to see them reconciled to God. Love does not always caress and soothe and say kind things. Sometimes it scourges. Its mingled goodness and severity are the reflection of the perfect love of God, who leads His children along rough ways to repentance, that He may at last have the joy of giving them the kiss of forgiveness.

FAITH.—Joseph is careful not to treat his brothers with any needless severity. His first impulse was to keep nine of them in prison, and to send one back to bring his youngest brother down to him. But after confining them all for three days, he decides to send nine home and to keep only one as a hostage. He gives them his reason in the words, 'I fear

[1] Oort.

God' (v.[18]). This is admirably characteristic of him. The fear of God is his religion. He has the name of God continually on his lips. He thinks and speaks of God as naturally as he breathes. He always expresses his faith in God in the simplest and fewest words, and it is worth while to bring all these brief pointed utterances together, that we may feel their cumulative effect. 'How can I sin against God?' (39[4]). 'Do not interpretations belong to God?' (40[8]). 'God will give Pharaoh an answer' (41[16]). 'What God is about to do He hath showed unto Pharaoh' (vv.[25, 28]). 'God hath made me to forget all my toil' (v.[51]). 'God hath made me fruitful' (v.[52]). 'God be gracious unto thee, my son' (43[29]). 'God hath sent me before you to preserve life' (45[5]). 'God hath sent me to preserve a remnant in the earth' (v.[7]). 'It was not you that sent me hither, but God' (v.[8]). 'God hath made me lord of all Egypt' (v.[9]). 'These are my sons, whom God hath given me' (48[9]). 'Fear not: for am I in the place of God?' (50[19]). 'Ye meant evil against me, but God meant it for good' (v.[20]). 'I die, but God will surely visit you' (v.[24]). The faith of this man—an ideal to all the Hebrews who came after him—is simple, strong, unwavering. These short sentences reveal his whole inner life. The thought of God is as familiar to him as the face of a friend, and gives the note of sublimity to everything he says. The current of his spiritual life is still and equable. We do not read of any wrestling and struggling, nor even of any vowing and covenanting, in his life. When he was yet a child, his heart was somehow drawn to God; when he left home, a lad of seventeen, 'the LORD was with him'; when he stood before Pharaoh at thirty, the Spirit of God was in him; and his habitual realisation of the presence of God was the motive-power of all his actions. It is evident that his religion was an inward principle, not a code of laws, a set of propositions, or an array of ceremonies. His creed—his central enthusiasm for God, the thing which he really believed — determined his life. It is remarkable that so early a book as Genesis should present us with an ideal of true religion as something entirely separate from outward forms, as simply and purely the life of the human spirit in contact with, and under the influence of the Divine Spirit. One often hears it said that it does not matter what a man believes, provided his life be right ; as if a stream might somehow be pure though the fountain is polluted, or as if we might expect a fine crop of grapes from a thorn-tree. The story of Joseph teaches us rather that nothing is so practical as faith ; and all the wisest men bid us covet 'such a sense of God as shall be the habitually ready principle of reverence, love, gratitude, resignation, obedience.'[1]

CONSCIENCE. — In the same chapter in which we read of Joseph's fear of God, we read also of his brothers' fear. 'Their heart failed them, and they turned trembling one to another, saying, What is this that God hath done unto us?' ($42^{28}$). 'They were afraid' (v.$^{35}$). Joseph's fear of the LORD, the holy reverence which is the beginning of wisdom, is a noble, beautiful, honourable sentiment, issuing in a good conscience and a tranquil mind. His brothers' fear of God is an anxious, restless, troubled feeling, issuing in the pain of remorse and the dread of punishment. Their trials turn their eyes into their very souls. Memory does its stern work in them. Their past life rises before them with awful clearness. They confess that they are verily guilty (literally 'guilty, guilty') concerning their brother. Joseph profoundly pities them as they stand before him with the abject mien of culprits. It is their religion—true religion as far as it goes—that terrifies them ; their belief in God that alarms and torments them. Their imagination conjures up spectral forms and voices out of the past. They have sinned against a child (v.$^{22}$), and the pitiful distress which they would not regard, the pleading voice which they would not hear, the fields of Dothan, the pit, the Ishmaelites, the ill-gotten gain, the coat dipped in blood, the shameless lying—all the details of their crime now come back

[1] Butler.

to torture them, and even the shuddering suggestion that their brother's 'blood is required' (v.²²)—though they had once made sure of escaping at least *that* charge (37²². ²⁶)—awakens no protest in their minds. They bow their heads in guilt and shame; they stand condemned at the bar of their own conscience; and they expect the righteous judgment of God. It is an awful moment for any man when he finds that the past is not past. 'If it were done when 'tis done!' But it is never done till justice is done. That is why 'it is hell on earth already begun when a sinner begins to remember.' [1]

NEMESIS.—Joseph takes Simeon from among his brethren, binds him before their eyes, and retains him as a prisoner and hostage, while he allows the others to go home (v.²⁴). Simeon is the villain of the piece, the evil genius of the family, the arch-plotter of mischief, to whom a period of detention will do no harm. At the same time, his imprisonment keeps the others from being elated at their own release. They see that the governor means to retain his power over them, to make them feel his hand laid upon them when they are far away, compelling them to return. There is that in their conscience which prevents them from uttering a word of complaint. When they reach home, and find that their money has been sent back in their sacks— which they would at one time have counted a piece of uncommon good fortune—their alarm is intensified. What is this that God has done to them? (v.²⁸). They have a vague restless sense of insecurity, as if they were walking among snares and pitfalls. Guilty men fear where no fear is. They tremble at the rustling of a leaf. 'Suspicion always haunts the guilty mind.' [2] Whereas the man who has a good conscience is at peace in a sea of trouble.

> 'Thou shalt not be afraid for the terror by night,
> Nor for the arrow that flieth by day . . .
> There shall no evil befall thee,
> Neither shall any plague come nigh thy dwelling.' [2]

---

[1] Dr. Whyte.     [2] Shakespeare.     [2] Ps. 91⁵. ¹⁰.

PROVIDENCE.—When Jacob's sons returned to Canaan, and told him what had befallen them in Egypt, they seemed to infect him with their own fear. He refused to see anything but the dark side of things. There is a plaintive cadence in his words :

> 'Me ye have bereaved of my children ;
> Joseph is not, and Simeon is not ;
> And ye will take Benjamin away :
> All these things are against me' (v.[36]).

And he adds forebodings of mischief, grey hairs, sorrow, and Sheol (v.[38]). Melancholy Jacob's faith is not yet perfected. Nursing his sorrow, saturating his mind with self-pity, he finds a dreary pleasure in counting his troubles, and inferring that they are all (the grand total is three !) against him ; while we, who know how the drama is unfolding, perceive that all the things in question, and many more, are working together for his good, and that he will live to confess that God has redeemed him out of all evil. God conceals 'His bright designs' in order that His servants may learn to trust Him in the dark as well as in the light. It has been finely said that 'the secrets God keeps must be as good as those He tells.'[1] And as our knowledge of Him increases, we find

> 'That more and more a providence
> Of love is understood,
> Making the springs of time and sense
> Sweet with eternal good.'[2]

---

[1] George Macdonald.          [2] Whittier.

## BROTHERHOOD
### Genesis 38, 43, 44

''Tis but a brother's speech we need,
Speech where an accent's change gives each
The other's soul.'—BROWNING.

PRAISE.—Judah, the fourth son of Jacob and Leah, is the hero
of this chapter. When his mother gave him his name she said,
'This time will I praise the LORD' (29³⁵). It was long before a
new significance was read into the name : 'Judah, thou art he
whom thy brethren praise' (49⁸). In his youth Judah gave
no sign of living up to his great name. His mother could not
praise God, nor his brethren himself, for the kind of life he lived.
His boon companion was an Adullamite (38¹· ¹²· ²⁰), and his wife
a Canaanite (v.²); and in his riper manhood his association with
the heathen inhabitants of the land, and his conformity to their
customs, led him into very miry ways. He was one of those
who conspired against Joseph, and it was at his suggestion that
the dreamer was taken out of the pit and sold (37²⁶· ²⁷). But a
few more years wrought a singular change in his character.
Somehow his strong and passionate nature was purged and
ennobled. From the fourth place in the brotherhood he rose
by force of character to the first. He merited the pre-eminence,
his elder brothers being intellectually and morally smaller men.
He became the recognised leader and spokesman of the family,
who commanded his father's confidence, and whose word carried
conviction. Clear-headed, great-hearted, strong-willed, he was
the man for an emergency. No one could reason so forcibly
or plead so pathetically as he, and his eloquence was only the
sincere and artless expression of the great thoughts of a noble
and simple nature.

PURITY—Tamar, Judah's daughter-in-law, is one of those strange, pathetic figures which serve to show us what ancient heathenism in Canaan must have been. According to the standards of her time and country, she passed for a 'holy' woman. She was mistaken for a priestess of one of the sanctuaries of the land. But what was holiness at these heathen temples? What was the sacrifice which a priestess offered at the shrine of her god? It was the sacrifice of her virtue to the worshippers at the temple. The holy places of ancient Canaan, like the shrines of modern India, were cesspools of iniquity, in which consecration meant prostitution. This fact indicates, more clearly than anything else can, what was the tremendous task which the Hebrews had to accomplish as the chosen people of God. To identify religion with a pure ideal, to make moral discipline the leading object of worship, to demand a righteous life as the essential condition of the divine favour, to purge the sanctuary, the home, the nation, to make Canaan really a Holy Land—nothing less than this was their mission. Even if they only partially succeeded, it was a splendid achievement, to which we owe that moral idealism which can never cease to be the salt of the earth.

RESIGNATION.—Remembering the sad fate which was supposed to have overtaken Joseph, Jacob at first refused outright to let his youngest son, Rachel's only other child, go down to Egypt ($42^{38}$). Reuben tried to change his mind; but Reuben's character had little weight, and his offer to let his own sons be slain if he failed to bring Benjamin back was too preposterous to have any good effect. But when Judah undertook to become surety for the beloved son, promising to bear the blame for ever if he did not restore him to his father, Jacob at length summoned up courage to face the facts and bow to God's will. He commended his sons to the care of Almighty God (El Shaddai); and the upward glance gave himself strength. The things which he so much dreaded appeared less formidable the moment he looked above them to God; and there is a certain noble pathos in the calm words in which he expresses his acquiescence in the Divine will: 'And if I am bereaved of my children, I am bereaved' (43¹⁴). Such words, it is true, are sometimes uttered with only a Stoical calm.

> 'We waive our claim to bliss, and try to bear;
> With close-lipped patience for our only friend,
> Sad patience, too near neighbour to despair.'[1]

But a believer in a God of love can face the inevitable sorrows of life with a different kind of resignation. He can surrender his fondest hopes and dearest desires with unmurmuring patience, because he believes that the Lord and Giver of life does all things well. He can be calm and tranquil, if he cannot yet be happy and joyous, in a life bereft of love, because he feels that he is accepting, not the decrees of an inexorable fate, but the appointments of an unerring love. Every man is sooner or later familiar with death; every man has to utter his Amen, his So be it, somehow; and there is no better way than this: 'The Lord gave, and the Lord hath taken away: blessed be the name of the Lord.'[2]

CONSCIENCE.—The story of the second visit of Jacob's sons to Egypt is a rapid, picturesque narrative, alive with human interest, abounding in dramatic situations, and leading up to a thrilling *dénouement*. All the movement and incident are made subordinate to the unfolding of character. There is intense excitement in the minds of the eleven brothers who come down from Canaan, and an expectation scarcely less intense in the mind of the one who awaits their arrival in Egypt. Things doubtful and mysterious will soon become clear. What manner of men will Joseph find his brethren to be? How will they stand the test to which he has subjected them? He earnestly hopes and longs for the best. Fear is the predominant feeling in the hearts of his brothers, and a command which they receive to dine with the

[1] Matthew Arnold.                    [2] Job 1²¹.

governor only increases their alarm. What does it mean? Are they going to be taken as thieves, as they were before taken as spies? ($43^{18}$). Joseph's steward — a man who echoes his master's devout speech—endeavours to calm their fears, bringing forth their captive brother, and conducting them into his lord's house with every mark of courtesy and respect. But in the guest-chamber another very strange thing happens. Their host arranges them at table in the exact order of their ages. Does the man know their private history? And if he does, what other dread secrets may not soon be torn from their breasts in this Egyptian hall of mystery? Though they try to enjoy the feast that has been spread for them, and even to be merry with their host (v.$^{34}$), their central fear remains. Their conscience has been aroused and cannot be appeased. Their superficial mirth does not still their raging inward unrest. With bated breath they await the something which they know is coming. The suspense is almost too much to bear.

SYMPATHY.—Joseph's personality stands out very distinctly in this part of the narrative. He is a man of action, whose hands and hours are full. It is no light task for him to be Pharaoh's grand vizier. He does not leave the practical part of his work to subordinates. He is at his government house, apparently as usual, early on the day on which his brothers chance to arrive (v.$^{16}$). He has to attend to an immense variety of interests, governing a country without oppressing it, feeding a people without pauperising them. Every faculty of his mind is awake. He makes haste, and expects others to do the same ($43^{30}$ $45^{9.\ 13}$). We see his alertness, lightness, swiftness, freedom, and resource. We think of him as grave and calm and strong, accustomed to issue orders and to receive instant obedience. Yet we see, too, that the man is not sunk in the official. If he does not wear his heart on his sleeve, it beats steadily enough in the right place. If there is a man of feeling in the world, it is the Egyptian governor. When he catches sight of his brothers on their second arrival, his heart leaps up and his eyes devour them. Is there among them the face he longs to see—of one younger and fairer than all the others? Yes, that is he—his own brother Benjamin. When he saw him last, he was a little child of seven, playing in the green fields of Beersheba, at their father's tent door; now he has grown to stalwart manhood. At first Joseph scarcely dares to look at him. He wishes to be master of himself. Giving some hasty orders about the reception of the Hebrews, he plunges again into work, and remains immersed in business until noon, when he comes home and endeavours to talk calmly and rationally. With a great man's air of condescension he asks his guests if this is the brother of whom they spoke on their former visit. But when he turns his eyes full on 'his brother, his mother's son,' and tries to give him a grave paternal blessing, it is too much for him ; he has to seek 'a place to weep in,' and hurries into his chamber to weep there (v.$^{30}$). He is like one who said :

> 'The pretty and sweet manner of it forced
> The water from me, which I should have stopped,
> But I had not so much of man in me,
> And all my mother came into mine eyes,
> And gave me up to tears.'[1]

Strong men are more than half ashamed of giving way to emotion. They wish they had their feelings under completer control. But in truth their great-heartedness, their magnetic quality of brotherly sympathy, is the secret and measure of their power. The heart nourishes, as nothing else can, the hidden roots of both the mental and the moral life, and in a great administrator the gift of sympathy acts like a charm, transmuting in his hands the iron rod of justice into the golden sceptre of love.

FIDELITY.—Joseph resolves to subject his brethren to a final and decisive test. They have brought their brother Benjamin down with them to Egypt. What are their real feelings toward

[1] Shakespeare.

this brother? Envy and malice, or loyalty and love? Will they be true or false to him in an hour of danger? If his life or his liberty is threatened, are they capable of leaving him in the lurch? If they are put to it, will they think first, or think last, of their own safety? To settle the matter, Joseph orders a cup to be put in Benjamin's sack of corn, and when they have all started for home—happy that Simeon and Benjamin are safe, astonished that all has ended so well—his steward comes riding into their midst, hurls at them a charge of stealing the governor's cup, and presently has Benjamin arrested as a thief, while the others are told that they may go. The men are appalled, but they do not show a moment's hesitation. Their brother is accused of a crime, and whether he be guilty or innocent they will never forsake him. There is only one thing to do, and they do it at once. With rent clothes they hurry back 'to the city,' and prostrate themselves before the man who has their brother's fate in his hands. Joseph has his answer before they speak a word. The men have come through the ordeal well. The anguish of their faces speaks of a great and genuine love in their hearts.

INTERCESSION.—Judah is spokesman for his brethren in this critical hour. We see him rise with them from the ground, and stand forth before the governor, his garments rent, his face pale, but with a singular nobility in his mien. His nature is stirred to the depths, and all the tenderness of his strong manhood leaps into the light of his eyes and the cadence of his voice. For simple and natural eloquence his speech—extending to seventeen verses— is almost matchless in literature. Luther says he would give anything if he could pray to God as Judah prayed to Joseph. True prayer is the spontaneous utterance of a deeply moved heart. Judah has a theme which makes him a perfect intercessor; he is pleading for a brother whom he loves, and for whose safety he has pledged his own honour. If our English literature contains anything that is worthy of being placed side by side with this Hebrew masterpiece, it is Jeanie Deans' intercession for the life of her sister Effie at the court of Queen Anne. Speech and writing of this kind always give one the impression of a certain unique artless power. We feel, but cannot analyse the charm. The same is true of the Bible as a whole, of which Heine has said : ' There is not a vestige of art in it. It is impossible to criticise its style.' Inspiration, the breath of God touching men's spirits to finest issues, is higher than all art.

ELOQUENCE.—At the outset Judah feels his impotence to utter a word. 'What shall we say to my lord? What shall we speak?' (v.¹⁶). Many a great speech has begun just in that way. The cause to be pleaded is momentous, the speaker is helpless to begin. There are certain important things to say—O for an angel's tongue to say them ! But lips of common clay have often worked wonders when they have been inspired by a glowing heart of love. The more fervent a man's affection, the less does he feel fit to express it—until he begins, and then comes self-forgetfulness ; and that very sense of incapacity for speech gives every word that is spoken a tenfold power. Pleading on behalf of his dead friend, Mark Antony said :

> 'I am no orator . . .
> But as you know me all, a plain blunt man,
> That love my friend . . .
> For I have neither wit, nor words, nor worth,
> Action, nor utterance, nor the power of speech,
> To stir men's blood : I only speak right on.'

That is the kind of speaker who *does* stir men's blood. Hebrew or Roman, Celt or Saxon, he plays like a musician upon human heart-strings and makes them vibrate till they almost snap.

SELF-SACRIFICE.—Judah is constrained to begin with confession. The bitter truth is wrung from him that sin lies upon his own conscience and the consciences of those who are with him. Whether Benjamin is innocent or guilty, his brothers at least are guilty. God has found out their iniquity (v.¹⁶) ; justice is overtaking them ; and their hearts tell them that they ought to suffer. 'Behold, we are my lord's bondmen' (v.[16]). But Joseph interposes. He has no accusation to make against Benjamin's brothers ; he simply wants to do justice ; he will make a bond-servant of the man whose guilt is evident, while the others are free to go their way. Then Judah, begging leave to 'speak a word,' pleads for all he is worth. The elements of his speech are simple. As we listen to it there rises before us the pathetic figure of an aged father mourning the absence of his youngest son and longing for his speedy return ; we catch a glimpse of a dear departed mother ; we think of a darling son who left home and never came back— believed to have been torn in pieces ; we are afraid to imagine what the father's anguish will be if he is bereft of his other son ; and then we are thrilled as we hear the speaker himself passion-ately pleading that he may be accepted as a slave in his brother's stead, because he cannot bear to go home and witness his father's intolerable sorrow. As we read, we feel that Judah's offer to renounce the things which are dearest to the human heart—home and country and liberty—raises him to a place among the heroes of the Bible. His moral strength is matched by his tenderness. He is glorified by the spirit of self-sacrificing love. 'Judah, thou art he whom thy brethren shall praise' (49[8]). He is worthy to be the founder of the tribe which is always figured in history as a lion, and to have as the greatest of his posterity One who is at once the Lion of the tribe of Judah and the Lamb of God.

FATHERHOOD.—To such a son as Judah the word 'father' is one of the most sacred words in human speech. He uses it fourteen times in his intercession for his brother, and it is his final, climacteric word which gathers into itself all the pathos of his noble appeal. The real meaning of common words depends to a great extent upon our own sensibility, and to Judah the word father has not always had such a rich and tender content as it has now, because he has not always regarded his father with the same reverence and love. He deceived his father. He conspired to commit a crime which lacerated his father's heart. But as he grew older, he became more filial. His eyes were opened. He realised his indebtedness to his father, witnessed his father's lonely sorrow, and understood the real nobility of his father's character. And now he responds to a true fatherhood with a true sonship, and proves it by his willingness to endure the last extremity of hardship rather than let his father be stricken with another sorrow.

TEARS.—Judah did not know what chords he was touching in the heart of the man with whom he was pleading. He thought he was appealing to the clemency of a judge, but he was moving and melting the heart of a brother and a son. Such words would have drawn tears even from the eyes of a complete stranger, however unused to weep, and to Joseph their pathos is overwhelming. He could not have 'refrained himself' any longer even if it had been necessary, and, happily, the need is now past. His doubts and fears are dispelled. He is convinced that his brothers are changed men. Gentler, kinder, truer, they have proved themselves loyal to their brother in his hour of trial and danger, and one of them had shown himself a pattern of heroic manhood. Joseph feels it is time to unmask. Hastily ordering his retinue to withdraw, since it is not fitting that the eyes of strangers should witness a scene so intimate and so sacred, he lets the flood-gates of emotion burst open, weeps aloud, and says to his brothers—speaking now in their own language—'I am Joseph.' At his words their hearts leap and pause ; their faces are a picture of terror and dismay ; a stupor of amazement holds them dumb. When he begins to speak to them, they cannot answer him (45³). Shall all guilty men one day be thus appalled before the innocent whom they have persecuted ? 'They shall look on him whom they have pierced, and mourn.'[1]

PROVIDENCE.—But Joseph has no thought of humiliating his brothers. He thinks only of making them better and happier

[1] Zech. 12.¹⁰.

men. He hastens to speak gracious words to them, lifting up their thoughts to God, on whom his own mind is habitually fixed. They have acknowledged their sin, and are grieved and angry with themselves (v.[5]). Remorse has done its work. Let them now look away from themselves and their sin to the God who is behind all events, who guides and controls all human affairs, who has been overruling all his and their actions for their common good. We mark his characteristic reiteration of the divine name. 'God did send me before you to preserve life. . . . God sent me before you to preserve you a remnant in the earth, and to save you alive by a great deliverance. So now it was not you that sent me hither, but God' (vv[5, 7, 8]). His purpose is not to deny or diminish the guilt of their actions, which must be judged by motives rather than results, but to show them—and they will be lost in wonder to see—that God in the end brings good out of evil, and that even while they have been thinking thoughts of hatred regarding another, God has been thinking thoughts of love regarding themselves. Here it is intensely interesting for us to look into Joseph's mind, and get an understanding of his outlook upon life. The meaning of suffering is luminous to him, and he hastens to make it clear to others. He sees God's hand in what He has permitted as well as in what He has appointed. He sees that his brothers' actions have merely been links in a wonderful chain of providence, by which God has fulfilled His purpose of grace. He sees that slave-dealing Ishmaelites, Potiphar and his faithless wife, Pharaoh and his forgetful butler, dreams and interpretations, plenty and famine, have been other links in the chain. He believes that every man's life is a plan of God. He knows that God does not violate men's freedom ; they are responsible moral beings, who choose good or evil with open eyes ; yet all their actions are woven into the plans of that amazing providence which transcends the vision of men while it shapes to nobler ends their rough and rude designs. This is a truth which all men need to know. Many people miss the meaning and the blessing of life because they never see beyond the malignity of second

causes. They are blinded by passion. They cry out against
human depravity. It is as if Joseph said in wrath : ' Simeon and
Levi did this, the villains ! Potiphar's wife did that, the adulteress !
The chief butler did the other thing, the ingrate ! ' We know
that Joseph had no such thoughts in his mind. To one and all he
could calmly say : ' You have neither made nor marred my life ;
I can neither thank nor blame you ; it was not you, but God, that
did it all.' The same thought runs through all the finest Hebrew
literature. ' This also cometh from the LORD, who is wonderful in
counsel and excellent in working.' [1] Only inspired thinkers, men
of great faith and profound reflection, could ever have reached
such a grand and tranquillising conclusion.

HUMILITY.—Joseph has to speak to his brothers of his own
wonderful success, and to ask them to carry tidings of it to his
father. He tells them that he has become a ' father ' [2]—counsellor
and benefactor—to Pharaoh, master of all the royal house, and
ruler over all the land of Egypt (v.⁸). ' Ye shall tell my father,'
he says, ' of all my glory in Egypt, and of all that ye have seen '
(v.¹⁸). Does this sound like boasting ? Hebrew history of a much
later date tells of a great man who was made to eat grass like the
oxen for seven years because he boasted of the might of his power
and the glory of his majesty.[3] But Joseph is not a man of that
stamp. He is entirely free from the taint of boastfulness, and for a
simple and sufficient reason : he praises God as the Author of all
his greatness. ' He hath made me a father to Pharaoh. . . . Haste
ye and go up to my father, and say to him, This saith thy son
Joseph, God hath made me lord of all Egypt' (vv.⁸, ⁹). He knows
that nothing delights a simple-hearted father like tidings of a
son's success in the great world. But he does not proudly boast
that he is a self-made man ; he realises and acknowledges that
he is a God-made man. We remember he had a youthful
presentiment that he was destined to greatness ; yet, when
greatness comes to him, no one seems to be more surprised at it

[1] Isa. 28²⁹.　　[2] Compare our ' city fathers.'　　[3] Dan. 4³⁰.

than himself. It is the LORD'S doing, and it is wonderful in his eyes. 'For neither from the east, nor from the west, nor yet from the south, cometh promotion ; but God is the judge ; He putteth down one, and lifteth up another.' God shows Himself willing to put the reins of government into the hands of a man who will always use it for His glory.

LOVE.—Joseph has tried to comfort his brethren with words. But somehow the wisest and kindest speeches fail to cheer the heart in its darkest and deepest sorrows. There are, however, other means which do not fail. Joseph lets Nature have her way. 'He fell upon his brother Benjamin's neck and wept ; and Benjamin wept upon his neck. And he kissed all his brethren, and wept upon them' (vv.[14, 15]). Till this moment his brethren have been tongue-tied. What have guilty creatures to say when they stand before their judge with all their sin found out ? They are conscience-stricken ; they are covered with confusion and shame ; they cannot, they dare not, speak a word. But now what signify those warm-flowing tears in the eyes of the man whom they have wronged ? And those kisses—what message do they convey to the hearts of the unhappy culprits ? They convince them of what seemed before incredible—that the man before whom they stand condemned and miserable is more than a judge, more than a benefactor, he is a tender-hearted brother still. 'And *after that* his brethren spake to him' (v.[15]). Genuine tears have a kind of magical virtue, without which the most charitable words and deeds are comparatively powerless to dissolve the barriers which have long divided those who ought to be friends. For genuine tears can only come from a whole-hearted love. Coleridge is right when he says :

> 'He that works me good with unmoved face
> Does it but half ; he chills me while he aids,—
> My benefactor, not my brother man.'

## ATTAINMENT
### Genesis 45:26-46:34

'With still a flying point of bliss remote,
A happiness in store afar, a sphere
Of distant glory still in view.'

BROWNING.

FORGIVENESS.—Jacob's sons come back from Egypt like men in a dream. As they ride across the desert, they have in their hearts the incredible comfort of forgiveness. They have on their lips the kiss of peace. They are tasting the quality of mercy, and finding it sweet. They have experienced the joy of reconciliation. The nameless terror which has so long haunted their minds is gone, and their hearts are at rest. The gloom in which they have walked is dispelled, and their sky is clear and blue again. They now know that there is in the world a love of which they have hitherto had little or no conception, a love which uplifts even while it humbles, forgives even while it condemns. As they think of all they have seen and heard they are lost in wonder. Something of their bitter remorse and shame will remain ; but in the end it must be swallowed up in the sense of a brotherly love which weeps and heals and blesses, and a Divine charity which in some mysterious way brings only good out of evil.

HOPE.—When Jacob received his sons at the door of his tent he eagerly scanned their faces to see if they had all come home. He saw that Benjamin was there, and Simeon was there, and that they were all happy, and had evidently fared better than they expected. But now what amazing tidings were these that they poured into his ears ? 'Joseph is yet alive, and he is ruler over all the land of Egypt' (v.²⁶). The old man listened, and 'his heart fainted.' He would have fallen if some strong arm had not supported

him. The sudden shock his mind received well-nigh made his heart
cease to beat. For twenty years he had mourned for Joseph as
one who was 'without doubt torn in pieces.' If he had for a while
cherished the forlorn hope that he might still see his son alive, the
hope had long since perished. And as eyes long accustomed to
darkness are blinded by excess of light, so hearts that have made
grief their element grow faint at tidings of joy. It is not easy to
turn back the whole tide and current of one's habitual thoughts
and feelings. Jacob 'would not believe' his sons' message. His
imagination refused to entertain the idea presented to it. His
mind reeled under the weight of an inconceivable joy. Joseph
alive and ruling a nation ! It was incredible, it was preposterous,
it was a cruel and bitter jest. And yet, here is Benjamin clad
in the richest apparel of Egypt ; here are beasts of burden laden
with the treasures of the Nile ; and here are wagons enough to
transport the largest household over the desert. These are sub-
stantial things which cannot be explained away. The voices of
the messengers, too, have an unmistakable ring of truth. These
men evidently believe what they say ; and as they fill in their
narrative with more and more circumstantial details, Joseph the
ruler of Egypt at last becomes visible to the old man's astonished
imagination. Jacob's spirit revives (v.[27]). His eye rekindles.
He has something yet to live for. Southward he sees gleaming a
beacon of hope, and his resolution is quickly formed. He has
been a wanderer all his life, and he will wander once more. 'It
is enough : Joseph my son is yet alive : I will go down and see
him before I die.'

> 'Death closes all : but something ere the end,
> Some work of noble note, may yet be done . . .
> 'Tis not too late to seek a newer world.'[1]

GUIDANCE.—When Jacob began this journey southward, his
mind was visited by certain natural fears which made him pause.
Eager as he was to see his son, he wondered if it was right for

[1] Tennyson's ' Ulysses.'

him to leave the land of promise. It was Joseph's will and Pharaoh's that he should come down to Egypt; and it was his own will to go; but what was God's will? It was a hazardous movement, both for himself and his people, on which he was venturing. He had reason to be afraid of Egypt. Abraham had gone down to it, and had not come back with honour. Isaac had been forbidden to go ($26^2$). Jacob was offered the rich lands of Goshen, the finest in Egypt, as a dwelling-place; but in the Vale of Shechem, the finest in Canaan, the Hebrews had not done well, and might they not meet with still greater temptations in Egypt? If Jacob left the land of promise, ought he not to go by faith, with a sense of God's presence and guidance? Under the influence of these thoughts and feelings, Jacob comes to Beersheba, where he lifts up his heart in the act of sacrifice to the God of his father Isaac. Once more a night-vision brings him light, and convinces him that he is on the right path. His Divine Guardian promises to go down with him to Egypt, to make of him a great nation there, to bring him (that is, his people) up again, and to give himself the comfort of having his son Joseph with him at the last (vv.[3, 4]). His fears are dispelled; he sees the guiding hand of God.

REUNION.—Jacob went down with all the Hebrews to Egypt, and 'sent Judah before him to Joseph, that he (Joseph) might show him (Jacob) the way unto Goshen' (v.[28]). Judah was chosen for this interview because he was fittest and worthiest. There were no two princelier men living in the world at that time than Joseph and Judah. They had risen by merit to the pre-eminence among the sons of Jacob. Judah delivers his message to his brother, and then comes the most touching scene in the Book of Genesis. 'Joseph made ready his chariot, and went up to meet his father; and fell on his neck, and wept on his neck a good while' (v.[29]). At last, at last, father and son meet again. They do not speak; they crowd all their pent-up love into a long embrace; and somehow the fullest tides of gladness always touch the source of tears. But the sadness of hearts over-happy is no intolerable pain!

For a companion picture we have to take this one of another son :
'And he arose and came to his father. And when his father saw
him, he had compassion on him, and ran, and fell on his neck, and
kissed him.'[1] One son comes back to his father's embrace with all
life's battles won, crowned with glory and honour. Another comes
back with all life's battles lost, his honour trailed in the dust. The
love which welcomes the one is as great, if not quite as wonderful,
as the love which welcomes the other. But can we doubt for a
moment that the stainless life is the ideal for every son whose career
in the world, with all its infinite possibilities, lies still before him ?

ATTAINMENT.—'Now let me die,' are Jacob's first words
when Joseph at last releases him from his close, warm embrace.
Till this rapturous day, death has seemed to him a thing to
be dreaded rather than desired. But the ecstatic moment has
come ; he has quaffed the full cup of earthly joy ; he
has reached the summit of being ; and now without a murmur
he could lie down and die. Let death come to him when it
will, it cannot now be untimely. He has lived, and loved,
and been loved. He has won the prize of life ; let death crown
him. 'Thus with a kiss I die,' says one of Shakespeare's
people. Pessimists think it must be good to die because life is
so empty. Optimists think it must be good to die because life is
so full. 'One crowded hour of glorious life,' and then—death !
When the eye is satisfied with seeing, the ear with hearing, and
the heart with loving, the silver cord may well be loosed.

> 'Glad did I live, and gladly I die,
> And I lay me down with a will.'[2]

The classical illustration of this feeling is the most sacred of all.
'When the parents brought in the child Jesus, then Simeon
received Him into his arms, and blessed God, and said, Now
lettest Thou Thy servant depart, O Lord, in peace : for mine eyes
have seen Thy salvation.'[3]

[1] Luke 15$^{20}$.     [2] Stevenson.     [3] Luke 2$^{27-30}$.

## SERVICE
### Genesis 47:1-48:20

'Therefore to him it was given
Many to save with himself.'—ARNOLD.

GOSHEN.—Jacob and his sons have the land of Goshen assigned to them as a dwelling-place. Pharaoh makes it over to them, for Joseph's sake, with a royal good will. He is exuberant in his expressions of kindly feeling and his assurances of what he will do for them. He is giving them 'the good of the land of Egypt'; they are to eat 'the fat of the land' (45[18]); they are to dwell in 'the best of the land' (47[6]). The rich alluvial plains of Goshen, the garden of Egypt, the proverbial land of plenty, become the resting-place of the Hebrews. In this goodly heritage, under the fostering care of a benignant monarch and his viceroy, they will rapidly increase in numbers and in power; and here in the providence of God they are destined to sojourn for centuries, until they become a great nation.

KINGSHIP.—The Hebrews were to be workers, not idlers, in the land of plenty. Some of them obtained an interview with Pharaoh, and the king's first question was, 'What is your occupation?' (47[3]). When he learned that they were shepherds, he bade Joseph pick out the ablest of them and make them rulers over his cattle. The royal herds grazed on the pasture-land of Goshen, and the sons of Jacob, that cleverest of stock-breeders, would make excellent graziers. The fact that this Pharaoh was himself of Shemitic origin—one of the Hyksos or Shepherd kings—made him partial to Hebrews and shepherds. He had a quick eye for 'any able men' (v.[6]), men of knowledge, capacity, energy, the best that could be found to do his work. Nothing so clearly indicates a man's fitness for the business of kingship as his unerring judgment in the choice of his servants. Pharaoh finds the right man to be 'ruler' over his people, and the right men to be 'rulers' over his cattle ; and if he finds the right men for all the intervening offices of state, he cannot fail to be one of the most successful monarchs of the land.

GREATNESS.—Joseph brought his father into the palace, and presented him to Pharaoh. The meeting between the Egyptian king and the Hebrew patriarch is one of those traditional incidents which can never cease to strike the imagination of mankind. Many other presentations — of princes, nobles, ambassadors—had taken place, and would yet take place, at that Egyptian court, but they have all been forgotten, while this alone is remembered. The scene represents the ideals of kingliness and saintliness. The two most eminent men in the world meet and converse as equals. Rank and power, titles and dignities fade into nothingness when they realise their common humanity. Days and years, earth and its pilgrimage, good and evil, are the same to a king and a shepherd. If there is a difference, Jacob is the greater of the two. Pharaoh counts it an honour to receive his blessing, 'and without dispute the less is blessed of the better.'[1] All the characteristics of Egypt and Israel are embodied in these representative men. Pharaoh stands for a nation which has long excelled, and is destined yet to excel, in secular wisdom and power ; Jacob, for a people who are destined to attain spiritual greatness, blessing others because they themselves have power with God and prevail.

LIFE.—'How many,' the king asks the patriarch, 'are the days of the years of thy life?' The question is somehow tenderly suggestive of the silvery hairs and wistful eyes and tottering steps of extreme old age. Jacob's years are evidently many. But his answer seems to come with a sigh : 'Few and

[1] Heb. 7⁷.

evil have been the days of the years of my life' (v.⁸). That life
is so short and so sad is the universal complaint.  What is
Jacob's life, Pharaoh's, any man's?  A pilgrimage, a tale that
is told, a handbreadth, a dream, a sleep, a vapour, a shadow,
a fading flower, a wind, nothing, vanity.  That is empirical life
as all men find it.  'What shadows we are, and what shadows
we pursue !' ¹

> 'A moment's halt, a momentary taste,
> Of being from the well amid the waste,
> And, lo ! the phantom caravan has reached
> The nothing it set out from—Oh, make haste.' ²

Is life itself, then, evil?  Does Jacob, whose days have been few and
evil, think so?  Is he one of 'the weary pessimists, life's tired-
out guests,' who cry that life is not worth living.  No, it is only *his*
life, or any actual man's life, that is evil.  Life, the gift of God, is
worthy of the Giver.  To every true Hebrew and every true man
life is essentially, wonderfully good—if only it were longer, and we
better !  Our sorrowful complaint that our days are few and evil
is the pathetic evidence of the presence in every human soul of a
craving for life as God meant it to be—an ideal, a perfect life.  We
hunger and thirst for it—for a life sweet and pure and everlasting.

> 'Whatever crazy sorrow saith,
> No life that breathes with human breath
> Has ever truly longed for death.
>
> 'Tis life, whereof our nerves are scant,
> Oh life, not death, for which we pant ;
> More life, and fuller, that I want.' ³

STATESMANSHIP.—As a stateman, Joseph took hold of Egyptian affairs with both hands.  There was a steady resistless force
in his movements and actions.  'He went throughout all the
land of Egypt.'  He was here, there, and everywhere.  His name
was known and his power felt by prince and peasant.  He had
to rule a populace now faint, now frantic, with hunger.  From
Nubia to the sea he heard that saddest of cries, 'Give us

---

¹ Burke.          ² Omar Khayyam.          ³ Tennyson.

bread,' and he had to be the dispenser of blessing to millions. He resolved that none should perish of want. The work required a vast, organising, far-seeing genius, and he proved equal to the task. He won the eulogies which are bestowed on a great ruler by a grateful nation. 'Thou hast saved our lives,' they said ; and when they cried 'Abrech,' and bowed the knee to him, it was not the mechanical homage of servile fear, but the sincere reverence of whole-hearted gratitude. As an administrator, Joseph has sometimes been accused of abusing his power, of snatching an unfair advantage in a time of national distress, of creating a 'corner' in wheat, and compelling a hungry people to pay extortionate prices. There is no real ground for bringing these charges against him. His contemporaries were better judges of his policy than we can be, and they were unanimous in their praise of his administration. What he did as a famine-minister was to sell corn first for money, then for cattle, and then for service. At the same time he seized the occasion to do a thing which probably greatly needed to be done—to nationalise the land. He made the proprietors of the soil 'servants' of the crown, tenant-farmers who paid a fifth of the produce of the land as a rent—an extremely moderate tax when the Nile Valley is yielding its normal harvest. 'The power of the old aristocracy was broken as completely as it has been in Japan in our own day,'[1] and probably with as good results. It is by such master-strokes of wise and energetic legislation that statesmen convert the passing misfortunes which visit a nation into great and permanent blessings.

FUTURITY.—Jacob lived seventeen years in Egypt, and then the time drew near when he must die ($47^{28}$). And he said to Joseph, 'Bury me not, I pray thee, in Egypt ; but when I sleep with my fathers, thou shalt carry me out of Egypt, and bury me in their burying-place' (vv.[29, 30]). It is evident that the two things, Jacob's sleeping with his fathers, and his being buried in the cave

[1] Sayce.

of Machpelah, are perfectly distinct. He will sleep with his fathers : God will see to that. The disposal of his body will follow : Joseph will see to that. The spirit will return to God who gave it, and dust mingle with kindred dust. But what is meant by sleeping with one's fathers? Sleep is in every language the natural image of death. When a Greek poet says of one of his heroes, 'He slept an iron sleep,' and an English poet of one of our kings, 'After life's fitful fever he sleeps well,' our thoughts scarcely go beyond the sleep-like stillness of the body. But the Hebrew idea of sleeping with one's fathers meant more. It took the imagination as far as it could go into the unseen world. It indicated the prevailing belief in a Beyond or Hereafter where the fathers were in some sense still alive. In regard to the other world, there are two things about which we Christians feel certain—first, that the dead are alive ; and, second, that they are with God. Of the first of these things the Hebrews had no doubt ; of the second they were far from sure. To them, death was a going to the fathers ; to us, it is a going to the Father. The difference is immense ; but between the meagre Shemitic idea and the full Christian faith there were the intuitions and instincts which prompted the larger Hebrew hope that after death there would not be less but more of the Divine Presence. 'I shall sleep with my fathers' was not a satisfying, though a peaceful, thought ; but the Hebrew saint learned ere long to say, 'I shall be satisfied, when I awake, with Thy likeness.'[1]

RETROSPECT.—A dying man's backward glance upon the life he is leaving is always full of interest. What incidents of the way does he recall at the end of the journey? What scenes stand out fresh before his mind when others have faded away? What voices, long hushed, does he now hear? When Joseph takes his two sons to see their grandfather, he finds him reminiscent of far off things and days of long ago (48[3. 7]). And Jacob

[1] Ps. 17[15].

tells his son what he sees. Two Places and two Persons crowd out everything else from his vision—Bethel, where God appeared to him, and Ephrath, where Rachel was taken from him. Faith and love—a great religious blessing and a tender earthly happiness—have made him the man he is, and sum up his life. Two supreme experiences have become an integral part of his being, and can only perish if the soul itself dies. There have been times when his better nature has almost been swamped by sordid and selfish cares. But his ideals have saved him. No man who believes with all his soul can ever remain sordid, and no man who loves with all his heart can ever remain selfish.

SHEPHERDING. — In token of a great love, Jacob adopts Joseph's two boys as his own (48⁵), thereby giving his favourite son a double heritage — the portion of a firstborn among the tribes of Israel. Joseph then brings his sons to receive the patriarch's kiss and blessing (v.⁹). No children ever got a more precious legacy to carry with them through life than these two. The benediction is perhaps the finest ever uttered by dying lips. Jacob puts into it his most thankful and joyful thoughts about God. He invokes Him as the God before whom his fathers walked—the God of history ; as the God who has shepherded himself all his life long—the God of providence ; as the Angel who has redeemed him from all evil—the God of grace ; and he prays Him who has been all this and done all this to bless the lads (vv.¹⁵· ¹⁶). Past, present, and future are sweetly linked together in the blessing. The God who has been tried and proved by the old who are going to their rest, will show Himself as gracious to the young who are rising up to take their places. Jacob's Shepherd, who has been tending and leading and feeding him so long, will do just the same for the lambs of His flock. Our English version misses something of the beauty of Jacob's words. The translation 'who hath fed me' is too meagre. We need to say, 'who hath shepherded me.' The same word is the keynote of the finest of all the Psalms : 'The

Lord is my shepherd.' It is a beautiful metaphor, which comes with an exquisite pathos and a profound significance from the lips of a dying shepherd. The poets of a later age could only echo his words : 'Give ear, O Shepherd of Israel, Thou that leadest Joseph like a flock.'[1] All the tender grace of the Old Testament religion is found in this lovely conception. It was not one man or two, but a whole nation that learned to believe in God as a Shepherd : 'We are His people, the sheep of His pasture.'[2] No other ancient nation ever expected from God such loving care and unerring guidance, no other nation ever promised such meek submission and faithful following. And while the Hebrew temple and sacrifice and priesthood have passed away as the shadows of better things, the Hebrew thought of a Shepherd-God will live for ever.

REDEMPTION.—The succeeding words of the benediction are equally fine : 'The Angel[3] who hath redeemed me from all evil bless the lads' (v.[16]). Much would have been lacking if Jacob had not spoken these words. They are of the nature of a palinode ; in speaking them he recants certain things which he said before. In his dark days he spoke in dirge-like tones of trouble and sorrow, gray hairs and Sheol ; he counted his many miseries, and said that all these things were against him ($42^{36}$). But in the retrospect he sees that he was wrong. All things have worked together for his good, and God has in His mercy redeemed him from all evil. As the ransomed of the Lord he has obtained joy and gladness, and sorrow and sighing have fled away. So his dying testimony pulsates with gratitude and hope. Let Joseph's sons know that life is good to every one who has a Redeemer. In our saddest days we would pass on to others the pessimist's gloomy creed :

> 'The happiest youth, viewing his progress through,
> What perils past, what crosses to ensue,
> Would shut the book and set him down and die.'[4]

---

[1] Ps. 80[1].　　[2] Ps. 100[3].　　[3] Vol. i. p. 91.　　[4] Shakespeare.

But the real lesson of llfe is the optimist's cheerful faith :

> 'That the procession of our fate, howe'er
> Sad or disturbed, is ordered by a Being
> Of infinite benevolence and power,
> Whose everlasting purposes embrace
> All accidents, converting them to Good.' [1]

SOVEREIGNTY.—Jacob is represented as crossing his hands in the act of blessing Joseph's sons, thus putting his right hand on Ephraim's head and his left on Manasseh's. Joseph supposes that his father is doing this unconsciously, as if it were the natural mistake of a frail or an absent-minded man, and tries to correct him. But Jacob's mind has never been clearer or stronger than it is in these last days. He does not need to be told which is the firstborn : 'I know it, my son, I know it.' He is guiding his hands quite wittingly ; and tradition represents him as thus symbolically foretelling that Ephraim will have a nobler name and a greater power than Manasseh. Genesis seems to be written for the purpose of overturning all our ordinary ideas of the rights of primogeniture. It advocates the divine rights of younger sons. It teaches us that God's choice is rarely pitched where man's would be. God prefers Isaac to Ishmael, Jacob to Esau, Judah to Reuben, Ephraim to Manasseh. Even the modern principle of the careers open to the talents falls short of the Divine method of working ; for God often passes by men of the most brilliant gifts, and uses the most unlikely instruments to do His work. Not that He ever acts arbitrarily ; He has a reason for all His actions and all His choices. But He exercises His sovereignty and bids us exercise our faith. 'None can stay His hand, or say unto Him, What doest Thou ?' [2]

[1] Wordsworth.　　　　　　　　　　[2] Dan. 4[35].

# FAREWELL
## Genesis 48:21-50:13

'O! but they say the tongues of dying men
Enforce attention like deep harmony :
Where words are scarce, they are seldom spent in vain.'
SHAKESPEARE.

DEPARTURE.—Jacob's old age is serene and grand. We found little in his youthful character to admire except the one great quality of faith in the unseen ; but that faith has gradually transfigured him, making the last part of his life the best. No other deathbed scene is so vividly depicted in the Old Testament as that of which he is the centre, and it is not in the least gloomy or depressing. On the contrary, his end is calm and majestic, like the setting of a summer sun, which is never so grand and beautiful as just before it disappears. He makes an ideal departure, which will teach multitudes of Hebrews in all ages how to 'yield up the breath.' The Hereafter might be dim and uncertain, but the present life, at any rate, was something great and holy, a wondrous gift from God, a glad and glorious experience to be taken leave of with high solemnity and dignity. Let the end of life be what it might, it was not the bursting of a bubble, the fading of a dream, the turning down of an empty glass. On this side it was a saint's calm surrender of his spirit into the hands of a faithful Creator ; what it was on the other side he could not tell ; he went to see.

HOPE.—By faith Jacob, when a-dying, leaves his children a legacy of hope in God. He looks upward in faith and forward in expectancy. His religion makes him sanguine and prophetic. 'Behold,' he said, 'I die, but God shall be with you' (48²¹). The words are suggestive of infinite possibilities. The One remains while the many change and pass.  When man dies, God lives on, and faith in the real presence of a living God is the spring of eternal hope.  Faith is the power by which men grasp the future, the unseen, the Divine, by which they maintain their expectant look, by which they remain optimists in spite of all the evil of the world.  Dying saints are enabled to bequeath messages of comfort to after ages, because they are sure that the God who has so greatly blessed themselves has greater blessings in store for their posterity.  True religion bids them expect a brighter day to dawn and a happier society to come into being. Jacob, dying in Goshen, the proverbial land of plenty, sees something still better than Goshen.  His conviction of the goodness of God kindles an ardent and unquenchable hope of the amelioration of the state of his people.  The vision of God is always accompanied by the vision of a better and happier world.

CHARACTERS.—The forty-ninth chapter of Genesis is usually entitled the Blessing of Jacob.  The designation is not strictly accurate, as some of the utterances contained in it are judgments rather than blessings.  It is sometimes called the Last Will and Testament of Jacob.  It is really a great and ancient poem, terse in expression, vivid in imagery, in which, while individuals are addressed, we may see the personified tribes of Israel mirrored as they actually appeared in the days of the Judges and the beginning of the monarchy.  The characterisations are keen and trenchant, such as a quick-witted and full-blooded people delight in.  If the criticism is unsparing, the appreciation is generous.  No doubt every phrase became ere long proverbial, and the portraits served as types to imitate or to avoid.  Tribes and nations, as well as individuals, have characters to keep or to lose.  Some have virtues which mark them out for success and happiness ; others have vices which doom them to failure and sorrow.  One tribe is lacking in moral strength, a second in love, a third in enterprise ; and, while prophecy may pronounce their doom, their own weaknesses are their real curse. Others, strong in character, rich in grace, abounding in energy, are helped by the Mighty God of Jacob, and win for themselves great happiness and renown.

CHASTITY.—Jacob is represented as denouncing some of his sons with the stern sad anger of a Hebrew prophet. The three eldest are failures. Reuben the firstborn had every natural advantage—the right of primogeniture, his father's strength, a certain native dignity and power. His youth was full of promise, and he might easily have retained the pre-eminence. He had good impulses and much kindness of heart ; he was averse to inflicting pain, and easily moved to tears. But he forfeited all his advantages, lost his supremacy, and sank into obscurity, through lack of self-control. Unstable as water, he could not excel (v.⁴). He vitiated his nature by animal passion. He made himself vile and despicable. He was wanting in the first attribute of manhood—chivalrous respect for the honour of womanhood. He let lust extinguish the light and glory of his soul. He transmitted to his posterity a vicious taint which they never eradicated. While other tribes were rising in power and fame, Reuben was decrepit and decadent. No judge, or prophet, or ruler had Reuben's blood flowing in his veins. Sensuality enervated the race, and Reuben became effete.

> ' Methinks I am a prophet now inspired,
> And thus expiring do fortell of him :
> His rash fierce blaze of riot cannot last,
> For violent fires soon burn out themselves.' [1]

BROTHERHOOD. — Simeon and Levi are characterised as 'brethren,' or kindred spirits, in evil. In their secret societies they hatched conspiracies so dark and foul that all good men were constrained to avoid them. 'O my soul, come not thou into their council ; unto their assembly, my glory, be not thou

[1] Shakespeare.

united' (v.⁶). The soul of man, here wonderfully called his 'glory'—that divine radiance or image within him which it is his task and duty to keep undimmed—would be darkened almost as much by a hatred like Simeon's as by a lust like Reuben's. The swords of Simeon and Levi are weapons of violence. Jacob denounces their vindictive spirit, their fierce anger and cruel wrath. Their treacherous slaughter of men and senseless mutilation of cattle at Shechem have not been forgotten. Their character will work out its own punishment. They will be divided in Jacob and scattered in Israel (v.⁷). While love is a uniting, hatred is a disintegrating, force. Conspirators are notoriously suspicious of one another, the same selfish spirit which makes them ruthless to their enemies making them also jealous of their friends. They stand by each other only so long as self-interest unites them. The violent man finds himself in the end alone. Brethren in evil are brethren only in name.

DOMINION.—With glowing colours and warm enthusiasm the poem describes the greatness, the glory, the prosperity of Judah. He bears a great name, of which he is worthy. He is victorious in battle : we see his hand upon the neck of his prostrate foes, and his brethren bowing before him in lowly submission. He is powerful as a couchant lion, and on his mountain fastnesses no one dares to disturb him. He receives into his strong hand the sceptre of dominion, and he will never let it slip till a heaven-sent Peace-bringer shall come, when he shall at length gather the peoples and unite them in willing obedience. His happy abode is described as a land flowing with wine and milk (vv.⁸⁻¹²). The vigorous metaphors of the first part of the prophecy are easy to understand. They exactly describe the proud position won for Judah by the military genius of David. We cannot be so certain of the meaning of the word Shiloh ; but it is probably connected—like Salem, Siloam, Solomon— with the root-word which signifies peace. If so, the idea is both intelligible and beautiful. In the land of Canaan, whose

mountains and valleys were the scenes of almost endless civil
and international strife, peace was the ideal state for which all
good men longed and prayed. If God would only send a Prince
of Peace to end all cruel and bloody wars, then the sovereignty of
Judah would find its fitting consummation, as the material power
of a great dynasty would be merged in a vaster kingdom of
grace! This is one of the greatest ideals which came from the
heart of the Hebrew race. Has it been realised? Judah certainly
won and retained the sceptre. His prophets and poets, more
than his kings, became the spiritual leaders of mankind—'dead
but sceptred sovereigns who still rule our spirits.' The land of
Judah (Judea) became the most sacred country, and the sons of
Judah (Judeans, contracted to Jews) the most wonderful race,
that the world has seen. And out of that land and that people
the great Peace-bringer at length came. 'Judah, thou art he
whom thy brethren shall praise' (v.[8]). It has been well said that
'the name of Joseph, first among the sons of Jacob at the
beginning of the nation, grows pale as history advances before
the name of Judah. Even the great word Israel dies before it.
It is the Jews, the men of Judah, that fill the records of the world.'[1]

SEAMANSHIP.—Zebulon is regarded as the father of a maritime
race. 'He (his people) shall dwell at the haven of the sea; and
he (his land) shall be for a haven (or beach) of ships; and his
border shall be upon Zidon' (v.[13]). His children shall be familiar
with the sound of clashing waves and the glory of setting suns.
They shall do business on great waters, and trade with foreign
lands. They are bidden elsewhere to 'rejoice' in their 'going
out,'[2] that is, in the enterprises of a seafaring life. They shall
'suck the abundance of the sea'[3]—a more graphic touch than our
'reaping the harvest of the sea.' Dwelling not far from Zidon,
the great maritime city of the Phœnicians, they in some respects
resemble their powerful neighbours. It should be observed,
however, that Zebulon was isolated among the Hebrew tribes

[1] Stopford Brooke.      [2] Deut. 33[18].      [3] Deut. 33[19]

in his naval pursuits. Israel as a whole never took to the sea, never became a sea-loving nation like Greece or England. Handicapped by the absence of natural harbours, they never had a fleet worth speaking of, and never fought a naval battle. They had their dwelling by the sea, but never their home on it.

STRENUOUSNESS.—Issachar's portrait is drawn with a few plain, masterly strokes. He was a husbandman, strong, easy-going, indolent. In his rich inland valleys he led a life of placid content. 'He saw a resting-place that it was good, and the land that it was pleasant '(v.[15]). He entered into possession, and had his heart's desire. He was pricked by no higher ambition. He should have been as strenuous as he was strong; but with wealth and comfort apparently secure, he did not see why he should exert himself overmuch. He loved the ignoble ease which has been called the vice of rich lowlands all the world over. In one trenchant phrase he is described as 'a strong ass.' He was well aware of his strength, but did not know that he was an ass. In the end he paid the price of indolence. As he was stretching his lazy length 'between the sheepfolds,' he forgot that his goods needed guarding. The lassitude which disinclined him for labour equally incapacitated him for self-defence; and when strangers cast their covetous eyes upon his fat acres and swooped down upon his peaceful homesteads, he and his possessions become an easy prey to the spoiler. And then, as he would not toil for himself when he was his own master, he must even toil for another master, 'bowing his shoulder to bear, and becoming a servant under taskwork' (v.[15]). So Issachar becomes a warning rather than an example. He points the moral that 'the prosperity (or careless ease) of fools shall destroy them.' [1]

' Then, welcome each rebuff
That turns earth's smoothness rough,

---

[1] Prov. 1[32].

> Each sting that bids not sit nor stand, but go !
> Be our joys three parts pain !
> Strive, and hold cheap the strain ;
> Learn, nor account the pang ; dare, never grudge the throe.'[1]

WARFARE. — Geographical conditions tended to make one tribe mercantile, another industrial, another military. Dan and Gad are both warlike, and none the less dangerous that they are small. 'Dan shall judge (defend) his people, as one of the tribes of Israel' (v.[16]). Dan became famous as a border raider. From his bare highland fastnesses he would make a sudden descent upon the rich plains of Philistia and return laden with spoil. His hero was Samson. The metaphor in which the tribe is described is graphic. Dan is an adder (horned snake) lurking in the way, which darts out and bites the passing horse's heels, making him madly plunge and throw his rider in the dust (v.[17]). The figure gives us the idea of a subtle, stealthy race, which knows how to lie low and bide its time, and then strike a blow with deadly effect. Gad is equally warlike, but gains his victories by more open means. There is a play upon his name, which resembles the word for a troop. 'Gad, a troop shall troop upon him, but he shall troop upon their heels' (v.[19]). It is not wise to underrate his skill or valour. When he seems to be having the worst of it, he knows how to turn the tide of battle and drive his enemies in headlong confusion.

HAPPINESS.—Asher, as his name indicates, is in many respects 'happy.' He dwells in the fertile plain of Jezreel, the garden of Palestine. He is described in the Blessing of Moses as 'dipping his foot in oil.'[2] He has enough, and more than enough, of earth's richest products, so that he can send exports to his neighbours ; and kings are pleased to have his dainties on their tables (v.[20]). Nothing is here said of the spirit of Asher ; but we learn elsewhere that he, like Issachar, was too fond of ease, and that in times of national peril he proved recreant.[3]

[1] Browning.      [2] Deut. 33[24].      [3] Judg. 5[17, 18].

He never furnished a hero to the Hebrew race ; and for all he was called so happy, he missed the glory and the joy which only the brave and self-sacrificing know.

LIBERTY.—Naphtali is a northern mountaineer, dwelling 'upon the high places of the field.'[1] He has a highlander's love of liberty, and is ready—as we see in the instance of Barak, the tribal hero—to risk all in its defence. He is compared to 'a hind let loose,' gambolling at its sweet will, breasting the steep mountain side, breathing the free air of heaven. The beautiful figure 'fully expresses the feelings which are bred by the health, the spaciousness, the high freedom and glorious outlook of Upper Galilee.'[2] Naphtali has, in addition, the gift of graceful and forcible speech—'he giveth goodly words.' In the absence of any historical explanation of this sentence, we may find some pleasure in a poet's fancy. Jacob was wearily awaiting the second return of his sons from Egypt, when suddenly one of them bounded into his presence.

> '''Twas Naphtali who hastened,
>     And, ere the rest arrived,
>   Poured into Jacob's wondering ears
>   Sweet news, to wrestle with his fears,
>     How Joseph still survived.
>
>   When Jacob lay a-dying,
>     At sight of Naphtali
>   The memory of the past returned,
>   The runner was again discerned
>     As in the hour gone by.
>
>   Then thus the father blessed him,
>     " Like hind 'mong mountain herds
>   Outstripping all, art thou my son,
>   Thou didst thy brethren all outrun,
>     Thou broughtest goodly words!"'[3]

BLESSEDNESS.—The Blessing of Joseph is by itself a little poem of much beauty. In spirit it is at once patriotic and

[1] Judg. 5[18].    [2] G. A. Smith.    [3] Poet's Bible.

religious. It praises the son who is worthy to receive a crowning blessing, extols the God who is his Guardian, and indicates the splendour of his heritage. Joseph is compared to a young fruit-tree (Ephraim meaning fruitful), a vine planted by a fountain, whose branches run over the wall—symbols of a fine race inhabiting a rich country and rapidly extending its borders. Joseph's prosperity provokes envious rivals, who sorely grieve him, shoot at him, and persecute him ; but his own bow abides in strength, and his arms are upheld and strengthened by the hands of the mighty God of Jacob (v.24). The figure is simple and beautiful. As a father bends down over his young archer-boy, lays his great palm over the little hand that holds the bow, and instructs the child how to direct the arrow and draw the string, so Joseph has the great God behind him to teach and encourage him. Joseph alone would be weak as a child, but Joseph aided by the power and wisdom of God is unconquer-able. For who is his God? 'The 'Mighty One of Jacob,' whose defence never faileth ; 'the Shepherd' of Israel, who leadeth Joseph like a flock ; and 'the Stone of Israel,' the Rock of Ages, against which all weapons are hurled in vain.

> ' Rock of the desert, prophet-sung,
>    How grew its shadowing pile at length
> A symbol in the Hebrew tongue
>    Of God's eternal love and strength ! ' [1]

This God will bless Joseph with blessings of heaven above—sunshine and wind, rain and dew ; with blessings of the deep that couches beneath—fountains and streams issuing from the heart of the earth ; and with blessings of the breast and of the womb—a vitality sufficient to fill the land. There is promised an exuberance of 'blessing,' in the strict sense of the word. The resources of nature are duly appreciated only when they are recognised as the gifts of God. Light and air, dew and rain, life and love, are common enough things ; but they are transfigured when we see the hand of God bestowing them.

[1] Whittier.

> ' Thy bountiful care what tongue can recite?
> It breathes in the air, it shines in the light ;
> It streams from the hills, it descends to the plain,
> And sweetly distils in the dew and the rain.'

Finally, the blessings of Joseph (Ephraim and Manasseh) are described as surpassing the blessings of the perpetual mountains and the treasures of the everlasting hills (v.[26]). For there are better things comprised in them than all nature's bountiful store. 'They include national and political greatness and the high religious privileges implied in the promises.'[1] The material wealth of the tribes may be great, but the people themselves, so long as they are brave in spirit and true to God, will be their country's real strength and pride.

STRENGTH. — 'Benjamin is a wolf that ravineth : in the morning he shall devour the prey, and at even he shall divide the spoil' (v.[27]). His home was up among the mountains of central Canaan, and his high, isolated position had a marked influence upon his habits and character. Hardy and brave, proud and resentful, he made no secret of his delight in war and plunder. His name meant 'son of the right hand,' and as if in sheer perversity he acquired a deadly proficiency in the use of the left hand ; his slinging and archery became famous, and with his back to the wall he proudly defied all comers. The 'wolf' in him sometimes betrayed itself in acts of singular ferocity ; but he put his strength to a nobler use in the Hebrew wars of liberation ; and he gave the nation some of its noblest men.

SALVATION.—In the midst of these oracular utterances Jacob lifted up his eyes to heaven, and ejaculated the words, 'I have waited for Thy salvation, O Lord' (v.[18]). It is somewhat difficult to read the thought of the dying patriarch, and to define the salvation for which he longed. The waiting is easily understood. It was the characteristic attitude of all believing Hebrews,

[1] Driver.

living or dying. They waited, and they felt that it was good for them to wait, not in languid indifference, but with intense desire and eager hope, to see what God would do. Waiting was the attitude of people who had an ideal which they confidently expected to see realised, though there was sometimes an intense pathos in the use of the word, when hope deferred made the heart sick. Salvation is not so easy to interpret. When *we* hear a dying man say, ' I have waited for thy salvation,' we know that he is thinking of personal immortality. But we cannot be sure that this is the Hebrew idea. Just as the blessings which Jacob promises his sons are destined, not for themselves as individuals, but for the tribes of which they are to be the founders, so the salvation for which he has waited may be a happiness which is to be attained, not presently by himself, but in the distant future by the nation which shall trace its descent from him ; in which case this earth will still be the scene of the salvation. ' One of the strangest things in the Old Testament is the little place which the individual feels he has, and his tendency to lose himself in larger wholes, such as the family and the nation. When in earlier times the individual approached death . . . he consoled himself with the thought that he did not all die, the memory of the righteous was blessed. He lived, too, in his children and in his people ; he saw the good of Israel; his spirit lived and the work of his hands was established.'[1]  On the other hand, there certainly came a time in the religious development of Israel when this oblivion of self was no longer possible. 'With the growing sense of God's greatness and power came the conception that even the realm of the dead was under His control, and that the righteous might still hope after death to see the salvation of God.'[2]

TEARS.—Jacob's latter end is peace. There is no timorous starting at the approach of death, no shrinking back from the unseen. The dying man calmly speaks of his being gathered

[1] A. B. Davidson.     [2] Hastings' *Dict.*, art. ' Salvation.'

to his people, gives careful directions for his burial in Canaan, gathers up his feet upon his bed as if he were only going to sleep, yields up his spirit, and is gathered to his fathers. Yet death, however peaceful it may be, is a hard necessity. 'Joseph fell upon his father's face, and wept upon him, and kissed him' (50¹). Love must weep. The Book of Genesis indicates that man as we know him, man the image of God, ought to live for ever, death being an intruder upon the joy of life—the dark shadow of sin. Our instincts confirm this teaching. The heart untouched by grace can never really reconcile itself to the cruel stroke of Fate or the hard pressure of iron Law, can never do aught but hate 'the fell Fury with the accursed shears' that 'slits the thin-spun life'; and even the heart that trusts in the living God would break if it did not find relief in tears. The Egyptians, according to their custom, mourned for Jacob seventy days [1] (50³), while the Hebrews themselves mourned but seven [2] (v.¹⁰), and the difference may indicate that death was somewhat less awful to those who had the clearer and stronger faith. But the stern, inexorable fact remained. We can still see the long procession winding on, and across all the centuries hear that 'very great and sore lamentation.' Death needed to be abolished, life and immortality to be brought to light.[3]

## FAITH
### Genesis 50:14-20

'All I have seen teaches me to trust the Creator for all I have not seen.'
EMERSON.

FORGIVENESS.—After their father's death Joseph's brethren become strangely restless. Their anxious looks betray the fact that their minds are haunted with gloomy fears. They

[1] So Herodotus.   [2] 1 Sam. 31¹³.   [3] 2 Tim. 1¹⁰.

somehow feel that a day of reckoning has come, and that terrible things are going to happen to them. They are tortured with morbid suspicions of their brother. Though he has remitted their transgression, though he has heaped favours upon them, though he has never given them the slightest reason to suppose that he is secretly harbouring a grudge against them, yet they fear him. They feel that it is too much to hope that he has absolutely and finally forgiven them. He must still in his heart of hearts be their enemy. It has been the fear of grieving their father that has restrained his anger during all those years ; he must have been nursing a desire for vengeance in spite of all his apparent kindness ; and now that his father's commanding influence is withdrawn, it is only too likely that his smouldering wrath will at last blaze out against them. They can talk of nothing else than this : ' It may be that Joseph will hate us, and will fully requite us all the evil we did unto him' (v.¹⁵). Their conscience is needlessly alarming them. 'There are they in great fear, where no fear is.'[1] Unable to banish their obstinate doubts, they at length send this message to Joseph : 'Thy father did command before he died, saying, So shall ye say unto Joseph, Forgive, I pray thee, the transgression of thy brethren, and their sin ; for that they did unto thee evil : and now, we beseech thee, forgive the transgression of the servants of the God of thy father.' They could scarcely have pleaded more humbly if they had actually been under sentence of condemnation. They confess their 'transgression,' their 'sin,' the 'evil' they have done ; and while they urge their father's dying behest, they plead the fact that they are Joseph's brothers and servants of Jacob's God. They can only hope that filial piety and the obligations of a common faith may constrain their brother to be merciful. It is no doubt forcible pleading ; but the pity that it should for one moment seem necessary ! Joseph listens with growing amazement. It is a sore disappointment to his sunny and generous nature to find

[1] Ps. 53⁵.

that he is so greatly misunderstood. Are his brothers so incapable of appreciating true and warm love? Must they enlist their father on their side against him? Does he need the pressure of parental authority to keep him right—the dead hand to restrain him from deeds of vengeance? Have they really been regarding their father as the only bulwark between themselves and a brother's wrath? Must they persist in thinking of him as a judge and a foe? Yet their suspicions only serve to display the generous sympathy of his nature. As he realises what they have been suffering, he cannot keep back his tears. 'He wept when they spake unto him' (v.$^{17}$). These are not hot tears of wounded vanity and fretful impatience. They are tears of compassion, overflowing from a heart full of love. We read of many occasions on which Joseph weeps—when he hears his brothers' first confession (42$^{24}$), when he meets his young brother after a long separation (43$^{30}$), when he makes himself known to his brethren (45$^{14, 15}$), when he embraces his father again after many years (46$^{29}$), when he sees his father still in death (50$^1$), and now when his brothers doubt his love. It is never the thought of himself, but always the thought of others, that moves him. The strongest quality in Joseph's character is forgiving love. We see in him the personification of healing mercy and redeeming grace. It is 'the Christian spirit before the Christian time.'[1]

PARDON.—When Joseph's brethren fell down before his face and pleaded for mercy, he said to them, 'Fear not: for am I in the place of God?' (v.$^{19}$). His answer is at once far humbler and far more august than anything they looked for. They expected him to speak as a just, and it might be a merciful, judge. He speaks as a loving brother who is also a prophet of God. He turns their thoughts away from himself. He directs their minds upwards. He tells them it is with God rather than with man that they have to do. The meeting-place between the penitent soul and God is holy ground into

[1] F. W. Robertson.

which no man should ever dare to intrude. What saint or angel can stand in the place of God? Whoever puts himself, or lets others imagine that he puts himself, for a moment into that position is guilty of treason. Joseph will not do it. He refuses to acquit or to condemn. It is his part to forgive as far as man can, and he does so with all his heart and soul. From him there is nothing to fear. But man's forgiveness can never make an end of sin. Joseph's brethren, if they are wise, will go home thinking no more of Joseph. He cannot speak the word that will give them comfort and peace. They need to go and fall down before another Face and plead for mercy. They need to hear another Voice pronouncing their sentence of absolution. Who can cancel a sinner's debt, who can remit punishment, who can purge the soul from moral defilement, but God alone? And, on the other hand, where is the judge who can condemn, if God hath justified?

PROVIDENCE.—Joseph restates to his brothers his doctrine of providence, which is to penitent minds at once so humbling and so comforting. 'And as for you, ye meant evil against me; but God meant it for good, as it is this day, to save much people alive' (v.[20]). Joseph recognises more clearly than ever a divine order in the story of his troubled life. He sees a line of light shining through all deeds of darkness. He discerns a definite purpose to bring good out of evil. The very wrong which once occasioned 'the anguish of his soul' (42[21]), has wrought out results which fill his heart with gratitude. His brothers meant it for evil, God meant it for good. They were thinking only how they might blight the prospects of a brother whom they disliked; but God—who is the God of Egypt as well as of Israel—was thinking how He might save a multitude of people for whom He cared in a foreign land. The LORD permitted them to follow the devices of their own hearts, but wove all their schemes into the wonderful web of His own gracious providence. Man is free to do everything except one thing—to thwart God's purpose of love. 'To the man who is not attuned to the will of God it is a thought full of dread that God has control of all the issues of life, the smallest and the greatest, the high and the low ; but to the man who is willing to make his will God's will, it is a thought full of rest and peace.'[1]   We may wonder how Joseph came to know so well, and to say so confidently, what God 'meant.' Though he may seem to be guilty of presumption, he is entirely free from it.   He speaks what he knows.   The truth is that there is a very intimate connection between doing and knowing.   It is by faithful obedience to God's will that we gain a clear understanding of God's ways.   Where a clever intellect fails to discover the hidden meanings of providence, a childlike and submissive heart succeeds.   'The secret of the LORD is with them that fear Him.'[2]

HOPE.—Joseph spent all his remaining years in Egypt.   He lived to see his children of the third generation (v.[23]).   When his end was drawing near, he spoke, as his father had done, words of hope.   'I die,' he said to his brethren, 'but God shall visit you, and bring you out of this land into the land which He sware to Abraham, to Isaac, and to Jacob' (v.[24]).   This is the dreamer's last dream, a waking dream.   It is rather the prophecy of a believing heart, the vision of God's gracious working in the near or the distant future.   The characteristic of waning life is said to be disenchantment.   Old men in general are inclined to check the zeal and damp the ardour of their younger followers.   A shrewd observer of life has said that youth is an illusion, manhood a struggle, old age a regret.[3]   'How many young men,' says a great idealist, 'have I not hailed at the commencement of their career, glowing with enthusiasm, and full of the poetry of great enterprises, whom I see to-day precocious old men, with the wrinkles of cold calculation on their brow ; calling themselves free from illusion when they are only disheartened ; and practical when they are only commonplace.'[4]   But believing men

1 Martineau.          2 Ps. 25[14].          3 Disraeli.          4 Mazzini.

experience no disillusionment. The leaves of hope never wither on souls that are rooted in God. Joseph when dying looks forward with calm and perfect confidence, knowing that glorious things, and ever more glorious, must be, because God is. 'What is this Better, this flying Ideal, but the perpetual promise of the Creator?'[1] God lives though a hundred Josephs die. The two characteristics of the Hebrew mind were the upward and the forward look, the one directed to God in the present, the other to His coming in increasing power and grace in the future. Optimism was the distinction of the Hebrews. 'In the absence of Hope and of an ideal of progress, we strike upon one great difference between the classical Greeks and the Hebrews.'[2] Among the ancient races the Hebrew was like a watcher standing on a high mountain top, scanning the horizon and catching the first beams of coming day, while others were still hidden in darkness. The very heart-cry of the Hebrew race is heard in such words as these:

> 'My soul looketh for the LORD
> More than watchmen look for the morning;
> Yea, more than watchmen for the morning.'[3]

FAITH.—On his deathbed Joseph bound the children of Israel under an oath to carry his body out of Egypt at their exodus and bury him in the land of his fathers. In accordance with his wish his body was embalmed and put in a coffin in Egypt (v.[26]); and after some centuries 'Moses took the bones of Joseph with him: for he had straitly sworn the children of Israel, saying, God will surely visit you; and ye shall carry up my bones away hence with you.'[4] One of the Apostles has selected this dying 'commandment concerning his bones' from among all the incidents of Joseph's career as the outstanding proof of his faith.[5] Amid all his Egyptian achievements and successes he kept his heart humble and his faith simple. Egypt was the scene of his struggles and temptations, his honours and triumphs; it was the

---

[1] Emerson.  [2] Professor Butcher.  [3] Ps. 130[6].
[4] Ex. 13[19].  [5] Heb. 11[22].

land of his adoption, in which he lived nearly a century, making history; but he never ceased to feel himself a stranger in it. The glamour of Egypt never withdrew his eyes from the glory of Canaan, and in his dying dreams he saw the land of Abraham, Isaac, and Jacob. He never ceased to be a true Hebrew. Sometimes he affected to be more Egyptian than the Egyptians, —a diviner who swore by the life of Pharaoh—but this was no more than a light play on the surface of his mind. He spoke the Egyptian language, married an Egyptian wife, served an Egyptian king, but he was never Egyptianised. His heart was 'true to the kindred points of heaven and home'; and if he could not live in Canaan he was minded at least to sleep his last sleep in it. We feel that it is characteristic of him that his last recorded utterance contains the name of God (v.[25]). His ruling passion is strong in death. His loyalty to the God of Israel is the outstanding fact in his story. In the wealth of Egypt's commerce, in the magnificence of her temples, in the learning of her colleges, he saw nothing to make him swerve from his allegiance to the God whom he learned to love as a child. He maintained his detachment of spirit; he served his God with twice the zeal with which he served his king. 'It is easy in the world to live after the world's opinion; it is easy in solitude to live after our own; but the great man is he who in the midst of the crowd keeps with perfect sweetness the independence of solitude.'[1] Pure and gentle, noble and generous, high-minded and true-hearted, Joseph dies as he has lived, in faith. To think of him is to think of youth, beauty, and victorious strength, of temptations resisted, of God-given gifts well used and the crown of earthly glory won. The cities in which he lived and laboured have disappeared; the multitudes which filled the air with the hum of their voices and the din of their industries have melted away; and scarcely one stone of Memphis rests upon another. But his spirit lives on, his virtues and graces silently passing into the lives of others, and his story bearing fruit through all succeeding ages.

[1] Emerson.

# INDEX

Affection                148, 208
Aspiration               154
Assurance                174
Attainment               328, 331
Authority                116
Awakening                269

Beauty                   185
Bethel                   229, 236, 246
Birthright               146, 203, 209
Blessedness              27, 174, 247
Blessing                 219, 222
Brotherhood              47, 56, 316, 342
Buoyancy                 347
Business                 179

Canaan                   223
Character  15, 118, 152, 206, 341
Charity                  121, 127
Chastity                 186, 342
Childhood                244
Comfort                  194, 284
Compassion               149
Conscience               282, 293, 309,
                         313, 318
Consecration             104, 236
Consolation              275

Counsel                  86
Courtesy                 177, 187
Covenanting              78, 103, 237

Dawn                     258
Decision                 49
Departure                340
Dependence               37
Destiny                  46, 225
Detachment               19
Diligence                164
Discipline               42, 59, 160, 229
Divinity                 64
Dominion                 84, 343
Dreams                   277, 281

Education                114
Eloquence                322
Encouragement            234
Endurance                85
Enough                   260
Experience               21

Faith        22, 77, 105, 109, 156,
             163, 210, 229, 248,
             311, 351, 356

| | | | |
|---|---|---|---|
| Farewell | 190, 340 | Importunity | 122 |
| Fatherhood | 102, 246, 323 | Individuality | 20 |
| Fear | 209 | Industry | 185 |
| Fellowship | 60, 285 | Influence | 125, 268 |
| Fidelity | 183, 273, 320 | Inspiration | 303 |
| Flight | 292 | Integrity | 139 |
| Foreknowledge | 113 | Intercession | 120, 321 |
| Forgetting | 308 | Interpretation | 302 |
| Forgiveness | 328, 351 | Israel | 257 |
| Fortitude | 167 | | |
| Freedom | 94 | | |
| Friendship | 45, 112, 216 | Joy | 144 |
| Futurity | 335 | Judgment | 119, 138 |
| | | Justice | 82 |
| Gain | 126 | | |
| Girlhood | 263 | | |
| Godliness | 98 | Kindness | 187 |
| Goshen | 332 | Kingship | 61, 332 |
| Grace | 80 | Kinship | 134 |
| Greatness | 28, 214, 333 | | |
| Guidance | 329 | | |
| | | Labor | 245 |
| | | Laughter | 143 |
| Happiness | 346 | Leadership | 58 |
| Harmonics | 194 | Liberality | 65 |
| Heaven | 199 | Liberty | 32, 70, 186, 215, 298, 347 |
| Hebraism | 14 | | |
| Hebrews | 23 | Life | 106, 333 |
| History | 203 | Light | 82 |
| Honor | 67, 139, 304 | Love | 88, 193, 239, 249, 267, 274, 279, 307, 329 |
| Hope | 239, 328, 340, 355 | | |
| Hospitality | 108, 188 | | |
| Humility | 122, 326 | Manhood | 301 |
| | | Marriage | 182, 218, 227 |
| | | Meditation | 192 |
| Iconoclasm | 270 | Meekness | 213, 216 |
| Ideals | 13, 233, 277 | Memory | 243, 299 |
| Idyllic | 181, 239 | Mercy | 97, 129 |
| Immortality | 198 | Merit | 304 |

Ministry 305
Monogamy 243
Morality 132, 294
Mother-love 220
Mystery 257

Nationality 26, 103
Nature 137, 230
Nemesis 304
Nobility 180
Nuptials 266

Obedience 30, 165, 220, 272
Observance 95
Old Age 195, 209
Oracles 204

Paradise 51
Pardon 353
Patriotism 25
Patterns 16
Peace 63, 262
Perfection 99, 158
Pilgrimage 176
Power 31, 97, 252
Praise 142
Prayer 130, 204, 252
Probation 159
Promises 24
Prophecy 73, 168
Protection 28, 74, 250
Providence 172, 179, 315, 324, 354
Purity 126, 262, 264, 271, 292, 317

Readiness 219
Reassurance 72
Recompense 51
Reconciliation 259
Redemption 338
Reflection 71
Renunciation 48
Resignation 317
Responsibiliy 211
Rest 34
Restoration 44, 269
Restraint 226
Retribution 136, 242, 309
Retrospect 336
Reunion 197, 330, 338
Revelation 18, 173, 213
Reverence 122, 172, 235, 276
Reward 75
Righteousness 77, 123

Sacrifice 161, 170, 272
Salvation 349
Scripture 107
Seamanship 344
Self control 170
Self examination 93
Self judgment 300
Self knowledge 90
Self sacrifice 322
Sensibility 224, 291
Sentiment 178
Service 28, 57, 265, 295
Shepherding 337
Silence 265, 295
Sincerity 142
Sonship 169, 217
Sorrow 175
Souls 33
Sovereignty 101, 205, 339

| | | | |
|---|---|---|---|
| Stars | 75 | Valor | 57 |
| Statesmanship | 334 | Veracity | 213 |
| Stewardship | 287 | Victory | 53, 290 |
| Strength | 349 | Vindication | 247 |
| Strenuous | 345 | Virtue | 87, 265, 285, 288 |
| Style | 157 | Vision | 91, 150 |
| Success | 123 | Vows | 68 |
| Sympathy | 81, 171, 297, 319 | | |
| | | Warfare | 54, 346 |
| Tears | 148, 324, 350 | Watchfulness | 37 |
| Temperance | 133 | Watching | 249 |
| Testing | 310 | Watchnight | 255 |
| Thanksgiving | 64 | Wealth | 43 |
| Tragedy | 212 | Wifehood | 111 |
| Trial | 251, 289 | Womanhood | 185, 228, 240 |
| Truth | 39, 141, 153, 221, 251, 278, 283 | Work | 287, 306 |
| | | Worship | 35, 100 |
| | | Wrestling | 250, 256 |
| Unity | 261 | | |
| Universalism | 29 | Zeal | 128 |